LADY CHARLOTTE GUEST

LADY CHARLOTTE GUEST

An Extraordinary Life

REVEL GUEST

AND

ANGELA V. JOHN

TEMPUS

First published in 1989 by George Weidenfeld & Nicholson
This edition first published 2007

Tempus Publishing
Cirencester Road, Chalford
Stroud, Gloucestershire, GL6 8PE
www.tempus-publishing.com

Tempus Publishing is an imprint of NPI Media Group

British Library Cataloguing in Publication Data.
A catalogue record for this book is available from the British Library.

ISBN 978 0 7524 4252 5

Typesetting and origination by NPI Media Group
Printed and bound in Great Britain

CONTENTS

ABOUT THE AUTHORS

Revel Guest, the great grand-daughter of Lady Charlotte, began her career as the youngest-ever woman parliamentary candidate. In 1960 she joined the BBC's *Panorama*, as its first woman producer/director and in 1968 formed Transatlantic Films, which has made over 150 award winning films and series. She is married with two children and retains strong ties to Wales where she farms in Powys and is Chair of the Hay Literary Festival. Her other book is *History's Turning Point*.

Angela V. John is a historian and biographer. She was, for many years, Professor of History at the University of Greenwich and now lives in Pembrokeshire. Her other books include a biography of the actress and suffragette Elizabeth Robins (also published by Tempus) and a life of the war correspondent Henry W. Nevinson.

ILLUSTRATIONS

ACKNOWLEDGEMENTS

Numerous people have helped in the years of preparation for this book. It would be impossible to mention them all by name but we are grateful to them. Special thanks are due to Viscount Wimborne for the use of Lady Charlotte's journals and to the Dowager Viscountess Wimborne for her interest, hospitality and permission to use unpublished material. Other descendants to whom we owe thanks include the Earl of Bessborough and Lord Eliot. Thanks also to Mark Schreiber. Particular thanks are due to Nicholas Shakespeare for all the work he did in the early stages.

We have benefited from the specialist knowledge of the following: Hélène Alexander, Dr Rachel Bromwich, Aileen Dawson of the British Museum, Menna Gallie, Madeleine Ginsberg of the Department of Costume and Textiles, Victoria and Albert Museum, Dr Brinley Jones, Professor Gwyn Jones, Professor Ieaun Gwynedd Jones, Dr Irvine Loudon of the Wellcome Unit for the History of Medicine (Oxford), Michael and Richard Keen, Dr Ceridwen Lloyd Morgan of the National Library of Wales, John Mallet, Keeper of Ceramics, Victoria and Albert Museum, Sylvia Mann, Nick Mansfield of Cyfarthfa Castle Museum, Peter Raymond, Judy Rudoe of the British Museum, Dr Elfyn Scourfield and John Vivian Hughes. We are especially indebted to Dr Aled Rhys Wiliam for his translation of the stanzas on the philanthropy of Lady Charlotte. Many people from the Uffington, Dowlais and Canford areas have been informative, chief amongst whom are Dr Eric Till, John A. Owen, Huw Williams, Geraint James, David Watkins, Derek Beamish, the Vicar of Canford, Michael Rathbone, Dr Thomas Morley and Alan Miller. Thanks are also owed to Dr Edgar Jones and GKN for permitting part of the manuscript of the company's history to be read, to Richard Morris for use of Lewis Weston Dillwyn's unpublished diaries, P.J. Simons for permission to use the copy of Phoebe Evans's transcript at Cyfarthfa Castle Museum and Dr Ted Ward for use of his unpublished manuscript of Lady Wimborne.

The staff of the following libraries, Record Offices and museums have been most helpful: Glamorgan, Dorset, Northampton and Suffolk Record Offices, the Victoria and Albert Museum Library, Department of Prints and Drawings and Department of Medieval and later Antiquities in the British Museum, the Department of Manuscripts and Reading Room, British Library and the British

Newspaper Library at Colindale, the Public Record Office, the London Library, the Guildhall Library, the Fawcett Library, Thames Polytechnic Library, Poole Public Library, Poole Records and Archives (and the Town Clerk of the Borough of Poole), the Archivist of Marlborough College, the National Library of Wales, Merthyr Tydfil Library, Merthyr Tydfil Heritage Trust, Dowlais Library, Cardiff Reference Library and the Institute of Historical Research. The Worshipful Company of Fan Makers has also been of assistance.

Thanks are also due to Derrick Webley, Dr Peter Searby, Leonore Davidoff, Sue Corbett, Lynn Hughes, Marjorie Caygill, Herbert Williams and Professor Gwyn A. Williams. Paul Stigant and Bertie Guest kindly read the whole manuscript. Thanks to Robert Albert for his patient help and to Judith Burnley for her encouragement. We are grateful to Jasia Chrzanowska and Susannah Herbert for their help and to Suzanne Warren for typing. Juliet Gardiner and Candida Brazil at Weidenfeld have been both encouraging and helpful.

For the new edition we are especially grateful to Laurence Clark, Bertie Guest, Richard de Pelet, Lord Wimborne and Sioned Davies. We also wish to thank Sophie Bradshaw and Lisa Mitchell at Tempus for all their work.

NOTE TO THE NEW EDITION

Since this book was first published in 1989 there have been a number of publications that throw further light on Lady Charlotte's life and world. She and Rose Crawshay were the subjects of Angela V. John's essay 'Beyond Paternalism: The Ironmaster's Wife in the Industrial Community' in Angela V. John (ed.) *Our Mothers' Land. Chapters in Welsh Women's History 1830-1939*, Cardiff, 1991 and 1997 and she was included in Kim Reynold's study, *Aristocratic Women and Political Society in Victorian Britain*, Oxford, 1998. She also features in Keith Strange's *Merthyr Tydfil. Iron Metropolis*, Stroud, 2005.

In 1999 a conference was held at the University of Bonn to celebrate the 150th anniversary of the publication of Lady Charlotte's translation of the *Mabinogion* and the papers were published in English and German (Bernhard Maier and Stefan Zimmer with Christiane Batke, *150 Jahre 'Mabinogion' – Deutsch-Walisische Kulturbeziehungen*, Tübingen, 2001). In the United States Erica Obey's *The Wunderkammer of Lady Charlotte Guest* is forthcoming. Sioned Davies's publications have included 'A Charming Guest: Translating the *Mabinogion*' in *Studia Celtica*, XXXVIII, 2004, pp. 157-178. She has done her own translation, the first by a woman since Lady Charlotte, for the Oxford World's Classics Series (Sioned Davies, '*The Mabinogion*', Oxford, 2007).

New editions of Lady Charlotte's translation have continued to appear: in 1999 the Dover Thrift edition, edited by Adam Frost, headed the Welsh Books Council's list of Bestsellers in Literature. The following year her translation was accompanied by illustrations by Alan Lee (the conceptual artist on *The Lord of the Rings* films) in a lavish publication by Voyager, an imprint of Harper Collins. There are several recent doctoral theses and monographs about Lady Charlotte's literary work whilst the enduring appeal and adaptability of the *Mabinogion* has been demonstrated in, for example, Cartwn Cymru's animated film 'Otherworld' (2003).

Lady Charlotte was the subject of Ann Eatwell's article 'Private Pleasure, public beneficence: Lady Charlotte Schreiber and ceramic collecting' in Clarissa Campbell Orr (ed.) *Women in the Victorian Art World*, Manchester, 1995, pp. 125-45. Henry Layard's links with his cousin Lady Charlotte were given fresh attention when an Assyrian bas-relief was discovered at Canford School and auctioned at Christie's for £7 million in 1994.

Lady Charlotte's original journals are now deposited on loan in the National Library of Wales, Aberystwyth where they can be consulted by the public.

September 2006.

LADY CHARLOTTE'S TIME

Year	Personal	Public
1812	May. Lady Charlotte's birth.	Birth of Charles Dickens. Wellington's victories in Peninsular war. Napoleon's march into Russia.
1814	Birth of brother Lindsey.	
1815	Birth of brother Bertie.	Battle of Waterloo. Peace. Corn Laws.
1818	Death of Lady Charlotte's father.	
1820		Death of George III. School established Dowlais.
1821	Lady Lindsey marries Rev. Pegus.	
1822	Start of pocket book. Birth of half-sister Mary.	
1824	Birth of half-sister Elizabeth. 1st trip to Paris.	
1826	Charles Schreiber born.	
1827	Proper journal replaces pocket book.	
1829		Roman Catholic Emancipation
1830		Swing Riots. Death of George IV.
1831	Lady Charlotte presented at Court.	Merthyr Riots.
1832		Reform Act. John Guest becomes 1st MP of Merthyr.
1833	Lady Charlotte marries John Guest and goes to live at Dowlais, nr Merthyr.	1st Govt. grant for education Start of Oxford Movement. Founding of Abergavenny Cymreigyddion
1834	1st child, Maria, born.	Poor Law Amendment Act.
1835		William Owen Pughe dies.
1836	The Guests buy Sully House.	Founding of Welsh MSS Society. Publication of Pugin's 'Contrasts'.
1837	Death of Elizabeth Pegus.	Victoria becomes Queen.
1838	Beginning of Lady Charlotte's translation of *The Mabinogion*. John Guest gets Baronetcy.	The Charter is published.
1839		Ifor works begun. Newport Rising.
1840	Lease on Spring Gardens house, London.	Opening of Taff Vale Railway.
1842		Chartist 2nd Petition. Strikes.
1844	Dowlais schools reorganized.	
1846	Purchase of Canford, Dorset.	Repeal of Corn Laws.
1847	10th and last child, Blanche, born.	Report on Education in Wales.

Year	Personal	Public
1848	Dowlais lease to expire.	
		Death of Lord Bute. European Revolts. Kennington Common demonstration.
1849	Publication of 3 vol. edition of *The Mabinogion*.	Henry Layard's *Nineveh and its Remains* published. Cholera hits Dowlais.
1851	John Guest sole proprietor Dowlais.	
		Great Exhibition. Ecclesiastical Titles Act. Dowlais Branch Railway.
1852	Sir John dies. Lady Charlotte takes over Dowlais Iron Company.	
1853	Dowlais Strike.	
1854		Crimean War (to 1856). Cholera returns.
1855	Lady Charlotte marries Charles Schreiber.	
1856	Ivor comes of age.	
	New Dowlais schools opened.	
1857	Schreibers move to Exeter House, Roehampton.	
1859		Publication of Tennyson's *The Idylls of the King*.
1862	Death of Augustus.	
1863	Gap in journal to 1869.	
1865	Charles Schreiber MP Cheltenham.	
		Death of Palmerston. Dowlais starts rolling steel rails.
1866		Women's Suffrage Petition
1867		Second Reform Act.
1868		Disraeli's 1st administration (Feb-Dec.)
1869		Start of ceramics journal.
1870		Elementary Education Act. Franco-Prussian War. Charles Dickens dies.
1871		Paris Commune. Founding of School of Art Needlework.
1872		Secret Ballot.
	During 1870s Schreibers spent many months in Europe travelling and collecting ceramics.	
1877		Russo-Turkish War.
1878		Congress of Berlin.
1880	Ivor becomes Lord Wimborne. Lady Charlotte treasurer of Turkish Compassionate Fund.	
	Charles Schreiber becomes MP for Poole.	
1882	Last European collecting tour.	Brymer Schreiber in charge of artillery in Egypt. Bombardment of Alexandria. Cairo occupied by British troops.

Year	Personal	Public
1883	South African voyage.	
1884	Charles Schreiber dies.	
1885		Presentation of catalogue and ceramics to South Kensington Museum.
1886		Langham Place Cab Shelter opened.
1887		Queen Victoria's jubilee.
1888	Volume 1 of *Fans and Fan Leaves* published.	
1889	Lady Charlotte moves to Blanche's home.	
1896	Sale of furniture, china Christie's. Vol. 2 of *Fans and Fan Leaves*. Farewell visit to Dowlais.	
1891	End of journal. Granted Freedom of Fanmakers. Fan collection goes to British Museum.	
1892	1st vol. published on Playing Cards.	
1893	2nd vol. published on Playing Cards. (3rd pub. posthumously.)	
1894		Death of Henry Layard
		End of Gladstone's 4th and last Ministry. Rosebery succeeds him.
1895	Lady Charlotte dies in January at Canford.	Freud publishes his first work on psycho-analysis. The term 'motor car' comes into use

INTRODUCTION

'The Depository of my dreams.'

Lady Charlote's life virtually spanned the nineteenth century. Born in 1812 and christened Lady Charlotte Elizabeth Bertie, she survived until 1895, outliving both her husbands, Sir John Guest and Charles Schreiber. It was a life of action, achievements and variety, yet she still found time for reflection and her thoughts are recorded in the copious journal she kept from 1822 until 1891. What started as a daily habit became a life-time companion and eventually a piece of social history. A translator, a businesswoman, a collector, an educator: these are someof the labels with which people have tried to describe Lady Charlotte. A life which straddled so many activities defies too neat a definition. And even today she is remembered in a number of different ways. For the people of rural Lincolnshire she is recalled as the eldest child of an illustrious family. Her father was the Ninth Earl Lindsey and she grew up at Uffington House near Stamford. Her relatives' graves can be found (some camouflaged by nettles) in the churchyard opposite the grounds where once her home stood. At Dowlais, above Merthyr Tydfil, in the very different terrain of the South Wales valleys, the heart of what Raymond Williams once called the 'Industrial Convulsion' and site of the Dowlais Iron Company, Lady Charlotte is identified as the wife of one of the great ironmasters. In 1833 at the age of twenty-one she had married the widower Josiah John Guest,[1] giving him status and support in return for love and wealth. An inhabitant of Dowlais sums up the local response: 'to us Lady Charlotte is Dowlais and the works'. Not only was she deeply involved in the community and works for twenty years but, in mid-century when her husband died, she ran for a time what was the largest ironworks in the world.

Some Dowlais people have direct links, having been educated at a school originally founded by Lady Charlotte. People will also mention, as will any Celtic scholar, her translation of the twelve medieval Welsh tales which she called *The Mabinogion*. Lady Charlotte learned medieval Welsh when newly married, whilst interspersing motherhood and successful Society seasons in London with promoting Whig politics (her husband was Merthyr's first MP). Her unprecedented literary publication made her a revered name and *The Mabinogion* remains a classic.

Yet in Dorset where the Guests bought a large estate in 1846, the images of her shift yet again. Here she is best remembered as the lady of the manor at Canford, near Poole, and it is in the churchyard at Canford that Lady Charlotte is buried. For the second half of the century, home was London. After marrying a second time in 1855, Lady Charlotte and her new and much younger husband travelled extensively on the Continent, returning periodically to their home in London where they amassed the treasures collected on their trips. Today they are honoured for their pioneering work with china and their vast and very valuable collection, known as the Schreiber collection, which can be seen at the Victoria and Albert Museum in London. In 1885 Lady Charlotte had presented their ceramics (and a catalogue prepared by herself) in memory of Charles who had died the previous year. She is also well represented in the British Museum. Here can be found her many fans and playing cards, two more areas of collecting expertise in which she excelled. She produced five folio volumes describing and reproducing her fans and playing cards which kept her busy until her death in her eighty-third year.

Despite the preservation of her collections and literary achievements (and she maintains some presence in popular historical fiction),[2] surprisingly little remains today of the visual landmarks of Lady Charlotte's life. Uffington House no longer stands. Dowlais House and Lady Charlotte's schools no longer exist though the stables have become flats and the splendid Guest Memorial Hall, built as a tribute to John Guest, remains. The modest ironworks started in 1759 by his grandfather have been translated into Britain's gigantic manufacturing company, GKN. Dowlais itself was less fortunate. Although Guest, Keen and Nettlefold Ltd would flourish in the late nineteenth century as producers of steel, by 1930 the main section of the Dowlais works was closed. 1987 marked the end of a long era, with the closure of the Ingot Mould Foundry, the last remnant of Dowlais's 228 years of heavy industry.[3]

Yet old images die hard and some history has been remoulded into modern icons. In 1980 when Merthyr Tydfil celebrated its 1,500th anniversary, Welsh Brewers opened The Lady Charlotte public house at Dowlais. Known locally as The Charlotte its sign was based on a painting of Lady Charlotte by the artist Richard Buckner, and cut-price beer combined with pictures evocative of Dowlais in its Victorian heyday. Then came the Lady Charlotte café.

Perhaps more appropriately, Canford Manor is now a school, though a boys' public school is a far cry from the ironworks schools promoted by Lady Charlotte for the education of boys, girls, men and women employed at the works. This progressive school system earned Dowlais the nickname of 'The Prussia of Wales'. The rented houses in which Lady Charlotte lived at Brighton for short periods remain but gone are her London homes at 8, Spring Gardens (demolished to build the entrance to the Mall) and Langham House (11, Portland Place), now replaced by an office block.

Yet if architectural reminders are few, Lady Charlotte lives on though her many descendants. During those busy years at Dowlais she also had ten children (in thirteen years), five boys, five girls. All but two married and seven of the Guest children had families. Surviving also is Lady Charlotte's original journal (in the National Library of Wales). The pocket book begun in March 1822 was replaced from 1827 by a proper journal.[4] By now Lady Charlotte would only 'very seldom miss a day'. Eventually there would be thirty-one volumes filling thousands of pages. Diaries had become popular in the seventeenth century as a means of recording the state of one's soul but Lady Charlotte's journal was poised between the eighteenth-century tradition of letter-writers such as Lady Mary Wortley Montagu and the well-known Victorian diarists.

Like Lady Mary, Lady Charlotte loved writing, languages and travel and educated herself with the aid of family libraries, dictionaries and grammars, subscribing to Lady Mary's belief that 'Whoever will cultivate their own mind will find full employment'. But there were also parallels between Lady Charlotte and the famous late-Victorian diarist, Beatrice Webb. Both had experienced miserable childhoods and adolescence during which they turned to writing a diary, which Beatrice called a 'mental looking glass', for solace and friendship. Beatrice was to write close to three million words. Both women were self-censorious and distrustful of any forms of idleness. Like Queen Victoria who wrote about 2,500 words daily in adult life, they were industrious and imaginative in their personal writings. They found the habits of discipline engendered by regular journal-keeping more attractive than the enervating demands of Society. Whilst the world saw only competent and controlled women in command of whatever they undertook, in both cases, behind the exterior lay another self full of doubts and questions. At a time when the formalities of social life made it difficult to establish intimate contact and frank conversations, a journal perhaps fulfilled a more vital need than it does today for most people. It was especially valuable for somebody as conscious of her breeding and as shy as the young Lady Charlotte. She was a lonely child. In 1843 she recalled how 'In the old days when I was very unhappy and when I had no friend to pour out my grief to, I used to have recourse to my journal and find solace in recording my sadness'. Her half-sister Mary was nearly ten years younger whilst her brother – a simpleton – was far from being the ideal companion for her. With few friends as a child she found it difficult to establish close contact with women as an adult,[5] particularly since some of her activities involved her in what was seen as a man's world.

Her fifth child, Montague (known as Monty) once described his strong-willed mother as '...very self-possessed and calm, with an extraordinary control over her feelings. I can truly say that I never saw her angry or unduly excited in my life.' Although it would be misleading to suggest too conscious a link between the public and private person in pre-Freudian times, Lady Charlotte seems to have used the journal as a necessary outlet. She called it the 'Depository of my dreams'. It reveals her as a passionate, highly sensitive person who became skilled in 'putting on a face' in public: 'when I feel myself attacked, I am particularly careful not to betray by my outward demeanour', and she admitted to her 'very strong passions too carefully concealed'. Once, when she saw a Welsh dancer and harpist, she wrote 'one is always obliged to look careless and indifferent and everything Welsh speaks so keenly to my heart'. She understood that she needed to set the tone as the employer's wife. Her public sublimation of her feelings may also have been linked to her embarrassment as an adolescent at the public excesses of her stepfather. The self-control which her children noticed even in an age of formality, was deep-rooted yet never easily achieved.

During the traumatic years of growing up, regular recording seems to have given Lady Charlotte some stability and purpose. When sixteen she wrote: 'From a perfect child I have always been anxious to retain the recollection of events, and have had a singular predilection for being able to tell what I was doing on such a day a year or two years ago and this first put it into my head to make some memoranda of the principal things that struck my mind.' Quietly writing was a pastime young women were not discouraged from doing and in itself proved a valuable form of self-education. It enabled an exploration and testing of inchoate ideas with an audience which, to use Beatrice Webb's words, was 'dumb but not deaf.' It gave her a chance to tell her version of events and to make her own contribution to her family history.

Lady Charlotte took what she called 'journalyzing' seriously. In 1828 she read Isaac D'Israeli's *Essay on the Manners and Genius of the Literary Character*, little knowing that within a few years she would have a brief romance with the author's son, Benjamin. She carefully copied out extracts from volume one. Here he discussed the purpose of keeping a journal. She read Evelyn's *Memoirs* and Pepys was an especial favourite. Never quite sure how intimately she could afford to confide in her journal, she explained (when fifteen) that she felt some restraint in committing to paper the 'recesses of my own bosom' despite temptations to write volumes on 'the state of my mind'. She worried about the erroneous notions which could be conveyed by the 'careless and often ambiguous manner in which, one who keeps a journal of thoughts and sentiments must be often liable to express ...'. So, in her early years she vacillated between outpourings of emotion and tantalizing silences. Since there was at least a hint of Jane Austen's Catherine Morland in the young Lady Charlotte (by adulthood her propensity for Gothic was largely restricted to architecture), the reader cannot know precisely where her fantasies ended and reality began. Sometimes, like other diarists, she is cryptic; sometimes her thoughts are clear. The tension between the urge to tell all to what Virginia Woolf called the 'blank-faced old confidante' and the concern lest others read her words, was re-lived during her secret romance with Charles Schreiber, the tutor who became her second husband. Painfully aware of her children's resentment and conscious of the impropriety of a recently widowed lady in her forties indulging in a courtship with another and younger man, and an employee at that, her journal reverts to a complex mixture of suppressed emotion and elation. Almost in code, individual significant words are inserted to trigger her memory but not enlighten any unwelcome reader. It becomes once more like the writings of the adolescent Charlotte Bertie, swayed by her feelings for the Uffington tutor, Mr Martin, although the later journal shows a confidence and underlying happiness which is missing from the teenage writings.

Lady Charlotte enjoyed nostalgia and romanticization and periodically she re-read her past words – 'nothing speaks more to the heart than a journal'. When sixteen she had observed that 'Every line recalls something to my memory… Sometimes a single dash which I have placed under a word will explain more to myself than pages written explicative of the subject could to another person.' She was striving to 'note the current of my evanescent thoughts'[6] (a reference to D'Israeli's advice in his *Literary Character*) and she chastised herself whenever she thought the journal in danger of becoming a perfunctory record devoid of reflection.

Somehow she found the space and energy to sustain her venture. Fortunately for us, she became an addict. The entries for eight unhappy months before her first marriage were destroyed partly because she feared they might cause distress to John Guest, but unlike many journals which cease on marriage, Lady Charlotte's was resumed at this point. She now felt that she was writing for John though he does not seem to have paid much attention to her journal. She continued writing, even recording her husband's dying hours in November 1852. There is a gap between September 1859 and January 1863, whilst the volume which covered 1863 to 1869 appears to have been lost. Between 1869 and the early 1880s the journal details travels in search of china, and the 'Ceramic Memoranda' (or 'Notes Ceramic') are written in soft-cover note-books, smaller than the thick books she had been using.

She tended to write for about an hour daily, either late at night or in the early morning. Although she occasionally threatened to abandon this remarkable temporal record and several times lost or broke the key to an individual journal, she knew that 'I cannot forsake my old friend'. She always came back to it out of habit and it was blindness which finally forced her to give up in 1891 when her love of order was offended as the neat pages of decades gave way to larger script which could no longer be contained in straight lines. In a long life fractured by time, place and bereavement her 'old friend' provided a note of continuity, ending within four years of her death. A typed version of her journal (made for Monty at the beginning of this century) runs to over 10,000 pages.[7]

We all contradict ourselves daily yet often expect historical figures to have remained rigidly consistent to beliefs which we have probably pigeon-holed for them and which we are prone to judge by the standards of our own time. Lady Charlotte's journal demonstrates processes of change, showing how and why individuals and attitudes harden or soften over time and it demonstrates how complex is human nature; the same individual can seem to be utterly charming to one person yet equally intimidating to another. From this we can also gain a fresh, necessarily angled view of an industrializing and industrialized Britain. Virginia Woolf once noted that the biography should be less a focus *on* the subject than a means of studying *through* that person and in this way Lady Charlotte's story is also the story of the nineteenth century, seen through the perspectives of a noble-woman whose experience of life was not restricted to that of the great estate.

The truncated diaries of illustrious contemporaries such as Gladstone (he wrote one for over seventy-four years) read like telegrams alongside the vivid writings of Lady Charlotte. From childhood her prose was fluent and accomplished – if at times slightly pompous to the modern reader. Her spelling was impressive from the start, reflecting how 'books were a second life to me and literature a sort of fairyland'. Encouraged by Charlotte, her half-sisters Mary and Elizabeth Pegus kept journals. Yet although they began at the same age as Charlotte had done, their entries were infinitely more childish. Mary's opened with 'I skiped [sic] with Lindsey and Elizabeth in the gravel walk and picked some flowers for Mama'. At the stage when she was referring to toys and games, Lady Charlotte was concentrating on Chaucer, Hallam and all things oriental. Yet when especially depressed, then and later her style would petrify, the usual flowing sentences giving way to short bursts, interspersed with many dashes.

Despite becoming an expert on fan collecting, external appearances were not what mattered most to Lady Charlotte. As she grew older and, as Fanny Burney put it, time became 'more nimble than memory', the journal became a piece of history for her. She was impressed that the criminal reformer and Solicitor-General Sir Samuel Romilly had kept a diary during twelve extremely busy years so that something could be given to his children. She recognized the importance of documenting a life. It helped her understand her own development and decisions, and as time wore on it became a legacy for her large family.

Judith Schneid Lewis's recent work on childbirth in the British aristocracy (between 1760-1850) concludes that out of the fifty women she examined, including Queen Victoria, Lady Charlotte was probably the most individually remarkable person. Her intimate journals show how she reconciled the need to be a loving mother with achieving eminence in her chosen fields. Her Catholic interests and the extent to which she appeared to succeed in all her enterprises set her apart from many women. Yet the current expansion of biographies of those previously missing from the historical record is revealing a number of remarkable women whose voices deserve to he heard. Moreover the biographer is aware of 'the whole plot' which the journal writer had to experience painfully stage by stage. Lady Charlotte's life may now seem remarkable – she herself was intent that it should be so, seeing herself set apart with no wish for the ordinary – yet she discloses the apprehension and worries that she had to endure to secure success. Her journal also shows the interplay between the momentous and the mundane.

Lady Charlotte was personally interested in biography. Chronicling the Bertie history was one of her projects at Uffington. The family's lineage appeared to hold out more romance and interest than their present activities. Ironically, when twenty-one she moved to a place where present and future were all-important: Merthyr was the epicentre of the iron trade. Yet even whilst plunging herself into its midst, Lady Charlotte was just as eagerly exploring the remote past of *The Mabinogion*.

In 1950 and 1952 one of her grandsons, the Earl of Bessborough, published two volumes of 'edited highlights' from Lady Charlotte's journals. They have made available a selection of her writings from her marriage onwards, though they unfortunately have long since been out of print. This book is the first biography of this fascinating and sometimes enigmatic woman. It draws on the entire journal. Any journal is prejudiced but we cannot afford to be too censorious. Most people do not so conveniently lay bare their feelings and activities for us to criticize. Lady Charlotte chose not to have her journal destroyed and so has enabled us to put her life under the microscope. Using other contemporaries' correspondence, diaries, letters, business records, memoirs, Parliamentary papers and newspapers alongside the journal (and Lady Charlotte's other writings) helps to put her views into some sort of perspective and confirms her strong sense of recall and ability to synthesize material effectively.

Although her name is known today to many different people, her activities have tended to be compartmentalized. This biography shows how her different interests slotted together, how she juggled with so many contrasting demands. The book is broadly chronological but within the three parts (divided into her early life as Lady Charlotte Bertie, the Guest years in Wales and the later period as Lady Charlotte Schreiber) the chapters are thematic. Some aspects of her life – such as giving birth to and raising ten children – are given the attention they deserve although they are not what she is remembered for. Although Lady Charlotte was infinitely more fortunate than most women since she had ample help within the home and all the comforts available, she alone had to endure pregnancy and childbirth and manage the household. Nor did the misery of her youth give way to unalloyed happiness for ever more. Her hypersensitivity, her first husband's deteriorating health and the many and conflicting demands on her time and energy ensured that old doubts and worries resurfaced despite the increased security.

Research has thrown new light on some of her better-known activities. Her journal reveals for example the difficulties she had in negotiating with ironmasters during a strike in 1853. With the benefit of the complete journals used alongside other sources we have been able to examine carefully and critically the extent to which she was responsible for *The Mabinogion* and the nature of her achievement. Her journal not only reveals what she collected in later life but gives a glimpse into the mentality of the collector. She remained active in later life, even into her eighties. Not only can we see the capabilities of the elderly, but also that age could bestow a certain dignity and independence from the prescriptions of Victorian society.

Lady Charlotte's life warns us against broad generalizations. Her involvement in politics and social welfare does not mean that she was attracted to the early women's movement as might be expected. The fact that an ambitious and successful woman had five daughters does not necessarily suggest that she would seek similar lives for them. Within her own long life there were many contradictions. Yet there were also a number of curious and recurrent threads, as she never failed to observe. One passage written in the journal in 1839 seems to point most keenly to what, above all else, appeared to drive her on: underlying her vitality, ambition and perseverance was the determination not just to get by, not merely to succeed but, despite or perhaps because of her feelings of inadequacy, to succeed *par excellence*:

> But whatever I undertake, I must reach an eminence in. I cannot endure anything in a second grade. I am happy to see we are at the head of the iron trade. Otherwise I could not take pride in my house in the City and my works at Dowlais, and glory (playfully) in being (in some sort) a tradeswoman. Then again, my blood is of the noblest and most princely in the kingdom, and if I go into Society, it must be the very best and first. I can brook no other. If I occupy myself in writing, my book must be splendidly got up and must be, as far at least as decoration and typography are concerned, at the head of literature …

Part 1

LADY CHARLOTTE BERTIE

1
The Young Aristocrat

'That great object of my existence, improvement in my studies.'

Life really began for Lady Charlotte when she was nine years old. Her aunt, Miss Pegus, gave her a copy of Cowper's poems and her stepfather, the Rev. Peter Pegus, presented her with a pocket book. From her first staccato one-line entries in March 1822 through to the uneven lines written by the elderly widow of seventy-nine (with over forty grandchildren), Lady Charlotte carefully recorded both her action and thoughts. A simple yet poignant early entry seems to sum up her girlhood: 'I went to the play and sought a cure for the heartache.' Isolated in a grand, grey, stone manor house built in 1686 in the small Lincolnshire village of Uffington, the tale Lady Charlotte tells of her youth is a lonely one.

No bells had rung out for her birth on 19 May 1812. Albemarle, Ninth Earl of Lindsey and his second wife, Charlotte Susanna Elizabeth (eldest of the nine children of Peter Layard, the learned Dean of Bristol and Rector of Uffington), had produced their first child but not a son and heir. Four years later Marrat's *History of Lincolnshire* erroneously recorded that this daughter (who was to live until 1895) had only survived a few hours. Ironically, when in November 1814 a son was born, Albemarle George Augustus Frederick Bertie, he was dullwitted and simple. The brother and sister were as two sides of the some coin, each representing the extremes of intellect and ability. Albermarle inherited the family title but Lady Charlotte had a simpler prefix and invariably described him as 'poor Lindsey'. Another brother, Montague Peregrine (whom Lady Charlotte called Bertie) was born in 1815, the year of Waterloo and peace. He appears to have been a curious blend of his older sister and brother. A very silent, tall figure, he delighted in knowing pedigrees by heart, was said to be somewhat uncouth but devoted to his library. His namesake, Lady Charlotte's own son Montague, once described him as 'a voracious reader and crammed full of information which even with his great memory, he was totally unable to make any use of to himself or others'. He was as lazy as his sister was diligent.

A former army General and Tory MP for Stamford, Lady Charlotte's father was sixty-eight when she was born.★ He died when his daughter was only six. This was

---

★ See Appendix 1.

an especially traumatic time for the young Charlotte, who in the same year had a narrow escape from a house fire, one of the regular hazards of the time (Uffington House was eventually destroyed by fire in December 1904). The death of her father proved to be a double tragedy as in April 1821 Lady Lindsey remarried. Her new husband was a thirty-one-year-old cousin, a stout, fair-haired and mercurial character: the Rev. Peter Pegus. Although Lady Charlotte soon gained two half-sisters, Maria Antoinetta (known as Mary) and Elizabeth (Libdub), Charlotte's life was to become overshadowed by difficulties with her stepfather. Her mother, who had once been described as extraordinarily active and vivacious, rapidly retreated into the ailing lady, supine on the couch, so familiar in Victorian fiction. Lady Charlotte's journals are riddled with references to her mother's illnesses and delicacy but her retreat may also have been a means of allowing herself a little space of her own in the rather charged atmosphere of Uffington. The former Lady Lindsey was used to entertaining both gentry and nobility but coping with Pegus's fondness for drink was rather more trying. On one disastrous evening he imbibed a whole mug of lamp oil which he mistook for beer. On another occasion his impetuosity and temper led him to sack all the servants. His wife's withdrawal forced her eldest child into a premature position of responsibility. The power of the paterfamilias was of course not easily questioned at this time and his wife's indisposition meant that it was Charlotte who often received guests, paid social calls, replied to invitations and prepared early morning breakfast for Pegus before his shooting trips.

Uffington House possessed a strange mixture of charm and terror for the romantic young Charlotte. The garden was her refuge. It boasted the largest wisteria in the land and she spent hours and hours by the south wall and amongst the avenues of lime trees, especially her cherished 'second avenue'. Here she acquired her bookish wisdom. She loved the rides and on horseback could look out to the spectacular sight of Burghley House, the home of the Second Marquis of Exeter. Passionately interested in anything eastern, she nicknamed its pinnacles 'minarets'. Stamford, just a couple of miles from her home, she found both elegant and barbaric, with its fine architecture yet cruel custom of bull-running.

The interior world held less charms. She developed a hatred of indoors and stuffiness though even this was better than the city. The woman who became an inveterate traveller was, in her youth, a conservative girl who hated change and failed to he inspired by her first trip to Paris in 1824.

Always proud of her heritage, Lady Charlotte's family was in a slightly delicate social position. Her two half-sisters were not invited to the King's ball – unlike her, they were merely daughters of the clergy. It was a rebuff she felt keenly, particularly since she was personally powerless to do anything about it. Her mother's second marriage could not compete with the Lindsey pedigree (which included a commander of the King's troops during the Civil War Battle of Edgehill). Her insistence on the Lindsey lineage intensified as relations deteriorated with the man who had replaced her father. Pegus did bring with him an estate but it was in the West Indies and at the height of the movement against slavery he could find nobody to buy it. He had ambitions but he lacked position. He coveted the Uffington living. The church of St Michael and All Angels, just beyond the gates of Uffington House, was also just out of his reach since its incumbent was now his wife's brother, the Rev. Layard. A somewhat unchristian and fruitless feud developed between the two brothers-in-law. Lady Charlotte found herself apologizing on behalf of her family after Pegus passed round peppermints in church, sniggered through sermons and generally proved disruptive. When she was nineteen she wrote on his behalf to try to secure him a living elsewhere but to no avail.

In addition to enduring an atmosphere increasingly clouded by Pegus's frustrated ambitions, Lady Charlotte was, like all daughters growing up in the wake of reactions against the French Revolution, influenced by a stress on domesticity which counteracted the earlier call for the rights of women by Mary Wollstonecraft and others. The scope for a libertine lifestyle still remained greater amongst the nobility than with the aspiring middle class but whereas young gentlemen might be described as rakes getting into scrapes, young ladies had rather less freedom to misbehave. They did not have 'second chances'. Their lives were geared towards marriage and motherhood, their 'true' vocation and education. In sporting Lincolnshire, recreational activities were especially gendered with emphasis on rough, outdoor masculine sports for men whilst women's activities were largely restricted to genteel, indoor pursuits. Although aristocratic women had managed estates in the past and produced religious and political words of wisdom in the Civil War, the Evangelicals and the repressive atmosphere of the Liverpool ministry now ensured that the stress was increasingly placed on the value of the woman in her home. Lady Charlotte's journal shows the tension between her personal desire to achieve, to reject passivity, and yet a recognition of the need to conform – at least outwardly. She possessed a strong sense of propriety, of class and of Christian duty but she was equally aware of her own potential ability and that she was not 'of the crowd'. Sometimes her journal acted as the receptacle for her protests and so enabled her to conform in public.

The journal reveals her enduring rather than enjoying the society of Lincolnshire, the London season and the Brighton mini-season. 'The riding is congenial' but not 'the parade, the driving about, visiting, the stupid evenings, the continual ennui'. After dining at Lady Trollope's when fifteen, she pronounced the ladies 'very Missy and the evening extremely stupid'. She worked long hours for the sales of work for charity which were almost obligatory events in the calendars of the wealthy. A three-day bazaar at Stamford in 1829 spurred her into producing numerous pin cushions and bead books whilst her administration of the stall and account-keeping showed a side of her which would be developed much more strongly in later years.

Another interest outside the home was politics. From a young age Lady Charlotte followed contemporary affairs in the newspapers, commenting on local politics from the age of fifteen. She was able to observe the effects of the last labourers' revolt, the Swing Riots of 1830. This protest had begun in Kent and spread to most of south eastern England by November, then into Cambridgeshire and Lincolnshire. It was characterized by arson attacks and anonymous letters signed 'Swing'. It developed gradually into wages riots and, in particular, assaults on the hated threshing machine. Lady Charlotte's home county experienced rick burning and the firing of barns, farms and some country mansions. Her journal tells how 450 men were reported to be within ten miles of Uffington burning and breaking machines along the way. Special Constables were being sworn in and Pegus armed himself with two swords, a double-barrelled shotgun and a brace of pistols. The local gentry assembled with their home-made weapons, including a bugle horn and a walking stick containing loaded pistols. Lady Charlotte could see the comic side of this nineteenth-century 'Dad's Army'. They looked 'more like stuffed figures to shoot at than active combatants … it seemed like a revival of the old feudal times and a burlesque of them'. Her harp teacher feared that Uffington was about to be besieged but closer inspection (through the telescope) revealed that the invading army consisted of sheep and cows. Left at home to calm her nervous mother Lady Charlotte secretly sympathized with the rioters – 'how I pitied the poor deluded fugitives'.

By December the disturbances were over. In their place were more modern forms of protest, urging Parliamentary reform. The journal reveals that 'People can talk of nothing else but the alarming state of the country which threatens a grand revolution.' Probably with thoughts of Joan of Arc, the romantic Charlotte commented 'Who knows in these troublesome times but that I may have to shoulder a musket.' The neighbouring Marquis of Exeter was hooted by the Stamford crowd. Lady Charlotte knew him well on a social basis but was privately unsympathetic to this landlord who evicted tenants who did not support his politics. She believed the present electoral system (there had been no change since Charles II's reign) was unfair and Stamford was a rotten borough. Back in office after a long gap, the Whigs now sought to remedy the situation. In London Lady Charlotte met lords hostile to reform whose windows were being smashed. She read avidly newspaper reports of the Parliamentary debates on the Reform Bill and always claimed that it was Lord John Russell's speeches to the House of Commons which turned her, the daughter of a Tory MP, into a lifelong Whig. She was especially disappointed in the way the Lords threw out the bill, a 'haughty and ill judged' measure 'utterly in defiance of the people'. To her delight the Reform Act was passed in June 1832.

During these years her companions tended not to be her own age. They were people like the Rector of nearby Barnack, who was also the father of the Christian Socialist and author of *The Water Babies*, Charles Kingsley. The Rev. Kingsley taught her to etch and introduced her to Ariosto. The Bishop of Peterborough (whose son Herbert Marsh was considered by the family as a possible suitor for Charlotte) was another older mentor. One afternoon, after she had fed strawberries to the Bishop's tortoise, he showed her the Koran and a lock of hair with some spidery correspondence that had belonged to the explorer Burckhardt who discovered Petra. Such moments, along with the discovery of a new author, interested her passionately. At one point she wrote, 'I have affection for certain books and certain copies stronger than for any human beings.' A reader could be forgiven for presuming that she was actually with the writers and composers she mentions. There are frequent entries such as 'after breakfast in my garden, for nearly two hours with D'Israeli', 'revelling with Ariosto in the sun' and 'walked out with Dante'. Authors received the devotion which she so badly wanted to bestow on others. 1826 marked her first 'acquaintance with Beethoven'. When she obtained an Arabic grammar it was 'a new oriental friend'.

These years provide some valuable clues to the self-discipline and direction of Lady Charlotte's later work. Although there are obvious dangers in reading too much into early events and identifying significant traits with the benefit of hindsight, it is striking how well she utilized formative intellectual experiences whilst at the same time her personal life did seem to follow certain recurrent patterns. She was personally fatalistic. On several occasions she, like many others, visited the phrenologist who read bumps on the head to determine intelligence and particular gifts. She saw certain numbers and dates as significant and sym-bolic, possibly influenced by the fact that her father was born and died on the same day of the year. She saw a chain or circle of circumstances developing over time. Keeping a journal must have enhanced the likelihood of spotting patterns and, perhaps influenced by the mysticism of the east, she believed that more than coincidence was at work in many of life's events. It is certainly the case that her past kept boomeranging back in later years.

By making reading her reality, Lady Charlotte was educating herself at a time when training of character was considered of more importance for girls than the acquisition of academic knowledge. The religious writer Hannah More stressed that 'The profession of ladies is that of daughters, wives, mothers and mistresses of families.' In the early nineteenth century young ladies such as Charlotte did not attend school but received suitable teaching within the confines of the home. Wanda Neff has described the process: 'To get ready for the marriage market a girl was trained like a race-horse. Her education consisted of showy accomplish-ments designed to ensnare young men. The three R's of this deadly equipment were music, drawing and French administered by a governess at home.' Lady Charlotte's upbringing was conventional in the sense that she learned suitable accomplishments: She played music, sang, etched on copper plate[1] and, when in London for the season, had dancing lessons (which she hated) and instruc-tion from an Italian tutor to whom she afterwards sent packages of work. In the autumn of 1826 she was learning geography, arithmetic and Latin with a tutor at home. One French governess clearly influenced Lady Charlotte but she left rather hastily after being seduced by Albermarle Layard, the black sheep of the Rectory.[2] The unfortunate French governess was replaced by Miss Galway. Although Lady Charlotte thought her of 'sweet disposition for the little girls', languages excepted, she was very ignorant. Lady Charlotte added, somewhat condescendingly, 'However she is very young and anxious to improve.'

The household's major emphasis was, however, on the boys' education. Lady Charlotte's somewhat erratic training in academic subjects was no doubt affected by the difficulties which faced tutors in trying to teach Lindsey. So, for much of the time, she fell back on her own devices. Her accounts of her self-education and great self-discipline are reminiscent of the working-class autodidactic tradition made familiar through nineteenth-century autobiographies of working men who also had to combine work with their long hours of study. Lady Charlotte's journal describes her devouring the books in the library, reading Ariosto at 4 a.m., reciting in the garden and setting strict routines:

> Italian, Latin exercises, my journal and practising till dinner which is at one thirty. Then I read, refer to Moreri etc. for a fuller account of persons characters and things mentioned in my morning's Russell, read Latin with Mr Martin (I am re-commencing *dear, dear* Virgil) and walk or drive in the open carriage till half past five tea time. I amuse myself in various manners till we assemble to desert at 7 o'clock. After this we have music to please Lindsey, and then Mamma reads from the Literary Gazette while I work at my bead-work which advances rapidly. After tea we retire for the night and next morning recommence the same routine.

Before long, however, she had found new and more absorbing pursuits. On 6 August 1829 'At five minutes past eight (I hope an auspicious moment) I commenced my Arabic studies in the garden.' When Richardson's *Arabic Grammar* arrived (specially ordered from Mortlocks, the Stamford booksellers) she wrote, 'Had there been a heaven higher than the seventh I should have been placed in it.' As a small child Charlotte had listened to her mother reading the 'Arabian Nights'. On her first trip to Paris she saw 'Alladin with wonderful lamp' but 'I was not pleased with it as the story was quite different to that in the "Arabian Nights"'. The Bishop of St David's pamphlet was a valuable aid in working out the alphabet. From now on she was captivated by the east, it was a 'deep-rooted and hourly increasing oriental mania'. Close on 200 of her copious notes on oriental subjects survive, detailing subjects such as eastern commerce, travels to Turkey, Egypt and Syria, Persian sonnets and Turkish bread. There are also examples of Persian translation. In London she met Sir Gore Ouseley, the elderly diplomat and scholar. Whereas she found fittings for her Court dress 'excruciating', this was a memorable occasion. Impressed that an Englishwoman should choose to learn Persian for 'her own amusement and oriental partiality', he lent her books from his library, showed her old manuscripts, spent hours discussing the east and introduced Lady Charlotte to the Royal Asiatic Society which he had founded. She wrote, 'I who am accustomed to cold hearted calculation find delightful relaxation with this old man.' At Brighton Major Keppel enthralled her with his conversation. She had read his account of his journey from India to England and had long been anxious to meet this man whose writing 'proclaimed him so clever, and whose account of this very journey through Persia, Baghdad etc. had so much pleased me'.

Lady Charlotte's son Montague later recalled how, even at the age of seventy-five, his mother still hankered after a trip to India. In the 1820s when a visit to London took the family twelve hours, it must have seemed especially remote and magical.

Lady Charlotte had met Major Keppel at a dinner party hosted by the flamboyant Duchess of St Albans. She did not much enjoy the balls or studied public visibility in this resort made so fashionable by George IV when Regent. She soon saw through the veneer and predictability where 'one is almost always sure to meet every day in the same places, and at the same hours and in the same occupation, that of parading up and down the cliff and gazing at each other in listless indolence'. She was, however, fascinated by the Duchess with her coffee-coloured pugs and almost somnambulant second husband who was Grand Falconer and exercised his hawks on the Downs. Before marrying her first husband, the millionaire eighty-year-old banker Thomas Coutts, the Duchess had been Harriot Mellon, an actress, and Lady Charlotte still felt her 'considerable and not unpleasant tinge of the theatrical'. The theatre was another of her own passions and much of her life she presented as an unfolding drama. Her very first line in her pocket book had recorded a visit to the Theatre Royal in Stamford, one of the country's earliest provincial theatres, and she collected playbills of the Stamford Players, writing critical comments on the back of them. She possessed what she called 'theatrical mania'. Even in her seventies she acted as patron to her maid's sister, engaging her in charity shows and securing introductions to leading actors and managers. She approved of Miss Tennison's perseverance despite adverse circumstances, understanding such love of the theatre – 'I had it very strongly in my youth and it is not thoroughly extinguished in me now.'

Yet another subject which took a firm and lasting hold of Lady Charlotte was medieval history and legends. She described reading Hallam's *Europe in the Middle Ages* as 'an era in my life'. In 1829 she copied out large chunks of this in her neatest handwriting. This and Chaucer were later to be used in the explanatory notes accompanying her English translation of the Welsh tales she called *The Mabinogion*. The lake poet Robert Southey was another favourite as were Hazlitt's essays (which may have had some impact on her longer passages of descriptive prose). To relax she read Sir Walter Scott's novels. Delving into her own family history also appealed to the romantic within her and she spent some time piecing together the 'Bertie Book' and tracing the deeds of her ancestors such as Baron Willoughby of Eresby who sat in Parliament during Elizabeth I's time. 'Sitting under the beech I read of Queen Elizabeth at Tilbury, so I said Why should not I ride as well as Queen Elizabeth – so I rode – and I got over my fears.' Reading (and riding her horse Ronshun) enabled her to escape into a world which she saw as infinitely preferable to the one around her.

She recognized that her interests were not really those of most young ladies of her age. When, just under seventeen, she was offered Sismondi's *Italian Republic* to read, she was not so much concerned at its size (sixteen volumes) as at 'the prospect of alarming others'. She was aware that advice books disapproved of too much learning in a woman.Yet, 'Much as I have heard the learning of Latin disapproved of in a female, I still persist in it, nor do I see that it can be of any harm.' She saw at first hand the psychological oppression of a life of leisure, observing her mother's health and spirits deteriorate.

A glance at journals kept by other young ladies of the period helps put Lady Charlotte's interests into some sort of perspective, though the intellectually confident and articulate women journal keepers should not necessarily be seen as representative of the aspirations and achievements of the majority of middle- and upper-class women. Emily Shore kept a journal from the age of eleven to her premature death from consumption aged nineteen. She had learned Latin and Greek and read widely before she was thirteen and then graduated to Babbage's *Economy of Manufactures*. Anne Jemima Clough studied Euclid and German, and like Lady Charlotte rose early and deplored laziness. Both nursed ambitions. Lady Charlotte felt impelled by her ancestors, 'I cannot believe a Bertie can ever abandon, an enterprise once begun, from fear of difficulties which others have conquered. Shall I degenerate?' Anne Clough wished '… never to be forgotten, to do something great for my country which would make my name live for ever'. She added, 'But I am only a woman.' Her father's failure in business meant she had to care for her mother though she did also run a small school from home. Lady Charlotte proved to be one of the lucky ones who was able to realize many of her adolescent dreams. Yet unlike some of the successful intelligent women of the nineteenth century – for example the daughters of the physician and lecturer Sir George Paget – Lady Charlotte did not receive active, direct encouragement from her elders. The one person who recognized and appreciated her talents at Uffington was the tutor Mr Martin. Not surprisingly, he became the target of her affections.

Her first love had been Augustus O'Brien, the son of a local squire. He later became MP for Stafford and Secretary to the Admiralty. He was associated with Disraeli's Young England movement, and his family lived at Blatherwycke Hall. Lady Charlotte first met Augustus when she was fourteen and she later described this occasion as 'decidedly the happiest day of the happiest year of my life'. She celebrated that summer of 1826 as an anniversary for many years – even fifty years later it still merited a mention in her journal. Time seems to have encouraged her to invest some events with greater significance later than they may have had at the time, though in this case Lady Charlotte may have been wary of committing too many of her young thoughts to paper lest anybody see them. Her first waltz with Augustus at Lord Exeter's ball was later recalled with tenderness, though Pegus, who had a knack for breaking the charm, had intervened and hurried her home. He summoned her to his study and expressed his displeasure. Her mother later declared that she would sooner see her daughter in her grave than married to Augustus. Thwarted love brought out the full force of Lady Charlotte's romantic nature. When her garden patch was destroyed to make way for more ambitious schemes, she felt that everything she cared for was being plucked from her. All that remained on the earth was one white rose on the first bush she had planted. She poured out her grief in her journal:

> My own happiness is quite wrecked for ever … my spirit is quite broken – in an evil hour I trusted to my own strength which of course sank – too truly as Southey said 'think, if a man will fight the devil at his own weapon he must not wonder at finding himself over-matched'. So the yielding to a momentary temptation has embittered the brightest daring year within my memory and has perhaps cast a shade over my whole life. I must go quietly on with my irksome duties and seem calm while the canker is eating deep within … when I look to the light hearted hours of 1826 they seem to have been too bright for earth – now have changed – this beautiful, this blessed day must be gone through mechanically with the forced smile of the agony upon my fevered brow … I am only fit for dreaming now.

In a last dramatic gesture as she was about to leave for Brighton, she attempted to pluck the white rose. It snapped and fell 'turned downwards to the earth alone, exposed for the next hasty footsteps to crush and destroy it'.

Sadly she did not realize that she was not the only teenager to feel that her hopes and dreams were, like the rose, crushed, even though not all adolescents would have quoted Southey in the process. Her tendency towards introversion and dramatization had been intensified by the Pegus's and O'Briens' hesitancy about whether the families were or were not suited to each other. On balance it was decided that they were not. Lady Charlotte's mother declared that 'the name of O'Brien has been a curse to me', the families quarrelled and Augustus was promised to a young girl who was not yet twelve. Lady Charlotte, who would never forget the white rose, declared that 'the whole object and end of my life is withdrawn'.

Yet if her family were concerned about her feelings for young O'Brien they were even more disturbed by the attraction they detected within their own home. On 22 May 1827 Lady Charlotte had recorded 'At 1 o'clock Mr Martin came.' Frederick Martin was the new Latin tutor. Originally from Liverpool, Martin was now in his mid-twenties, intellectually inclined and fascinated by genealogy (in the mid-1840s he was to publish two volumes on the subject). At this point Augustus was centre of Lady Charlotte's attention so although she appreciated the tutor's learning she did not say very much about him. As the boys were destined for Eton he did not stay long and ironically moved to Blatherwycke Hall to tutor the O'Brien children. Unfortunately public school was not a success for the Berties. Lindsey was bullied, locked in a desk and on one occasion forced to drink tobacco and water. He was quickly removed and Mr Martin returned. Unlike everybody else, he seemed to appreciate Lady Charlotte. He recognized her intelligence and encouraged her studies. Through him she learned 'how extremely disgraceful was the state of my ignorance'. He provided her with inaccessible books such as Sir William Jones's *Persian Grammar*, obtained Southey's autograph for her and it was he who introduced her to Virgil and Sir Walter Scott. He was in short, 'the very best friend I ever had', a real compliment from a young woman whose only friends were illustrious authors. Fact and fiction once more became blurred. Martin was like a figure from Scott's *Guy Mannering*, a 'full, thin, kind-tempered man in black who used to teach me my letters and walk out with me'. He talked of Cambridge, showed her 'where to find fresh objects of admiration in literature and sources of information which, however essential, had never been guessed at'.

Impressionable and prone to hero worship, she soon aroused suspicions amongst her family. At a time when a network of espionage permeated political society to an unprecedented degree, Lady Charlotte felt that she too was being spied upon: 'How cruel to be so watched in every word and action and look.' As a result she drew even closer to Martin, 'This continued espionage is so base, so unworthy... to me disagreeably revolting.' Not understanding that her swings of temperament were typical for a young woman of her age and only too aware of her brother's state of mind, she began worrying about her own sanity, intellectualized some of her fears and intensified the teenage tendency towards self-absorption. The darker side of the romantic spirit came to the fore with all its 'picturesque falsehood'. In 1831 her creative imagination combined with her fears and the journal became punctuated with references to madness – 'have been very mad this last week' and 'I feel often insane – the state of doubt and perplexity is intolerable'.

Lady Charlotte had no close girl friends – she liked the O'Brien sisters Emma and Angelina but they were soon pronounced *personae non gratis* and she could not confide easily in her mother. She once wrote, 'My great ill luck has been that I have never had a friend.' Her books and literary heroes offered no clue to coping with her emotions. To make matters worse she suffered frequent head-aches which today would be diagnosed as migraines. She did not know that there was a direct relationship between them and the frequent bouts of depression she experienced. For a time she also suffered from a nervous disease, a skin complaint called erysipelas or St Anthony's fire (because of the red blotches it caused) and she had to have her head shaved, take daily baths and don spectacles.

As her feelings for Martin intensified and she became further alienated from her family, so the journal suggests an impending crisis. By July 1831 she was writing 'How will all this sad thing end – this is the crisis and something should be done.' Her prose no longer flows so easily and there are increasingly euphemistic refer-ences such as a 'deceitful, hastily assumed smile'. She describes herself as 'shattered in mind and body by anxiety; and illness and writing under the influence of very strong passions – too carefully concealed'. The full force of family displeasure was vented at the slightest sign of any intimacy between Lady Charlotte and the tutor, and her uncle, the Rector, accused her of attempting to engage Martin's affec-tions. On hearing about this, Lady Charlotte rushed out to the second avenue: 'The wind was high, I cared not for my anger boiled.' Martin became elevated into the wronged hero and she pledged never to give him up. Pegus more and more assumed the role of the classic wicked stepfather.

The cryptic entries in the journal and the fact that some lines were later erased by heavy black ink make it impossible to know exactly what took place in these months. Her guilty discovery of her own burgeoning sexuality and what she called 'my own personal wickedness' made the journal a receptacle for her confused outpourings. Her pride forced her to 'assume an air of indifference' whenever possible which only enhanced the contrast between her apparent composure and her intense emotions. The diary of Lady Charlotte's half-sister, Mary, during this time records the family at prayer – but without Charlotte. Mary's diary suggests a far more harmonious picture than Lady Charlotte ever portrayed but Pegus was her father and Mary a placid, gentle girl who simply saw Mr Martin as the tutor. Lady Charlotte in contrast was a dreamer who tended to depict people as all good or bad. Pegus, once the 'noble-hearted', was now blocking any hopes of happiness with Martin, and presented as frequently intoxicated and rude to Lindsey. Despite his profession, piety does seem to have been in short supply. When Lady Charlotte made her first communion he was indulging in his favourite sport, grouse shooting in the Fens. Monty later added, 'He was an awful sinner really'.

Lady Charlotte's intense emotions were also linked to the pressures of living with Lindsey. He was a sorry figure whose chief delight seemed to be scraping away on his fiddle 'in such a style as nearly to induce toothache'. When Martin's saint-like patience gave way to ill-health, Lady Charlotte offered herself as Lindsey's instructor in an act of self-sacrifice. She felt that the honour of the family depended on him. Turning lessons into instructive games she tried hard to awaken some interest in her pupil, but it was eight months of torture for her. Her propensity for hyperbolic language led to analogies with slavery and her 'sad thraldom' was exacerbated by the knowledge that Lindsey did not really like her. Many daughters acted as unpaid governesses to their younger relatives but poor Lindsey was no ordinary relative.

The full extent of his simplicity will never be clear. Monty remembered him as a hopeless case, 'a poor imbecile who had to be watched and treated like a baby' but by that time his uncle had probably deteriorated considerably. Lady Charlotte could know little about theories of mental health, though like many of her voyeuristic generation she had visited the unfortunates at Bedlam. Here she saw another example of a family split like her own. Jonathan Martin the incendiary of York Minster was there: 'I was told that he continues his ranting and the sad idea of his being a prophet.' She was struck by the contrast between him and his talented brother the artist John Martin, whose idea of 'The Hollow Deep of Hell' was not a lunatic's cell but brilliant illustrations for Milton's *Paradise Lost*.

The visits to Uffington from Dr Francis Willis of Greatford were probably not merely social calls. He ran a lunatic asylum at nearby Shillingthorpe and had been one of George III's consultants. There was nevertheless some attempt (if only pretence) to give the Earl an education despite the 'glaring wildness and awful smile'. It is somewhat ironic to read of Charlotte desperately trying to get her brother to parse Horace whilst her own academic education was largely dependent on her own devices to improve herself.

Lord Lindsey's problems did not pass unnoticed in the local community. Lady Charlotte recalls how he went missing one night. For once this succeeded in bringing together the warring factions of the manor and church and Pegus and Layard set off in search of him. For a time a Miss Posnett (whom Charlotte suspected of giving her brother a 'taint of duplicity') had been encouraging this titled minor at dances. Lindsey was discovered with her. A scene had taken place which adds a new veracity to Wilkie Collins and popular romantic fiction. After encouraging Lindsey to drink (but not eat), a mock marriage ceremony had been enacted, encouraged by the O'Brien family. Somebody had donned a white sheet and read the marriage service as a hiccoughing Lindsey gazed into Miss Posnett's eyes. Pegus had great difficulty in persuading him to return home.

Yet Pegus soon entered into his own intrigues about Lindsey's future. His dreams of marrying into money had been thwarted, partly by the fraudulence of a lawyer handling the Ninth Earl's affairs. As Lindsey's majority drew nearer so Pegus attempted to secure a better future. A scheme was devised to marry him to a rich heiress worth £400,000 a year. The plan collapsed once the prospective father-in-law set eyes on Lindsey. Worse was to follow. Lady Charlotte, who had accompanied her stepfather and brother to London, was drawn into a plan which horrified her. The men visited a woman who had formerly been the mistress of Sir Keith Jackson (an acquaintance of Pegus's). After a trip to the opera with this woman, Pegus proposed that Lindsey accompany her to Brighton for a fortnight. The mock marriage incident had already resulted in Charlotte's mother being appointed Lindsey's sole guardian and the twenty-year-old Lady Charlotte now tried in vain to persuade Pegus to await his wife's permission. Pegus was however determined to see through this liaison between Lindsey and 'a woman of no character or principles'. The idea of '… such an acquaintance for a boy of Lindsey's mind distressed me … I was most difficultly and delicately placed; it was a case of which no girl of my age and of my happy inexperience could be supposed capable of giving an opinion and most distressing was it to me to do so: my mind was in a dreadful state.'

In desperation she appealed to the Lord Chancellor who was already aware of some of the family's problems. A secret meeting was arranged with the aid of a servant delivering messages and Lady Charlotte found herself in a private interview with Lord Brougham. He told her that he very much approved of her conduct. She had acted 'very wisely, and judiciously …'. Pegus was forced to cancel the trip to Brighton, his wife took her daughter's side and Lady Charlotte experienced a nightmare journey back to Uffington with an enraged Pegus who spoke his mind: 'It was horrible to hear. I heard so much that I was but more thankful that my brother was rescued.' In future any attempt to remove Lindsey without his mother's permission would necessitate applying to the Lord Chancellor. Pegus became more determined than ever to remove Lindsey from the protection of Martin and at the same time prevent his stepdaughter from fulfilling any foolish plans she might have hatched with the tutor.

Some of the high drama of the journal in the early 1830s can be explained by its writer's fears not just about losing Martin but also being sacrificed to some highly unsuitable husband. After the episode with Lindsey and the heiress Lady Charlotte dreaded what plot might be being hatched for her: 'they would next amuse themselves with some horrible plan for me'. As Lindsey got closer to twenty-one, her fears for the future increased. She was now 'Disliking the present, not daring to look upon the past and already dreading deeply the future.' Since the age of fifteen there had been veiled references to various gentlemen who had been 'laid out' for her as suitors. In September 1832, thanks to some scheming by her mother, a sprightly sixty-seven-year-old appeared on the scene. Robert Plumer Ward was a politician and novelist already twice widowed. He proposed to Charlotte. Her fear of being sacrificed only increased her feelings for Martin but he was about to be sent away from Uffington for good. Her own mother had married a man over sixty. Lady Charlotte believed that 'my morning of life is over – twenty summers have changed me … I know all is passed for me'. Later she recalled how Plumer Ward was the cause of so much misery to me'. She refused to marry him.

On a visit to Westminster Abbey with Bertie and Martin, she had found the tomb of 'my own Chaucer who has written such commentaries on my own inconstant heart.' This was one of the moments she cherished. She was close to Martin and 'as we paused a moment my hand was detained'. Yet she knew that her family were implacably opposed to him and the hopelessness of a future with him was perhaps confirmed by a trip to the north of England (recorded by Mary) where Charlotte saw in Liverpool 'the wretched small house in which poor Martin's father used to live'. Prophetically Lady Charlotte copied out a translation from an Arabic inscription: 'thy love for thine own land is a manifest weakness; go abroad that thou mayst find a change of men; water becomes putrid by stagnation; the moon by changing becomes bright and perfect'. On 30 April 1833, a few weeks before her twenty-first birthday, Lady Charlotte left Uffington for London and there she met her future husband.

Lady Charlotte later burned her journal entries for the period between late September 1832 and May 1833, fearing that they might cause pain to those who read them. Some of the events can however be pieced together from her later references and from Mary's diary. When Lady Charlotte packed her books for London her spirits must have been especially low with the prospect of a season ahead, living in Eaton Square with a family for whom she retained little respect. Once there, however, her life was to assume one of the many dramatic shifts which she would experience over the years. The first notable event was a meeting with Benjamin Disraeli. Lady Charlotte's cousin, Henry Layard, who knew him well described him at this time, wearing 'waistcoats of the most gorgeous colours and the most fantastic patterns with much gold embroidery, velvet pantaloons and shoes adorned with red rosettes … his black hair pomatumed and elaborately curled and his person redolent with perfume'.

On 18 May Lady Sykes invited Disraeli and Lady Charlotte to the opera – 'He and I soon got acquainted. We talked about several things. He is wild, enthusiastic and very poetical.' At this stage he was a romantic young writer and traveller with some leanings towards radicalism. He was trying to get into Parliament.

> His Contarini Fleming was written in Egypt – He knew Ibrahim Pasha and gave me anecdotes of him. He told me he thought Southey the greatest man of the age … The brilliancy of my companion infected me and we ran on about poetry and Venice and Baghdad and Damascus and my eye lit up and my cheek burned and in the pause of the beautiful music (Tancredi) my words flowed almost as rapidly as his … With all his enthusiasm and contradictions he pleased me and we were very good friends I think.

They were. Two days later Disraeli bought flowers for Lady Charlotte and, accompanied by Lady Sykes, they attended a morning concert. Lady Charlotte's old enthusiasm had returned. She confessed to never before having liked the violin (hardly surprising given Lindsey's renderings). Mr Disraeli had 'less of eccentricity than on Saturday'. She wondered whether he had then thought '… by his brilliancy to take my imagination by storm. I liked him better today – we agree on very many points and his details interest me. If I had time I would put down much of his conversation – His admiration for Southey and Hallam both of whom he knows well personally, would redeem a great many sins. He is a follower of Beethoven in taste though not musical. I learnt from him that he is preparing a new Oriental story placed in remote times in Syria.'

Many of Disraeli's observations were culled from closer quarters. In the opening pages of *Sybil* (1845) there is a reference to 'waltzing with the little Bertie' at an assembly at Lady St Julian's, whilst in the same novel Lady Joan Fitz-Warene is described as: 'certainly not beautiful; nobody would consider her beautiful … and yet she had a look, when … she was more than beautiful. But she was very clever, very clever indeed, something quite extraordinary … languages and learned books; Arabic and Hebrew, and old manuscripts.'

Having recently had his proposal of marriage rejected by Ellen Meredith, Disraeli wrote to his elder sister, Sarah, two days after his second meeting with Lady Charlotte. 'By the bye would you like Lady Z – for a sister-in-law, very clever, 25000L and domestic? As for "love" all my friends who married for love and beauty either beat their wives or live apart from them. This is literally the case. I may commit many follies in life, I never intend to marry for "love", which I am sure, is a guarantee of infelicity.'

Still hoping that Ellen would change her mind, Sarah (who had heard rumours about Plumer Ward and knew of Lindsey) was not impressed by Lady Charlotte. She correctly expressed doubts about the reputed fortune and reminded her

brother of the 'improvident blood' that 'more than half fills her veins'. By the
summer of 1833 Disraeli was having an affair with the chaperone, the married
Henrietta Sykes.

There were, however, to be a few curious twists to this story. In 1839 Disraeli
did finally marry. His wife was the older and widowed Mrs Wyndham Lewis.
Her first husband had been a grandson of one of the founders of an ironworks
at Dowlais in South Wales. Wyndham Lewis's partner (who actually ran the large
works) was Josiah John Guest. Coincidentally it was this same Mrs Wyndham
Lewis who first introduced Lady Charlotte to her future husband at one of her
London dinner parties on 17 June 1833. Many years later she was also to introduce Lady Charlotte's eldest son Ivor to his future wife, Lady Cornelia Churchill,
and it was Disraeli who was to recommend Ivor for a Peerage.

After the atmosphere of intrigue and real or imagined conspiracy at Uffington,
the meeting with a practical, middle-aged iron manufacturer must have seemed
almost providential. John Guest had come to London to take his seat in the
House of Commons as Merthyr Tydfil's first MP after the reform agitation which
Lady Charlotte had so keenly followed. Lady Charlotte was never one to pay
much attention to physical descriptions of people and had not been encouraged
to see herself as a beautiful or even attractive young woman. Whereas others
would see her as slim, with thick black hair and very large, expressive eyes, she
could only recognize her short sightedness and lack of inner poise. Yet Disraeli
had paid attention to her and now the curly haired John Guest, acknowledged
to be handsome, was giving her many compliments. Although the widowed
Mr Guest was forty-eight, in comparison with Plumer Ward the age difference
hardly seemed to matter. Most importantly, John Guest was not associated with
Uffington and represented a real and independent escape from a world in which
as eldest daughter she had faced responsibility without real power and learning
without most people's appreciation. The wealthy iron manufacturer was, like herself a slightly hesitant outsider in titled London Society. Lady Charlotte's mother
was somewhat worried about the connection with trade[3] though Pegus probably felt adequately compensated by the tales of fabulous wealth surrounding the
Dowlais ironmaster.

The young and innocent Mary provides a few details of the courtship. Her
journal for June and July refers frequently to Mr Guest. Before long he was
endearing himself to Mary by giving her a toy and Elizabeth a purse. There were
trips with him to the Botanical Gardens and frequent carriage rides. Mr Guest
came to dinner regularly, he accompanied Charlotte to church and by 22 July
Mamma had decided to postpone the return to Uffington. On 12 July John had
proposed to Charlotte in Kensington Gardens.[4]

Years later Monty found some pages torn out of an old notebook of his
mother's. Written on 16 July they alluded to a final clandestine meeting with
Martin, whom her parents had forbidden her to see. 'What then of today's excitement! I go in one hour to see you for the last time before my marriage to another.

I go in purity of heart – in gratitude – to you whom I look upon (as I always must) as my best and kindest friend – after my husband – God bless you as he has blessed me.'

Unfortunately Martin did not seem to be blessed. The years following his abrupt departure from Uffington were extremely unhappy ones and, try as she might, Lady Charlotte could not easily exorcize the sense of guilt which clung to her. She feared that she had ruined his career and his happiness. He made attempts to enter the Church but this did not prove easy despite Lady Charlotte's efforts to help. By the 1840s he seemed 'broken and changed' and 'quite unfit for any of the serious business of Life'. She never forgot the tutor who became 'the wreck of the bright hopes of former days'.

Meanwhile, on 29 July 1833, Lady Charlotte Bertie and John Guest were married by the Bishop of Gloucester at St George's, Hanover Square, the fashionable church where the Countess of Lindsey had married the Reverend Pegus in the 1820s. Even on her wedding day, Lady Charlotte puzzled her mother: 'Poor Mamma drew me aside alone and asked me if I were not now very happy. It is a peculiarity of mine never to like to be asked this question, and it is in human nature never to acknowledge happiness, but rather to complain. I answered waywardly, "No, not particularly. Much as usual." Seeing however, that she took this in a literal sense I was forced, ere I said good-bye, to assure her that all was well ...'

Uffington celebrated with a ball and an ox roast. The Guests honeymooned in Sussex and, whilst travelling, Lady Charlotte began to learn about the vast Welsh ironworks and community at Dowlais near Merthyr. This must have seemed as remote as Damascus to the young English lady who had never seen mountains, let alone the raw industrial settlements of South Wales.

Part 2

LADY CHARLOTTE GUEST

2

The Wife and Mother

*'And behold I have settled down into a quiet unambitious wife and mother
– But the old fires are not quite extinct and they will blaze up for a moment
or smoulder rather painfully sometimes.'*

Lady Charlotte's timing was impeccable. She was not the only one to be experiencing a 'New World' of tumultuous change. The rapid growth of the iron trade transformed rural hamlets into densely populated industrial communities whilst the Guest family itself was an object lesson in how, within a couple of generations, a family's fortunes could be realized.

Josiah John Guest's grandfather, John Guest, was 'a plain homely man', a small freeholder brewer and coal dealer who, in about 1758, left his native Shropshire and rode on horseback over the mountains to Wales.[1] He helped start a furnace at the Plymouth works at Merthyr and in 1767 took over the management of a new venture at nearby Dowlais, perched high on Gwernllwyn hill at the northern end of the parish of Merthyr Tydfil. He built himself a house near Dowlais, his son Thomas succeeded him at the works and in turn, his grandson, Lady Charlotte's husband. John Guest had been born on 2 February 1785. His mother (Jemima Revel, née Phillips from Shifnal, Shropshire) had worried about him making a living but, as an old carpenter told Lady Charlotte, she was mistaken 'for he has got his bread and cheese pretty well in this world'. For a time he stayed with an uncle in Shropshire attending Bridgenorth Grammar School but he took over the works after his father's death in 1807.

By the time of his marriage to Lady Charlotte the Dowlais Iron Company was poised to become the largest ironworks in the world. It was one of four major ironworks in the district. The Company's historian has compared the establishment of Dowlais, Cyfarthfa (owned by the Crawshay family), Plymouth (Anthony Hill), and Penydarren (Thompson and Forman) to the rise of the oil industry in Texas. Together this 'capital of the iron and coal' produced 40 per cent of British pig iron.

Merthyr was simultaneously a symbol of the achievements and atrocities of industrialization. The local historian Charles Wilkins called it 'the great realm of Cyclops which would have appalled even tribal Cain'. A future Company Trustee declared that 'no one lived there by choice'. Yet for Lady Charlotte, 'long buffetted by storm and sorrows', her new home by the works – a recently built Georgian house with a columned portico – must have seemed like a dream existence. Its novelty made it a source of delight and romance. Up above the narrow Taff Fechan (little Taff) valley stood the remains of thirteenth-century Morlais Castle from which Ifor Bach had attacked Cardiff Castle. Her eldest son was named after him and another son christened Merthyr (which she henceforth called her husband). Her relatives were less captured by the surroundings, Lady Lindsey fearing that they were 'wild enough for banditti'. Mary pronounced Dowlais 'a very odd looking place as are all bits hereabouts' and allowed herself a few uncharacteristically dramatic lines about the 'gushing smoke and whizzing, curling steam. Its wild bursting glares, its million wheels rushing round with their everlasting roar, and its cinder capped mountains.'

Influenced by Rousseau and Romance and deterred from touring Europe by the Napoleonic Wars, travellers were mesmerized by the awful grandeur of 'these regions of smoke'. A member of the King of Saxony's entourage echoed writers and artists when he declared of Dowlais that 'one could easily have believed oneself transferred to the blazing city of Dis, mentioned by Dante!' *The Morning Chronicle* agreed: 'The scene powerfully affects the imagination, for it has vastness, suggestiveness and mystery. Dante might have borrowed hints from it – Martin alone could paint it.' Lady Charlotte's acquaintance John Martin whose illustration for *Paradise Lost* had so captured the imagination, had indeed been there.

Lady Charlotte saw her new surroundings as part of the artist's canvas. On her first walk into the works, 'In the glare of the fires (from a little distance) the workmen formed groups which might yield fine studies for the painter'. Her sentimentalization was preferable to the language used by many visitors. George Borrow was not alone in referring to 'throngs of savage-looking people' and when Bishop Sumner consecrated St John's Anglican church in 1827 (for which Guest paid £3,000) he told the first incumbent, the Rev. Evan Jenkins that in this 'heathen' (Nonconformist) community he was 'as a missionary in the heart of Africa'. For Lady Charlotte this was to become 'Dear Wales! How tame every place is after such loveliness and grandeur.'

For an Earl's daughter, the ironmasters must have seemed almost as strange a breed as the workers. Acutely aware of the intricacies of rank Lady Charlotte cast a critical eye over them: 'Mr Anthony Hill is a gentleman – Mr Bailey has a low born purse proud cunning – Mr Thompson is the Alderman in every sense, and has not the uprightness which I should be inclined to give most City Merchants credit for – the Harfords are Quakers of rather an American stamp.' As for the head of the Crawshay 'dynasty', William II, he was 'beyond all rule and description and is quite one of those meteoric beings whom it is quite impossible to account for'. He drove his family to church in a coach and four with liveried coachman. His equally ostentatious son, Robert, lived in 'splendid misery' at Cyfarthfa Castle, Merthyr (built by the family for £30,000) and boasting fifteen towers, battlements and seventy-two rooms. Lady Charlotte had more in common with his young wife, Rose Mary from Caversham, near Reading. Well-read and highly intelligent, in later years she became the first woman on Merthyr's School Board, a Suffragist and promoter of literature. In the mid-1840s however, she was a shy young bride of eighteen and not real company for Lady Charlotte. Considering the ironmasters as a whole, Lady Charlotte found herself '… far from disposed to be pleased with them and am glad there is but little occasion for mixing in their society'.

At the same time Society associated the Guests with ironmaking. That observer of social niceties Lady Greville saw trade as a 'disgrace', placing its votaries 'beyond the pale of Society'. Lady Charlotte understood and deplored this:

> Though my husband is peculiarly formed to shine and rise, and is infinitely more eloquent than half the lordlings that I meet, and though I have my own rank which is high enough to assist me, the consciousness frequently obtrudes itself that in this aristocratic nation the word Trade conveys a taint. I am determined to overcome the prejudice, I will force them, whether or no to disguise, if they do not forget its existence in my case. For myself I care not … But the children shall never feel that there live any on the earth, who do or who dare look down upon them, and their own feelings on this head will go far in giving the tone to those of others towards them.

Nevertheless there were occasions when she found herself recoiling from some of the less desirable manufacturing parvenus. Encountering one Staffordshire iron-master on a train, she declared him 'not of the first refinement – Such a specimen! No wonder there exists such a horror of everything connected with trade, as far as Society is concerned'. Ironmasters at this time needed to be skilled, practical men and whilst Guest's background exemplified the virtues of self-help soon to be extolled by Samuel Smiles, the 'top drawer' of Society remained cautious, particularly since he possessed some disqualifications.

His father had been a Wesleyan lay preacher – though interestingly John became an Anglican. His first wife, Maria Ranken, had been Irish. Early industrial Britain displayed distinctly xenophobic tendencies with the Irish becoming convenient scapegoats for many problems. Nor would John's Welshness have enhanced his image outside Wales, particularly since, after his mother's early death, he was looked after by a nurse known as 'Mari Aberteifi' and a turkey breeder.

Marriage to Lady Charlotte, more or less coinciding with a new Parliamentary career, represented a significant juncture in John's fortunes. Although increasingly impoverished, Lady Charlotte's family had standing based on time-honoured rank. Lady Holland (who was unsuccessfully enlisted in support of Frederick Martin's career) wrote to her son: 'I have got acquainted with a very remarkably clever, distinguished woman, reckoned by many extremely handsome, Ly C. Guest, nobly born, married to an immensely rich man, who wanted what the Spaniards call *Sangre Azul*, and gave her wealth which she wanted. They seem perfectly happy; his riches are in Wales … Did they ever fall in your beat?'

With his wife by his side, John began to move in high circles. The Queen was sponsor for their son Montague's christening and in 1838 John was offered a Baronetcy. Lady Charlotte was not sufficiently impressed: 'my dear Merthyr was elevated (if so I must call it) to the rank of Baronet. I consider it a paltry distinction and was much averse to his taking it but he liked to secure something which would descend to Ivor.' Her aspirations were premature. The only industrial Peer with a comparable background was Edward Strutt who became Baron Belper in 1856 after John had died.

Yet John Guest left £500,000 in his will and a vast country estate in Dorset. He had recognized the need to found a dynasty by more subtle means than Crawshay, the rich man in his castle. Successive generations of Guests consolidated the family's credibility. In 1880 the eldest son, Ivor, was created Baron Wimborne. He married into the Marlborough family and owned over 80,000 acres of land in Dorset, Wales and Scotland. The Canford-based family got a Viscountcy in 1918. Other members of the family made 'good' marriages too.★

Yet if marriage to Lady Charlotte gave John a new footing and added some cachet to his constituency (Merthyr newspapers reported on the glittering London events graced by the Guests), what did she gain from her new husband? Added to a fortune (one wedding anniversary present was the Empress Josephine's ear-rings) was a new peace of mind. After years of passionate sobbing, the somewhat contrary Charlotte did not shed a single tear at her wedding. With new-found confidence she could now exclaim: 'I am ambitious ... I have youth and riches and rank and beauty – yes – even beauty –They say so now even of me who used to be so differently considered in that respect ... I who were as nothing and worse than nothing once now have all these advantages and is it not enough to make me ambitious?'

Even her relationship to her journal altered (at least for a time), 'For not now as in the winter can I say that the only friend I had to confide in was my journal. Now every care and every joy, every sorrow and every delight is shared and sympathized with.' At times it almost seemed too good to be true: 'Sometimes I fear I am too happy; the contrast with the old days is so very striking, I almost tremble lest it should not last' but for the time being she was '... with Merthyr and loved to feel that I could be his companion as well as his wife'.

Yet there was a slight catch. If John was not the obvious choice of husband for a daughter of almost impeccable lineage, neither was Lady Charlotte fully prepared to play the part of the conventional wife. She did try. She interspersed her reading with books such as Mrs Ellis's *Wives of England* (a present from her husband). This contained some disturbing passages. Mrs Ellis warned that where there had been great advantages of wealth or station on the wife's side or 'in the ease of a highly gifted woman, even where there is an equal or superior degree of talent possessed by her husband, nothing can be more injudicious or more fatal to her happiness than an exhibition even of the least disposition to presume upon such gifts ...'. How could this be squared with her ambitions?

★ See Appendix 2.

... even I, a woman, and under peculiar disadvantages – have dreamed that I might have achieved something worth remembering – From a child the idea has haunted me, and even now, that I feel my path lies only among the quiet duties of domestic life, I sometimes start with a flush of emulation when I hear and see what has been done by others and what I once hoped I had strength and energy to have at least equalled myself – It was a vain dream, but it is hard to discard it – the langour of delicate health unites with my position to crush the aspiring (hopes) – Yet sometimes a flash of the old fire will sparke for a moment spite of all my reason and circumstances can do to extinguish it.

Such feelings had somehow to be reconciled with her desire to be a good and dutiful wife. She did, after all, seek to excel in whatever she undertook. Yet no wife, especially one like Lady Charlotte, could hope to fulfil all the demands of the advice manuals all of the time. Too much had to be sublimated. Mrs Ellis stressed self-effacement, duty and sacrifice. She warned that a woman's 'real existence only begins when she has a husband'. Yet married women found in practice that this was precisely where their independent existence ended. The noted jurist Blackstone had declared that 'the very being or legal existence of the woman is suspended during marriage'. In those days wives could not own property, make contracts, sue or be sued. The Victorian feminist Barbara Leigh Bodichon put it succinctly: 'In short, a woman is courted and wedded as an angel, and yet denied the dignity of a rational and moral being ever after.' After Sir John's death his lawyer wrote to Lady Charlotte about the valuation of his estate adding, 'I can by no means guarantee that the office will not consider your jewels and ornaments Sir John's property for this purpose.' Men had power, women influence. The woman's qualities were seen to complement the aggressive, masculine qualities of their husband's public world. As one magazine put it, 'Home is a woman's proper sphere and the performance of home duties her chief and peculiar mission.'

Even the privileged Lady Charlotte dreaded (quite apart from personal loss) the implications of losing John – 'a breath could destroy all; for with me everything hangs upon one hope, one blessing, one husband'. *The Saturday Review* explained that 'Married life is woman's profession ... by not getting a husband, or losing him, she may find that she is without resources. All that can be said of her is, she had failed in business and no social reformer can prevent such failures.' When Lady Charlotte's imagined fears were materialized into justified concern for John's health, she saw herself facing more than the loss of the person she loved. Her influence was also threatened since, despite submerging her separate identity through marriage, marital status also gave her greater credibility and influence than she could possess on her own.

Although radiantly happy as a new wife, Lady Charlotte's journal nevertheless betrays a tension between her naturally impulsive, independent and creative self and the need to conform as a loyal, Christian wife of an eminent manufacturer.

As the novelty of marriage receded, as she matured and found outlets for not inconsiderable talents, so it became increasingly difficult to sustain an equanimity.

Lady Charlotte read Hannah More's *Coelebs in Search of a Wife* (two volumes published in 1809). Here was a model of an evangelical household. The hero's wife had to be elegant, sensible, prudent and informed as well as well-bred, consistent and pious. All these qualities helped her as 'directress for his family, a preceptress for his children, and a companion for himself'. Charlotte Guest could see beyond such prescriptions (and possessive pronouns) whilst still paying lip service to them. Her own upbringing had queried the meaning of the happy family and she did not intend to become like her own mother. Intellectually she was challenged and depressed by woman's lot. Through her journal some of the contradictions were aired. In a passage reflecting her reading of *Coelebs* she revealed her ambivalences, particularly through her use of caveats and parenthesis:

> How deeply I have felt this inferiority of sex and how humiliated I am when it is recalled to my mind in allusion to myself! Knowing that most wives are but looked upon as nurses and housekeepers (very justly too) I have striven hard to place myself on a higher level – and dear Merthyr, who knows how sensitive I am on this point and who really does think that some women are rational beings – has always aided and encouraged me – I have given myself almost a man's education from the age of twelve when I first began to follow my own devices – and since I married I have taken up such pursuits as in this country of business and ironmaking would render me conversant with what occupied the male part of the population – Sometimes I think I have succeeded pretty well – but every now and then I am painfully reminded that toil as I may, I can never succeed beyond a certain point and by a very large portion of the community my acquirements and judgements must always be looked upon as those of a mere woman.

This particular analysis was prompted by a difficult exchange with John. She had asked his opinion about an idea she had and he had replied, half in jest and half seriously, that he would never seek his wife's view on such a subject. Characteristically she agreed and laughed 'Yet the words he had spoken sank deeply into my heart and clouded all that evening.' When he occasionally kept matters from her – such as a rumour of machine-breaking – she was hurt, 'I did not think he gave me credit for such a weak mind as to tremble at a shadow; nor do I know why I should be more frightened at a mere report than himself.'

She found it difficult to fit into any pre-defined slot or to follow only one pursuit. She felt herself to be somewhat apart, not just from the crowd but even from many women of her own class. Sometimes she delighted in being differ-ent and daring. On an expedition to see a viaduct she found that there was too much scrambling involved for some of the ladies, 'I believe I was the first female that ever crossed this bridge and at the height of some seventy or eighty feet it appeared a perilous undertaking.' It is tempting to ask what the visiting ladies and ironmasters' wives made of this. The following day the party rode out again. 'The scenery was suited to the wild and somewhat pensive mood which I was in', so she left the group and rode off 'singing my Welsh airs'. At Uffington she had shocked Lady Carbery by riding with a gentleman: such 'scruples surprised and almost made me laugh', and she persuaded Mary's husband to give her rifle-shooting lessons. At a time when even the home was divided into masculine and feminine space Lady Charlotte cheerfully breached the areas which were seen as male preserves. In her youth she had acquired a penchant for billiards and continued to play for many years. The library was a predominantly masculine haunt in many homes but this was where Lady Charlotte was most often to be found, 'I have been very happy there more so than in any other spot upon earth.'

Thanks to her birth and acquired wealth Lady Charlotte could at least enjoy a qualified freedom which exceeded that of most contemporary women. Many would have understood her sentiments yet been more hidebound by circumstances than herself: 'The spirit will rebel sometimes against this uselessness – and when I venture to tell what I feel to Merthyr he chides me for it. Indeed it is almost the only thing that has power to vex him with me yet I cannot help the emotion – I see every day men, even though not encouraged, and though perhaps uneducated, I see men planning and carrying through enterprises – their minds have scope and they have field for action.'

Her cousin the explorer Henry Layard described her as '... an extraordinary woman and her character a remarkable one – in some respects resembling Mme de Staël in the union of feminine and masculine qualities'.

There were moments when Lady Charlotte felt especially despondent. In November 1840 she wrote, 'I have learned that there is but one answer to the question I have so often asked myself "What can a woman do?" "Nothing"! Yet that nothing conspires that she can love and be happy and perhaps she ought not to wish for more, but leave all higher aspirings to those whom she feels to be painfully her superior in mind (not in heart) both by nature and education.'

Yet she never quite convinced herself with such contrite comments and continued to worry at the problem. Reasoning from within the parameters of a notion of separate spheres it is hardly surprising that she could not come to a satisfactory conclusion and so could sometimes claim to be 'quite careless of all but matters of domestic solicitude' or state that 'to remain in quiet and undisturbed pursuance of my duties is now my only wish'. The timing of such sentiments is, however, significant. They almost invariably followed a particularly active period of literary or business activity and were at the same time one way of adjusting to the fact that she was about to produce yet another child.

One of the ironies of the Victorian wife's position is that at the same time as she was portrayed as weak and fragile, obedient rather than commanding, she was also expected to bear a number of babies and spend many years surrounded by dependants. Lady Charlotte had ten children in thirteen years. 1760-1850 was the period of the greatest fertility in the history of the English aristocracy. A study of fifty women aristocrats of this time, including Lady Charlotte, shows that the pattern was for such women to marry at twenty-one and have about eight children, giving birth to the last child when thirty-nine. Nearly half had their first child within a year of marriage. Lady Charlotte had five boys and five girls. Mary had fourteen children, also equally divided by sex, though not all survived. Lady Charlotte also had a miscarriage between her second and third child. For much of her marriage, especially in the early years, she was pregnant (for roughly ninety months in all) and there were only eleven months between the births of her first and second babies and gaps of twelve and thirteen months in the case of four of the others. Whilst this was not particularly remarkable then,[2] the circumstances were unusual since her pregnancies more or less coincided with the production of her literary masterpieces.

In the early nineteenth century pregnancy and childbirth were especially hazardous. Despite the advantages of servants, nurses, youth and the care of her husband, Lady Charlotte was in a vulnerable position. John's first wife had died in childbirth, Merthyr had no hospital and not until Queen Victoria's use of chloroform for anaesthesia in the 1850s did this become generally acceptable. Quite apart from personal danger, the number of deaths among children under five in Merthyr was way above the national average. Though cushioned, the Guests were not immune. Asiatic cholera had already reached Britain and Merthyr was to have more than its share of cholera victims. The house was not in isolated splendour and problems in breast-feeding necessitated using local girls as wet nurses.[3] The Guests did have the option to move elsewhere but Lady Charlotte was keen, if at all possible, for her babies to be born in Wales. She shocked her own mother when planning to have her second child at Dowlais. Mamma's timidity made her wonder whether 'I ought to be frightened at having country medical advice' but it could not actually dissuade her. When about to have her fifth baby she wrote, 'It is a trial that my child should not be born in Wales. Besides I am always happier there than in any other place in the world.' Most of her children were born at Dowlais and all christened there. When Ivor was born the workers had a day off.

Lady Charlotte's first child, Maria, was born on 3 July 1834. She recorded in her journal (writing it up three weeks later from daily pencil notes) that she had 'suffered about as little as possible'. She had expected to spend time writing with John in the library but 'in this world our intentions (even the very best) are sometimes foiled ... at two my dear child was born. I was soon pretty well.' Merthyr's birth was even easier. After a walk and long before the doctor arrived, 'I was confined of my fourth child, I may say almost without pain ... my suffering was so very slight that it seemed to me perfectly miraculous'. According to her journal she finished her night's rest 'as if nothing had happened' and it was the nurse who was ill. Yet this should be seen alongside her determination not to be weighed down by circumstances. The consciously matter-of-fact descriptions of childbirth as one more facet of a busy and literally productive life perhaps also suggest a hint of bravado, as if she were trying to convince herself (let alone any

possible reader) of the ease with which she took to motherhood and its reconciliation with her other roles. Her account of Constance's birth shows this. She was
by now a very experienced mother about to have her ninth child. On 17 October
1844 she walked to the furnaces with her husband, learned some German poetry
and read in the library. She was about to dress for dinner and rang for the maid,
'But my dressing was never accomplished for I was suddenly taken ill and had to
send the maid for the nurse. The works bell rang six o'clock just as I got into bed
which I did forthwith. In less than twenty minutes later another dear baby was
added to our family.' Her husband had no idea that anything was the matter and
'indeed had parted from me quite well in the works not two hours before'. At ten
o'clock she went to sleep and had a good night's rest. The description of Enid's
birth suggests fortitude and resignation to inevitable pain: 'I look forward to my
trial with hope and gratitude' and she did concede 'a night of racking pain' after
Katherine's birth, though added 'Nobody can have been stronger, better than I
have been all through my confinement and I have got up wonderfully strong.'
In this year there were over thirty-two times as many deaths from childbirth in
England and Wales than there are today, though upper-class women were the
most likely to survive their childbearing years. The birth of Lady Charlotte's tenth
and last child in August 1847 did lead to illness. She was now thirty-five. Although
at first she seemed fine, a fainting fit followed soon after giving birth. She became
delirious, apparently close to death from exhaustion, and had to remain indoors
for some weeks – childbed fevers tended to cause more deaths than childbirth
itself. In October she wrote 'I am a poor shattered unenergetic thing. How unlike
the enthusiastic daring girl of those meteor days.'

Yet if most of her deliveries were accomplished relatively easily (certainly compared to many women's experiences), pregnancy itself was another matter.[4] Lady
Charlotte frequently felt sick during the early months and was sometimes quite
ill, especially when expecting girls. The journals of both her half-sisters are punctuated with references to Charlotte being poorly when visiting Uffington. When
expecting her sixth child she had four months of 'excessive sickness'. She hated any
incapacitation. During her first pregnancy she exclaimed 'feel unable to take part
in his [John's] quiet pursuits, such as reading or writing. However I trust when I
become more accustomed to my present indisposition, I shall be able to overcome
much of this lassitude, and be again interested in all that interests or concerns my
dear affectionate husband.' She worried because her Persian studies were suffering
from lack of energy and feared that perhaps she was too old to learn and 'must relinquish all my highflown prospects'. Yet despite frequent bouts of depression (which
she did not really understand and for which she gained no sympathy from others)
the twenty-two-year-old had over half a century of studying still in front of her.

Her problems were compounded by her determination to be a dutiful wife
and stay by John's side. This was difficult since he made frequent journeys, many
of which were lengthy and tiring. She suffered on a business trip to Cornwall not
long after a miscarriage. She worried lest John became ill without her, so tried to

accompany him even though it meant 'risking a *little existence* which is very dear to me'. Mary, who could never quite fathom Charlotte's behaviour, recorded how her mother gave her a long lecture about doing 'too much for her strength', living at Dowlais and when in London sitting up late for her husband when he went to the House of Commons 'and more of which the person appealed to (I am sorry to say) seemed not to care much about'.

Pregnancy frustrated Charlotte's ambitions, 'It pains me much sometimes to think how much I once did – How steadily I applied to particular subjects – and how little I ever attempt to do now.' On another occasion she cried out in her journal 'Everything I do now seems wrong, I can please nobody and I have myself the gnawing thought that I can never be useful and that every pursuit I have most attended to is vain – my time has been thrown away and because I am a woman there is no profitable way of spending that which remains.'

She later acknowledged that this was somewhat exaggerated, but still fundamentally true. Despite all her advantages and force of personality, the strictures on all wives and mothers, the frustrations and the weariness became focused during pregnancy. In 1858 even Queen Victoria wrote to her daughter that despite the 'unbounded happiness' which marriage could bring, pregnancy spelt 'aches – and sufferings and miseries and plagues – which you must struggle against – and enjoyments etc. to give up – constant precautions to take, you will feel the yoke of a married woman'. She added 'I had nine times for eight months to bear with those above-named enemies and real misery (besides many duties) and I own it tried me sorely; one feels so pinned down – one's wings clipped – in fact, at the best (and few were or are better than I was) only half oneself – particularly the first and second time … And therefore I think our sex a most unenviable one.'

Although even four years after marriage Lady Charlotte could declare that 'the Honey Moon is not over', John had some difficulty appreciating her heightened sensitivity during pregnancy. Like other Victorian fathers he remained remote from childbirth, upsetting his wife by returning to London (to vote on the Irish church bill) once her second child had been born. Such disappointment she kept to herself, consoling her spirits by going over the history of the steam engine in her mind, though a slight fever necessitated taking a little opium. A fortnight earlier she had made four dresses for little Maria, an appropriately maternal gesture which delighted her husband. Given the dangers of childbirth and her powerful imagination, it is not surprising that her first two confinements were heralded by prayers for safe delivery and forebodings of tragedy.

Lady Charlotte's desire to maintain 'business as usual' during pregnancy rather challenges the conventional image of pregnant Victorian wives hidden away in the home. The study of childbirth of fifty aristocratic women also suggests the continuation of active social lives at this time. Lady Charlotte danced at a ball in front of the King and Queen on 20 June 1834 and on 3 July gave birth to Maria. In the later months of her pregnancies she regained strength and kept as active as possible. Even sedentary pastimes were pursued with gusto: before one birth she knitted twenty-four pairs of socks. After giving birth she would be itching to resume her studies. Doctors and nurses were stricter than she liked; the custom was to keep mothers very still and like 'a close prisoner'. Fortunately this could not prohibit mental exertion. After Ivor's birth Lady Charlotte relearned Chaucer's *Prologue* (she could recite it in thirty-five minutes), resumed Persian and Arabic and, just two weeks after the birth of her sixth child, was immersed once more in translating Welsh.

She was extremely fortunate in that all ten children survived to adulthood – 'How few are blest with so much cause for contentment' – but there were anxious moments. Soon after birth Maria had convulsions. Lady Charlotte feared that Ivor had only been 'lent for a short time' and worried that Monty might die from an illness he contracted as a tiny baby. Since her maid Susan and a succession of nurses (one of whom she feared was drunk or insane) looked after the babies much of the time, she was not always sure just how ill they might be. John was not always understanding: he was 'so annoyed at my being constantly in the baby's room that today I consented to go out in the carriage'. Most years there was some worry about childhood illness. Virtually all the family had measles soon after Constance's birth. Then, as always, it was Merthyr Bach (little Merthyr) who gave the greatest cause for concern. Some of the children were evacuated to the Guests' seaside home at Sully, on the South Wales coast. The doctor visited Dowlais House five or six times in twenty-four hours and, for a time, hopes for Merthyr's survival seemed faint. Although six, he was given milk from a wet nurse, shaved and blistered and journal writing was suspended for a month. In a state of delirium he sang hymns and nursery songs, crying out 'I wish I could go to heaven when I die'. It was a nurse who died from the illness. Lady Charlotte came her closest to playing the role of housekeeper and nurse and caught measles herself. After three anxious months Merthyr rallied although he continued to be a sickly child. Some years later he contracted pleurisy: his lungs were distended, his heart out of place and Lady Charlotte remained at home for a week 'aged beyond my years, surrounded with blessings but the spirit wearied and the whole heart sick'. The illness went but recurred in the 1850s.

Despite efforts to minimize (at least on paper) the disruptive effects of motherhood, Lady Charlotte did not find adjustment particularly easy. The greater separation which existed then between children and adults would, however, have literally given her some space since the little ones spent much of their time in the nursery and ate separately. Considering the size of her family, the journal is remarkable for its relative lack of references to her babies. Many days could pass without mention of the fact that she had recently had a child. Although a devoted mother, she was clearly someone for whom small children could not provide adequate company for long. She did once write 'I am sure if a woman is to do her duty as a wife and mother that the less she meddles with pen and ink the better … It is quite right that I should have done with authorship', but this came after completing a hefty chunk of literary work and proved to be merely a writer's pause for breath. Within a month she was back at her Welsh.

The children spent quite a lot of time away from their parents. Enid once claimed that Miss Kemble the governess had been 'more of a mother to us all than ever our own mother who was far oftener away from us'. Miss Kemble had joined the family in 1843 when Enid was three months, staying until her marriage in 1868. Enid's journal depicts Lady Charlotte as a slightly formidable figure, described as 'the Mother' or 'The M'. Admittedly this is only the view of one child – and one who had lost her father when nine and experienced her mother remarrying when she was still young. Certainly, responsibility for a large family can never have been easy, particularly with so much travelling. Before the Great Western Railway shortened the journey to Wales, even getting there from London took much time. Travel could be hazardous: the heir to the Crawshay business was killed in one of the storms that plagued the boats crossing the River Severn. Transporting the Guest family was quite a feat, and, on one trip to Dorset, the ten children plus servants generated eighty-one pieces of luggage.

Lady Charlotte once remarked, with some justification and some exaggeration, 'I toil and strive to controul [sic] all the servants and dependents until really my life is rather that of a steward than a lady.' It is easy to dismiss the lives of wealthy ladies as devoid of responsibility but the wife's position was somewhat analogous to that of a works manager, with the husband as the owner with full and ultimate control and the wife chosen to manage (in both senses of the word) everyday affairs. Lady Charlotte also did time-consuming monthly household accounts. Once when the governess was ill she declared 'I feel now that I have completely sunk into the mere drudge, to look after servants and check expenses and writing accounts, or to supervise tutors and governesses'. Admittedly her journal was the one private place where she could moan and indulge in some self-pity and a little poetic licence. Nevertheless, the private side of the public lady should be remembered because it can so easily become submerged and minimized. For all the smart London dinners there were also 'trades people, shopping, dentists, physicians' to visit.

House-guests needed entertaining at Dowlais too. Arrangements for the visit of the Grand Duke Constantine of Russia were made from London, and Lady Charlotte engaged the fashionable firm Gunters to handle catering. Far more troublesome than this was the visit of Mr Martin, once her tutor but now thin, drawn and exuding a 'painful abandonment of hope, the wreck of his prospects, the almost nine years expectancy of a living, and the continual disappointments'.[5] Increasingly desperate letters had culminated in a brief personal visit. John left the guilt-ridden Lady Charlotte to talk to him, and the children ran in and out of the room. Lady Charlotte wrote 'I think Martin must have been assured that ours was a house completely united and full of domestic happiness and love' and she understood that this might have upset him even more.

A rather more welcome visitor was the mathematician Charles Babbage. His wife had died after eight pregnancies in thirteen years and he involved himself in the intellectual development of his children. Lady Charlotte sought tips on this score, feeling him to be a kindred spirit. He stressed the value of posing questions to the young and encouraging their empirical reasoning: 'one thing he said struck me much – that we should be ever forming opinions or judgements upon everything and everybody we see at first sight and then watch carefully how the experience of time would bear out such opinions by which we should gain a habit of judging correctly and also acquire a knowledge of the worth of our own judgement.' Lady Charlotte remembered his advice on first impressions and wrote down his suggestions 'because I think they may, especially those relating to children, be useful to me one day or another'.

She was an ambitious teacher: Maria had to listen to Blunt's lectures on Elisha when only seven. Lady Charlotte usually read to the children after meals, and when they grew older, like the Dowlais scholars, they were encouraged to write essays for prizes. Pleasing such a gifted mother cannot have been easy. Maria was so anxious to excel at a French class that she worked herself into a fever. Although not acknowledging it, Lady Charlotte's eldest daughter was in many ways a replica of herself when younger: 'She is a peculiar child – easily depressed and made to feel at a disadvantage with others – although cleverer than most girls of her age – and when she feels this depression it seems to paralize [sic] all her energies …' The difference was that Lady Charlotte was more skilled at disguising her inner feelings. Fortunately not all life was work. The size of the family gave Maria and the other children scope for theatricals and charades, especially popular at Christmas. Maria was, like her mother, a passionate actress.

For many years the girls' education was under the control of the reliable Miss Kemble.[6] The boys had less continuity. There was a succession of tutors, some of whom were dismissed for excessive strictness or temper: one struck Merthyr, splitting open his ear-drum. It was decided, with some reluctance, that the older boys should go away to school. This was never considered for the daughters, though girls' secondary education had not yet been reformed and the education the Guest daughters received at home (not entirely segregated by sex) was probably much more academic than the subjects which would have dominated a school curriculum. Ivor found preparatory school difficult and Harrow even worse. He was accused of using 'wicked language' and being a bad influence but enquiries revealed that he had become a scapegoat for the boys and he was removed forthwith. Monty was also unhappy there. To Lady Charlotte's dismay he then entered the army, but 'it is his *bent* so I cannot withstand it'. In the early 1850s Augustus showed the greatest promise as a future ironmaster, and in January 1852 Ivor went abroad with a tutor,[7] filling in the gap before university like many young gentlemen who sampled the arts of Europe. Lady Charlotte gave him a Bible and a book on Palestine. Sir John's parting gift was Milton's works.

As early as 1844 Lady Charlotte had observed her husband's 'worn and anxious look' and feared trouble. Medical consultation confirmed her fears. Her journal acquired a solemn importance: 'Sorrow is come at last, and in its most gnawing form. I feel that I must confide it somewhere and to no living being may I tell my grief.' Despite assurances to the contrary from eminent London surgeons, the Dowlais doctor's diagnosis of a serious kidney complaint proved to he correct. Benjamin Brodie, medical advisor to three monarchs and later President of the Royal Society, was the authority on gall stones. He had popularized lithotripsy, which involved crushing the stones with instruments, and his operations had a good success rate but were performed without anaesthetic or antiseptics. Some temporary relief was gained through Brodie's operations performed on the sofa whilst an extremely anxious Lady Charlotte peeped through the door. Fatalistic, she was already writing 'It is over. It is over. At the best I know that all gladness has passed away from me.' She resolved never to contradict Sir John, portraying herself as 'an automaton, a drone' in contrast to the days when 'the poetry of enthusiasm was around me'. Sir John rallied temporarily in the second half of the 1840s but he was never again really well.

When John married Lady Charlotte he could have had little idea of the extent to which they would both be saddled with the problems of her relatives. She never completely broke from her home. This is hardly surprising given the Victorian emphasis on the family, her belief in the institution and sense of redeeming family honour. She also cared deeply about some of the individuals concerned, though the extent to which she was used as mediator and diplo-mat for her distant Lincolnshire relatives is somewhat ironical given her lack of legal rights as a married woman. From the start, John's money and Lady Charlotte's 'know how' were irresistible. He lent (in practice gave) £1,000 to cousin Brownlow Layard to enable him to marry without even knowing him:[8] Lady Charlotte was persuaded to help Bertie get a commission in the Guards even though John was simultaneously calling for the reduction of the Guards and Pension List in Parliament.

Mr Martin pestered them with pleas for financial help. Pegus refused to sign a testimonial for the Bishop of Norwich to ordain him and was furious when the Rector of Uffington did so. Further unpleasantness resulted from the Guests din-ing with the latter on a visit to Uffington in January 1834 and Pegus challenged John, declaring that 'if he chose to call him out he would meet him'. Marriage gave Lady Charlotte greater strength to resist her stepfather and the couple left the next day on a pretext of business. Yet despite deploring the way Pegus 'so often tyrannised over my family with impunity' Lady Charlotte recognized that her mother suffered from estrangement and so sometimes relented. Later that year, for example, Pegus christened the Guests' daughter.

A genuine tragedy rather than one of the frequent storms in a teacup occurred in 1837. Close on the death of John's brother, Thomas, came news that little Elizabeth had been drowned.[9] Mary wrote poignantly in her journal: 'My dearest sister Elizabeth was drowned and is now an angel in heaven.' Yet Charlotte never again mentioned Elizabeth in her voluminous journal. When real tragedy befell her it got deeply buried.

Meanwhile there was another relative who was very much alive and demanding attention: poor Lindsey. The Tenth Earl seems to have been happy enough in his own way but was clearly totally irresponsible. His life was punctuated with unfortunate incidents: inadvertently shooting a favourite dog of John's, setting himself on fire whilst dressing, and increasingly suffering from fits. Charlotte's own journal betrays little of the details of his lack of coordination but a letter from the caricaturist George Cruikshank to Charles Dickens reveals something of his problem. Since Lindsey was keen to meet some of the 'Live Lions' of society Dickens had sent him to Cruikshank with a letter of introduction: 'Your "Lion" hunter call'd. The same I suppose who hath been slightly of character of the wild animals himself.'

Cruikshank explained to Dickens:

It is well you took the precaution of ommiting [sic] to mention any of his *Lordship's* peculiarities in your note for I found his Lordship had carried it off with him, what a rum "un eh? – My wife saw him first and came and told me that there was a man either drunk or mad – I said, 'Show him up' – and when he got into my room hang me if I do not think that he thought he was making hay – he pitched the papers about so!

To the Guests' dismay Pegus persuaded Lindsey to cut off the entail to his estate. Lady Charlotte felt that he used Lindsey to further his own plans and she refused to lend her brother money, which anyway would have acknowledged that he was of sound mind. Pegus in turn frightened Lindsey with stories that the Guests wanted to take out a Statute of Lunacy against him, more than once threatened John with legal action, and ensured that Lindsey made a will excluding by name all Lady Charlotte's offspring from ever succeeding to the Uffington estate.

He even seemed to turn his wife against Lady Charlotte. This provoked much bitterness in the journal: 'I should have thought a mother would not have given up a child so easily, but that unfortunate second marriage laid the foundation of all this misery.' She added that 'she ceased to be my mother in becoming the wife of that wretched man whose only excuse is that he is half-mad. Indeed I have often heard Mamma herself say that she feared he would lose his reason when in some of his violent paroxysms of rage.' When her mother ignored her, Lady Charlotte was equally obdurate and denied her the chance to see her grandchildren.

Caught in the middle, Mary was not happy with the way Charlotte tried to draw a distinction between her position as half-sister and friend and her role as part of the Pegus family. Yet even she depicted her father as 'amusing himself quarrelling with the lawyers' whilst her husband's diary described how Pegus kicked up 'a precious hulla-bulloo' at Fentons Hotel. It was the Guests rather than her own parents who launched Mary in Society, arranged her trousseau and held the reception for her marriage to Charles Huntly (who in 1853 became the Sixth Earl of Aboyne and inherited an impoverished Scottish estate).[10] The Huntlys later had their share of troubles and received financial support from Sir John for their Orton Longueville estate near Peterborough. Even after Sir John's death his successor at Dowlais, G.T. Clark, advised the widowed Mary, lent her money and warned her of her son's gambling debts.

There was even financial scandal surrounding the Rectory. Lady Lindsey's brother, Brownlow Villiers Layard, had twelve children from two marriages and found it difficult to pay his bills. His debts were probably compounded by demands from his son, Albermarle, who had a criminal record. Eventually in 1843 the long-expected 'crash at the Rectory' took place, the Rector fleeing to Boulogne where he stayed. Pegus and then the Rector's son, John, held the fort at Uffington. Although there was talk of resignation on terms mutually agreeable to the Rector and his creditors, he remained the formal, though absentee, incumbent. Seven years later Lady Charlotte saw him, now without 'position, fortune and three of his promising sons'. His wife, she felt, had the 'benignity of a Guardian Angel'.

Meanwhile Pegus's behaviour was far from angelic. To Lady Charlotte's horror, on the pretext of health he had 'bought a connection' for Lindsey. She deplored this 'atmosphere of sin – permitted, acknowledged by a man who ought to have screened his poor weak mind from such things – and that man too a clergyman'. For once Lady Charlotte almost ran out of words in her indignation and 'my consternation was greater still' on finding that Bertie was also staying at Mrs Maitland's house. The 'tone of morality' was very low but with her mother doting on Bertie she felt helpless to intervene though prayed fervently that her own boys would be protected from the influence of a man 'so hardened in vice as Mr Pegus'.

Bertie was soon 'rescued' by marriage. To Lady Charlotte's relief his wife, Felicia (née Welby, herself the daughter of a clergyman), seemed eminently suited to cope with the family. For a time Pegus was 'in a state bordering on ecstasy' about his daughter-in-law but his enthusiasms were soon absorbed in railway matters which now seemed to engross him, particularly when there was a chance of securing financial arrangements with companies in return for assurance that the Peer Lord Lindsey would support railway bills in Parliament!

In November 1858 after a bout of bronchitis, Lady Charlotte's seventy-seven-year-old mother, stone-deaf and world-weary, died. Her will was a minor triumph for Pegus's opponents. The Berties were to live at Uffington with Lindsey. Pegus was to be offered the Uffington living when it became vacant and in the meantime paid an allowance.

Pegus vented his wrath on Felicia – 'he applies to her the most infamous appellations' – and told Lindsey that the Berties were seeking to poison him.

Afraid that he might abduct Lindsey, they became terrified of leaving the estate. It was Lady Charlotte who had to take action. Anxious to respect her mother's last wishes she paid off Mrs Maitland (whose daughter had recently been entertaining Lindsey) and then took a bolder step. Pegus was 'deposed' and banished from Uffington by a legal settlement which denied him the living and the management of the house and estate. He was granted an annuity. Lindsey confounded everybody by signing the agreement 'with a clearness and propriety of words and thought'.

The very next year Pegus disappeared from Lady Charlotte's life. After staying with Mary he had moved to Baker Street, London, where he died from dropsy on 21 April 1860 'without any friend or relative near him'. He studiously refused to see Charlotte throughout his illness though somewhat perversely never failed to ask if she had been to enquire after him. She also could not expunge the complicated links with her stepfather and enquired after him almost daily.

He was buried by the side of his wife at Uffington. Lady Charlotte watched the funeral from the house 'and it was a strange feeling that he who has so troubled our family for so many years should be no more – but I believe he was not accountable for his actions at all times – and certainly he often had good and kind impulses – so let his memory rest'.

Lindsey, who was patently not accountable for his actions almost all of the time, died in March 1877. He never did marry. The title passed to Bertie who now had an heir christened with those familiar family names of Montague Peregrine Albemarle. Lady Charlotte returned to Uffington for her brother's funeral: 'It was a mercy to feel that his blameless life had ended without actual suffering. We cannot reget him though it seems so sad that he should no longer be among us with all his little innocent, childlike ways, in the midst of which he was always so kind and affectionate to everybody. It was a curious state of existence to have lasted sixty-two years – what a romance I might write on the incidents connected with it!'

As the funeral cortege gathered, they tried to dissuade her from following 'as no other woman did so. But as his only sister I could not forbear paying him this last tribute of respect and love.'

Once again there was a glimpse of a woman for whom Victorian conventions, though commanding her attention for much of the time, could also act as a constraint which she could not and did not accept.

3
The Educator of The People

*'We talked about the poor and the feeling of
the lower classes to the rich and the
necessity of educating, of humanising, the
lower grade. But I know one cannot make
people good and religious by Act of
Parliament. The first step is to make them
comfortable and happy.'*

Lady Charlotte wrote these words on 13 April 1848, just three days after a massive
Chartist demonstration on Kennington Common, London. She had been talking to Mr Gifford, a curate. She described this time as 'one of the most important
weeks of my life', adding 'a new era seems to have commenced'. Chartism was
the first national working-class organization in the world, a movement dedicated
to achieving Parliamentary democracy. It helped persuade Lady Charlotte of the
need for closer involvement in practical work for the people of Dowlais. Like a
number of wealthy employer families, the Guests developed educational and leisure
facilities for their workforce. Lady Charlotte sought to be an educator in the widest
sense, providing not just schooling but an appropriate climate and culture. As in so
many facets of her life, the results were somewhat extraordinary. With the zeal of
the converted she recognized in 1848, 'How much I have to do. How much I have
neglected. But in truth I mean to work if it pleases God to give me power and
health. May he also give me energy and a blessing on my work!'

Reared in the world of traditional aristocratic patronage but living in the fast-
changing society of the industrial magnate, she helped in the transition to an
ordered and rational industrial workforce.

The shift in Lady Charlotte's conscience and consciousness of what needed to be
done can be best appreciated by looking first at how, in the years before 1848, her
husband attempted to 'make people good and religious by Act of Parliament'. In this
work he was actively supported by Lady Charlotte. John Guest had been elected as
Merthyr's MP at a significant turning point in electoral history. The 1832 Reform Act
sealed the power of a new middle class. It was a time of government growth, increased
state intervention and a developing professionalism amongst both Whigs and Tories.
Between 1826-31 John had represented the West Country constituency of Honiton.

His early Parliamentary career shows that he was then most closely linked with the Canningite Tories, supporting their three 'C's' of corn, currency and Catholic reform. By the time of his re-election in 1830 (when the Whigs finally regained power), he was increasingly describing himself as an 'Independent' MP and urging Parliamentary reform. His stance during the Reform crisis – his electoral posters billed him as 'The Poor Man's Friend' – cost him his seat.

He considered one of the new Glamorgan County seats but within two days of the news that Merthyr was to have its own Member, he was invited to stand for his home constituency. John's one-time support of truck (Dowlais had run a Company shop) and harsh treatment of trade unionists in the wake of the Merthyr Rising were counteracted by his attacks on the Corn Laws, cries against excessive expenditure – as Gwyn A. Williams has observed 'whenever Guest spoke at length in the House, someone lost money' – and his call for Church reform. The Merthyr electorate was tiny, only 502 men in 1832, chiefly shopkeepers and publicans.[1] Only one in seventy had the vote in the reformed Parliament. The local Radicals appreciated the way he increasingly identified himself with the views of the Philosophical Radical, the Scotsman Joseph Hume. Between 1833–4 John voted with him on thirty-one out of thirty-seven occasions and Hume once declared that 'there was no more able man in aiding him than Mr Guest'.

Although, like all women, Lady Charlotte lacked the vote, she nonetheless recognized the possibilities of influence. Her political activities were never primarily concerned with women's rights. Unlike the younger Rose Crawshay who became friendly with the leading Suffragist Millicent Fawcett and spoke for and financially contributed to the cause, Lady Charlotte never singled out this issue for her approval. Nor did she, like her daughter-in-law Cornelia, formally register her disapproval.[2]

Her background and forceful personality aided her involvement in public affairs on behalf of her husband. Her sense of wifely duty suggested an active endorsement of John's views but she also maintained her own strongly held opinions. Many of her judgements were astute and, quite apart from the value of her unpaid secretarial help and publicity, she had style. Apathy had no place in Lady Charlotte's vocabulary. John welcomed the advantages of a female touch. He probably also learned that it was futile trying to dissuade her from sharing in a subject that interested her.

It was fortunate that politics did not bore her. 'Corn Laws all dinner' was not everybody's idea of entertainment. Political receptions and dinners were statutory. The Guests even attended some dinners held by the opposition since John's partner's widow married Disraeli. Lady Charlotte was distressed to see how the former Mrs Wyndham Lewis was ridiculed by those around her. She was, however, influential and gained a reputation for distributing appointments and helping to write election speeches.

Lady Charlotte thought the Whigs somewhat arrogant in power and joked that 'as they will take no notice of me I will contrive once or twice to keep my husband from their most important divisions'. In practice she took John's Parliamentary work very seriously, seeing it as a way of effecting improvement in society. She understood the need for routine constituency and Parliamentary work. One morning she wrote thirty-six notices to friends and acquaintances to 'help us obtain' a second reading of a bill on the Poor Law in Ireland. She wrote out speeches for John, noted down progress on bills and even Mary had to help fold petitions. When support was needed for the Dowlais Market Bill, she tracked down her husband's business adviser, Edward Divett (MP for Exeter), and persuaded him and the Swansea Member John Vivian to vote in time to save the bill. She later canvassed several Peers for the Lords' debate and when it passed declared 'I consider this quite my own bill.'

Lady Charlotte was both powerless and powerful. She used her connections to enquire about suitable seats for those close to her. When John's nephew, Edward Hutchins, was elected at Falmouth after her advice for him to stand there, she wrote: 'All the five vacant boroughs have now gone in our favour and the Tory cry of reaction must at least be checked.' She wrote: 'I never failed to exert myself when I have it in my power to do anything that would be advantageous to my party.' She did not manage to persuade Lindsey to support the Whigs but when her new brother-in-law, Henry Schreiber, wanted a clerkship in 1860, she saw Palmerston (as First Lord of the Treasury) and persuaded him 'for the sake of old times', even though Charles Schreiber supported the Tories.

Her anomalous position was summed up by her relationship to Parliament. She was not impressed by the Commons in 1834:

> The House seemed to me a miserable little hole. If I thought the House of Lords of puny proportions, how much less admirable did this appear. The libraries of both Houses seemed paltry to me, and bitterly was I disappointed in the little that remains of the Painted Chamber ... Though I saw the death warrant of Charles I, I was gratified by one thing, viz, Merthyr's pointing to the place he generally occupies. I can now fancy *exactly* where he is during the many long hours that we are parted.

As the wife of an MP she admired her husband's conscientiousness but found that increasingly 'I am becoming a slave of circumstances' since 'The House of Commons quite destroys my domestic comfort'. Sessions were very long, John often not returning until the early hours of the morning. Perhaps Lady Charlotte was comforted to hear that he was one of the minority who voted in 1842 that no public business of consequence should be debated after midnight.

Despite her interest in proceedings, Lady Charlotte could not easily attend debates. Although ladies had once sat at the back of the Strangers' Gallery, they were banned from attendance in the late eighteenth century. (When the French socialist Flora Tristan visited London she slipped in to a debate disguised as a Turk.) After fire nearly destroyed both Houses in 1835, women were allocated some space in the new temporary accommodation but were confined to a ventilating shaft up above the chandelier. When the House of Commons was rebuilt, a Ladies Gallery was included for forty visitors. They were, however, forced to sit behind a grille. In the 1880s a number of empassioned speeches stressed how ladies deplored 'that horrid thing' and urged its replacement by a rail. The Member advocating such change was none other than Lady Charlotte's son, Monty. Not until 1917 was the grille finally removed after pressure from Suffragists who cannily organized a petition signed by the wives of 264 MPs.

On 14 February 1842 Lady Charlotte braved the heat, smoke and frustration of seeing little to attend a debate on the Corn Laws. These laws had been imposed in 1815 to perpetuate the monopoly enjoyed by British farmers during the Napoleonic wars. They kept the price of corn artificially high and infuriated manufacturers like the Guests who favoured Free Trade. In 1839 the Anti-Corn Law League, a pressure group to repeal the laws, was founded. With the support of the Tory Prime Minister Peel (whom Lady Charlotte admired despite his party affiliation), the laws were eventually repealed in 1846. The debate Lady Charlotte heard introduced her to the thrill of some political speeches. Palmerston combined 'poetry and expression of truth'. His call for cheap bread made her feel 'perfectly carried away by it. It was a new sense to me – an excitement of which I had never had the slightest idea before.' She was vehemently opposed to 'that wicked tax on corn' but despite Palmerston's rousing words 'the majority for opposition was 123'. She returned to the Commons two days later.

As well as hating the Corn Laws, Lady Charlotte was vehemently opposed to the new Poor Law. Her husband's handling of the 1834 Poor Law Amendment Act, however, indicates his readiness to adjust his views in the light of constituency pressure. The law centralized and systematized the control of poverty, abandoning centuries of parochial responsibility for the poor and mitigating concern about high Poor Law rates by attempting to abolish outdoor relief to the able-bodied and, through its principle of 'less eligibility', ensuring that only the truly desperate entered the workhouse. As Dickens commented through *Oliver Twist*, it forced the choice of 'being starved by a gradual process in the house, or by a quick one out of it'. Lady Charlotte understood only too well the long-term implications of this legislation. The Whig plan, consistent with Benthamite thinking that control must be asserted against a chaotic system, challenged the old order more effectively than had Parliamentary reform. The ageing Radical William Cobbett declared that the bill threatened to 'totally abrogate all the local government of the Kingdom' divesting the gentlemen and justices of their power. As part of that old order and married to a man who sought to extend his influence at the local level, Lady Charlotte could sympathize with the 'Tory Radicals' who opposed it.

At first John supported the Whig law. He later claimed that he had always felt some reservations but, if so, he seems to have kept them to himself. His position was in line with his political mentor Joseph Hume. In contrast Lady Charlotte 'hated the effect of these poor laws' from the start. She conceded that 'Their principle is a sound one ... but some of the details are too bad for any but slaves.' At the end of 1836 Merthyr and eight other parishes formed one Poor Law Union, and John became Chairman of the new Poor Law Board. Lady Charlotte was 'not at all fond of' this position and was convinced that 'the next riot at Merthyr will be owing to this new Poor Law'.

Her apprehension was justified. In 1837 Merthyr produced 9,460 signatures against the law. A huge meeting of workmen on Aberdare Hill resolved not to be represented by any supporter of the Poor Law. John produced an explanatory address. For once his faithful 'secretary' appeared to have lost it so she reconstructed it from memory. On perusing Lady Charlotte's version John found it 'not quite according to his views' so dictated a fresh version to the Works Manager. Aware of local opposition he now protested in Parliament about the segregation of the sexes in the workhouses. During what she called the 'meridian of its madness' Lady Charlotte surveyed the Beacons 'proud and free before us', appalled to think that, 'we could even consider with common patience the law by which our fellow creatures are to be immured in a Workhouse by no other sin other than that of being poor and afflicted. It seemed to me a strong exemplification of the strange anomalies of which life is composed.'

The local Board of Guardians resisted the full implementation of the law. Not until 1853 did the town have a workhouse.[3]

When first elected for Merthyr, John had stated that 'Knowledge is Power and I wish that power to be extended to all ranks of Society in order that they may become better and happier men.' 'Knowledge is Power' was the slogan proudly displayed by the influential *Poor Man's Guardian*, a newspaper which deliberately refused to pay the tax on newspapers and advocated far-reaching changes such as universal suffrage (the vote for all males over twenty-one) and the secret ballot. John was wary of manhood suffrage but, influenced by Merthyr Radicals and Joseph Hume, he supported the ballot. Here Lady Charlotte dissented from her husband. In June 1835 John went to a debate on the subject, intending to vote for it. Lady Charlotte had 'foolishly expressed an idea that his doing so might detriment me in Society and he kindly said he would forbear voting at all'. Once he had left she felt guilty and hoped he would not be swayed by her. He was not; though secret voting only became law in 1872. During this period John was largely 'Whig in party and Radical in opinion'. The measure of his Radicalism was tested several times as elections propelled him into the limelight. Never one to stay in the wings, Lady Charlotte saw her support as a means of helping the people.

At first she expressed some caution but this soon gave way to more positive words and action. Before the 1835 election she wrote, 'I had taken great pains not to say one word to any one touching the canvass, thinking that women have nothing to do with politicks [sic] and being very anxious that Merthyr should not think I interfere in what I could know nothing though, perhaps, a wife might be sometimes excused, if in the course of the conversations she is present at, she is led to express some feeling and interest …'

She was skilled at arguing her way through her own writing and so convincing herself. Even though 'informed of (and sometimes even consulted upon) every move' the task of keeping quiet would, she felt, be more difficult than translating a French pamphlet on hot air blast. And the very next day she went out canvassing.

When in the 1880s the Corrupt Practices Act forbade the payment of canvassers and the Third Reform Act widened the franchise, women's involvement in canvassing became widespread.[4] Millicent Fawcett advised the Liberals to make 'all possible use of every available woman in your locality'. Long before this Lady Charlotte was an avid canvasser. She mentioned that some Tories had said she should not take part in the election but her friends had countered this by declaring her 'the right sort of woman, for I was not afraid and entered into the spirit of the thing'. Early Tory canvassers were not unknown: the landowner and business woman Anne Lister canvassed her Yorkshire tenants in 1837. Lady Charlotte accompanied her husband canvassing and sought votes herself. She and Thomas Guest covered Blaen Dowlais to Penydarren, securing sixty-three promises of votes and no refusals. It was a difficult constituency to cover as it encompassed Aberdare as well as Merthyr and was divided by a mountain ridge; so all help was welcome. The works surgeon flattered Lady Charlotte by telling her she was 'the best canvasser after all, for that I was soliciting a vote at Pont Storehouse [the most notorious district in Merthyr] at nine o'clock the foregoing night'. Her surprise at the ease with which votes were promised to her husband betrays a certain *naïveté*. Declining to pledge a vote was rather more difficult than promising it for such an influential employer.

When one man who had worked fifteen years for Crawshay (who was behind John's opponent) appeared at Dowlais House, Lady Charlotte carefully asked for his vote in Welsh. She also patronized a play 'which shall famously hit the opposite party'. A few days before the 1837 election she made her own dramatic entry, dismounting from her pony in the middle of a crowd. She was cheered by them and had been 'cheered at Gellifaelog and got a shout at Penydarren'. Over 100 women and children had hailed her at the Plymouth works. She walked alone to the polling booth on election day, proudly adding 'I suppose they expected as usual to see me where everything was going on for I found a chair prepared for me of which I took possession and there I remained speaking to the voters and thanking them as they left the booth.' Before long a fight broke out between the two sides and the Riot Act was read. (Some years later Lady Charlotte witnessed some 'hard fighting' at a Poole election. Rotten eggs, apples, turnips, balls of flour and stones were thrown at speakers. The effect was 'very ludicrous, the flour sticking where the egg had already taken effect and giving all the party on the hustings the appearance of being so many millers'. One poor Whig already at the receiving end of some rotten eggs inadvertently got into a crowd of Tories and received a blow on the head. The next day Lady Charlotte spent in the Whig Committee Rooms. The Tories had the doors of their Committee Rooms broken down by a hammer.[5])

Her contributions to the campaign included writing an anonymous political squib (aided by Edward Hutchins) 'as severe as we could make it'. It must have been, for the printers 'in timidity' suppressed it for several days. The *Merthyr Guardian* soon provoked her into a second effort. She also wrote a 'sharp letter' to the ironmaster Fothergill (who professed Liberal principles but was not helping her husband). This was printed in Welsh and English. She persuaded the Guest supporters to put Welsh on to the flags, she ordered waistcoats in purple and yellow and dressed little Maria in these colours and in Welsh flannel. At the election dinner to celebrate John's success in 1835 (the Tory Walter Meyrick had finally withdrawn and so left the seat uncontested), Lady Charlotte was the subject of a toast from Taliesin Williams, son of the radical antiquary Iolo Morganwg:

> Gentlemen, I have seen, during my many years residence in this town, several English families settled among us, who, notwithstanding their various grades of respectable intellect, still could not surmount their national prejudices and unjust animosities; hence, in their imprudence, uncharitableness, and injustice, they have viewed our national habits and our indefeasible attachment to our ancient language with jealous unkindness ... Gentlemen, a distinguished lady, from the noble House of Lindsey, now resides among us: her lofty mind is, from exalted sympathy, attached to our towering hills; she has adopted our costumes – and our language, from the first day that she honoured Merthyr with her residence, has been the object of her successful study; and beyond all, she has visited the widow and the fatherless, and fed the poor and the needy.

According to the *Hereford Times* this speech was received 'with the most astounding cheers'. John then read out a letter from Lady Charlotte. Half of it was in Welsh.

Although she did not attend the actual election dinner in 1837 where John declared that 'I am not of high birth; my father and grand father raised themselves and I have done the same by the labours of my countrymen', Lady Charlotte did listen to the speeches from the far end of the room. Then at the right moment she walked its length with two-year-old Ivor in her arms and received a toast to his health.

John had defeated John Bruce Price the Tory candidate.[6] In Dowlais he had got all but two of the votes – and they were abstentions. He also stood for one of the two County seats in 1837 (as a 'Liberal and Free Trader'). Lady Charlotte did her bit, attending Swansea races – 'It was very hot and very stupid, but it was considered I should be there.' She took declarations of affiliation so seriously that she refused to be godmother to John's niece's child since Sarah (who had no vote of her own) was not supporting her uncle. The County seat provided opponents more in tune with Lady Charlotte's background than John's. Viscount Adare the Tory headed the poll and C.R.M. Talbot (of Margam and Penrice) came second. Talbot, a Liberal, would eventually become the 'Father of the House', sitting for sixty successive years until 1890.

Mrs Gladstone is reputed to have been the first woman to accompany her husband on the campaign platform but Lady Charlotte clearly saw herself as an active part of her husband's campaigns. Sometimes she exaggerated her importance in political decision-making. For example in 1841 she wrote that Crawshay wanted to see her 'to try to sort out the second Whig candidate for the County in case of a contest for Merthyr Tydfil'. Yet, though her actual influence was probably less than she fancied, it mattered to her that her contribution was stressed in the journal as she badly wanted to be involved in decision-making.

In 1852 the wily William Crawshay wrote to her about attacks by the 'Bute thumbscrews' on the Liberal candidate at Cardiff, and flattered Lady Charlotte by reference to 'the interest which you take in political matters' and urged her to exert influence against the Bute nominee, presenting this as a quid pro quo for the lack of opposition to Guest at Merthyr. Lady Charlotte was shocked by some political practices. She found a farmer who had been given seven glasses of gin by Crawshay in an attempt to sway his vote. Back in 1830 she had felt that the Marquis of Exeter 'richly merited his reverse' for intimidating tenants and she now deplored Tory landlords who threatened political evictions, 'treated' in the public houses and promised spirit licences in return for votes. 'It is very wicked to influence these poor peoples' minds for political purposes.' The *Merthyr Guardian* just as confidently accused Guest's side of corrupt practices. Meanwhile Lady Charlotte read (and found familiar) Dickens's *The Pickwick Papers*.

Part of the secret of John Guest's success as MP for Merthyr (especially in 1835) lay in his support from the unrepresented, those without their own votes but able, in a constituency like Merthyr, to exert a powerful influence on the minority who were enfranchised. This was done through large open air meetings and through tactics such as exclusive dealing – buying only from those shopkeepers who supported their chosen candidate and policies. Since the 'shopocracy' constituted the majority of voters in Merthyr, the measure was calculated to succeed. Yet it cannot have been easy juggling the demands of an increasingly articulate local population with the Guests' lifestyle and the demands of John's political masters. On the one hand he supported expelling bishops from political functions, admitting Dissenters to universities and appointing Welsh-speaking clergy for Welsh dioceses. On the other hand he personally abandoned Nonconformity for the Church of England. He voted for the ballot and shorter Parliaments but, unlike an increasing number of Merthyr Radicals, was not prepared to go along the road to Chartism (which included the ballot and annual Parliaments as two of its six-point Charter).

A few months after the 1835 election he was invited to dinner with Lord John Russell. The latter is 'I evidently perceive to become his leader in politicks [sic]' wrote Lady Charlotte. 'He finds so much illiberality amongst the Liberals that with very little or no change of opinion or mode of action, He will I think assume the name of Whig.' Whereas in 1834 he voted with the Whigs on only four out of nineteen occasions, the following year John supported them in ten out of twelve divisions.[7] In 1836 Lady Charlotte commented on his 'very grand speech, whereof he is not a little vain – but in that he resembles all the men that ever were in the world'. At this point he deliberately refrained from supporting a radical measure espoused by Hume attacking a large military presence in peacetime and 'so proving he is a Whig'. His former track record – attacking military flogging and aiding Hume in an anti-Pensions List campaign – suggests the symbolic significance of this new 1836 stance. The Tory *Merthyr Guardian* often exaggerated but it does seem to have been close to the mark when it described him as the 'Ultra Liberal' who became a Whig and 'general supporter' of Lord John Russell. Meanwhile Hume would go on to support the Charter.[8] John, soon to be Sir John, took a different route.

The timing and demands of Chartism reflected disappointment with the 1832 Reform Act and subsequent Whig measures. Whereas middle-class reformers had boasted that 1832 represented the victory of the people, Chartist analysis provided a different definition of the people, appealing instead to those who had been left out of the political equation by the Reform Act, which transferred power to the middle class but 'left the people as helpless as before'. The movement also drew on earlier radical demands, fusing them into a forward-looking programme published in 1838 as the People's Charter. It was a time of severe economic upheaval and distress. Chartists did not deliberately seek out violence but within such a massive organization with support the length and breadth of the country, disillusionment at the failure to achieve constitutional democracy by peaceable means goaded some into contemplating using physical force. Considering that the movement lasted for over twenty years (the last Convention or conference was held in 1858, the year when one Chartist point, abolition of property qualifications for MPs, was achieved) the violence was remarkably contained. For the majority of Chartists, the movement was a means of self-education, education by the people. It helped provoke Lady Charlotte into efforts for the people of Dowlais.

She first mentioned Chartism in her journal at the end of 1838 when she estimated that Merthyr had about 700 Chartists. Her initial response (based on newspaper reading) was dismissive. They were 'about one million of idle and ill informed people who wish for nothing but revolution and misrule, and call it reform'. Bearing in mind the history of popular protest in Merthyr – 'the Welsh being well known to be inflammatory' – she was defensive. On Christmas Day Chartists met at Dowlais and she admitted that it was 'rather a nervous thing'. They occupied themselves in 'inventing what diversions were in our power in order to keep as many of our population away from the meeting as we could without appearing to do so'. About 400 uniformed Oddfellows did the trick, marching in procession with their flags.

Chartist strength grew in the early months of 1839. The first Chartist petition to Parliament in favour of their six-point Charter contained over a million signatures, more than 14,000 of them coming from Merthyr. The town had an active Working Men's Association but John's earlier radical stance was such that the local Chartists were hardly strangers. Morgan Williams of Penrheolgerrig, their leader, was a small-scale web and flannel manufacturer and had sat on John's 1835 election committee. Along with Lady Charlotte he was one of the best canvassers. Although by the late 1830s Merthyr Radicalism had split – largely but not entirely along class lines – John Guest's political pedigree was impressive. His grandfather had been one of the town's two subscribers to the pro-Jacobin *Cambridge Intelligencer*, delivered to him by none other than Morgan Williams's mother.

The man whom it was later rumoured had been the original choice to lead the 1839 Newport Rising when the town became the 'cockpit of the kingdom' was well known to the Guests. The flamboyant Dr William Price of Porth y Glo had also been 'one of our best friends at the last election'. Lady Charlotte knew him through her Welsh literary activities – 'he is a clever man and on Welsh subjects well informed'. This surgeon was also, in the eyes of many, 'a fit subject for the lunatic asylum'. He drove around in a carriage drawn by goats and wore full Bardic costume 'of red and green and his lambskin on his head with the four lambs tails hanging about his eyes', a sight which terrified the young Maria. It was Price who, years later, was responsible for the legalization of cremation after his court case over the burning of his illegitimate child, whom he had called Jesus Christ. The Guests hoped to influence him, so he was summoned to Dowlais House. Lady Charlotte explained that 'he owned being favourable to Charterism [sic] but disclaimed all idea of physical force which he said had almost determined him to abandon the doctrine altogether'. John warned him of the danger of 'lending his countenance to any society of the kind – and he seemed grateful for the advice'. Yet after the Newport Rising he felt the need to flee the country. His love of dressing up proved handy, as he disguised himself as a woman and escaped to France.

Confident that she and her husband had a rapport with their community, Lady Charlotte was secretly amused to think how 'The idea of such a long interview as mine with a Chartist leader would be sufficient to frighten many of my friends. How much people and things are exaggerated.' She carefully distinguished between the local Chartists and 'the rabble of Birmingham', a reference to the Chartist Bull Ring Riots – for which her hardest words were reserved for the magistrates and police who had displayed 'great want of promptitude'. Her journal recounted Chartists marching in an orderly manner with flags and music, taking over pews at Merthyr's parish church – 'The church was quite crammed with Chartists', many wearing the distinctive waistcoats from Morgan Williams's factory and sporting blue ribbons attached to button-holes.

By 3 November 1839 the atmosphere was more ominous. There were reports of Chartists marching east over the mountains, keen to release the popular orator Henry Vincent from Monmouth Gaol, and Lady Charlotte heard about the manufacture of pikes. She later saw one of them, a blade concealed in what looked like a walking stick. Always good in a crisis, she refused to believe everything: 'There were absurd rumours that the bridge was to be broken down and all coaches stopped.' The march of 7,000 Welsh Chartists early on 4 November actually resulted in about twenty deaths and many injuries after confrontation between the Chartists and soldiers stationed at the Westgate Inn in Newport. It has been called 'the most serious clash between people and government in modern industrial Britain'. Yet after barely twenty minutes the 'poor deluded creatures' took flight (John used the term 'poor deluded persons' in a letter to

Bute later that month). Lady Charlotte added, 'It is said to have been lamentable to see the droves of these poor tired and defeated men returning from their ill-fated expedition.' Some Dowlais men had joined marchers between Newport and Ebbw Vale and two were now imprisoned but on the whole Merthyr and Dowlais Chartists do not appear to have been centrally involved in the Newport Rising. There were rumours that Merthyr Chartists had been awaiting news of a successful attack on Newport as a signal to take their own town but many local Chartists, Morgan Williams included, called themselves 'moral force men' and opposed physical confrontation. Rumours were rife. Hearing about a projected attack on Dowlais House, Lady Charlotte wrote (with some bravado): 'The idea of a siege and defence only inspired me with anything like dread on account of the children.' Dowlais House had been attacked during a strike in 1816 and John barricaded inside. Now they had thirty stand of arms and 450 Special Constables had been sworn in on 4 November. Influenced by reports in *The Times* about plans to capture the town, five children and three nurses were escorted out of Merthyr before 4 a.m. the day after the rising. That morning up to 600 gathered at the Big Pond above Dowlais then marched to Rhymney and put out blast furnaces. Several hundred remained to hear Sir John's plea for a return to Dowlais. The next day his men resumed work. Lady Charlotte retained utter confidence in the loyalty of the workforce. 'If anything had happened I should have walked into the forges which were in full work and where I am sure I should have been quite unmolested.' Blame was placed elsewhere. 'Our own men are good and true and stick to their work gallantly. It is of the Hill people that apprehensions are alone entertained.' She nonetheless recognized her vulnerability, 'It is an uncommon thing to feel that a mine may at any moment explode beneath one's feet. Their secrecy is beyond all comprehension.' As a believer in social harmony she had difficulty in appreciating the urgency or rationale behind this 'extraordinary infatuation'. One way to cope with it was to provide education to 'humanize' and so show the disaffected the folly of their ways.

It also helped to explain away the situation by romanticizing the Welsh – 'I do not believe that any but Welshmen could be brought up to such a pitch of enthusiasm.' Certainly there was only one event like the Newport Rising and the particular conjuncture of historical grievances and social composition of the industrial valleys gave Welsh protest an especially sharp edge. Yet it would be misleading to see Welsh Chartists in isolation or to claim that the movement (which started in England and was led by an Irishman) had less significance in other parts of Britain. Lady Charlotte's knowledge of Welsh history was derived from accounts of dashing and daring ancient heroes. In 1843 Sir John sat on the Grand Jury to try the Rebecca Rioters, impoverished farmers who had attacked the toll gates of West Wales disguised as women. Crossing the River Severn at the end of the year, the Guests were approached by John Hughes 'the personifyer [sic] of Rebecca himself'. His attack on Pontardulais toll gate had resulted in a sentence of twenty-one years' transportation, and he was on the first stage of his long journey to Tasmania. He described the Welsh farmers' problems. Lady Charlotte (who had just read Carlyle's indictment of modern society in his *Past and Present*), showed some sympathy for 'my poor Welsh rebel with all his faults and all his grievances and all his romance'.

The aftermath of the Newport Rising saw a 'silent warfare' with informers abounding and South Wales on the alert for several months. There were rumours of incendiary attacks, that Guest was a marked man, and local shopkeepers helped ensure that a company of the 45th Regiment was quartered in the Dowlais Stables (something which the Guests found inconvenient and expensive). Home Office correspondence suggests that most other local employers had rather less faith than the Dowlais master in their workforces. The Guests also dissociated themselves from their Rector's recriminatory approach. His vindictive pamphlet *Chartism Unmask'd* denounced Chartists as followers of evil practices. Lady Charlotte remarked that 'a kind of feud' developed between the Guests and the Rev. Evan Jenkins for many months because of this. Sir John refused to buy or distribute the pamphlet whilst Edward Hutchins gave secret instructions for a parcel of these pamphlets, 'the entire sentiment of which I do not approve', to be burned.

In 1841 local Chartists adopted the popular tactic of putting up a candidate at the hustings before an election. Although not going to the poll it enabled the Chartists to test the populace's feelings by a show of hands and provided an opportunity for denouncing the real candidates in a fiery speech. In her account of her husband's re-election Lady Charlotte omitted to mention that Sir John was actually defeated on a show of hands (after a recount) by Morgan Williams at the hustings. Her silence was probably due to Williams's denunciation of Guest for not being 'What he professed to be – the friend of the people.'

Although Sir John was returned unopposed in the actual election, it was the Tories who were now returned to power nationally. The early years of Peel's ministry saw severe economic depression. In January 1842 Dowlais laid off 150 men and the price of bar iron plummeted. Wage reductions fostered talk of strikes and the centre of Welsh Chartism now appeared to be Merthyr. Returning to Wales from London, Sir John went to Dowlais 'to the certainty (almost) of a riot and perhaps to any great danger'. Lady Charlotte did not appreciate being left in Cardiff: 'I am not allowed to be with him.' It was 'a great trial to be sent away like a child, while he is in danger'. Penydarren and Cyfarthfa workers were on strike for a resumption of 1839 wage levels. The events in Wales mirrored those in northern England where Chartists and trade unionists were stopping production by pulling plugs out of the boilers. With a comment which summed up her life more generally, Lady Charlotte remained 'very calm in appearance, very anxious in reality'. Yet the Dowlais workers 'never stopped for an hour in any department'. Within a few weeks peace was restored generally in the area and Chartists dismissed from work. The following year a spy told the Home Office that Dowlais men now sought help from Merthyr Chartists. The latter were only prepared to join a national strike and upbraided the Dowlais Chartists for remaining aloof the previous summer. It was Lady Charlotte who was eventually to experience the problems of a major Dowlais strike.

By April 1848, when Lady Charlotte discussed with Mr Gifford how best to educate the people, Chartism was once more resurgent. With a background of European revolts (the overthrow of Louis Philippe in France made people especially nervous), the collapse of the railway share market, a very severe winter and some rural rioting, Lady Charlotte and others like her were sharing 'many an anxious hour'. The Chartist 'threat' was in many ways illusory but concern was whipped up by the Government in the hope of provoking a final confrontation between the 'evil' of Chartism and the forces of law and order. Writing in London on 9 March Lady Charlotte referred to 'a tumultuous meeting of rabble' (a term *The Times* also used) in Trafalgar Square. She carefully distinguished between respectable workers and the rest: 'some knots of ill-looking people' (an ambiguous description) remained in the streets and 'seemed to have scared away the respectable part of the ordinary population'. This meeting had cheered the 'People of Paris and the People's Charter'. Apart from having their doorbell rung at intervals during the night, the Guests were undisturbed. Yet musing on the situation, Lady Charlotte believed that there was real cause for concern:

> What is to become of our unemployed? I was almost going to say our uncared for! Chartist meetings are being held in all our manufacturing places and they intend to make a great demonstration in London within the next few days. Who can say if the starving meet the troops, that there will not be bloodshed, and what implacable hate will not blood engender. I shudder to think of the future, the immediate future I mean, for all I feel sure will ultimately settle down into what is right. But we must all be brave and determined in the cause of Order.

Unlike some of her contemporaries, who seemed concerned only about the threat to property and people, Lady Charlotte dwelt on the plight of the poor, her concern exacerbated by worries that the non-renewal of the lease on the Dowlais land which ran out in 1848 and consequent run-down of the works was causing great distress at Dowlais. She asked, 'How can we expect these poor breadless creatures to be wise and not fall into the delusions of the tempters?' The works surgeon was distributing 'little charities' for her at Dowlais. Lady Charlotte recognized that her husband might see this as interference but 'my heart bled for Dowlais and I could not help it'. In London 'all the respectable people are being sworn in as Special Constables or are preparing with their estates or workpeople to support the cause of order. It is fearful to think what might ensue should there be a collision between these poor misguided men and the military. God only knows how it will end.'

Many thousands of Special Constables were recruited for the Kennington Common meeting and presentation of the third petition, almost the entire Metropolitan Police were mobilized and over 8,000 troops. Wellington was brought out of retirement (Lady Charlotte later talked to him about Chartism 'which he thinks more seriously of, than I should have expected'), artillery in the Tower prepared for use, the Bank of England barricaded and a war sloop positioned in the Thames. The Queen hastened to the Isle of Wight. Lady Charlotte's Society friends could talk of nothing but 'the expected turmoil' and the Railway Secretary hinted that there were 'a number of foreigners in England doing their best to promote anarchy'. Sir John refused to let Lady Charlotte accompany him to the Commons, 'These are anxious times. The consideration of them threw a gloom over me all day which I could not even try to shake off.'

By the date of the meeting (10 April) Lady Charlotte was safely installed in Dorset. Telegraphic communication told her that Feargus O'Connor had not persisted with the procession to Parliament and the petition was instead conveyed by two cabs. He had however addressed what would become the century's largest public gathering at Kennington Common, south of the river. (In 1842 Feargus O'Connor, the Chartist leader, had 'very politely assisted' Lady Charlotte at breakfast at Rugby railway station.) On 11 April she wrote, 'It was all admirably managed and the 10th of April must be remembered as a great triumph for order and peace.' On the same day *The Times* declared 'The 10th of April 1848, will long be remembered as a great field day of the Constitution.' It has been suggested that the demonstration and build-up to it reveal more about the fears of the propertied classes than about Chartism.[9] The concern, though abated, did not disappear. There was stone-throwing, and police charged a crowd in early June – 'They say it is all quiet again now but I suppose the violence may explode again at any moment.' Rumours abounded again. At one ball Lady Charlotte heard that the Chartists had taken possession of the City. At another she was told they planned to burn London in the course of the night. The poor servants had to sit up all night 'nor did I sleep much myself.'

In the wake of Kennington Common Lady Charlotte reiterated her worries about responsibility: '… while other nations are in such an awful state of confusion and anarchy we have great cause for gratitude to God for our present safety. But it must not blind us to the future. Something must be done for our unemployed, the events of yesterday must not lull us into security and make us overlook this duty, this necessity.'

From this time can be seen most clearly Lady Charlotte's commitment to educate the people. Her recognition and repeated use of the term 'unemployed' – forty years before it became widely accepted as a concept – suggests the influence of her cousin Henry Layard,[10] then at his most radical phase (he had been present at Kennington Common). It also shows her recognition that her husband's work through Parliament and aided by herself, was not enough, something demonstrated by the appeal of Chartism. One positive way of improving society was through the education and influence of the respectable working class who could set an example to others. Helped by Henry, Lady Charlotte now redoubled her efforts to provide schooling and recreation for the people of Dowlais.

For some years Dowlais had prided itself on its schools. Initial inspiration came from John Guest at a time when there was no statutory right to schooling and many felt no responsibility for providing it. The first government grant for education allocated less money for the entire country than had been spent on Windsor Castle stables. Apart from private schools, some of which were very inadequate – Merthyr and Dowlais had twenty-one Dame schools in the mid-1840s – education was dominated by two religious societies, the Rev. Andrew Bell's National Society (founded in 1811) and Joseph Lancaster's non-denominational British and Foreign School Society used by Nonconformists. Keen to provide some elementary and technical education for his future workforce, John adopted the organization and principles of the Bell system (so the catechism was taught in his schools) but the Company, employees and pupils financed them. The first ironworks school in Wales had opened in Monmouthshire in 1784. Others expanded in the first half of the nineteenth century, stimulated by the exclusion of children under ten from working in underground mining and the appeal from the North Walian Hugh Owen for the development of elementary education, and encouraged by the belief that schools were successful antidotes to political unrest. It was pointed out that the Blaenavon area, where a works school had existed since 1816, was free from disturbances. The rapid growth of population at Dowlais further stimulated the development of schools there.

When she first came to Wales Lady Charlotte was, (unlike the horrified government Commissioners), amused to hear a little girl reply to the question 'Who was St Luke?', with the answer, 'An Ironmaster'! She does not appear to have been very involved in the early phases of the Dowlais schools but did help with their reorganization in 1844. The Dowlais day schools boasted a number of progressive features. Children remained in school until they were fourteen and, unlike most schools where pupils were taught together in large halls with tiered seating (the juniors relegated to the galleries), classes were held separately, sectioned off by curtains or partitions in what was known as the Prussian or German system. The Guests had toured the German mining districts in 1842 and their visit to Prussia (where education was compulsory between six and fourteen) had an impact on their plans for Dowlais.

Perhaps most importantly, the Guests used trained teachers. South Wales did not have its own training college before 1848, so they turned to the London colleges. When Lady Charlotte first came to Dowlais the schoolmaster was Thomas Jenkins, an 'excellent, painstaking creature, the very beau ideal of a country school master'. He was succeeded in 1844 by a new type of teacher. Matthew Hirst was a Yorkshireman trained at the Normal College in Battersea (his widowed mother received financial help for this from Lady Byron). He was personally recommended by James Kay Shuttleworth, one of the school's founders (and Secretary to the Committee of the Privy Council on Education). He was the first certificated schoolmaster in Wales and remained at Dowlais for forty-eight years. He married twice and both his wives were Dowlais schoolmistresses. A schoolmistress was chosen (with the help of Mr Kingsley) from the eminent Whitelands Training College, and in 1849 she was replaced by Esther Lamb. According to Lady Charlotte's description, Miss Lamb lived up to her name as a 'calm, mild' person but also 'judicious and quite the right sort of person to manage so difficult a post'. The government Inspector was so impressed by her that he felt it would be beneficial for mistresses from other parts of South Wales to 'finish' their education with a spell at Dowlais under Miss Lamb. Male and female assistants were drawn from Battersea, Westminster, Cheltenham, Chelsea and Whitelands colleges, were better paid than pupil-teachers and secured for the scholars (according to a commissioner) 'incomparably superior advantages'. There were also some pupil-teachers, learning as they taught.

Infant schools were developed in the mid-1840s. Lady Charlotte had already seen the school developed by her sister-in-law Anne Guest at Cardiff: 'I think, as I thought then, that such an institution may be very useful as to keeping little animals out of mischief, and I am going to establish one at Dowlais where the children abound in all parts of the streets, and are constantly meeting with accidents, particularly from the steam engine and trams.'

The first English infants' school had been started in Westminster in 1819, founded by a group which included Brougham, the Lord Chancellor, whom Lady Charlotte had appealed to in her youth. She had not been to school herself and found that it did not agree too well with her sons but she made sure that her children were taught from an early age and that the Dowlais community had an educational ladder. Inculcating from infancy the importance of attendance and punctuality combined with an appreciation of learning would, it was hoped, encourage pupils to stay on at school.

Not receiving financial help from the National Society, there was no obligation for the schools to be inspected. The Guests, however, wisely recognized the advantages of inspection. They gained excellent publicity through it. The HMI, the Rev. Longueville Jones, repeatedly praised these schools as the best in his district. Most employers were more suspicious of the prying eyes of inspectors and commissioners. In Wales sensitivity was heightened due to the infamous education report published in 1847 and known to this day as *Brad y Llyfrau Gleision* (*Treachery of the Blue Books*).[11] In the Parliamentary debate which led to the enquiry, Sir James Graham had singled out the efforts of Sir John and members of his family as evidence of improvements made since the Newport Rising. The three Commissioners who headed the enquiry were, as David Williams has pointed out, very able but ignorant of Nonconformity and the Welsh working class. Not understanding the English language was made synonymous with illiteracy and backwardness, and although the provision and standard of education in Wales did leave much to be desired, the accompanying cultural insensitivity (revealed in such comments as 'his language keeps him under the hatches') fanned tensions between the English and Welsh and more specifically between the Nonconformists and the minority of influential Anglicans in Wales.

Although most of the thirty-seven schools in the Merthyr and Dowlais area were criticized (only three were deemed even moderate), the Dowlais schools were praised and the boys' upper school room described as 'by far the best provided in Wales'. There senior boys discussed international trade and 'a thoroughly good, even superior education' was provided. The publication of this report was a stimulus to Lady Charlotte's renewed efforts in education from 1848. Whereas previously John had been the one most committed to educational development (especially promoting the potential of the senior boys), now Lady Charlotte, who had recently completed her translation work, increasingly turned her attention to education as a means of improving the condition of the people. Her sentimentalization of Welsh 'warmth', where 'I am happy, I am free. It is a sense of love to and from all that no cold English decorum can ever supply', encouraged her to put something back into the community.

Lady Charlotte recognized that 'there is more here to occupy me than months or even years could accomplish' but 'if I can but do a little I must be grateful'. Educational developments gave Lady Charlotte a chance to forward her own ideas in unison with her husband but in such a way as to permit scope for some independent thought. She specialized in furthering the extreme ends of the educational ladder, the infants and the teaching of adults. Her concern about Chartism was reflected in the provision of adult education and Dowlais was the first place in Wales to develop evening schools for adult men and women. In the autumn of 1848 she explained that she was trying to establish a night school for the young women employed in the works, many of whom had come from rural Carmarthenshire with no formal education. Others had been in the Dowlais schools when young but wanted to learn more: 'the idea has pleased the girls themselves'. Numerous applications were received from young women over sixteen and on 9 October the new school was opened for the winter months. Out of 177 only twenty could read and write, some did not know their letters at all and anyway found English a difficult foreign language. Yet 'they seemed most anxious to learn, most grateful to be taught'. Some of the agents' wives helped out. It was 'a touching sight. I had been nervous about the experiment, but what I saw tonight quite repaid me.' An adult evening school for men (two-thirds were miners' sons of eleven to twenty-six) proved very popular. Cwmavon Copper works and the Neath Abbey works also evolved their own evening classes with emphasis on technical instruction. For a time Dowlais provided some morning instruction in the library for workmen studying higher mathematics. To complete the scheme were seven Sunday schools catering for all ages in Welsh and English. Lady Charlotte occasionally gave 'a sort of lecture' to a class for girls. Although she found their English poor so kept her talks short, she did not attempt to address them herself in Welsh. The Minutes of the Committee of the Council on Education show that in mid-century the total school attendances (excluding Sunday school) were over 1,000. By 1865 this had risen to over 2,000.

Leslie Wynne Evans points to the Guest schools as 'undoubtedly the most important and also the most progressive in the industrial history not only of South Wales, but of the whole of Britain during the nineteenth century'. This perhaps requires some qualification though their innovation and example were unequalled in Wales and many parts of Britain before the 1870s. When Lady Charlotte visited the progressive, radical New Lanark schools in Scotland in 1839, she commented that 'They did not appear to me to be better than our own Dowlais – if indeed so good.' Owen's New Institution included a playground for infants and Dowlais too developed an enclosed play area with circular swings. Both places used wall displays in their classrooms. Owen and the Chartist William Lovett (who developed educational theory and practice) saw education as the key to social change and shared with the Guests a recognition of the value of education in training minds and character from an early age. Although the Guest schools were not as visionary as Lovett's plans, they were much more enlightened than most schools of their kind, forming a refreshing contrast to the mindless contemporary custom of relying on learning by rote, so graphically portrayed in Dickens's *Hard Times* (which Lady Charlotte read in 1854). Lady Charlotte's efforts were appreciated. A Merthyr printer, Rees Lewis, eulogized her philanthropy, paying tribute in verse to her provision of 'the finest golden gift of education.'★ In 1850 the *Merthyr Guardian* declared that 'Education has in her one of its greatest promoters.'

Most days and evenings when back at Dowlais in the autumn of 1848 Lady Charlotte visited schools – whatever the weather. She even recorded going over the mountains to Banwen Infants in deep snow. On 8 October she wrote that she had been at the schools every week day for the past few weeks excepting one day when she had so much writing at home that she could only manage a visit to the Works Manager's wife to discuss school plans.

She had spent much of the past week at the girls' school where she set the first class history, 'making a short epitome of it from dictation which interests them, I think, more than their dry routine of writing copies'. Despite her own interest in Welsh literature and history, unlike Lady Hall who encouraged Welsh and English at her Abercarn schools, Lady Charlotte does not seem to have appreciated the value of the children studying their own language or history. Her emphasis on English language and affairs was consistent with contemporary teaching in general and such a tendency was intensified by the publication of the 1847 education report.

When she left Dowlais briefly in mid-October she observed that 'all my new interests bind me to it more than ever'. She held frequent discussions with the Rector about 'my people' and was especially faithful in attending the young women's night school. In late November she wrote that: 'Merthyr has lately been annoyed at my going to the schools and this vexes me.' The old contradictions were resurfacing.

> I feel it my duty to go and on the other hand I cannot bear to do anything he the least disapproves. I know that in real truth he sees it also to be my duty and does not seriously wish me to give it up, but just at the moment it ruffles him and the children see this. Now it must not be that they or anybody suppose that I should act in any way against his wishes. The effect would be incalculably bad. So this morning I forced myself to come to an understanding with him and the result is that I have

---

★ See Appendix 3A.

made a promise only to go to two evenings a week, at the most, and he has promised to allow this cheerfully.

That very evening John's nephew Edward Hutchins arrived to stay. Lady Charlotte could never resist any opportunity to show off the schools so, 'I took this for one of my nights and went with him to the schools'. She only visited them one other evening that week though she spent many hours in the day schools, interviewed the teachers and purchased anatomical diagrams 'which will be a treat I hope for my schools'. The next week a representative from the National Schools arrived so she was permitted an extra evening out. So regular was her attendance that on Boxing Day she declared like one of the teachers, 'I feel it a holiday too to be exempted for one week of all charge about the schools.' Her involvement included trying to get the girls 'into a tidy way of keeping their hair', providing infants with Welsh woollen dresses and encouraging regular attendance reports. The evening classes were designed to cover the winter months but she kept on a skeleton staff in case there was demand for classes in the summer months.

Leading scientists such as David Brewster and Sir Charles Wheatstone toured the schools and gave lectures on subjects like 'remarkable earthquakes and undulations'. To further her own knowledge Lady Charlotte read books such as *The Social Condition and Education of The People* (two volumes) by Joseph Kay, the barrister brother of James Kay Shuttleworth. Kay praised the educational system the Guests had sampled in Germany. It was a work 'that interests me very much – Having so much to do with masses of people I think it is right to turn my attention as much as possible to subjects of that kind and they have a deep interest for me.'

She also had to sort out problems of authority. The wrangle between Church and State for control of schooling was exemplified by the Rev. Evan Jenkins and Matthew Hirst. Since Jenkins' school was nominally under the banner of the National Society, he saw himself as ultimately responsible for the schools and resented the schoolmaster taking independent action. He complained to Lady Charlotte after Hirst ordered books from the National Society without his knowledge. Nor was this

the first or second time that Mr Hirst has tried to cast me overboard. I know I am an impediment in his way – and his wife was at the same game when she had the girls' school – If Mr Hirst is allowed to act quite independently of me there is at once an end of my influence over the School – and it can do no good there … I am willing to go on but I must have full authority, under your Ladyship – and through me from your Ladyship to the Schools – unless this will be the case I can have no influence for good – Of course if your Ladyship wishes Mr Hirst to act independently of me I have no alternative but must respectfully beg of your Ladyship to accept my resignation of the management of the schools.

If anybody was skilled in dealing with the ruffled feelings of clergymen it was Lady Charlotte. She also had to restrain the Rev. Evan Jenkins from exercising his authority too clearly. She was not happy when he publicly expelled some scholars. On another occasion she found herself pleading to her husband for clemency. An evening scholar had been caught taking coal from the works and 'on my begging' Sir John agreed not to prosecute but warned her that 'I am never to ask again' for such favours. The Rector was a strict Sabbatarian and objected to the company allowing men to work on Sundays. It was to Lady Charlotte that he complained, just as she had to deal with a schoolmistress who attended a 'convivial' party on Good Friday. Teachers were public figures who both demanded and expected respect and were hastily rebuked if they could not command it. Reacting to one tiresome anonymous letter about the conduct of a schoolmistress, Lady Charlotte remarked 'How much worry there is in *my* world and how brief are my intervals of peace.'

At the end of each term Lady Charlotte held prize-givings. Classrooms were decorated, work displayed and oral examinations held. The more advanced evening-school pupils had written examinations in subjects such as arithmetic and Holy Scriptures. Scripture papers included such questions as: 1. Write out the Commandment which teaches you your duty to your parents. 2. How, and within what time was the world created? Describe the creation of man. Prizes were also given for regular attendance and general progress. Lady Charlotte was pleased to see the progress made by the young women in 1849, 'Many can write, can cypher, can work, and I think the influence in a moral point of view has been greater still.' After the presentation she admitted: 'These speeches always rather excite me, they require so much care and fact, to please, give no offence and yet be serviceable.'

Unfortunately Sir John was rather less impressed by the whole event, declaring the presentation evening 'dull and ill-managed'. To her credit, Lady Charlotte took these gatherings as seriously as any she attended. She was sent in advance lists of the best-qualified pupils from which she picked prize-winners, and she selected prizes in the Lowther Arcade in London. When an evening scholar married she was presented with a personally inscribed family Bible. Lady Charlotte supplied materials for needlework and approved the purchase of teaching resources. Letters from Hirst to her read like modern pleas from head teachers to their local education authorities justifying necessary expenditure and urging immediate further supplies.

By the autumn of 1850 Lady Charlotte was well acquainted with school management. Although she had felt shy about visiting the young men's evening school, she felt they wanted 'a little supervision' so 'overcame my feelings in this respect, and arranged their classes, started their singing, and I think was of use in setting them to work'. The next month she took their classes whenever there was a shortage of teachers. Teaching was not new to Lady Charlotte but tutoring brothers or offspring was very different from conducting classes for adult workers. Her own background and standards made her initially somewhat unrealistic. After one examination she wrote that 'some young ladies of ten years old could not spell Thessalonica'. She soon learned that this was the least (and least relevant) of their problems. From 1848 she had stepped into the breach whenever a teacher was required for the girls or young women, acting as an extraordinary 'supply' teacher. She experimented with teaching methods, using cards and pictures, for example, to illustrate scripture for the infants – 'I am very anxious to make everything as attractive as I can.' Miss Kemble and Maria were soon pressed into service and cousin Henry Layard, now famous for his discovery of Nineveh, rendered 'invaluable assistance'. She recognized that he could provide 'a great impetus to the people' of Dowlais. After one concert with the pupils at which Henry played the flute, Lady Charlotte remarked somewhat ambiguously, 'These fluxions of classes for rational and humanising pursuits are very valuable.'

Lady Charlotte visited schools at Swansea, Llandaff and London. She approved of Mary's village school at Orton Longueville and travelled with her husband to see the Worsley schools established by the Ellesmeres in Lancashire. By the autumn of 1851 plans were underway for new schools at Dowlais. Charles Barry was commissioned to design them and John Gabe (a local builder experienced in chapel work) got the building contract. The Dowlais Central Schools were a showpiece containing seven schoolrooms and a large central hall lit by four perpendicular traceries windows. They accommodated 650 boys and girls and 680 infants. The total cost of the land, design, buildings and fittings reached £20,000 – the same amount as that set aside for the schoolroom building of England and Wales in the first government grant of 1833. On 11 September 1855 Lady Charlotte attended the formal opening of the schools – thousands of school-children from all over the district were treated to tea and plum cake. The impressive educational system at Dowlais was complete.

Educating the people involved more than political education and schooling. It meant helping to inculcate and implement a wider social culture based on employer support yet respecting self-help. Lady Charlotte helped develop a Dowlais Savings Bank (which probably provided the model for the Post Office's National Savings scheme). Frugality was encouraged by sobriety and, to combat the appeal of Dowlais's numerous beerhouses, Lady Charlotte set about turning free time to good purpose. 'Mental elevation' was encouraged by supplying local hawkers with books of 'good tendency and of a popular description' (along with generous commissions) to combat the 'trash' they were used to peddling. In the mid-1840s Lady Charlotte helped form a workmen's library with 200 volumes and a 1s 6d subscription.[12] In 1853 this became a free library. A decade later the Guest Memorial Hall was opened, its colonaded Tuscan portico and pediment displaying Sir Charles Barry's signature. A purpose-built workman's hall with reading room and library, it had been planned as a monument to Sir John from the people of Dowlais, though costs outran subscriptions and the Company took over its responsibility. The money raised for Sir John was instead used to finance yearly scholarships for Dowlais schoolchildren.

The Guests actively supported the Friendly Societies which fostered self-help, offering benefits for sickness, old age and death based on regular contributions into a common fund (the Company also operated a scheme for the relief of the sick and employed a surgeon, the costs defrayed by a levy on wages). The Oddfellows named a lodge The Lady Charlotte and their patron graced some of their social functions.

Lady Charlotte believed that women of the ruling class could play a particularly valuable role in promoting social harmony. When in 1856 she read about a dinner for workmen and agents hosted by her Society acquaintance the widowed Marchioness of Londonderry, she noted: 'She made them a speech on the occasion – a most excellent and sensible one – No man could have done better – few things have pleased me more of late than this little circumstance – It is a move in the right direction and as coming from a woman is deserving of greater consideration – If our aristocracy will avail themselves of such occasions to mingle with and advise the people, they will do much good for both classes – I greatly rejoice at this one – and feel it the more as it reminds me of my old days of power.'

Attracted by the contemporary interest in 'rational recreation' Lady Charlotte sponsored a recreation area for Dowlais workers, a converted field where the brass band played and skittles, bowling and gymnastics flourished. The most ambitious scheme was, however, tried out in the pattern shop. Here evening parties were held to bring together the employer and the respectable workman, to 'humanise and civilise'. Sir John and H.A. Bruce originally suggested the idea but it was developed by Lady Charlotte working closely with Henry Layard. It was a popular idea amongst Radicals at the time – for example the Chartist Ernest Jones held soirées or 'evenings with the people', though his events combined poetry with politics. The first Dowlais evening party took place in October 1850 in the increasingly conciliatory atmosphere which seemed to mark mid-century politics. By no means all Dowlais workers would have appreciated the marked note of paternalism which surrounded such events, but simply dismissing them in terms of a crude social control suggests too much coercion on the one side and excessive blind acceptance on the other. There is plenty of evidence to suggest that for the artisan elite, such as the highly skilled puddlers, such gatherings were welcomed as educative.

It was Lady Charlotte who wrote out the personal invitations and supervised arrangements. As with all her parties, whether in Merthyr or Mayfair, masses of evergreens were displayed. Entertainment at these 'intellectual feasts' included Henry lecturing on Nineveh, an ode composed in his honour and read by the scholarly tradesman Thomas Stephens, a rendition of Handel's choruses by the choir coached by the talented ex-miner Rosser Beynon, an anthem composed by one of the choir, songs from the Dowlais Glee club and the scholars and even a piano recital from Lady Charlotte. After one event attended by between 500 and 600 people, Henry who 'always furnishes me with material for thought' discussed with Lady Charlotte and an old clergyman friend 'every sort of subject especially all that might be done for the lower classes – in this place as elsewhere – it was a most agreeable little talk.' Paternalism was clearly not the prerogative of rural society – nor of men. Industrialists' wives like Lady Charlotte were instrumental in cementing social relations in their communities.

Yet despite the broad programme of education, liberal endorsement of different religious sects and generous provision of places of worship and pleasure, the Guests do seem to have had a blind spot. They may have believed in the civilizing effects of hard work and the opportunities of industrial development enhanced by education but they paid scant attention to improving homes and the physical environment. Between a quarter and a third of the local population were housed in workers' cottages. Some of the best-paid Dowlais workmen speculated in housing with money borrowed from the company. Yet although the best houses tended to be those erected by the iron companies, local housing left much to be desired. Even more disturbing was the lack of sanitary amenities. The cholera epidemic of 1849 when 'the streets were black with coffins' took over 500 lives in Dowlais alone. Although the Dowlais Iron Company appears to have been less bound up in self-interest than the other local works – demonstrated by Lady Charlotte's exchanges with the Merthyr Board of Health in mid-century, attempting to secure for Dowlais a separate and decent water supply – at the end of the day there was more concern to cleanse the community morally than to provide practical help in alleviating the shocking physical conditions of employees living in the shadow of the ironworks, which in itself was hardly conducive to good health. The return of cholera in 1854 'in a most virulent form' was a commentary on the employers' abdication of responsibility in a district which never ceased to horrify visitors unused to its lack of the most basic facilities. In 1848 the year when Lady Charlotte sought to 'humanise' the lower classes, Merthyr's mortality rate was the highest in Wales and the third highest in the kingdom.

Unlike the vast majority of Merthyr's inhabitants Lady Charlotte moved away from this environment. She did make return visits to the schools after the 1850s but only occasionally. After one visit to the Talbots at Margam[13] and the Vivians at Swansea (where she visited their school at the Hafod Copper works) as well as seeing the Dowlais schools, she wrote 'I had seen much that interested me, and rejoiced very much at the prosperity of the schools.' Her final visit to the Dowlais schools was in 1890. She was seventy-eight and called it 'my farewell visit to dear old Dowlais'. She and her granddaughter Alice spent two days in the schools – there were now 2,090 daily pupils.'[14]

Yet despite their evident success, it was individual examples of initiative and opportunity through education which afforded Lady Charlotte the greatest pleasure. An unexpected example of this happened in the summer of 1873, three years after Forster's Education Act introduced secular rate-supported elementary schools (run by School Boards) throughout England and Wales. Lady Charlotte and her second husband, the Cambridge Fellow, Charles Schreiber, were on the cross-Channel steamer. Many of the passengers were bound for the Iron and Steel Congress at Liège. They included:

> … a well-dressed middle-aged man, who introduced himself to me, as a former Dowlais schoolboy, and told me he was now a partner in a rolling mill near Stockton-on-Tees. He said, having been a poor boy, he owed all his success in life to his teaching in the Dowlais schools, and remembered on one occasion, my having patted him on the head and told him to be a good boy! (oh! how many years ago). He seems to have well obeyed my instructions. His name he said, was Prosser. I shall enquire more about him.

4

The Society Lady

*'Even pleasure is but a business – for balls and
parties are only pleasure to me as contributing
to one of my objects – Society.'*

Throughout her life Lady Charlotte maintained a love-hate relationship with
Society. She needed it but was not always convinced that it needed her. She certainly wished to succeed in this sphere of life as in every other. Her concern to
reach an eminence in all she undertook, her acute awareness of the implications
of marrying into trade and newly acquired wealth, alongside ambition for her
children, fuelled her determination. Yet somehow, full participation in fashionable aristocratic Society seemed to require more effort, even hard work, than her
other occupations, though they might appear to us as more onerous. Helped by
dogged perseverance and the Lindsey name, she did make her mark. Yet her high
standards, sensitivity and acute grasp of social gradations prevented her from taking anything for granted, and she pursued Society as if it were a valuable business
contract which had to be secured and then carefully monitored lest either side
threatened its validity. Her journal enables later generations to glimpse the rituals
of the London season, her detailed entries guiding us through its rules and pitfalls
at a time of great social and economic change. Challenges to the 'old order' were
producing ever more elaborate regulation of behaviour and acceptance and a ruling class which was more fractured than the image it sought to present. Although
Society provided the one opportunity for some women to exert an influence in
public, for Lady Charlotte it was an area over which, initially at least, she had little control. Her ability to see through much of the protocol and the pretensions
provides us with perspectives which are missing from the etiquette manuals.

Even before her marriage, Lady Charlotte's visits to London and Brighton
had produced 'ennui' rather than exhilaration. There had been a few high spots
– Madame Giuditta Pasta's rendering of 'Mary' helped compensate for the 'very
intense misery and awkwardness' felt in a London dancing academy. She reluctantly conceded that Brighton could be amusing. Its inhabitants included Mrs
Fitzherbert, who had secretly married George IV (though his father later made
the contract invalid). Although it was rare for Lady Charlotte to mention everyday
dress, she did describe the oriental style pink and silver tunic with bird-of-paradise

feathers worn to Mrs Fitzherbert's fancy dress ball. Pegus went as Hamlet but had agonized over the suitability of his costume and his own heroic potential. Lady Charlotte was captivated by George IV's exotic creation, the Brighton Pavilion. The combination of Hindu, Chinese and classical was irresistible, especially the Chinese gallery with its clawed dragons climbing from the bamboo chimney to the peach-blossomed ceiling. The Chinese scenes were actually painted in Sussex and the bamboo effect achieved by cast iron but it was enchanting enough for Lady Charlotte, particularly since the sun flowers of the Music Room evoked her favourite 'Arabian Nights'.

Yet within months the mere mention of returning to Brighton or Paris (where Pegus 'liked the champagne very much') produced outpourings of 'horror'. Lady Charlotte was greatly relieved when a plan to send her to Italy came to nothing. Part of the problem was that few real people could live up to the expectations produced by literary heroes. In 1828 she wrote 'The height of my ambition this year is to remain quiet at dear Uffington, amusing and improving myself in peace and retirement'. Fifty years later she would have scoffed at such introspection. When her honeymoon route lay through Brighton some of the old ambivalence returned as she dubbed it 'my old friend or rather enemy for I was grievously ill there'. Yet years later she sent her children there for the air and rented a house in Marine Parade only a few doors from the lodgings taken by the Pegus family in 1828.

Soon after the first Brighton season Lady Charlotte learned something of the workings of Society. She attended a ball at which the Duchess of St Albans and Augustus O'Brien were present. After dancing with 'the person who has engrossed almost all of the little feeling that my unfeeling self ever possessed' she impetuously dashed up to the Duchess (resplendent in green velvet) and asked if Augustus could accompany her to the Duchess's home at Holly Lodge. The Duchess promptly refused and Lady Charlotte backed away: 'I never asked a favour in my life that I was not refused.'

As she grew older she soon picked up the rules of the game. Her first trial was 'coming out'. She had described presentation at Court as 'part of the business I sincerely wish to escape' but by 1831 it could no longer be delayed. She felt 'degraded' by the whole experience and a letter from Mr Martin was 'quite an oasis in this desert where I am shut out from all I care or have interest in'. 'I fear I acquitted myself very ill', she wrote after the presentation to William IV. Her family spent the season at 8, Cumberland Place and she attended balls. She was not naturally gregarious and was prone to 'frozen fits'. She once wrote, 'I always feel so solitary at all the gay things. I am shy and proud (or rather from extreme sensitiveness I seem so).' Yet contemporaries did not have the advantage of reading her journal confidences, and her impeccable manners must have camouflaged her inner feelings. She never enjoyed dancing and the following rhyme she composed (in about 1847) about dancing at her London home seems to sum up her feelings.

Dancing, 8 Spring Gardens

Oh dancing is the bane/Of my whole life

It gives me jealous pain and envy rife

When I go round and round so does the room!

I sit down on the ground, my usual doom!

I can't quadrille or 'lance', I can't 'cotill'

I can't dance any dance they make me ill.

I cannot 'Polk' or valse, I'm fat and slow!

But supper never palls, that's why I go.

Most balls she dismissed as 'stupid'. Though having a slightly less derisory mean-ing then than it has today, she deliberately used the term to register her lack of interest in such events. There was a problem. Young ladies were expected to find suitable husbands within two or three seasons at the most (not least because seasons were costly). As we have seen, the young men Lady Charlotte had liked in the past met with her family's disapproval whilst the not so young men her parents put forward evoked an equally hostile response from her. When the fam-ily decided against taking a London house for Christmas 1831, Lady Charlotte's reaction was mixed: she was glad to escape yet 'I feel it will be the greatest pos-sible disadvantage to me'. In May 1832 she felt self-conscious going out with her brothers: 'I feel quite aged'. A year later she was married and wrote with relief 'Now that my fate in life is fixed, there is no need to go to gaieties on the chance of making a grand conquest – of all things most abhorrent.'

Her marriage gave her a vital injection of confidence. She wrote with mock gravity about John's attentions to her: 'he was very wild and did not behave with propriety; so I here record that if he in future insists upon kissing me in the mid-dle of Regent Street in broad daylight I will not take him down to the House of Commons again after dinner'. She admitted 'I never felt so comfortable in London before' but there were now new hurdles to face. At Court in 1833 the King had asked the age of her brother. She was so surprised at this attention that by the time 'I had given the answer and made the required curtsey I began to doubt whether I had any brother at all'. Now she had to be presented again as significant life changes such as marriage required renewed introductions. An individual had to be sponsored by somebody already 'in' Society and the more elevated, the better. Although it might seem that Lady Charlotte could glide back in, she and her family knew that real acceptance (particularly in the light of her marriage) was not easy. Pegus was anxious for Lady Stuart de Rothesay to 'assist me in Society'. She declined (via a note) to present Lady Charlotte who had to fall back on the friendly but less prestigious Mrs Heathcote. Lady Charlotte had been wary of Pegus's suggestion: 'The wide political difference between him [Lord Stuart] and Merthyr would be an obstacle – Then he might be one of those who would be glad to be civil to me as a bribe for obtaining my husband's vote and I should not consider it fair to let him entertain any idea of ever getting that, and thus as it were receiving his kindness under false pretences.'

Yet a patron was needed to get on. At the end of 1835 Lady Charlotte summoned up the courage to approach Lord Stuart at an afternoon party held by the Duchess of St Albans. 'He was very kind and seemed inclined to render me his assistance in attaining that Society to which I feel entitled, and beneath which I am unwilling, at least without a struggle, to sink; but, he said, he should consult his wife, and I cannot help feeling she, from her cold manner the other day, may frustrate my schemes and his good intentions.'

As was often the case, her fears were well-founded. Four days later Lady Stuart had still not responded and, to make matters worse, Lady Brown had refused tickets for Almacks. These gatherings were strictly regulated affairs run by a coterie of hostesses headed by Lady Jersey. Lady Charlotte might have consoled herself with the knowledge that the Duke of Wellington had apparently been turned away twice for not wearing knee breeches. On the night that she was refused, her iron-master husband in his most radical phase was voting in the House of Commons for the secret ballot.

The London season was always crowded and it was important not to double-book events in the social calendar. When Lady Charlotte met Lady Stuart at Lady Stepney's Drawing Room she was dissuaded from holding a concert as it clashed with a ball for which Lady Stuart was a patroness. The latter did hold out the carrot of introductions to the ambassadors but 'did not seem inclined to forward my going to any of the large parties going now'. Lady Charlotte's relative, Lady Willoughby, only allocated her one Almacks ticket and that at a time 'when she knows that nobody cares to be there'. Lady Stuart advised her to put off having her own ball until the following season. This was a far cry from Dowlais where the only opposition to balls came from strict chapel and church-goers who still remained indebted in various ways to the powerful Guest family.

Lady Charlotte attempted to maintain some critical distance between herself and the rest of Society. Earlier in the season she had written:

I had intended to study Society and attempt success in it – The object would have amused me the aim was not great enough to give me the least disappoint had I failed – This idea was hastily adopted and more because I wanted the excitement of aiming at something other than from ambition (which relating to Society I cannot feel) but I have quite given it up and I am glad I have – it is useless to catch an ugly butterfly not worth having – it would be worse than useless – criminal – to waste time on the pursuit of it; but that I would never have done.

The problem was, however, that her husband needed to be in London for Parliamentary duties. For Lady Charlotte, duty lay in accompanying him, and once in London she could not easily shrug off the desire to move in elevated circles. Nor was she being strictly honest with herself when she claimed that failure would not disappoint her. Failure was not something she could accept easily, and despite her ability to see beyond the shallowness and pettiness of much of the life of London Society she found herself attracted to aspects of it. She also wanted to rescue the family name from her mother's second marriage – not always that easy as Pegus had a disconcerting habit of popping up in London just when she least wanted to see him. In 1836 she reviewed her immediate objectives. They were: 'Society, Next getting Lindsey to go with the Whigs (which I see is all but hopeless owing to Mr Pegus's prejudices) – Then the amassing such a fortune for the babies as to make them very well off hereafter – Society is by far the most difficult of these.'

No doubt the fact that most of her other occupations were chosen, whilst this was seen as necessary, influenced her perceptions. To wifely duty was added maternal responsibility and social redress through the next generation.

The price was high. A punishing round of balls and parties all laced with polite and correct conversation and demeanour could soon take its toll, particularly since most events continued into the small hours and Lady Charlotte was pregnant for much of the time. A typical week in June 1852 included the following events:

> Monday – dinner and dance at the Londonderry's
> Tuesday – ball at Lady Cavendish's
> Wednesday – concert Lansdowne House
> Thursday – French play
> Friday – Maria's fête for 8th birthday. Duchess of Bedford presided at tea table for adults. Dined Lady Kinnoull's
> Saturday – dinner Duke of Somerset's.

When Lady Stuart came to return a call, Lady Charlotte read between her polite lines. She

> … was remarkably civil, staid [sic] half an hour and talked about nothing …she says she is delicate about introductions which is to say she will make none. She says it is extremely difficult to get to any of the good parties, and does not offer to assist me to any of them. Even introducing me to the foreign Ambassadors, which at first she said she could accomplish, she now cannot promise, and I think her offer of giving some of my cards to young men was the only result of the half hour's conversation. I spoke to her coming to dine with me and she talked of Lord Stuart's coming alone and she said she seldom went out except to Balls with her daughter. This I should like much better as he is delightful and she is at best very stiff. So much at present. I believe I must depend on myself for getting on.

In order to 'get on' an elaborate code of conduct had to be observed. As Leonore Davidoff has pointed out, it is perhaps significant that the word 'etiquette' means 'labelling' or 'ticketing'. By 1800 the French custom of printed cards had spread to Britain and they would be left on an initial visit. The two ladies would not actually meet since a servant would deliver the card. A card would then be left in reply. Calls had to be returned by calls, generally lasting about fifteen minutes in the afternoon. Sundays were outside the regular calendar, being times for family, friends and church (even pews could be rented for the season). Lady Charlotte had been used to social calls from an early age.[1] If a person were considered undesirable, the opposite of calling, the 'cut', was adopted. When John's niece was pursued by 'that horrid scamp' Lord Glentworth, Lady Charlotte requested her to '... cut him with all imaginable speed'. Needless to say, Lady Charlotte 'cut' Pegus a number of times.

Lady Greville observed that 'men and women are divided between those who are in and those who are out of Society'. Yet within this there was some demarcation according to gender. Just as the social call was the ladies' concern, so was the club the gentlemen's preserve. John was a founding member of the Reform Club, established in 1836 'for the purpose of bringing together the Reformers of the United Kingdom' and sat on the initial provisional committee of fifty. Joseph Hume was the club's first chairman.

During the 1835 season Lady Charlotte underwent the statutory round of calls despite feeling ill (Ivor was born in August). The elaborate and hierarchical network of introductions helped regulate entry to the higher echelons of Society. Persons of lower rank were always introduced to those of higher rank. Marital status, age and, above all, rank, were crucial determinants. Sometimes an introduction was refused. Lady Stuart 'politely declined' to introduce Lady Charlotte to the Duke of Wellington. Undeterred, she looked elsewhere: Mrs Tollemache was 'a great bore' but could make a useful introduction so 'if she effects this I must have her to my concert'.

Lady Charlotte's first concert was in May 1834. She saw it as 'a great undertaking and one in which I should most probably fail'. It provoked one of her old sobbing fits. The date she had singled out was being used by Mrs Wyndham Lewis for a party. Lady Charlotte could not offend the wife of her husband's business partner but, as Lady Greville put it, a concert was 'a necessary evil for a lady in Society'. Lady Stepney suggested consulting Lady Clarendon but, not knowing her, this was not possible. 'This scheme has already given me more trouble than it is worth', wrote Lady Charlotte. Relative newcomers needed to have their entertainments sponsored by well-known ladies of fashion. Lady Charlotte let Lady Stepney choose the date and was dismayed when Ascot Day was selected. Lady Lindsey was summoned from Uffington 'as I am very ignorant about arrangements'. The morning concert was a success. Two of the leading ensemble from the Queens Theatre in the Haymarket performed, also the passionate soprano Giulia Grisi and the tenor Giovanni Rubini. The Neapolitan Conductor De Costa directed the music. The concert had been advertised in the *Morning Post* and the house was full – 'If this day last year I could have foreseen all this, how surprised I would have been.'

The following season her concert was not the success she wished: the music was good, and there were plenty of people but not those she wanted, 'In fact I was annoyed to find exactly those I wished to have staid [sic] away.' Lady Lansdowne and Lord Liverpool both had parties on that day so 'I, of course, had no dance'. Lady Stepney had invited some of the guests herself, a custom undertaken by those patronizing newcomers. About 300 guests attended, and Mary helped deliver invitations and put up flowers. Lady Charlotte was even more dismayed by a dinner party held for a mixture of family friends and her husband's acquaintances and graced by Lady Stepney. One guest was Mrs Wyndham Lewis. Not renowned for her tact or delicacy, after dinner she told 'a shocking story'. 'All the Mammas looked grave and the young ladies shocked, and I was red with anger that such a thing should have happened in my house.' Even John's gift of the late Lady Antrim's jewels could not compensate for this *faux pas*.

Unfortunately entertainment in the home was crucial. Amongst the highly regulated elite a sense of place mattered. The more public and accessible social centres of the eighteenth century – the Pleasure Gardens of Vauxhall and Ranelagh for example – were giving way to more privatized entertainment where coveted invitations gave limited entry now that industrialization was producing a new wealthy class. Success was not allowed simply to spell acceptance. Despite having to struggle initially to be accepted herself, Lady Charlotte had taste and 'breeding' on her side. It is interesting to note her reaction to the *nouveau riche* provincial wife of George Hudson the 'Railway King', whose fortune was made by the same development which helped secure the wealth of John Guest. Alderman Thompson the Penydarren ironmaster (and MP for the City of London) invited the Guests to a dinner party:

> Conceive the horror of seeing a fat woman sit opposite to one in a *yellow* gown, and an *amber* cap with *red* flowers, and the still greater horror of that fat lady claiming to be an acquaintance. She proved to be Mrs Hudson, and the only other people in the room that I knew were Major Gore Brown and his wife, with his sister, Miss Buryon. The Browns and the Hudsons were almost the only two families in London that I have taken pains to avoid having any communication with, so that I was supremely unlucky to have met them there.

Here London was being made synonymous with Society.

Yet when she met the refined Mrs Waddington, Lady Charlotte was saddened by her story of rejection at Court.[2] Her marriage at sixteen to a wealthy merchant had diminished her social significance despite her earlier influence at Court through her aunt Mrs Delany, friend of the writer Fanny Burney. Once Mrs Waddington was married: '… no longer was she the adored niece … no longer I *may* add, the lovely Miss Port who carried away all hearts. She was married and married to a merchant.' She became a 'pariah' in Court circles. Her husband had amassed 'great riches in trade' and, like Lady Charlotte, she followed him to Wales to live. The parallels were clear as was the importance of royal patronage.

The season was intrinsically linked to the Royal Family: In 1830 George IV's illness had delayed Lady Charlotte entering Society, and 1843 was a dull and empty season as the Queen's confinement meant no Drawing Room. Ladies were presented at Drawing Rooms; held at 3 p.m., some were very crowded. In 1850 girls fainted in the crush and heat and it was said that one made her way by sticking large pins into all who blocked her path.

After a few seasons Lady Charlotte had some power. Pegus's friend Sir Keith Jackson wanted her to present his wife at Court. So: '... although I feel myself nobody in Society, and neglected by those who ought at best to be civil, I find that my introduction is an object to some people not so well off in that respect, even as myself.'

In 1836 she was disappointed that 'The Queen scarcely vouchsafed a civil bow' though the Duchess of Kent was 'well aware that my husband was a good friend to the little Princess in the House and was as firm a Whig as she herself could desire'.

That 'little Princess' became Queen in June 1837 at the age of eighteen. When John took his oath of allegiance in the House of Commons Lady Charlotte noted that the young monarch 'read her speech extremely well. They say she has put herself in Lord Melbourne's hands.' She added, 'I cannot help thinking there is much Toryism at heart in some of those high quarters'. The following day she watched the Proclamation from a room at the corner of St James's Street. She was later told that Victoria was 'crying all the time' that she appeared at the palace window.

The accession marked a new stage in the Guests' acceptance in Society. It was the Coronation Honours list of July 1838 which gave John his Baronetcy. This, perhaps combined with his more cautious political line and the Queen's dislike of what she called 'the vile Tories' put them in a more favoured position. Lady Charlotte made her first appearance at Victoria's Court in April 1838. She was presented by Lady Lansdowne, then in turn presented Mrs Divett, the new wife of John's London business adviser, a former Miss Ross who had once been 'considered' for Lindsey. The Guests also found favour with the Whig Duke of Sussex, the Queen's uncle. He presented John at the levee where he received his title. John had shrewdly been one of a minority who voted for an increase in the Duke's pension – a somewhat unusual step for a Member known to be parsimonious on such issues! The Guests attended the Duke's party in May, such a crowded event that it took two hours for the string of carriages to reach their destination. 'The low and crowded rooms were very hot and there was nothing very agreeable in the party, but all trouble and inconvenience were fully repaid by the pleasure of seeing the Queen receive. Her manner was perfect, so self-possessed and so courteous, that it was more like one sees in very good acting on the stage than anything else.' This was praise indeed from Lady Charlotte.

The highlight of the season was the Coronation. Lady Charlotte witnessed events from the Record room of Westminster Abbey, describing it as 'very amusing and inter-esting' but adding that it lacked animation. Later in the same year the Guests observed the Coronation of Emperor Ferdinand I as King of Lombardy.[3] The feeble-minded

inheritor seemed an unworthy successor to the crown which had once graced
Lady Charlotte's hero Charlemagne. They were amazed by the excesses of the
ceremony in Milan. Velvet, satin and ermine abounded, though the symmetry
of the Cathedral impressed Lady Charlotte rather more, as did Pasta's singing.
She was amused by the banquet since etiquette dictated that nobody ate any
of the magnificent courses which were placed before them. She decided that
the whole tawdry event with its exaggerated parade was but a 'mockery of joy'.
Excessive pageantry was not in vogue with early nineteenth-century English
people.

On the night of Victoria's Coronation the Guests went to the Duke of
Wellington's ball followed the next evening by a ball at Lansdowne House
attended by all the Royal Family. There Lady Charlotte met Joseph Hume 'of
economical notoriety'. The Third Marchioness of Lansdowne proved a more
valuable ally than Lady Stuart, introducing Lady Charlotte to Prince Esterhazy
(the Austrian Ambassador) and promising further introductions to 'some of the
first English families'. She made out a list of such people and gave advice about
the party to celebrate Sir John's elevation. Approaching Lord Lansdowne in the
first instance had made Lady Charlotte tremble so much that 'I nearly fell to the
earth' but it proved to be worth it, and 'Altogether to my surprise my party was
brilliant and quite successful.' Attended by ministers and foreign ambassadors it
was a great relief to find '… that affairs have taken this turn. I have striven hard
to place myself in the situation of life in which I was born and from which my
mother's unfortunate marriage so long excluded me – and now I really believe I
have accomplished it and need not henceforth toil through pleasure for the sake
of Society. My children now I hope and believe will have none of those struggles
to make which I have felt so humiliated by.'

A party and ball at Count Strogonoff's, then a ball held by the French Ambassador
Marshal Soult 'on a very magnificent scale' followed. When Lord Stuart saw Lady
Charlotte at an exclusive gathering at Lansdowne House she fancied that he did
not 'I thought, look pleased at my being there without his introduction'.

Lady Charlotte's first visit to Buckingham Palace was for the Queen's ball.
Queen Victoria was its first resident monarch; George IV had died before its
completion and William IV had not liked it. The architect of Canford, Edward
Blore, supervised alterations before Victoria moved there. Lady Charlotte was
'quite surprised, after all I had heard to find it so handsome. When the Pink Pillars
are taken away there will not be much fault to find with it.'

In 1840, when Victoria married Prince Albert, Lady Charlotte had a place in
Queen Anne's room at the Palace from which she could observe events. She now
consulted Lady Lansdowne about situations at Court 'as I have had rather a fancy
to be about the Queen, respecting whom I feel a very great interest'. However
the only appointment for which she was eligible was Lady of the Bedchamber
'and as that will under the present system bring me rarely in contact with her I do
not think it worth while to trouble myself further on the subject'.

In some respects this seems incongruous given Lady Charlotte's repeated insistence on disliking Society. She described her experience of one ball as 'about ten people all sitting in a row, boring each other to death'. At another the 'company was egregiously dreadful'. She longed to return to Wales to 'my old wild delicious home' having received so little gratification and intellectual stimulus from the season: 'I was delighted to get away from London where I have no sort of amusement and nothing excites my sympathy.' At the same time she felt that if she did become involved in something she must do it well and go to the top, 'my blood is of the noblest and most princely in the kingdom, and if I go into Society, it must be the very best and first. I can brook no other.'

She never again mentioned a royal appointment in her journal, though in 1848 on a visit to the Aboyne estate in Scotland it was Lady Charlotte who prepared the rooms in the village inn for the royal party who were passing on the way to Balmoral. When the Queen, Prince Albert and their three eldest children arrived, Victoria talked to Lady Charlotte and Mary as the children took some broth, pudding and oat cakes.

On balance, London provoked regret rather than relief: 'And now begins once more the barren record of a London life' which spelt 'Nothing but visits and parties and a great deal of trouble' devoted to 'people one does not care a straw about, and very little time left for any rational occupation of enjoyment'. She did try a little careful mixing of the world by introducing Welsh flannel into the London season. She wore Welsh costume to the Cambrian ball, 'such a thing I believe had never been seen before in London and it caused quite a sensation'. At a party in 1850 'our Welsh harper played'. This was Mr Thomas, now sponsored by Ada, Countess of Lovelace, the daughter of Byron and a close friend of Charles Babbage, one of the few people in London Society whom Lady Charlotte really admired.

Babbage straddled several of Lady Charlotte's spheres of interest. He visited Dowlais, was concerned about the effect of social habits on life expectancy, stood as a Whig candidate and was popular in London Society. In the 1830s Lady Charlotte attended his soirées where could be found key social and 'literary stars'. Above all she enjoyed serious discussions with him as 'the mind is expanded while the imagination is pleased'. In addition to inventing safety measures for trains, producing the first comprehensive treatise on actuarial theory, inventing the heliograph and opthalmoscope, he anticipated the basic principles on which the modern computer works. His pursuit of mathematics by mechanical means dominated his life. He was the first to work out logarithm tables by machinery, and spent twenty-seven years perfecting his Difference Engine and then the more sophisticated Analytical Engine. For the first calculating machine he received a government grant but soon needed more financial support and appreciation. As Lady Charlotte explained, 'He feels much how his invention is beyond the power of the age to appreciate and this mortifies him more than it should do.' His son gave Lady Charlotte several lectures on the machine whilst

Babbage concentrated on combining business and pleasure: 'His society is always delightful and I began to be very much flattered at so clever and celebrated a man thinking it worth while to spend a whole hour with me, when I found that he wanted something.' His request was 'merely that Merthyr ask a question about his machine in the House of Commons if the subject came forward there', something which Lady Charlotte felt to be quite reasonable.

The Welsh harpist had been playing at Lady Palmerston's. The sister of the Whig leader Lord Melbourne and reputed to have double his energy, she was the principal political hostess. It was said that an invitation to one of her Saturday evening parties at Cambridge house helped to determine wavering votes. Another London hostess was Lady Cork, who had been a friend of Dr Johnson's. Although confined to the couch it was said that she knew exactly what was going on in Society. Lady Charlotte found the eighty-eight-year-old Dowager dressing for dinner: 'The dressing was performed in the dining room, and her Footman received a lecture about wearing gaiters, while her maid was taking off her morning gown, and I was writing, in her name, an invitation to a child of six years old to come to her breakfast.'

The elderly Whig hostess Lady Holland was equally relaxed. Lady Charlotte recounted how, on one visit to her, Lady Holland was writing with a servant 'kneeling before her rubbing her feet, which she continued to do all the time I was there'. Lord Holland sat at the other end of the room 'his hand tied up with gout'. Both were 'exceedingly agreeable'.

A leading Tory hostess was Lady Londonderry. Despite their differences in politics, the Guests were invited to her gatherings which Lady Charlotte called 'immense crush receptions'. She held court on Saturday nights at her Park Lane home, sitting on a dais under a canopy, taking little notice of her guests and 'blazed among the peeresses'. Disraeli had described the Coronation banquet given by the Londonderrys as 'the finest thing of the season' and in that season many tried to excel. The life of Frances Ann, wife of the Third Marquis of Londonderry, had encompassed travelling and mining interests. Her husband had been at the British Embassies in Vienna and St Petersburg. After he died in 1854 she spent much of her time at Seaham Hall near Sunderland managing her extensive collieries and 4,000 pitmen. Like Lady Charlotte she developed educational facilities for the workforce, though the Londonderrys' relations with their workers was never the same as the Guests'. Neither, despite Lady Charlotte's approval of her hosting dinner for workers and agents, was Lady Londonderry's conception of political rights close to Lady Charlotte's: she felt that tenants should vote as she dictated. Up until 1832 the nomination of Durham City was in her exclusive gift. Lady Londonderry's daughter married John Churchill, Marquis of Blandford, who became the Seventh Duke of Marlborough and the father of Cornelia Churchill, Lady Charlotte's future daughter-in-law. Cornelia's sister, Fanny, was to marry Edward Marjoribanks (later Lord Tweedmouth). This family was linked through business to the exclusive family banking firm of Coutts.

The heiress to the Coutts fortune was also known to Lady Charlotte and a number of similarities existed between these two ladies. Reputed to be one of the wealthiest women in Europe, Angela Burdett-Coutts was the first woman to become a Baroness in her own right (in 1871). Her inheritance had come from her grandfather via his wife Harriot Mellon, that same Duchess of St Albans who had so intrigued and upset Lady Charlotte. Her aunt had married the First Marquis of Bute.

Miss Coutts (as Lady Charlotte called her) also enjoyed the society of scientists such as Babbage and Wheatstone and was close to Lady Charlotte's cousin Henry Layard. Like Lady Charlotte she had been fascinated by the Orient for many years and in later life the two women helped organize the Turkish Compassionate Fund for refugees. At the age of sixty-seven Angela Burdett-Coutts shocked Society by marrying her thirty-year-old secretary. Queen Victoria dubbed it 'the mad marriage'.

For decades Lady Charlotte attended parties at the Coutts' home, Holly Lodge, lying in sixty acres of Highgate. Her children (Maria in particular) were very fond of its owner. The Duke of Cambridge described her as 'an English institution' and today this daughter of the Radical MP Sir Francis Burdett is best remembered as a benefactress. She gave away considerable sums of money to the London poor, her good works including a home for 'fallen women', help to the watercress and flower girls and the development of model housing.

Although in later years Lady Charlotte would become involved in a number of charitable works in London, during her married life she largely compartmentalized her concerns, and her interest in social welfare was mostly confined to Wales. She did, however, view some model lodging houses for single men in the Bloomsbury and Covent Garden areas in 1848. She hoped that she and her husband might pick up 'some useful hints' there. London at this date was the largest and richest city in the world, yet the high society in which Lady Charlotte lived and moved was geo-graphically confined to one small area in the West End. Indeed so small was it that on one occasion when the carriage inadvertently dropped her off at the wrong house for a party, she found herself at the home of her acquaintance Mr Bunsen, the Prussian Ambassador. Beyond lay not only many villages which are today part of London, but at deceptively close quarters another city could be found, the one discovered by Henry Mayhew and extended to the reading public in his mid-century articles for the *Morning Chronicle*. Here, as well as skilled artisans, unskilled labourers and all the workers who made possible the London season – dressmakers, for example, for whom the season determined the rhythm of their labour – could be found the 'submerged tenth', living in abject poverty.

Lady Charlotte's journal presents London in a one-dimensional form that was based on her own direct knowledge. Only very occasionally were there forays into the unknown such as the trip she and Bertie made on an omnibus (an adventure in itself for them). They went to Pentonville and briefly saw 'wretched poverty' at first hand. On another occasion Lady Charlotte and John glimpsed a London which would probably have only been familiar to them through Hogarth: 'My greatest ambition was to go inside a gin shop, and the view of several very gay ones renewed my curiosity. At last we made for one, but thought it prudent to reconnoitre ere we entered it. We looked in accordingly through its half open doors. Such a collection of debased squalid-looking wretches I never saw … Many the laugh of drunkenness on their brow.' She did not see a single woman there. They decided against entering in the clothes they were wearing. Lady Charlotte's journal also relates how they felt it too risky to enter a gin shop in the Oxford Street area as it was so close to their neighbourhood that they might 'fall in with someone who was accustomed to opening the door for me at some friend's house'.

In 1837 the Guests had bought Lord Wilton's house at 13, Grosvenor Square for £10,000. In a moment of rashness Lady Charlotte chose to furnish it in arabesques and rich red satin draperies. Despite self-doubts about her taste in furnishings she conceded that her drawing room was 'certainly perfect'. The house soon proved too small for the growing family and was sold for £19,000 after two years. The London home with which they became most closely identified was 8, Spring Gardens, where the ground rent was £800 per annum (paid to the Duke of Bedford). It remained in the family's hands until 1856. It was at one of the grand balls in Spring Gardens that the Vandyke collar originated. It was so hot that the gentlemen turned down their collars and this remained the fashion for the rest of the season. At another ball there 'a little Russian boy' played the piano after dinner. Aged thirteen he was making his European debut that year and would soon become the world-famous pianist, Rubinstein. When he had first appeared in public in Moscow aged ten, he was so small that he had to be placed on a table to be seen by his admiring audience.

Lady Charlotte's balls had become a big success. She would illuminate the gardens and fill the house with masses of flowers and ribbons. In 1844 she commented with satisfaction: 'I know the ball was beautiful, for I have never seen anything equal to it in London and I consider the success comprehensive.' The season was now far less of an ordeal. She also enjoyed attending art exhibitions At the Royal Academy in 1846 Sir John was so impressed by Richard Buckner's work that he immediately commissioned him to paint Lady Charlotte. Two years later her portrait was hung at the Exhibition at the Royal Academy, though friends considered it unexpressive so she underwent a further sitting. Portraits were of course important accompaniments for country houses and the Royal Family's interest in art helped stimulate picture collection more generally. The Guests had both been painted by A.E. Chalon soon after their marriage and Lady Charlotte had also sat for the Merthyr artist Penry Williams, once patronized by Crawshay but now settled in Rome. In his painting she wore a Vandyke dress of white satin, sported a scarlet poppy and had her hair in ringlets.

Being seen at the opera and theatre were also important and posed no hardship for Lady Charlotte. In common with other fashionable people the Guests took an opera box some seasons (a season of sixty performances cost about 180 guineas).

In the mid-forties they took a box on a long lease. The opera house (rebuilt in 1790) was in the Haymarket and the two 'top' theatres were Drury Lane and Covent Garden. An evening's entertainment was at least that, lasting the whole evening: opera would be followed by ballet; a play would be succeeded by a farce and pantomine which might continue until well after midnight.

Private theatricals were also popular. The Duke and Duchess of Bedford held annual New Year parties at Woburn Abbey. Here the highlight was the acting. The Guests stayed for a week in 1843. There were over thirty to dinner daily. Lady Charlotte made what the Woburn playbill called her 'first appearance on the stage', playing the part of Lucretia in *The Rendezvous*. She was extremely nervous beforehand but 'the soul of acting was strong within me, and spite of all my apprehensions I was compelled to persevere'. A few days later she acted in front of an audience which included Edward Ellice the former Gentleman Manager of Drury Lane and Lord John Russell, whose quiet congratulations and praise 'was to me the most flattering and sincere of the many testimonies of applause that I received'. A year later however, when the events were repeated, her husband told her she was overacting.

Lady Charlotte had to prepare her children for their role in Society. She ensured that they had ample opportunity for learning accomplishments and attended morning parties. John was especially insistent that Maria should have company, and when just under seventeen she had a lesson in 'the mysteries of making curtsies and kissing the Queen's hand'. Her Court dress was purchased in Paris on a family holiday. Here Lady Charlotte had wryly observed how 'We who, like all England, fancy we wear nothing but things in the latest French fashion' were stared at by the Parisians. Maria's first ball was in France. She was soon immersed in London parties and attended a fancy dress ball (at which the Queen was present) dressed as Charles II's sister. Her father wore black velvet and her mother went as the Princess de Conti. Young ladies had strict instructions to be chaperoned at parties and they were not expected to have more than a couple of dances with one partner or sit out a dance with a young man. Such codes helped exert control over suitable marriage partners. Lady Charlotte expected her daughters to adhere to this regime despite her early days of waltzing[4] with Augustus O'Brien. When Katherine danced at a ball in Swansea just before she came of age, she disgraced herself dancing three times with the same young man. Her 'very naughty' behaviour led to a scene between mother and daughter which made Lady Charlotte feel 'quite ill' for some days.

Maria's first season included a play at Devonshire House patronized by the Queen in which Charles Dickens acted. At another gathering was the Whig historian Macaulay 'the life of the party and most amusing' according to Lady Charlotte. Two huge parties were planned for Maria, 900 attending the first. Her birthday party never took place since she caught chicken pox.

As Sir John's illness gradually took hold, so the Guests withdrew a little from the full frenetic diet of Society, and by 1852 it was extremely difficult for Lady

Charlotte to manage the gaieties of the season. At a hot, crowded ball at Lady Ailesbury's she 'sat quite still, without speaking, alone' while the dance music played, 'my thoughts dwelling upon him that I have left so ill at home'. She attended an immense party held by the Duke of Wellington who 'seemed almost asleep' in the stiff and formal atmosphere. In the autumn the Duke finally died and the Guests made what was to be their last journey home to Dowlais.

Lady Charlotte's reactions to Society varied over the years, depending on circumstances. Her age, health, her husband's health and wealth, her children, her marital status, all affected the degree of social acceptance and her perceptions. Yet throughout she always held a trump card. As an intellectual she knew not to take Society too seriously, even though initial rebuffs were painful. Most importantly she could see beyond it and wrote 'I have occupation and resource enough never to feel dependent on *Society* for amusement.' As Lady Charlotte Guest she was more fortunate than many Society ladies (though they would not necessarily have perceived their situations as she did). For many, the end of the London season signalled the start of a county version of it in their large residences, and, although the Guests themselves purchased a Dorset estate, there remained Dowlais. The very different social and business demands there marked Lady Charlotte off from most Society ladies for whom industrialization remained something one might profit from but did not participate in. Once at Dowlais: 'London and its turmoils, its visitings and etiquettes and nonsense were forgotten and my thoughts fell into older, more congenial and healthier currents.'

Lady Charlotte may have worn Society's war paint but she saw herself doing it as a means to an end. Her children's prestigious marriages and the elevation of her eldest son to the Peerage would seal her achievements in this quarter. And even within the season she found an alternative niche for herself. From the mid-1830s a new London location begins to feature in the journals with increasing frequency: the British Museum. Lady Charlotte's interest in studying old Welsh manuscripts (and the beginning of the translation of *The Mabinogion* in January 1838 coincided with the Guests' real acceptance in London Society) gave her a new purpose, complemented her husband's work in the Commons and made her city life profitable. Moreover her learning of the Welsh language was as significant as it was unusual. It set Lady Charlotte apart from most of the English ruling class who settled in industrial South Wales and proceeded to ignore the people's language.

5
The Intellectual in Wales

*'… If I occupy myself in writing, my book must
be splendidly got up and must be, as far at least
as decoration and typography are concerned, at
the head of literature, and I delight in the contrast
of the musty antiquarian researches and the
brilliant fêtes and plodding counting
houses …'*

The name of Lady Charlotte Guest is most widely associated with her translation into English of the medieval Welsh tales which she collectively described as *The Mabinogion*. The *Oxford Companion to the Literature of Wales* calls the 'Mabinogi' 'the Welsh people's greatest contribution to the literature of Europe'. By making available the richness of early Welsh culture, Lady Charlotte stimulated an interest in the subject which has lasted and spread. *The Mabinogion* (though no longer her translation) remains a classic which is reprinted almost yearly. The stories which she popularized in English fascinate all ages: the 'Mabinogi' tales have been turned into children's books, plays and even a Walt Disney film, whilst Arthurian scholars are especially interested in the three Romances.* The tales have appeared in modern Welsh, French, Breton, German, Czechoslovak and Japanese. Cambridge University students still boast a *Cymdeithas y Mabinogi* (a Welsh Society). In the mid–1860s Matthew Arnold gave four seminal lectures at Oxford University on the study of Celtic literature. Here he acknowledged the 'debt of gratitude' he and others owed Lady Charlotte.

Yet how was it that an English lady, largely self-taught and living in the midst of an iron-making community, should undertake such an audacious and ambitious venture? Such an occupation seemed unlikely for a young wife. John Ruskin summed up the contemporary perception of appropriate wifely knowledge in *Sesame and Lilies* (1865): 'a man ought to know any language or science he learns thoroughly; while a woman ought to know the same language and science only so far as may enable her to sympathize in her husband's pleasure, and in those of his best friends.' Moreover a weighty translation of Middle Welsh seems at first sight to be one of the most curious by-products of the Industrial Revolution.

---

* See Appendix 4A.

A closer look at Lady Charlotte's life and at the wider development of Welsh literature and Welshness makes this remarkable project more comprehensible. Lady Charlotte may have been a dutiful wife (keen to understand a language her husband spoke and valued) but she was never prepared to sublimate her own intellectual aspirations and follow Ruskin's advice. Her personality and early studies ensured this whilst the focus of the Romantic revival on the glories of medieval life and emergence of interest in things Celtic helped produce an increasingly favourable climate for the reception of early Welsh culture. To these factors were added intellectual developments within Wales. All this helped Lady Charlotte's work to become not only possible but successful.

She admired most those who gave her access to further learning. Her friendship with the Orientalist Sir Gore Ouseley lasted and soon after her marriage she joined the Oriental Translations Committee. She possessed eight volumes of the work of Sir William Jones, a lexicographer and Persian scholar who stressed connections between Sanscrit and the Celtic languages. A phrenologist who read the bumps on Lady Charlotte's head told her that languages came easily to her and an annotated note in the margin of the journal (by Monty) tells how her unscrupulous Italian master, Santagnello, published in his own name the translations which his young charge innocently and assiduously made for him in 1827.

Mr Martin, the tutor, played a more influential part in Lady Charlotte's life than he may have realized. It had been Martin who first introduced Lady Charlotte to Hallam's work and to Sir Walter Scott's novels.[2]

If tales of Arabian Nights formed her favourite childhood stories and Chaucer's *Prologue* her most cherished volume as an adult, then *Waverley*, *Kenilworth* and *Ivanhoe* seem to have been her choice in her teens. There were some interesting parallels between the well-bred English hero Edward Waverley who found himself involved in the Scottish rebellion of 1745 and Lady Charlotte who would develop her own version of Celtic present and past in Wales. Scott's novels took precedence for Lady Charlotte over Jane Austen's, although the latter's subject matter would have been more familiar to her. Perhaps it was for that very reason that this romantic young woman found them less palatable. She could pick up much British history from Scott, and his work, along with Southey's introduction and notes to Malory's *Le Morte d'Arthur*, appears to have influenced her approach to annotating *The Mabinogion*. Her penchant for the works of Southey and Scott was thus to bring her into indirect contact with two of the contemporary writers most interested in the revival of Celtic literature and language.

Much of her early knowledge of the Middle Ages was refracted through the Romantics, introducing her to the blending of myth and fact and alerting her to something of central importance in *The Mabinogion*: the handling of material far older than its written form and the ways in which versions of the past were mediated and reinterpreted through the changing concerns of the present. Above all she learned to see the Middle Ages as the time of Romance. Given her wish to escape from the present, remote time became an attractive refuge, and her love of medievalism did not diminish as she grew up. On a tour in 1842 she wrote 'During my stay in Belgium I may truly say that I lived rather with those of the fourteenth and fifteenth century than with any that actually moved around me'; her first trip abroad after marriage was a journey back into the reading of her youth 'the Romance will not leave me', and Venice was 'The scene of my early dreams of the Romances of the brain'.

Lady Charlotte was not the first person to attempt to translate what became known as *The Mabinogion*, but she was the first to succeed. Her success was in part due to timing. Before the Romantic revival only serious works of history were revered by Welsh scholars studying early literature. During the time of the French Revolution myth and history became intermingled as the Welsh created a past which had never actually existed and, thanks to that brilliant forger, Iolo Morganwg, soon excelled in an inventive literature. One of Iolo's contemporaries was a Welsh schoolmaster living in London, William Owen Pughe. This scholar and lexicographer translated *Paradise Lost* into Welsh, edited Dafydd ap Gwilym's poems and produced a two-volume dictionary (with at least 40,000 more words than Dr Johnson's English equivalent). He also planned to translate what he called 'The Mabinogion'. He published his translation of 'Pwyll' (the first of the four tales known as the Four Branches of the Mabinogi) in a work called *Relicks of the Welsh Bards* and much of the text and translation were serialized from 1796 in the first learned Welsh periodical, the *Cambrian Register*.

He regarded the *hen ystorion* (old stories) of the Mabinogion as the earliest Romance writings in Europe but he was easily diverted from his ambition to make them available. Diverted by the demands of a Welsh estate he had inherited, he also became immersed in the millenarian ideas which were so popular in the charged climate of revolutionary Europe. His mythological and Druidical dreamings merged with beliefs about the end of the world and he became one of the 8,000 or so 'deluded followers' of the West Country servant Joanna Southcott who proclaimed herself as Revelations' 'Woman clothed with the sun' sent to deliver mankind. William Owen Pughe was one of her four-and-twenty elders and even after her death in 1814 maintained his visionary fervour, some of which was now transferred to William Blake. Despite a new version of 'Pwyll' in 1821 and 'Math' in 1829 followed by the later tale of 'Taliesin', assurances about the imminent publication of his 'Mabinogion' were never translated into reality.

Much of Lady Charlotte's achievement was in the very areas over which William Owen Pughe could exert little control. He had recognized that an introduction was essential and that the tales would 'require a good deal said by way of illustration'. Yet his skill lay in translating words rather than in total production and unlike Lady Charlotte who always envisaged much more than translation work, he was easily side-tracked and had difficulty in raising subscriptions for publication. Although already known in print, he had made himself unpopular with some due to his orthography and inventions. Some of his words were based on a spurious bardic alphabet (*Coelbren y Beirdd*). In Southey's view he was so receptive to new ideas that 'a muddier-minded man I never met with'. Lady Charlotte, however, benefited from the publicity which he and his generation helped stimulate, whilst his *Dictionary* and *Cambrian Biography* provided useful detailed notes on key figures in the *Mabinogion* stories. Whereas Lady Charlotte could draw on a store of contacts and influential people to help further her research, William Owen Pughe's possible patrons were stern critics. One urged him to adopt a less servile mode of translation and remove obscurities. Welsh critics found him too 'fanciful' and his English translations 'so cramped and absurdly literal'. In contrast, Tennyson praised Lady Charlotte for using 'the finest English he knew' – he compared it to Malory's *Le Morte d'Arthur* – whilst Jones and Jones, her successors in the Everyman edition, describe her translation as a 'charming and felicitous piece of English prose …' Indeed, 'charming' is the word most frequently associated with her style.

Owen Pughe and Lady Charlotte based their translations on the Red Book of Hergest (*Llyfr Coch o Hergest*) of Jesus College, Oxford, a vast and important collection of medieval manuscripts thought to date from between 1382 and 1410. The antiquity of the tales is not fully known.[3] The Four Branches ('Pwyll', 'Branwen', 'Manawyddan' and 'Math') seem to have existed in manuscript form since about 1200, but they were most probably relayed orally over several generations before ever assuming written form. The *Cyfarwyddiad*, early professional story tellers, would have played an important part in their transmission. In a memorable passage in his Celtic lectures, Matthew Arnold recognized that the medieval storyteller was himself 'pillaging an antiquity of which he does not fully possess the secret; he is like a peasant building his hut on the site of Halicarnassus or Ephesus; he builds but what he builds is full of materials of which he knows not the history, or knows by a glimmering tradition merely; – stones "not of this building", but of an older architecture, greater, cunninger, more majestical.' Pioneer translators were therefore faced with unravelling as well as translating a varied and complex set of ancient tales.

The first result of Lady Charlotte's scholarship was published in 1838, just three years after William Owen Pughe's death. Other tales followed amounting to seven parts and then a three-volume edition appeared in 1849 with a total of twelve tales (including those already issued). Welsh and English versions were given and known versions in other languages were discussed or parts of them reproduced. Lavish illustration and copious notes (most detailed when concerned with Arthurian legend) accompanied each tale. Lady Charlotte extended William Owen Pughe's term 'The Mabinogion' to include not just the Four Branches, three Arthurian Romances and four independent tales★ but also added the later 'Taliesin'. Subsequent translations have tended to exclude this last tale which, unlike the rest, did not come from the Red Book of Hergest.[4]

Unfortunately *Mabinogion* is really a non-word. The term Mabinogi was originally applied to the Four Branches and both William Owen Pughe and Lady

---

★ See Appendix 4A.

Charlotte interpreted *Mabinogion* as the plural form (-ion is a common plural ending in Welsh). Yet the word only occurs once, at the end of 'Pwyll' where it is a short-word produced by the form *dyledogyuon* in the line immediately above it. A scribe appears to have inadvertently miscopied and so produced *Mabynnogynon*. The word *Mab* means 'boy' or 'son' in Welsh and Owen Pughe referred to the tales as 'Mabinogion or Juvenilities'.[5] Scholars now suggest that the word came to mean 'a tale of descendants'. Lady Charlotte made the association with youth and dedicated her work to her two eldest sons,

> To Ivor and Merthyr
> My dear Children,
>
> Infants as you yet are, I feel that I cannot dedicate more fitly than to you these venerable relics of ancient lore, and I do so in the hope of inciting you to cultivate the literature of 'Gwyllt Walia', in whose beautiful language you are being initiated, and amongst whose free mountains you were born. May you become early imbued with the chivalric and exalted sense of honour, and the fervent patriotism for which its sons have ever been celebrated. May you learn to emulate the noble qualities of Ivor Hael, and the firm attachment to your Native Country, which distinguished that Ivor Bach, after whom the elder of you was named.
>
> I am,
> Your affectionate Mother,
> C.E. Guest.
> Dowlais, August 29th, 1838.

Lady Charlotte viewed the tales as exemplary stories, demonstrating virtues for her sons to emulate. Chivalry was especially appropriate to Victorian thinking: notions of devotion, courtesy and protection of women finding many parallels in the cult of the idealized nineteenth-century lady so evident in Pre-Raphaelite art, poetry and prescriptive literature. And just as Owain's Countess in 'The Lady of the Fountain' was able to assume an authority actually denied her in medieval society, so too did Victorian culture contain and maintain beliefs about women which were inconsistent with reality. Honour, bravery and public service were applauded as masculine virtues, therefore the dedication did not include the eldest child Maria (though it is only fair to add that she had been born in England and was not as closely identified with Wales as the Welsh-born children). Lady Charlotte enjoyed reading the stories to her children and later her grandchildren. She proudly wrote 'I never saw anything equal to their delight' after reading 'The Lady of the Fountain' to Ivor and Maria. Rhiannon, the heroine of 'Pwyll' was a special favourite, as was Enid, wife to Geraint (one daughter was named after her). Lady Charlotte's translations went more or less in tandem with giving birth to her large family and must in part have been stimulated by the desire to make intelligible to them the ancient tales of the country to which she attributed so much of her new-found happiness.

Lady Charlotte first arrived in Dowlais on 15 August, meeting the Rector, Evan Jenkins, on 21 August. Two days later he gave her a Welsh lesson. Welsh, she explained, was something 'which I should wish to understand'. She did, however, sound a cautious note at this stage, 'in the multiplicity of occupations here, I do not find much hope that there will be time for it'. Yet over the next month she fitted in a number of lessons interspersed with visits to Welsh services. By 27 September she was engaged in translating part of St Matthew Chapter XI into English. On 14 November she declared: 'I am going to be very industrious, Prichard[6] my solid reading, Welsh my study, and Ariosto and Chaucer once again my relaxation. These are grand-sounding plans, and in a moment of comparative health I look forward with pleasure to accompanying thus the time, which I must necessarily spend alone …'

She also made notes on the Middle Ages, studied Latin and a little Persian and felt alarmed and dismayed by the effects of her first pregnancy. In a statement which must have caused her to smile in later years, she declared in 1834 that she was beginning to feel 'too old to learn, and must relinquish all my high flown prospects'.

Rather than surrendering, she began to organize time more effectively. In the autumn she wrote 'Baby leaves me but little time for anything and that time must be spent on Welsh.' The occasional Welsh word was smuggled into journal entries and Wales had become 'my own dear country'. A typical day (if such a word can ever be applied to Lady Charlotte's life) included a couple of hours of Welsh translation on the library sofa. After the birth of Ivor she and John would study and read together for several hours in the morning (they rose at 7 a.m.).

A number of scholars have had their names linked with Lady Charlotte's translation work, chief amongst whom are Tegid (Rev. John Jones) and Carnhuanawc (Rev. Thomas Price).[7] The Dowlais schoolmaster Thomas Jenkins has also been credited (erroneously) with teaching her Welsh. In July 1835 she read his lecture on the Welsh language but it was Evan Jenkins the Rector who began teaching her. Tegid and Price were invaluable in the protracted stages of preparing the work for publication but the scholar Elijah Waring provided the initial impulse for her particular project. The editor of a short-lived journal enlightening readers about Welsh history, the *Cambrian Visitor*, he was an English Wesleyan now living in Neath. When he came to Dowlais on business in October 1835, Lady Charlotte wrote, 'I find he is somewhat acquainted with ancient literature … He is the only person I have found so in this country except George Clark …' (George Clark was a friend of Sir John's who combined engineering with antiquarian interest and who eventually became resident trustee at Dowlais).

The next month they met again and 'our conversation turned much upon the superstitions and legends of Wales – I think it might be desirable to make a collection of them. His love for ancient literature is quite refreshing to me who have been so long deprived of everything like fellow feeling in that respect.'

Delighted that he enjoyed discussing Chaucer and Froissart, she dubbed him 'the only person with sympathy for my former studies'. He lent her his draft biography of his friend Iolo Morganwg. In January 1836 Lady Charlotte tried to persuade the latter's son, Taliesin Williams, to let duplicates of his father's 'most curious MSS be made in order to ensure their preservation'. It was to no avail: 'he is very avaricious of them'.[8]

Parallel to her growing interest in such manuscripts was Lady Charlotte's own romanticization of Wales. She declared that 'Wales is mighty it is romance and grows mightier every hour as the chivalrous days more and more recede.' Around her were vividly contrasting worlds – the medieval stronghold Morlais Castle, now a ruin, being excavated close to an ironworks which symbolized the modern source of power. Ironworks could probably only seem romantic to those who could escape labouring there. Lady Charlotte could romanticize the works and the place (Merthyr was, after all, named after a Celtic princess and martyr) and forge her own links with the past. In Wales her personal history and that of the country could come together. In his Celtic lectures Arnold described Wales as a land where 'the past still lives, where every place has its tradition, every name its poetry …' In the mid-1830s Lady Charlotte chose the peak of the Brecon Beacons as the place she wished to be buried in – 'Nobody that comes after me will love that rugged old mountain as I have done.' She even sketched the Beacons for the background of her portrait by Buckner.

Not long after marrying, the Guests visited Warwick Castle. Here Lady Charlotte mused over the fourteenth-century romance of the Dun Cow, a monstrous animal slain by Guy of Warwick, in his effort to win the hand of the Earl's daughter. Lady Charlotte posed a question which goes some way towards explaining why she translated *The Mabinogion*: 'Why should we disregard our own traditions … because they have not been handed down in Greek or Latin? For my own part, I love the old Legends and Romances as they teach us so naturally the manners and opinions of those who were, in fact, much more nearly con-nected with *us* of the present day than were any of the heroes of Rome.'

They then visited Kenilworth, home of the twelfth-century castle and abbey and site of Elizabeth I's visit, immortalized by Scott. The previous year they had read the novel *Kenilworth* together.

One further strand in understanding why Lady Charlotte became a translator lies in her secret hope for fame. In May 1835 she wrote, 'We must keep our minds in constant advance … I sometimes start with a flush of emulation when I hear and see what has been done by others and what I once hoped I had strength and energy to have at least equalled myself.' She also remarked how she 'once hoped not to have died unknown' and reflected on the days when 'the poetry of enthu-siasm was around me'. She battled against the depression and illness of pregnancy, 'The langour of delicate health unites with my position to crush the aspiring [hopes]' but she still found that: 'sometimes a flash of the old fire will sparke for a moment spite of all my reason and circumstances'.

The first journal reference to *The Mabinogion* was on 17 October 1837 after a meet-ing of Celtophiles at Abergavenny. Here the barrister Arthur Johnes promised to try to obtain Owen Pughe's manuscripts and notes. Johnes knew his son, Aneurin. It seems unlikely that this happened since the journal does not record him obtaining or lending it. Rachel Bromwich has compared pieces of translation of 'Pwyll' and 'Math' and finds that Lady Charlotte's translation 'clearly owes nothing to the earlier versions and is in several instances more accurate than Owen Pughe's'.

Later in the same month Johnes, Price and Tegid 'came in council with me about the Welsh Manuscripts Society', a new venture founded in 1836 to promote and publish old Welsh manuscripts. On 30 November a breakthrough was recorded. Mr Justice Bosanquet of Dingestow Court, Monmouthshire agreed through Tegid to lend his copy of the tales from the Red Book of Hergest, 'the Mabinogion, which I hope to publish with an English translation, notes and pictorial illustrations'. Price and Tegid pledged their assistance and 'by God's blessing I hope I may accomplish the undertaking'.

At dusk on 4 December Lady Charlotte read part of a translation made by Bosanquet of the native Welsh tale of 'Kilhwch and Olwen', commenting 'it pleases me much'. She found translation from the Red Book 'extremely difficult' but interesting, 'I think it will be a popular number if I can bring it out properly'. She was somewhat concerned when the Welsh Manuscripts Society wanted to take the venture into their own hands, 'believing that I have given it up'. This redoubled her determination: 'We have to arrange to prevent this, and also to go into some plan for translating Justice Bosanquet's copy, as I do not feel inclined to give up my scheme of publishing it myself.' Tegid took Bosanquet's manuscript 'to copy from it one story at a time in a fit manner to go to the press (viz., in modern orthography which will be more generally useful) and send them to me to translate'.

So, on New Year's Day 1838, after nine days of 'hard work making slippers for Merthyr' Lady Charlotte began translating *The Mabinogion*. Tegid chose the starting point, wisely picking the Romance tale 'The Lady of the Fountain' ('Iarlles Ffynnawn'). This tale of Owain was one with which Lady Charlotte would have been familiar through versions in other languages and easier to translate than the Four Branches which open most modern versions. The three Romances (*Y Tair Rhamant*) had a familiar Arthurian setting, their heroes being the figures of the British Heroic Age (*c.* the sixth century AD) engaged in the chivalric deeds which so fascinated Lady Charlotte. She had long admired Arthurian legend and named her horse Llamrei after Arthur's mare. Arthur himself she considered 'the noblest creature that ever lived in fiction'. Tegid translated one sheet which he then sent her and so this big project got underway. They soon evolved a routine of communication in which Price also played a key part.

In order to appreciate how this trio came together, we need to explore Lady Charlotte's relationship with the pro-Welsh gentry and in particular, with the Llanover circle. In the Merthyr district the predominantly English industrialists, Anthony Hill for example, remained scornful of Welsh.[9] One Cyfarthfa manager claimed that the language stultified intellectual development and helped transmit prejudices and bad customs. Yet outside the circle of owners and officials a pro-Welsh radical culture flourished and spawned the first working-class newspaper in Welsh, *Y Gweithiwr* (the *Workman*) in 1834. Merthyr also had its own Welsh Cymreigyddion Society in which Iolo Morganwg had been active. By virtue of their status within Dowlais the Guests were set apart from the Merthyr Welsh, although they did not share the anti-Welsh sentiments of their social equals. This helps explain Taliesin Williams's lavish tributes to Lady Charlotte after the 1837 election.

The centre of pro-Welsh influence amongst the gentry was at Abergavenny. On 22 November 1833, the year Lady Charlotte moved to Wales, the *Cymdeithas Cymreigyddion Y Fenni* (Society of Welsh Scholars of Abergavenny) was formed. The Guests were founder members. Thanks largely to the work of Price and Augusta Hall of Llanover it soon boasted seventy-five members, promoting Welsh teaching in Sunday schools and day schools, adopting Welsh names for Welsh children and holding competitions in Welsh poetry, singing, the harp and prose through an annual Eisteddfod. Lady Charlotte hired a nurserymaid to teach her first child Welsh, gave all her Welsh-born children Welsh names and became one of the most avid supporters of the society's Eisteddfodau.

Hall's mother was Mrs Waddington, whose story about being spurned at Court after marriage had moved Lady Charlotte. Mrs Waddington's elder sister, Louisa Port, had married in 1803 none other than that ill-fated Rector of Uffington, Brownlow Layard. Thus Lady Charlotte's aunt (her uncle's first wife) was also Lady Hall's aunt. There were further connections with the Guests. Augusta's husband, Benjamin Hall, was the Whig MP for Monmouthshire Boroughs (1831-7) and, like John Guest, was pro-Reform, liked things Welsh, and built schools. He was awarded a Baronetcy in 1838. Descended from the Crawshays, he was more gentleman-farmer than industrialist and this rather large man's posthumous fame mainly derives from his responsibility as First Commissioner of Works for the casting of the Parliamentary clock tower nicknamed Big Ben.

From their Jacobean-style home, Llanover Court, the Halls promoted Welshness like Renaissance patrons, subscribing to the publication of Welsh works, saving manuscripts and building up a large library. Welsh luminaries, including the antiquary Angharad Llwyd, graced events such as the house-warming party of 1837. Lady Charlotte wore fancy dress 'exactly similar to what the peasants wear about Merthyr except that the material instead of woollen was satin wove to the proper pattern on purpose, the hat was black velvet instead of beaver and that the whole had a sprinkling of gold over it to give candlelight effect'. She had made careful preparations for her costume since it was Augusta who had entered (anonymously) and won the 1834 National Eisteddfod with her work on the language and costume of Wales, later published with her coloured illustrations. This played a key part in fostering the idea of a national identity. Keen for Welsh women to wear local tweeds rather than cotton or calico, Augusta offered prizes for collections of traditional designs. From this came the concept of a national Welsh costume which, as Prys Morgan has pointed out, transformed the everyday dress of the *Gwerin* (common people) into something romantic and patriotic at the very time when the old styles and regional varieties were becoming obsolescent, thus giving another unity (albeit a manufactured one) to Wales. The red cloak worn over a petticoat and bed gown and the tall black hat (worn in the Abergavenny Eisteddfod processions) became a new national symbol used for example in *Western Mail* cartoons at the turn of the century to depict 'Dame Wales' and living on in St David's Day celebrations and holiday souvenirs. Whilst Lady Charlotte was reviving pride in Welsh literature through *The Mabinogion*, Lady Hall's imaginative romanticization was defining 'Welshness' in another way.

In 1891 Enid Layard (née Guest) wrote that the two 'had been contemporaries and rivals in Wales in their youth'. Yet a reading of Lady Charlotte's complete journals suggests rather an eagerness initially to emulate on her part followed by both women excelling in their own individual areas of expertise. When Augusta was identified as the Eisteddfod winner to a 'thunder of applause', Lady Charlotte, who never competed herself, declared that although some scoffed at her entry 'I should have been very pleased to have filled her place'. Maxwell Fraser's effort to rescue Lady Hall (she became Lady Llanover in 1869) from the autocratic image with which she, unlike Lady Charlotte, has been associated, has by the same token questioned Lady Charlotte's reliability and generosity of spirit. Not only did the latter remain full of praise for the Llanover circle with which she was closely linked throughout her years in Wales but she viewed Lady Hall's mother as the ideal mentor for her daughter Maria. John and Benjamin were Parliamentary allies, members of the same clubs, and both couples frequented similar social circles in London and sometimes stayed at Fentons Hotel. In 1848 when Benjamin was ill, Lady Charlotte immediately altered her travel plans, went to Wales specially to see Augusta, then travelled on her own to London, crossing the Severn in a hot cabin 'with men drinking rum and gin'.

The only critical journal entry was in 1856 when Lady Charlotte was understandably hurt by the way in which her erstwhile friend responded to her second marriage. Lady Hall was

... very mischievous and her manner vexed me when I saw her in London – I befriended her years ago when she was in trouble and when her husband's conduct made her grateful for sympathy (though I always assumed to *know* nothing that could hurt her or reflect upon him) and this has been my return – she is the only person in the course of all the differences of opinion about my marriage that has shown me personal coolness amounting almost to incivility.

If Lady Charlotte felt nervous on her first visit to Llanover in 1833, she soon learned to conquer, at least outwardly, her apprehension. Welsh gatherings became the order of the day. In 1834 the Guests attended the National Eisteddfod in Cardiff. Lady Charlotte approved of its encouragement of all artistic talent regardless of rank. She

> ... got a very good place in the front row opposite the platform. After a pause, Lord Bute opened the Eisteddfod. His speech was miserable, and made me tremble lest I should be betrayed into a smile. When it was at length, to my great relief, and I should think to his, concluded, Mr Price came forward and made one of the most beautiful and eloquent speeches that was ever heard. He traced the history of the Welsh and expatiated on their attachment to their country, their usages and their language. It was, indeed, most exciting.

She was invited to the platform and pleased when the Chair was awarded to Taliesin Williams. A blind old harpist so moved her that she had to hide her tears behind her little half-sister Libdub when he played 'The Rising of the Lark', 'simply, feelingly'. She then presented a prize for a geological sketch. The following day another harpist played 'Codiad yr haul' ('The Rising of the Sun') with such gusto that Lady Charlotte's imagination took flight, conjuring up 'an ancient Chieftain inspirited to fight and die by such a strain, for the sake of his country'. Her husband's speech was overshadowed by a child of four who apparently read Hebrew, Greek and Welsh upside down and quite won over Lady Charlotte, followed by a violent crash as the over-crowded platform gave way. Lady Charlotte now learned Welsh airs on the harp and one of the prize subjects she chose for the Abergavenny meetings was the history of the harp in Glamorgan and Monmouthshire.

She was therefore well placed to solicit support for the promotion of Welsh literature. She could also draw on non-Welsh patrons. She appealed to Babbage on behalf of the Welsh Manuscripts Society and the 'miniature Eisteddfod' at Abergavenny. Through her influence Henry Hallam attended the 1838 meeting, presenting a subscription prize of 60 guineas for the best essay on 'The Influence which the Welsh Traditions have had on the Literature of Europe'.

Enthusiasm did not cloud her critical faculties. She was wary lest the Cymreigyddion became too 'tamed down to the conventional rules of English taste', complained about the 'uncivil treatment' of a 'poor manufacturer' who had competed for a prize advertised in her name (and was assured that this would not happen again) and whilst Lady Hall would have nothing to do with the son of one of the Chartist leaders (Zephaniah Williams) Lady Charlotte was keen to promote the musical talents of this harpist. The Guests subscribed a guinea each annually to the Society and gave a number of 10-guinea prizes.

Through this Lady Charlotte had access to learned papers and read through compositions (including rejected essays) submitted for competitions. Central to the establishment and development of the Society were the two men who were crucial to the success of *The Mabinogion*, the Revs Price and Jones (Tegid). Thomas Price had been Vicar of Cwmdû, Crickhowell since 1825. He was a polymath, winning prizes for his knowledge of Welsh history, geography and the scriptures.

An accomplished harpist, etcher and carver, he did the engravings for the Welsh Manuscripts Society and may even have helped with *The Mabinogion* illustrations. In 1845 he won the principal prize at Abergavenny for his comparative essay on the remains of Welsh literature in Welsh, Irish and Gaelic. Between 1836 and 1842 he published his history of early and medieval Wales (in Welsh). His obituary in *The Critic* described him as 'an eminent living example of what the human mind can accomplish'.

The same journal described Tegid as 'a most profound scholar, and one of the greatest Welsh poets of the age'. His bardic name, Ioan Tegid, derived from Llyn Tegid (Lake Bala), his birthplace. An Oxford mathematics graduate, he translated the Book of Isaiah from Hebrew into Welsh and English. From 1823 to 1842 he was Precentor of Christ Church, Oxford, then, through Lady Hall's influence, obtained the Pembrokeshire living of Nevern, in the gift of the Lord Chancellor, Lord Cottenham. He stayed there until his death ten years later, the same year as Sir John died. A story is told that the visiting clergyman at Nevern suddenly had the sound of his voice drowned by the song of a thrush. At that moment Tegid died. Fourteen years earlier he and Price had helped make it possible for Lady Charlotte to publish *The Mabinogion*.

It is not difficult to imagine Lady Charlotte's New Year resolution for 1838. Her journal shows her busy on the translation of 'The Lady of the Fountain' throughout the first half of January. Despite finding it difficult she finished all that Tegid had sent her by 17 January, when baby Merthyr was born. Within a few weeks the dictionaries were out again. The tale was finished on 6 February and the following day Price came to stay. They discussed printing and publishing (done by Rees of Llandovery and Longmans in London).[10] After dinner, 'We polished my Translation slightly for the Press. But being willing to keep very rigidly to the original very little alteration could be made in my version, which will I fear appear rather clumsy English.'

Nevertheless Price stayed several days and they worked during this time. This set the pattern for subsequent tales. Rumours that Tegid might give a tale to somebody else were countered by a strong letter from Lady Charlotte.

The journal shows her constantly battling against time. No doubt frequent pregnancies and childbirth (with associated fears) contributed to this, as did other demands in her busy life as well as with her determination that nobody should outdo her. She made the most of every spare moment. On one trip to London the carriage was so crammed with books that a spring gave way before reaching Monmouth. Part of 'Kilhwch and Olwen' was translated at the Pyle Inn near Margam whilst John visited his Newton properties. During the 1838 European trip pencil translations of 'Geraint' were done whilst travelling and copied out whenever they stopped. Lady Charlotte was quick to notice that translation and transcription work combined with 'keeping up my journal and writing letters has not allowed me a single idle moment since I left England. As for Merthyr he does nothing at all.' She read Welsh in Milan, translated at Lake Como and Florence and copied at Zurich and Lausanne. She was still beavering away in early October, nervously anticipating the reception of her first number, 'I brood over it and fancy that I left several inaccuracies uncorrected (which however I *trust* is not the case) and sometimes I am very anxious for the result.' In her absence Price had corrected the proofs. It came out in late August but Lady Charlotte did not see it until back home in November; it was 'certainly got up most beautifully'.

In the midst of sorting out the translation of 'Geraint' came an unexpected problem. A Breton Count, Theodore Hersart de la Villemarqué came to Wales as part of a team commissioned by the French Ministry of Public Instruction to report on Welsh literature. He attended the Abergavenny Eisteddfod, seeking to re-establish Celtophile connections between Brittany and Wales. At first Lady Charlotte thought him 'a clever and agreeable young man'. He was struck by her linguistic ability and wrote to his father that '*ce qui m'intéresse surtout en elle, ce sont ses trouvaux sur la littérature galloise; elle publie en ce moment une traduction anglaise charmante qui ont un grand succès*'. Villemarqué stayed at Dowlais for several days and he and the Guests were at the Vivians' New Year house-party. He had previously transcribed for Lady Charlotte the romance of the 'Chevalier au Lion' of Chrétien de Troyes from the Bibliothèque du Roi in Paris. This she had published as an Appendix to her first number.

It seems that Villemarqué's real concern was to minimize the differences between Breton and Welsh and so claim that much old Welsh literature really originated in Brittany. By the end of January 1838 Lady Charlotte was becoming concerned about his behaviour. He was increasingly, 'wild in his notions and presumes on my good nature, because he corrected the press of the last part of the Chevalier au Lion (which it was necessary he should as no one could correctly read his transcript so vilely was it written) he writes insisting on Rees's signing his name to the printed copy and saying it is published by him. Poor Rees is annoyed. Of course I can consent to nothing of the sort.'

When Lady Charlotte learned that Villemarqué had persuaded Tegid to copy out for him the third of the Romances, 'Peredur' for immediate publication in France, she postponed her plans for publishing 'The Dream of Rhonabwy' in order to publish 'Peredur' first. Just before Monty was born she spent nearly twelve hours one day 'in the faint hope of getting it out before the Frenchman explaining 'I have much going on towards my book in different directions and every moment that I am not suckling my little infant is fully taken up.' To make matters worse little Merthyr fell seriously ill. Nevertheless the rush to the press paid off. Better relations were resumed with Tegid, Price gave his usual generous help and within seven weeks Lady Charlotte had 'transcribed it, translated it, written the notes, provided all the decorations and brought it almost out of the Printer's hands. I have had the interruption of confinement and of watching two sick children during the time, and have not had the slightest assistance except Mr Price's criticism during the short visit he paid us this week.' On 29 July she triumphantly received the first copies of 'Peredur' having beaten Villemarqué.

At the October 1840 Abergavenny Eisteddfod (when 'Geraint' appeared in print) Villemarqué entered an essay on the influence of Welsh tradition on European literature. Within this he made considerable use of Lady Charlotte's work with scarcely any acknowledgement, 'on the contrary he delicately insinuated that I did not write the book myself (a degree of moral turpitude which he dare not openly accuse me of). The secret of all this is his anger at being unable to forestall me in the publication of Peredur.'

Villemarqué had already published his *Baraz-Breiz* which proved not to be, as he claimed, authentic old Breton ballads. In 1842 his *Contes Populaires des Anciens Bretons* appeared. It included translations into French of the first three parts of *The Mabinogion* (from Lady Charlotte's contemporary English into contemporary French). Although containing a reference to her efforts and intelligence, it avoided any direct acknowledgement to her published English texts and so conveyed the impression that he had translated straight from the Welsh. Villemarqué actually knew very little Welsh.

Lady Charlotte's reaction was predictable: 'Altogether it is a most shabby proceeding, but the man is too contemptible to be noticed.' Her husband sent 'most kind notes from the House of Commons, doing all he could to soothe my ruffled feelings'. The Breton nationalist Rio sympathized, labelling his fellow countryman 'L'homme Marqué'. To add insult to injury the *Athenaeum* praised the book as if it were an original. Lady Charlotte and George Clark promptly concocted an explanatory letter to the editor. Fortunately a German version of the tales edited by Albert Schulz was 'in a very different spirit' and scrupulous in acknowledgement. Lady Charlotte was herself charitable enough to acknowledge in her three-volume edition the 'kindness and alacrity' with which Villemarqué had supplied her with the 'Chevalier au Lion'.

The demands of publishing were wearing, especially when combined with pregnancy. On one of Price's visits she had to put her work aside due to 'my health which now drags me down to the very dust'. She was 'desolate beyond expression' when translating 'Branwen'. Yet there were times when she felt stronger and less rushed. 'I did most completely enjoy this day. It was all so calm, and my work prospered nicely', she wrote when working on 'Rhonabwy'. By the end of June 1843 she had effectively finished her translations. There was a gap before the publication of the three-volume edition in July 1848. By 1845 the tales had appeared in seven parts. The Introduction for the complete edition was 'something which I am more or less appalled at'. She wrote this in 1848, trying it out first on Sir John.

This marked the end of the venture in more ways than one. Although Price spoke briefly about *The Mabinogion* at the 1848 Abergavenny meeting, within a month he was dead. This had been the first meeting held under the auspices of the Prince of Wales. It was also attended by Henry Layard. Three years later Lady Charlotte negotiated with her Llandovery publisher about producing Layard's Nineveh work in Welsh. Tegid was her original choice as translator but Rees feared (from a specimen translation) that his version would not be sufficiently popular so it was put in other hands.[11] Lady Charlotte corrected the proofs and discussed drawings.

At the 1848 Abergavenny meeting the major prize had been awarded to Thomas Stephens, a young druggist in Merthyr. His essay was published the following year as *The Literature of the Kymry* (in English to extend circulation). In 1921, the centenary of his birth, a correspondent in the *Western Mail* using the pseudonym of 'Ap Dowlais' questioned whether Lady Charlotte had actually translated *The Mabinogion*, claiming that in the Merthyr district there was talk that Stephens was the true translator. 'Ap Dowlais' referred to the 'joyful assertion that it was a Welshman who gave to the world these Translations and not the intellect of another race'. Clearly there was some difficulty in accepting that an English woman rather than a Welsh man had performed such a feat. A Swansea librarian (and member of a Mabinogion Society reading circle) came to Lady Charlotte's defence by publishing in the same paper (and later in a booklet) extracts about the preparation of her work from the journal, obtained earlier from Blanche. Although they do not include every reference to the work, they were sufficient to prove the point. Rhys Phillips also explained that Stephens was only sixteen when Lady Charlotte embarked on her work and that this young apprentice (son of a bootmaker) could not then have had access to the array of scholarship and books which were at Lady Charlotte's disposal. Stephens was anyway a highly principled young man who championed the cause of historical accuracy and honesty. Indeed his refutation of the Madoc myth (which claimed that the Welsh had discovered America) caused such a stir at the 1858 Llangollen Eisteddfod that his prize was withheld. Though he tended to be sparing in praise (and refreshingly self-critical) he wrote, after comparing *The Mabinogion* to the original Welsh, that he had 'uniformly found reason to think that our ancient tales have been exceedingly fortunate in being translated by Lady Charlotte Guest. Her version correctly mirrors forth the spirit of these antique stories and is as much distinguished for elegance as fidelity.'

Stephens's relationship with the Guests appears to have been good, though it only seems to date from 1848. Sir John paid for his publication (also with Rees and Longmans) whilst Lady Charlotte made enquiries on his behalf about the protocol for the presentation of copies to the Queen. She also helped correct his proofs and secure a suitable binder. Any profits were to go to him.[12]

In a French translation of *The Mabinogion* (published in 1889 with a second edition in 1913) Joseph Loth claimed that Lady Charlotte 'ne savait guère le gallois: elle a travaillé sur une version littérale d'un savant gallois et à force de pénétration, de conscience et de talent, réussi à en faire une traduction d'un grand charme et qui ne dénature pas l'original dans l'ensemble'.

As we have seen, she was newly acquainted with the language. She did not deny this. In the Preface to the 1849 edition Lady Charlotte forestalled possible criticism by acknowledging that: 'It may be considered rash in one who has but recently become acquainted with the Principality and its literature, to engage in a work like the present, while there are so many others by whom it would be much more ably executed.' Nor does her journal pretend that she found the new language easy. In 1836 she admitted that translating a history of Wales into English (something she was contemplating) would be very difficult. Half a page took a couple of hours and despite some work on this over the ensuing weeks, Katherine's birth signalled a welcome end to the venture. She admitted that the first tale she translated was difficult, 'being so little conversant with Welsh and the Mabinogion being in such a cramped and ancient style'. Yet she seems to have learned quickly. In July 1838 she read 'Geraint' on a journey. She had forgotten her dictionary and 'was quite surprised to find that I could understand the old Welsh without one'. Some tales were more tricky than others. 'Rhonabwy' was 'tiresome difficult Welsh' compared to the Romances.

There is not, however, evidence to suggest that Lady Charlotte had much knowledge of contemporary Welsh. Although she uttered the odd word on appropriate public and ceremonial occasions this does not necessarily denote a fluent Welsh speaker. Indeed, knowing even a few words would have delighted many since it was more than most English incomers and some Welsh people managed, and suggested she cared about the language. For example, a letter from John Evans of Machynlleth begging a mining job not only carefully stressed his abstention from liquor for the last five years but also commented on Lady Charlotte taking notice of a language 'abused, by her own Sons and Daughters who should Honour it with all their might'. As one of the 'meanest of the sons of Gwalia' he had written part of his letter in English since Lady Charlotte had taken the trouble to learn Welsh.

A rough draft of a letter she wrote in 1837 in Welsh to the Liverpool Cambrian Society suggests that, at that stage at least, her skills of translation of English into Welsh left much to be desired. Expert opinion suggests that her use of syntax, word order and literal translation of individual words indicate somebody at an elementary stage in learning the language. Yet the letter may well date from the beginning of the year, involved the use of modern Welsh and was certainly written before embarking on the long and educative task of translating the medieval tales. Lady Charlotte was a linguophile, very familiar with working with dictionaries and engaging in complicated translation work in languages which she did not necessarily speak. In a letter to his father, Villemarqué called her 'Une femme extraordinaire' who 'écrit le francais comme nous, elle sait l'italien, orientales …'. Her work for *The Mabinogion* was anyway concerned with translating Welsh into English and not vice versa. Lady Charlotte had long been an amateur but accomplished philologist.

The Welsh critic W.J. Gruffydd believed that the main credit should go to the two scholars who 'devilled' for her, Tegid and Price. Tegid's transcripts of the tales were essential, though this was openly acknowledged in the Preface where Lady Charlotte admitted her 'great obligations for the trouble he has taken to forward my wishes,

Part of a letter sent by Lady Charlotte to the Secretary of the Liverpool Cambrian Society in 1837. This was only a rough draft and some of the sentence construction, wording, etc., might have been tidied up in the top copy. It acknowledged her invitation from the Society, asks for Guest and herself to be included as members, and assures support for the muse, harp and language of the old Welsh.

with respect to publishing the MS as correctly as possible' (the 1877 edition also mentioned Bosanquet). Moreover, Tegid seems to have been happy for Lady Charlotte to translate his poem 'Ymweliad y Bardd'. Her English version of the four verses of what she called 'The Bard's Journey to Bala' was published[13] and later J.D. Jones of Ruthin printed it in Welsh and English in a popular series of sheet music (costing 3*d*).

If Tegid provided material from which she could work, then Price was of central importance to the translation. This elderly scholar visited Dowlais whenever Lady Charlotte had completed the first draft of a translation. Although the journal does not make explicit exactly how much assistance he rendered on each occasion, it is quite possible that his input was invaluable. Indeed the relationship between Lady Charlotte and Price was in a number of respects akin to that of pupil and teacher. Not only did they work together on the manuscripts but there was frequent correspondence between 'Persondy', his vicarage, and Dowlais House. Most people who wrote to Lady Charlotte adopted a suitably deferential tone; not so the Rev. Price. Most interestingly, Lady Charlotte seems to have accepted, without demurring, this alien tone. For example he responded to eight parcels of her work with, 'I am quite disappointed in your treatment of the Tair Gormes' (Three Plagues); He reminded her that the story within 'Lludd and Llevelys' was one of the most important in all the collection, and he wrote of the dragons in Dinas Emrys and the development of Merlin's magical powers, stressing that 'by your way of telling it you deprive it of much of the interest which it would possess if given as a literal translation' Lady Charlotte appreciated his advice. She always revered true scholarship and on first meeting Price had observed that he possessed 'a sort of universality and was conversant on what ever subject was started'. He admired Sir Gore Ouseley and probably alerted Lady Charlotte to Prichard's work.

Her Deed Box in the National Library of Wales contains hundreds of pages of translation and notes for the printers. Much is beautifully written out in her hand, though the Welsh text is presumably in Tegid's handwriting. There are also rougher versions, as an early translation for 'Rhonabwy' shows. A possible interpretation of the stages of development of *The Mabinogion* is that Lady Charlotte made the initial translation from the copy supplied by Tegid, and that Price then worked with her on this, improving it. The degree of amendment probably altered as she became more skilled and used to the material. She would then have turned this version into the graceful and elegant English which was her hallmark and with which she was so familiar, thanks in part to many years of journal writing. Gruffydd's charge of 'devilling' therefore seems unduly harsh, underestimating the complexity of the protracted undertaking now revealed by the Deed Box and the complete journals.

Criticism of Lady Charlotte as the sole editorial voice lies partly in her failure to acknowledge Price in her Preface. Yet despite this admittedly curious omission, he was thanked in the notes – both in name and on one occasion as a 'gentleman' who made the journey to Carn Cavall for the 'Kilhwch and Olwen' tale – and there is no evidence of his having wished to receive greater recognition in the separate numbers of the tales. He did of course die before the publication of the 1849 volumes and Lady Charlotte may simply have felt that there was sadly no point in now thanking him in a Preface. To the last he praised her and declared at Abergavenny 'we are indebted to the talents and liberality of Lady Charlotte Guest'.

Confusion over Lady Charlotte's linguistic ability has been compounded by the fact that the edited selections from her journal published in the 1950s by her grandson, the Earl of Bessborough, were based not on the original handwritten journals but on a typed version made for Monty at the beginning of this century. His anonymous typist(s) performed a mammoth task but did not understand Welsh and misread many Welsh words which were then copied in the Bessborough printed selections. Thus the *Llyfr Coch o Hergest* (as per original) became transformed into the *Llyfr Goch y Hugest* in the Edwardian typescript. *Englynion* became distorted into *engbynion*, 'Branwen' became 'Bauwen' 'Hanes Taliesin' 'Hones Taliesin', and so on; all errors from which Lady Charlotte is entirely exculpated. HerHis original journal is free from such mistakes yet the incorrect transcriptions gave a spurious fillip to her detractors.

Lady Charlotte's journal and correspondence suggest that the production of her *Mabinogion* was not unlike the shaping of the Four Branches. We shall probably never know the finer details of how the tales became transformed from oral to written form and assumed their familiar form in the Red Book (probably as the work of one redactor). So too Lady Charlotte's work represented the climax of scholarship which indirectly owed much to individuals such as William Owen

Pughe but more directly harnessed the talents of early nineteenth century clerical scholars. In the final resort it was Lady Charlotte who put it all together, and even allowing that the translation was perhaps more of a collaborative effort than she fully acknowledged, there is still no detracting from her superb achievement,. She ultimately transcends her critics, not least because it was she and she alone who possessed the foresight, ability, drive and means to oversee such a massive enterprise. A superb organizer and manager (as so many other aspects of her life reveal), she engineered not merely the translation of important Welsh medieval writings but an end product which was literally a Victorian work of art and in the production of such a *chef-d'oeuvre* appears to be the key to her success.

In order to fulfil her aims Lady Charlotte made the most of her resources. Assistance was sought from those closest to her. John copied and listened, the harp teacher took down some dictated translation and Mary did her bit, copying, reading aloud and correcting proof sheets. In a superb under-statement Mary's journal casually mentioned that she had sat with Charlotte and 'looked over the MS of the 2nd number of her book written chiefly in the carriage during her travels on the continent'. Clark proffered some criticisms of the translation of 'Kilhwch'. Predictably the former tutor Mr Martin sent notes on Romantic fiction, and just as predictably Lady Charlotte dismissed them.

It was, however, access to scholars and scholarship which put her in such an advantageous position. At a time when many old manuscripts were locked away in private hands or specialist libraries and not generally available to the public (which partly explains the relative ease with which forgeries were produced), Lady Charlotte could obtain material from such sources.[14] Within Wales she had assistance from *Yr Hen Bersoniaid* (the old literary clerics) of the Anglican church, men such as 'Gwallter Mechain' (Rev. Walter Davies) of Llanrhaidr. Like Price he helped in topographical work, locating places and place names especially vital in such onomastic tales as the Four Branches. Lady Charlotte recognized the value of this, the antiquity of the tales being demonstrated by their inevitably pre-dating the old place-names they mentioned.

She pored over manuscripts in the British Museum and sought expert guidance there. Joseph Ritson (who has been dubbed the 'first modern Arthurian scholar') alerted her to an Icelandic manuscript which she sensed to be the same story as the Welsh 'The Lady of the Fountain'. The museum's English version 'Ywayne and Gawin' she found to be translated virtually word for word from Chrétien de Troyes's French. Lady Charlotte found that all three of the Arthurian Romances had European analogues. According to Rachel Bromwich she was probably the first to 'discover and point out that closely parallel versions existed in French and other languages …'. This had important repercussions. It stimulated the development of Romance study and prompted energetic and somewhat chauvinistic debate around whether the French were indebted to the Welsh or vice versa. Prevailing current opinion seems to be that the Romances evolved in a bilingual environment (South East Wales seems the most likely area) not long after the Norman Conquest when French influences were absorbed by an unidentified authorship.

Part of the delight of Lady Charlotte's *Mabinogion* lies in the illustrations and notes. Her notes often cleverly utilized the extensive reading of her early life – Dunlop's *History of Fiction*, for example, first read in 1831 – and an inventory of her books shows also how she extended her reading.* A significant part of the 'total package', the illustrations are truly Victorian interpretations of chivalry and medieval life. The beginning and end of each tale (in both languages) contained illustrations and the notes included occasional sketches such as the funeral urn of Branwen. Lady Charlotte negotiated with 'the woodcut engineer' and the lithographer who made facsimiles from the Red Book and from manuscripts of other versions.[15]

Lady Charlotte's lavish *tour de force* was a quintessentially Victorian product, geared to a particular kind of readership and in tune with the allusive and florid style which contemporary readers understood and expected. Judgement of her translation has to take this into account. For example, Victorian propriety (and the fact that the stories were seen as tales for children) would have influenced her rendition. Arawn's return to his wife in 'Pwyll' was omitted as he indulged 'in loving pleasure and affection with her'. The need for delicacy can be appreciated by considering Mary's response to Charlotte's subject matter. Mary's journal records that she was 'much *shocked* [her emphasis] at its *impropriety*'.

Once published, *The Mabinogion* was duly praised, as was its translator. A sonnet dedicated to Lady Charlotte was published in *Lays From The Cimbric Lyre* in 1846, the poet (a Welsh speaker and Senior Wrangler at Cambridge University) using the pseudonym of Goronva Camlan. It ended with the lines:

> For thee, of English birth but British heart,
> Our Bardic harp neglected and unstrung
> Moved to the soul, and at thy touch there start
> Old harmonies to life: our ancient tongue
> Opens, its buried treasure to impart.

A few years later a Brecon poet dedicated his *Isolda, or the Maid of Kidwelly and Other Poems* to Lady Charlotte.

In the mid-1860s she was paid the ultimate, though erroneous, compliment of being described as Welsh. *A Cyclopaedia of Female Biography* providing sketches 'of all women who have been distinguished by great talents, strength of character, piety, benevolence or moral virtue of any kind' declared that Lady Charlotte was born in Wales, and has done much to elucidate its language and literature'. Through her efforts, much of the history of 'her' country had been 'sought out, set in order, and thus will be preserved'.

---

* See Appendix 4B.

Further afield, her work helped stimulate Ernest Renan's *Essai sur la Poisie des Races Celtiques* (1854), an unprecedented comparative approach to Celtic literature which called *The Mabinogion* the 'true description of the Celtic genius' which had transformed the 'imagination of Europe' and which, until Lady Charlotte's work, had been hidden from history. In 1876 Lady Charlotte revised her work into one volume with a new Preface. It was published the following year by Bernard Quaritch. Her translation was also the basis for *The Boy's Mabinogion* a decade later, with an Introduction by Sidney Lanier who had edited *The Boy Froissart* and *The Boy King Arthur*. Lanier dedicated it to Lady Charlotte 'whose talents and scholarship have made these delights possible'. Advertised as 'The Gift Book to the Younger for the Season' it cost a guinea and sought to appeal to the student of mythology and folklore as well as youthful readers delighting in 'tales of warlike and strange adventure of knights who encounter giants, goblins, and sorcerers, of Beauty wronged and redressed'.

Later scholars also emphasized their debt to Lady Charlotte. Rhys Phillips suggested that her range of knowledge and breadth of scholarship (English, Welsh and 'Continental') marked her out as 'one of the most remarkable women of that Victorian age'. Not until 1929, over ninety years after her first number was published, did a new translation appear[16] (by T.P. Ellis and John Lloyd), followed in 1948 by the magisterial translation by Gwyn and Thomas Jones for the Cockerel Press. Their version was, however, from the White Book of Rhydderch and not based on the Red Book of Hergest. They recognized that their predecessor took some liberties in producing a Victorian masterpiece out of the medieval Welsh – 'Hers are beauties indeed, but too often they are not the beauties of her wonderful original' – they also made it clear that they could not 'too emphatically pay tribute to so splendid an achievement'.

In the Preface to the 1877 edition (which omitted the Welsh texts) Lady Charlotte drew attention to an event which had 'interested a much wider circle of readers in the legends …'. This was the publication of Tennyson's *The Idylls of the King* which included 'Geraint and Enid' based on her translation 'Geraint the son of Erbin'. Tennyson wrote this and 'The Marriage of Geraint' in 1856 and first printed them the following year (with 'Merlin and Vivien') in six private copies. It was said that he learned Welsh for this – he certainly stayed in Wales in 1856. Lady Charlotte's translation was the first work he bought after his marriage. He altered one line of 'Geraint and Enid' after learning from her the correct Welsh pronunciation of the name Enid. *The Idylls of the King* proved to be the most popular poetic work of the Victorian period. Tennyson, like Matthew Arnold, owed 'a debt of gratitude' to Lady Charlotte. Her 'happy entry into the world of letters' (Arnold) enabled contemporaries to appreciate medieval Welsh literature and stimulated successors. In this sense she succeeded in her aim of putting herself 'at the head of literature'. Alfred Nutt, who reprinted her work in 1902, wrote that she had 'succeeded, beyond all others, in preserving for the modern world what is most distinctive and permanent in the charm of medieval art'.

6

The Businesswoman

'I am iron now — and my life is altered into one of action, not of sentiment.'

One of Lady Charlotte's objectives was to amass 'such a fortune for the babies as to make them very well off hereafter'. Not only was this aim fulfilled but she made certain that she played her own part in this process. At first she assisted her husband out of duty, but as her own understanding, knowledge and interest in business developed, she intervened more decisively. As Sir John's health deteriorated so Lady Charlotte correspondingly became more crucial to the enterprise, assuming greater and graver responsibilities. By late 1851 she was in practice virtually controlling the Company, a position which became formalized when he died.

True to form, Lady Charlotte wasted no time in acclimatizing herself to her new surroundings. After coffee on her first day at Dowlais, John took her through the furnaces and forges. After dinner they watched the casting of iron. This set the pattern for almost daily trips to the works which, after all, were on her doorstep. Brother Bertie's first comment on Dowlais House had been 'Well it's a capital house and you've got a *lucrative* view from the windows.' Whereas once the lime trees of Uffington had been her refuge, now 'I sauntered through the furnaces and mills' and listened to the 'musical clank of bars of rails'. She watched iron ore run into moulds as pig iron, saw the refining process where the metal was roasted, and admired the skilled peddlers kneading the molten metal into a bloom which was then hammered and taken red hot to the rolling mill. She observed the iron being cut, piled, rolled to produce the thousands of rails which made the firm world-famous. Some of her adjectives were not those commonly associated with ironmaking. She described making nail rods as 'the prettiest process in the world' and felt 'inspirited' when the wall of No.7 blast furnace was lit up by a rainbow as she ascended the cinder incline. The stream and smoke were likened to ostrich feathers. Lady Charlotte was determined that 'muck' would produce not just 'brass' but beauty too, 'as I bounded over the cinder tips and heaps of mine rubbish even they seemed to possess beauties'. One reason why she so disliked Sully, the holiday house on the Glamorgan coast, was because of the absence of noise and excitement which characterized Dowlais by day and night. Within six weeks of arriving she was commenting, 'I am now beginning to understand, and to become interested in what I see there, and Merthyr is always ready to explain to me all I wish to know.'

The gradual transformation of the aristocratic lady from rural Lincolnshire into an informed and competent businesswoman in the iron trade of South Wales can be seen as a metaphor for Britain's industrial development more generally at this time. The story of Dowlais's spectacular expansion dates from the mid-eighteenth century. In 1748, 2,000 acres of land, together with mineral rights, were leased from Herbert, Viscount Windsor to a Thomas Morgan of Ruperra, Glamorgan for ninety-nine years at a fixed yearly rent of £26. Morgan used the land for hunting. In 1759, however, it was subleased to Thomas Lewis of Llanishen, Glamorgan, and he with eight partners from Wales, Bristol and Shrewsbury (including the father of the inventor John Wilkinson) erected a small furnace. Today's manufacturing company, GKN, dates its development from their articles of co-partnership. Situated on the northern rim of the coalfield there were plentiful deposits of coal and iron ore, limestone and water power at the Dowlais Brook. Within a year 500 tons of iron had been produced and in 1763 a further twenty-two acres of common land were leased. As we have seen, the involvement of the Guest family dated from 1767.

A second blast furnace was erected in the late eighteenth century when demand was greatly stimulated by war in America and Europe. The invention of a puddling process known as the 'Welsh method' enabled coal to be used to make malleable iron and the adoption of steam power (a Boulton and Watt engine was in use from 1798) increased productivity still further. The Glamorganshire Canal was built in the 1790s, an impressive engineering feat which covered the 24 miles between Merthyr and Cardiff, and thanks to Richard Trevithick, the world's first steam locomotive ran on rails on the nearby Penydarren tram road in 1804. Three years later Thomas Guest died and his son John Guest became manager (sharing this with his brother-in-law's nephew until 1814). 1815 certainly spelt peace and prosperity for him. As principal shareholder he now controlled a concern producing 15,000 tons of iron annually. With a mind like a steel trap tempering technology into profits he continued the pioneering process. John Guest and Adrian Stephens are credited with the invention of the steam whistle and, in the year of his marriage to Lady Charlotte, Guest devised a 'running out furnace' which obviated the need for a wasteful cooling process.

There was, however, the proverbial thorn in the flesh. John, Second Marquis of Bute, was successor in title to the Windsors and from 1814 was the landlord. He received only a nominal sum (£100 until 1828, then £2,315) for the dozen or so leases under which Dowlais was by this time held. Not even paying royalties, Guest was meanwhile reaping huge annual profits – £55,000 for example in 1842 – whilst Bute looked on. Determined to remedy the error of his predecessors, Bute waged a battle for a more economic rent and compensation for encroachments on land. Between them, Guest and Bute kept lawyers very busy.

As an MP Sir John had helped Bute's plans for developing the port of Cardiff but his political views were anathema to the Tory Marquis. John Davies, Bute's biographer, has shown how his subject viewed Sir John as 'the ultimate source of all radical agitation in Glamorgan' and in 1841 even tried to tempt him with the renewal of the lease in return for withdrawing from the election. Bute was wary of all things associated with the Guests – Sir John was Chairman of the Taff Vale Railway Company (Dowlais accounted for 80 per cent of its iron cargo) which broke the monopoly of the Glamorganshire Canal. As if this were not bad enough, Bute suspected that, as Director of the Cardiff branch of the National Provincial Bank,[1] Sir John was seeking to ruin his credit. There were disputes over wharfs for Dowlais at the Bute dock, this and other excuses being used to delay the signing of the lease. Such action was, in Lady Charlotte's opinion, 'quite unworthy of a man, not to say a nobleman'.

In Lady Charlotte's journal Bute became the wicked and grasping landlord, the Guests' fortunes now being identified with industrial capitalism rather than the landowning interest. In practice their interests were not so neatly divorced – Bute, who already owned 22,000 acres of Glamorgan, had dreams of a rival ironworks at Rhymney, whilst Guest became landlord of the Newton Nottage estate and owned a number of farms in the southern part of Glamorgan. Yet their contest over the renewal of the lease was reminiscent of an ancient feud as Bute relentlessly used his ultimate control as a means of getting his tenant to do what he wanted. The tortuous story of the renewal of the leases culminated in a death bed scene as dramatic as any of the colourful incidents in Lady Charlotte's life.

By 1845 Dowlais had eighteen blast furnaces (the average number for ironworks was three), each producing over 100 tons per week. The site covered forty acres and the workforce numbered 7,300, many of them coming originally from South West Wales. A second works, the Ifor works, (named after the Guests' eldest son) was built to the north east of the main works in 1839, costing £47,000 to erect and equip. After buying out shares held by the Lewis family, Sir John completed his control in 1851 when he got the two shares held by his nephew, Edward Hutchins. He was now the sole owner of the company. Although wielding more power than ever, his illness ensured that he was less able to exercise it. Much of the running of affairs was delegated to Lady Charlotte who had already undergone a long, albeit unofficial, apprenticeship. Her journal became a repository for comments about the state of the works: alongside accounts of measles, *The Mabinogion*, Merthyr and Mayfair were equally detailed descriptions of the mills, the mixture used in blast furnaces and the week's make of finished iron. Her use of language is revealing. After feeling low one day she took her customary walk into the works 'the mills were as stirring and joyous as ever, this walk was certainly of use to me. I always feel here in my proper sphere.' Mrs Ellis would not have approved. After the literal confinement of childbirth (a few hours before Merthyr's birth she watched an experiment at No. 9 engine) it was with relief that she returned to the works 'where the noise and life and activity restored my satisfaction'.[2] When describing her emotions the metaphors were those of the works. She referred to the blazing fires and flames of her ambition, sought to demonstrate her strength and determination by declaring that she had become iron and wrote that 'in these days of railroads and excitement one ought to be as hard as the nails on the blocks'. She soon became quite proprietorial:

on a trip to Switzerland she was delighted to find the Guest Lewis mark on bar iron at a foundry, 'my own iron in this remote spot'. In 1839 she declared that she had so schooled herself into habits of business that 'it is now more congenial to me to calculate the advantage of half per cent commission on a cargo of iron than to go to the finest ball in the world'. She felt it important that 'We are at the head of the iron trade. Otherwise I could not take part in my house in the City and my works at Dowlais and glory (playfully) in being (in some sort) a tradeswoman.'

How was this identification (with its accompanying qualifications consigned, as usual, to brackets) achieved? As with everything else, Lady Charlotte approached her new environment with gusto. Not content with looking on the surface she also made a number of trips underground to see the coal and ironstone workings, even though this involved 'a good deal of scrambling and it was very wet sometimes'. She seized the opportunity for an initial tour when two visitors came to see the balance pit (where young women raised full trams of coal by lowering a tram full of water) and was at pains to tell her journal that she found being lowered from one level to another 'perfectly easy, no way alarming'. Mary's initiation in the balance pit (from a suitable distance) evoked a different response: 'All was very novel very astonishing and very awful.' Lady Charlotte would use whatever transport was at hand: travelling on the 'loco' or even bareback on the tramroad horse.

Some of her investigations could be quite perilous as this visit to a half-finished blast engine shows: 'Having no door, I was obliged to enter it by a ladder put against a window, and as the flooring was still wanting, my only way of going over it was by climbing along the rafters and machinery, and in one instance walking along the arm of a fly wheel.' Her poor eyesight did not help but John was keen she should see it so 'I suppose my neck is at his disposal'.

In 1834 Mamma came to stay and to her dismay found that she was expected to indulge in some highly unusual and inappropriate activities for a lady of her standing. They posed all sorts of new problems. How might one descend from a waggon gracefully? What could be said in praise of the steam engine that Charlotte so admired? Lady Charlotte must have upset a number of her mother's plans for her daughter's genteel future, settled as a wife and mother. Admittedly it was not that easy to be a conventional lady when you lived in the midst of a dirty, sprawling ironworks but did Charlotte need to be quite so enthusiastic about it all? Sarah Ellis had outlined the wife's position in the home as the antithesis of the workplace but at Dowlais such divisions were confounded. One morning as Lady Charlotte was dressing, the central boiler of the new forge burst, throwing down with it a 120-foot engine stack. For once even she seemed lost for words: 'I cannot on paper convey any idea of the crash and terror with which it was accomplished.' The house shook violently, the windows rattled, the frames breaking as well as the glass and 'a volley of stones darkened the air'. Pieces of iron weighing several pounds were speared into the wall and 'a large brick was found in my bed which I had not long left'. Everyone in the house escaped unhurt but in the forge three were killed.

Confused by Lady Charlotte's breaching of the golden rule of separate spheres for the two sexes, contemporary writers explained away her contribution to Dowlais in terms of complementarity, Lady Charlotte providing the qualities which Sir John lacked. Charles Wilkins, Merthyr's chronicler, observed that Guest's 'home life needed a presiding spirit' and argued that from the time of Sir John's second marriage dated his best and happiest projects. He then corrected himself: 'We should rather say their projects, for in all that he was deficient she excelled; and while we credit him with the honour of founding the greatest iron works in the world, and giving sustenance and substantial comforts to twenty thousand souls, it is chiefly to her influence that we must look for all that was done in the way of moral and mental elevation.'

Such descriptions portrayed Lady Charlotte as Lady Bountiful, leaving out what she defined as her proper sphere. A memoir to Sir John written for the Institute of Civil Engineers described how he was 'ably seconded' by Lady Charlotte, 'This estimable lady, whose literary powers are as well appreciated as her general talents and acquirements in branches of knowledge not usually presenting attractive features for ladies ...' It went on to show how she played her part by visiting the homes of the ironworkers, 'she administered to the wants of all around her; thus performing her Christian duties she extended the previously-acquired influence and power of her husband'. Interestingly, one-third of Charles Manby's memoir to Sir John is actually devoted to Lady Charlotte.

In order to consolidate her grasp of technology, at the end of 1834 Lady Charlotte began translating a French pamphlet (by P.A. Dufresnoy, the French Minister of Mines) on the advantages of using hot air in the manufacture of iron. James Neilson's invention of using hot blast in the blowing of furnaces dated from 1828. Most of South Wales favoured the expensive cold blast process but by 1839 Dowlais had adopted the hot blast method in a third of its furnaces. Lady Charlotte read about the subject and attended a relevant lecture at the Liverpool Mechanics Institute. Translating the French into English was difficult with so many technical terms but it was ready for publication within a year. For once attempting something which met with his stepdaughter's approval, Pegus tried in 1838 to obtain a copy of the pamphlet but found it sold out. Although the print run was probably small, Lady Charlotte was understandably flushed with her first (anonymous) effort in print – 'I hope my next attempt at publishing may prove as successful and popular.'

She was soon launched into an ambitious plan for providing a history of the iron trade. She read works such as Ferguson's study of hydraulics,[3] went to the British Museum in search of material and attended lectures on geology and chemistry. After hearing one talk on iron gas pipes she noted that a foreman had developed them but that the invention had been patented by his employer who should have shared the credit. At a Society of Arts meeting she found a scientist who had already written much on the manufacture of iron but was relieved to find that their research did not overlap. Some of her earlier reading may have helped. Like Mary Somerville the scientist (after whom the Oxford college is named) she had enjoyed Euclid in her youth and returned to his work in 1833. His *Elements of Geometry* would have given her the basis of mechanical science. Her husband spent time explaining the steam engine to her, going over lectures whilst she wrote notes and giving her practical lessons on subjects such as tapping a furnace. Joseph Richards explained the machinery in the engine house and she studied plans for a boring mill. She could often be found at the works perched on a wheelbarrow or coal tram until Will the butcher made her an iron chair. Her mixed reaction to this reflected the difficulty she had in being taken seriously, 'I felt flattered at the attention – but alas! that I should be at every step reminded of the feminine weakness of frame and mind.' This feminine weakness was actually contradicted by the Dowlais women workers, who spent twelve-hour days screening and raking coal, wheeling it in barrows, breaking limestone and performing other arduous tasks. Yet though physically strong, this did not mean that they were seen as equal to their male counterparts, something which was clearly reflected in their low pay and unskilled status.

The demands of Welsh, maternity and other distractions made Lady Charlotte despair of her history project. There is no evidence of it ever being published, though when George Clark wrote about the iron industry for the *Quarterly Review* he asked Lady Charlotte for some facts and figures. Her acquisition of knowledge was never wasted.

The Guests attended the yearly meetings of the British Association for the Advancement of Science at venues such as Southampton, Liverpool and Bristol. Although a few ladies attended it was of course the men who asked the questions in such public gatherings: John Guest asked one question after a lecture on his wife's pet subject of the hot blast method. On one London visit George Clark was much amused at Lady Charlotte's remarks on visiting a small steam boat works and foundry at the docks. She quite startled one of the partners by asking him '(perhaps rather abruptly forgetting that I was a lady and had no right to know anything) what sort of pigs they used'. Only too often was she forcibly reminded that although she had literally made it her business to understand pig iron and the world of manufacturing industry, it was clearly not a woman's domain. Not long after marrying she had gone with John to Liverpool and 'to my great disgust' was sent back to the hotel in a hackney carriage whilst he went to the Exchange to see some people about a contract for iron. Nevertheless she was soon accompanying him on visits to his mines in the Forest of Dean, to ironworks all over Britain, and to Europe.

With her Catholic tastes the ideal was to have a blend of mines and myths when travelling. In Cornwall they observed new mining methods at tin and copper works (Lady Charlotte later had to produce a 'sort of journal' for him of proceedings in Cornwall and Devon). They also saw King Arthur's birthplace. On one Scottish tour they saw mines, mills and forges, but on the next visit viewed Holyrood, Arthur's table, and Walter Scott country. German tours included observations on the Hartz mining district, the hard work performed by country women and the tomb of Charlemagne, 'a hero most dear to my imagination'.

Travelling was increasingly speeded up and facilitated by the railway. Many of the journeys in England were performed on trains running on Dowlais rails.

By 1836–7 Dowlais was producing 20,000 tons of rails per year. Back in 1833 Charlotte's mother had tried to dissuade her daughter from using such a dangerous conveyance but this was only the beginning of many train journeys, and rails were the backbone of the Guest enterprise. The firm had supplied some rails for the Stockton to Darlington railway. Their customers included the Liverpool and Manchester Railway Company, the Dublin and Drogheda Railway Company and the Berlin-Leipzig Railway. Cuba, Italy, Hungary, Holland and America bought rails, but the largest order came in 1844 for an unprecented 50,000 tons of rails for Russia.

The Great Western Railway also used Dowlais rails and the Guests proudly attended the opening of the South Wales railway in 1850 – 'The speed we went at was wonderful', wrote Lady Charlotte, and Paddington to Bristol took a mere two-and-a-half hours. The GWR's engineer, the renowned Isambard Kingdom Brunel, also worked on the much more modest Taff Vale railway. Guest and Anthony Hill were behind the scheme to link Merthyr by rail to Cardiff, and John and his brother Thomas were major shareholders. The line was opened as far as Abercynon in October 1840 and extended to Merthyr by April 1841. With her husband as the first chairman of the company Lady Charlotte was asked to perform the traditional wife's role of laying the foundation stone for the railway in 1837. Her performance was less conventional. Amidst cannon volleys and cheers she made an awkward descent into the valley and laid the mortar with a trowel but when the stone was lowered to its place and the engineer produced a 'Lilliputian hammer from his pocket for me to strike it with' she found the idea 'so absurd that I rebelled outright and insisted upon using the wooden mallet to the no small amusement of the workmen'. She then said the expected few words.

Even more theatrical was her visit to Cardiff for the opening of the Marquis of Bute's docks in 1839. This gigantic venture cost £350,000 of Bute's money and had been actively supported in Parliament by Sir John, despite the differ-ences between the two men. Sir John went ahead to Cardiff the night before the ceremony, leaving Lady Charlotte with the Halls at Llanover near Abergavenny. On impulse she decided to join her husband although it was after midnight, the rain was torrential and the journey 26 lonely miles across country. She set off in a carriage 'on my wild expedition', the poor servants having to walk some of the way leading the horses, so bad was the weather (no doubt they had stronger words than 'wild' to describe such an escapade). They reached Cardiff at 5.30 a.m., having rested for a few hours at the Westgate Inn in Newport. Just over a month later this very same inn was to be the scene of the Newport Rising. The opening of the docks provided further evidence of Lady Charlotte's love of an audience. When she saw her own steamer the *Lady Charlotte* sail into the dock she could not resist springing on it to a round of cheers from onlookers – 'the incident pleased the spectators and hundreds (I may say thousands) crowded after me'.

In August 1851 the Dowlais Branch railway was finally opened, connecting the works with the Taff Vale railway. A sick man by this time, Sir John left the proceedings early whilst a troubled Lady Charlotte maintained the role of smiling hostess to the visitors, who included the deposed King of Oudh. She had become used to standing in for her husband. When the Prussian Minister of Commerce and a Silesian manufacturer visited that same year it was she who explained the business. She also acted as interpreter for an Italian Inspector. She enjoyed entertaining distinguished visitors and once even spoke to the Duchess of Sutherland about the Queen's visit to Bristol 'thinking it not impossible that she might like to run across to Cardiff – go up the valley to see the Iron works as she is so interested in the Manufactures of the Country'. No more was heard of this.

Many of the leading contemporary scientists and engineers came to Dowlais at one time or another. There was Isambard Kingdom Brunel, who had a habit of arriving early in the morning and was a 'chain' cigar smoker. Lady Charlotte also knew his father, Marc, who designed the Thames tunnel. Since 'I like every form of enthusiasm' such individuals were welcome especially as Lady Charlotte felt that 'engineering is nearly allied to *my trade*'.★ After the British Association's meeting in Bristol in 1836 Charles Wheatstone, Sir David Brewster and Charles Babbage came on to Dowlais. Wheatstone (who invented the electric telegraph and the concertina) was so incensed at the Bishop of London forbidding the attendance of females at his public lectures on electricity that he resigned his Professorship at King's College. Babbage also believed in encouraging women in science and since his appointment as a Trustee of the British Association had been urging the attendance of ladies at their lectures. Lady Charlotte confided in him, explaining how daunted she felt by her ignorance of the works and her eagerness to teach Ivor about what went on. He admitted that he felt overawed by some subjects and found it helpful to concentrate on the large issues rather than allowing details to dominate. He encouraged Lady Charlotte to persevere and gave her Whewell's Bridgewater Treatise (on astronomy and general physics in relation to 'Natural Theology') to read.

Later that same month (September) Lady Charlotte became John's secretary, undertaking: 'To write all his letters and keep everything copied and arranged – If I find the work too much I am to resign it – But I hope I shall not for I think it will be improving for me and give me a habit of business.' To get into this habit she promptly saw to the writing and dispatching of twenty letters, 'This was beginning in earnest but I have been training for it for some time.' Earlier in the year she had done some writing for her husband. Her language had become that of the employee, though there were times when this role was not so attractive: 'Merthyr called me into his library to write for him' but 'I was vexed for everybody else went out to walk and I was almost angry at being obliged to give up society which I have so seldom an opportunity of enjoying'. Whilst he went to the House of Commons she handled his letters. The letters received had also to be catalogued and copies made of those sent. John Guest was an exacting employer. Within a few months she was worried as he 'seemed not quite satisfied' with her efforts. 'I had hoped to become useful to him some day with his correspondence if

---

★ Authors' italics.

I went through the drudgery of learning first all the details – But this I fear in vain for I have persevered since 26 September and am as ignorant as when I began.'

Perhaps she should confine herself to 'household and nursery concerns' and think no more of business 'which is not my province'? Somehow neither she nor John were fully convinced by such sentiments, no doubt prompted by the fact that she had, eight days earlier, given birth to a 'nice fat baby'.

In February 1837 Thomas Revel Guest died suddenly in Dublin from a bout of influenza. After a wild early life which supposedly included fighting a duel in France, fathering two illegitimate children (who were packed off to Australia) and being unfrocked, he dedicated his later years to the business, Wesleyan Methodism and opposing frivolity and trade unions. Recently he had worked closely with his brother, mainly conducting the Irish side of the business, and his loss increased the dependence on Lady Charlotte. She declared, 'I know the brightest and most dazzling part of my life is over. Merthyr's cares, and his business increase every day and with them my anxieties.' She was not even immune from correspondence in her boudoir: 'Merthyr had brought up an immense pile of letters which I had to dispose of – to answer – or – destroy – that had accumulated since my confinement – So when I went to bed I was quite knocked up and I felt the effects of it all the following day.'

Lady Charlotte continued as a faithful secretary for the family business like others before her – Sir Robert Peel's mother had for example written out most of the business letters for their family's cotton firm. There were intervals necessitated by childbirth or by John's impatience. On one occasion he told her she was 'idle and careless and caused him to neglect all his business' and hoped her successor would fare better. Yet she carried on, writing up letters with the Works Manager, John Evans, in the works office, making out abstracts of orders, sometimes until 11 p.m., and sorting out correspondence with the clerks at home. Even travelling involved designated tasks, marking out railroads on a map during a trip to Yorkshire and copying out business letters in Europe. At times she felt frustrated by her anomalous position. Being a secretary was (and is) one of the most elastic of all in terms of job description and Lady Charlotte was always more than an amanuensis. Added to this was her ever-conscious awareness of the problems facing her sex: 'I only perplex him as I have no appointed department – and then the humiliation of feeling that my femininity renders me incapable.' When in 1838 the Company opened an office at 7, Token House Yard in the City of London for transacting sales, prospects looked good but Lady Charlotte was personally cautious:

> For my own part I do not like it very much. Merthyr has weaned me from all my own pursuits and taught me to be fond of his business and now that I have got into such habits that business is almost the only thing that interests me, it is put out of my reach and I cannot follow it without perhaps going further than I ought. I feel it rather hard to have now to try and take up again the occupations which I have been led to abandon. But everything is for the best and all these little mortifications are good for me who as a woman must expect suffering and mortification.

Lady Charlotte also kept the private accounts. Historians have certainly underestimated the extent to which women were skilled at keeping household accounts and those of small businesses. In May 1834 she had recorded that her husband was going to teach her how to make up the books as she was to keep his accounts for him. He gave her lessons on balancing and winding up and supervised as she closed her first year's books. Whole days and many evenings were devoted to this job, which never really appealed to her. The task got bigger and more onerous over time. Childbirth was usually preceded by an extra flurry of activity. She finished posting the books at 8.30 one evening and Blanche arrived at 10.30 the next morning. After nearly seven years she had had enough: 'I have resigned my charge of the books and given up my cash.' Unfortunately, on rediscovering the burden of doing his own accounts Sir John was 'much annoyed that I do not write up all the Books as formerly'. So she was recalled.

She tried giving up secretarial tasks but this 'cost me many pangs'. It also had wider implications in terms of spatial segregation in her London home. Previously she worked in her husband's room or close to it as business necessitated constant communication. Now she was consigned to her own day room and 'I feel like a banished thing and know nothing of what is going on'. Even allowing for embellishment provoked by righteous indignation, it is clear that Lady Charlotte needed to be useful and occupied. Within a short time she had not only resumed her secretarial job but all the work reports were now channelled through her. She even took messages to the City office (known as the London House), increasingly operating in an overwhelming male business environment. Her comment on the Token House Yard office had included a reference to 'perhaps going further than I ought'. She now found herself pushing at these boundaries.

Increased involvement was to her taste: 'I always rally when I have plenty of work and today I had cheques to draw for the works and other things appertaining to business to attend to', buying horses for the colliery and doing Welsh translation. Her latest child had been born one month earlier. She soon acquired a new space of her own. In 1939 the firm opened a City office at 42, Lothbury and paid Lady Charlotte 'the compliment of fitting up a room for me there, and I think it is a retreat that I shall often be tempted to resort to from the gaieties and interferences of Grosvenor Square'. Mary recorded her stays in London with the Guests, finding that she was often left to her own devices: 'Char [sic] and Sir John are gone into the City and I am as usual about to pursue my daily avocations in solitude.' She also mentioned 'Sir John, Char and a clerk … cogitating over some large cash books.' In addition to regularly handling a veritable 'budget of letters' Lady Charlotte now hazarded opinions more frequently and Sir John in turn involved her in some negotiating. In 1836, after a meeting with Crawshay about the consolidation of the canal and railroad, Lady Charlotte proudly recorded that 'my opinion was asked'. Her response differed from the majority view but a few days later she was allowed to deal with the matter and write to Crawshay. Two years later he sent her to meet Mr Lucy (from a Bristol ironworks) on the subject of rails for the Midland Counties Railway. 'This is the weightiest piece of business with which I have hitherto been entrusted,' wrote Lady Charlotte and, tongue-in-cheek, she added that Mr Lucy 'a very agreeable Quaker seemed at first rather surprised at seeing me, but we soon began discussing questions of freight, interest etc. as comfortably as if I had not the mortification of being of weaker sex and intellect than himself'. It would be fascinating to know how Mr Lucy described the encounter.

Lady Charlotte sometimes represented the firm when her husband was away. She dealt with compensation claims from the Penydarren Company for land taken by the Taff Vale railway – 'Altogether I was harassed and never felt so great a responsibility.' After contacting solicitors and using procrastination tactics, she decided that her husband should be recalled, so wrote ten letters to seven different towns to track him down. On this occasion her cautious handling of affairs met with his approval. She was soon reporting on progress in Cardiff, dealing with advances of money to other ironmasters, writing statements on railway branch affairs and conducting voluminous correspondence via the London House with railway companies all over the world.

Sir John's impatience increased with his medical troubles. By 1849 Lady Charlotte was commenting sadly, 'I cannot now speak to Merthyr on any matter of business, he gets so vexed with me …' It was especially frustrating since at times he relied heavily upon her, expecting her to deputize effectively, make snap decisions and be abreast of the market situation. Yet at other times he either interpreted her interest as unwarranted interference or criticized her for a lack of professionalism when she had undergone no formal training and was expected to have acquired, as if by osmosis, the skill and expertise to handle complex international business. Running through all of this were the disadvantages of being a woman in the nineteenth-century business world. Not surprisingly, Lady Charlotte felt confused. In 1843 a letter concerning an arrangement with the ironmasters Bailey and Thompson for the supply of rails to Germany met a despondent response from Sir John. Only Lady Charlotte's journal was told her true feelings: 'I felt the same for I did not like the terms, but I had no right to express it and I am sorry that I did. Yet *once* I had so much part in everything that went forward that scarce anything of importance was done without my being admitted to full discussion on it, and it is difficult to forget old habits.'

She discovered that one way of avoiding (or at least postponing) her husband's displeasure was simply not to inform him about all her business activities. She was initially hesitant about such tactics but as Sir John's health deteriorated, so it seemed more justifiable and especially helpful in dealing with the Dowlais staff since their employer's fractiousness made them glad of a sympathetic ear and interceder. Lady Charlotte acted as a valuable conduit through which they could channel their grievances. As early as 1836 she had opened a letter of resignation from the Works Manager, John Evans, and without troubling her husband had calmly returned the letter to its sender (personally), advising him to think again. After her assurances Evans was apologetic and no more was said on the matter. Lady Charlotte had made a copy of the letter and did eventually show it to her husband. The following year it was the turn of the brother Thomas Evans (sales agent) 'the faithful, the trusted' to feel discontented. He went straight to Lady Charlotte, asking her to read his letter of resignation before giving it to her husband.'It came upon me like a thunderbolt', the letter pouring out a tale of physical and moral exhaustion and a serious dislike of the work. Lady Charlotte persuaded him to spend a month considering the situation. After three days she felt guilty about keeping this secret from John so sought out Thomas Evans. He confessed to having been quite miserable since he had spoken to her and was happy now to 'quite rely upon me and do as I advised'.

It is of course possible that Thomas Evans's deference in the presence of this aristo-cratic English lady, combined with Lady Charlotte's own sense of self-importance in recounting these matters, led her to over-estimate her success. We only have her side of this story, and certainly within a few years Thomas Evans was once more unhappy and confronting his employer with his problems. This time an ugly scene ensued in which the latter threatened to enforce his agreement with the Company and, if neces-sary, take him to court. Lady Charlotte suffered as much as they, 'It is killing work this parting with Evans', and she envied her husband's ability to compartmentalize affairs and set aside worries when not directly dealing with them. After a further scene in which Evans left the room in tears Lady Charlotte secretly walked to his home. 'It was a bold step and one that it was difficult to manage without compromising my posi-tion but I think I have carried it off perfectly well.' She explained that her husband might be angry if he knew but felt that a third person to mediate was invaluable. She appealed to Evans as 'an old servant' and dealt with his demands, in turn mentioning the possibility of percentage payments on profits rather than a fixed bonus. At the end he asked that it might appear that he had been compelled to remain at Dowlais. Lady Charlotte wasted no time in getting this in writing. Just as it was difficult for Thomas Evans to protest to this high-born lady, so was it easier for her with her effortless sense of superiority to deal with him than it was for her husband.

John had known Evans since boyhood and had been 'brought up in his views and interests'. To Lady Charlotte's disappointment Sir John was rather less than delighted on learning of his wife's rendezvous. Yet three weeks later he made a supplementary agreement with Evans offering him the very high wage of £1,000 yearly which was accepted. Evans had come to Dowlais in 1836 for 400 guineas a year and his brother John only earned £750 as General Manager. This did not last long, for Thomas Evans died in 1846.

Lady Charlotte received occasional pleas from the workforce. For example, a deputation of workmen appealed to her after they had taken advantage of the fortnightly advance of pay and gone off to drink 'leaving everything in disorder'. Probably flattered that they had appealed to her and recognizing that John Evans was notoriously strict on such matters, she was prepared to grant a pardon. Wives of coal and ironmasters were the ones to whom appeals for clemency were traditionally made. For example, at the Bridgewater collieries it was to the Countess of Ellesmere that the workers directed their plea to return to their old method of fortnightly pay.

The Guests had visited their Lancashire collieries in 1848. Unlike the over-whelming majority of employers, Sir Francis Egerton and his wife (who became the Ellesmeres) had sought to mitigate the sudden and harsh effects of the 1842

Dowlais Works:
Jane, a labourer, a bronzed muscular & very
Comely girl of 20, quiet & hardworking) filling
the trams with iron ore for the kilns.
Pencilled on spot, 26 Sept. 1865.

Left and opposite: Two sketches from
A.J. Munby, an English diarist and one
of the few Victorian middle-class men
not associated with the iron trade who
approved of these women and their work.

Mines and Collieries Act, which had forbidden all females employment in underground mining. Instead they had gradually phased out the work, had tailored it
to alternative employment opportunities and started a small servant's school for
ex-pitwomen. Most impressively, they had devised an early redundancy scheme
paying 1s weekly for a year to the families of those forced to leave the pits.

In 1841 Dowlais employed fifty-three girls and 327 boys under thirteen. The total
number of females was 411 but although the Children's Employment Commission
had revealed that some girls worked in the collieries – for example Ann Bowcott
told how she had 'kept a trap door' (opened and closed a ventilation door) since
the age of five – most of the female employment was above ground and therefore
not prohibited by the 1842 legislation. Women and girls worked with iron ore, coal
and in the brickyards. One job which was largely performed by female labour was
piling the lengths of puddled bars of iron ready for rolling. John Guest tried to ban
women from piling at night but soon found that his instructions were being ignored.
Lady Charlotte supported his views 'for the present mode is very demoralising'. The
Morning Chronicle report on South Wales in the spring of 1850 (most probably written by Angus Bethune Reach) credited her with having successfully discontinued
the practice. Yet it is interesting to note that, unlike this reporter, Lady Charlotte did
not condemn the women's surface work *per se.* As the employer's wife Lady Charlotte
defended the use of single women in mining day work and, living locally, she could
see at rather closer quarters than visiting reporters the effects of the work.[4]

By mid-century there were all sorts of new problems facing the Guests.
Worries and uncertainties about the renewal of the lease had led to some fairly

Dowlais Works:
Mary Davis, a robust
comely and extremely
nice girl of 20, oiling
tram-wheels at mouth
of Cwm. Cemwl in motion
hit. Pencilled on spot,
26 Sept. 185..

drastic trimming. Capital investment had been declining for a number of years and new workings were not being developed.

Surveys commissioned by Bute suggested that coal mines were being misman-aged and coal wasted at Dowlais. The company retaliated with a counter-report. Plans were mooted more than once for a Joint Stock company but came to nothing. Sir John was ageing, his sons were young and, with the cost of renewing the lease exorbitant, Lady Charlotte feared for the future of the works. In 1846 the Dowlais minerals were advertised in the press. Then Thomas Evans died, and, in her language of iron, the ever-fatalistic Lady Charlotte wrote, 'Poor Evans seems one of the links riven'. Ironworkers, who had no second home to which they could turn, held a large meeting and memorialized both John Guest and Lord Bute. Whereas, in Lady Charlotte's opinion, the latter's response was 'unfeeling and arrogant' – he claimed that the ironworkers' future was not his responsibility but that of their master – her husband replied with 'a few words expressive of his sympathy with the populace'.

By March 1848 six of the eighteen furnaces were idle. Although raised hopes for settlement restored affairs slightly the following year, the early 1850s saw a loss for the first time.[5] Buying out the Lewis share cost £200,000 whilst Edward Hutchins's two shares ate up a further £58,000. There were worries too about domestic expenses. Some decisions were made jointly – 'we went upstairs to read them the letters and to cogitate over our plans' – but, as the Company's correspond-ence reveals, it was Lady Charlotte to whom problems were now (not just literally) addressed. In Society circles she had already acquired a reputation for great wealth and style. There is an apocryphal story about her which was related in Roebuck's history of the Whigs. At a grand ball in London a horseman booted, spurred and mud-bespattered, appeared in the drawing room clutching a Dowlais balance sheet. Lady Charlotte glanced at the total and passed it to a banker who was close by. The accounts showed £365,000 17s 5d. 'Yes,' said Lady Charlotte, 'bad year, very bad but we do not make money as you bankers do. Better luck next year.'

By mid-century Lady Charlotte was working as hard as possible to try to secure the lease and shield her husband from the more troubling aspects of the business. For a time it was feared that the works might even have to close. Fortunately hard work was Lady Charlotte's panacea for all ills. In 1848, weary with health worries about Sir John and immersed in educational schemes, she wrote: 'No one can know what I have suffered, but the constant work, hard work, doing his business and my own has enabled me to keep up throughout.' In a life which saw more than many people's share of crises (real or imagined) she tended to thrive when the going was tough. Despite 'late hours and unceasingly busy days' in 1850 she kept up with her work 'very well, better than I ever did in my life before, and I have no arrears of business'. So closely was she associated with the Works that a fabricated tale circulated for some years about 'Lady Guest and her Book Keeper'.

When one of the firm's rails broke in Russia in 1851, Lady Charlotte was determined to keep the bad news from her husband. It had happened when Edward was running operations and was especially worrying as the Russians were their best customers. On New Year's Day 1852 she learned that a big Russian order was being challenged by a lower tender from Bailey of Nantyglo. It was galling since 'this order would have quite re-established us'. For as long as possible she kept the knowledge as 'a heavy secret, bowing me to the earth' but eventually was forced to explain. Sir John suggested coming to an agreement with Bailey so that whoever got the order should share it with the other. Dowlais eventually won the contract and had to keep their own promise.

Catherine Gladstone, born in the same year as Lady Charlotte and also for many years concerned about her husband's health, tended to censor William Ewart Gladstone's mail and apparently withheld some of his letters. A recent article about her direct intervention in the Prime Minister's political life suggests that 'Beneath the halo, wings and white robes was a woman of *iron determination* and great energies who attempted to do what she believed was her duty as best she could' for her husband. Lady Charlotte understood such sentiments.

In addition to reading daily reports from Dowlais and replying to them from Canford, the weight of mail from agents, accountants and solicitors alone ensured the consumption of considerable time. Letters such as one of June 1852 which began 'We are not going on at all well' did not refer to a dear friend's health but was a worried statement from John Evans about machines and engines and bad yields from the mills and forges.

It was by now even more unusual for women to be involved in big business than it had been in 1800. Retreat from the public world of the workplace was accompanied by the increasing privatization of the home for those families hoping to succeed in business. Many jobs became professionalized making it increasingly difficult for women, denied equal educational opportunities, to qualify even for entry to training. Women had a protracted battle in trying to prise open areas of employment which in some instances had once been open to them. Lady Charlotte had encountered some difficulties – she was, after all, based in a land where Nonconformist traditions militated against challenges to the gendered division of labour. She was, however, fortunate to have been born into a social class which gave her an entrée which was not possible for many Victorian women. Moreover she was careful to stress also her duty and support for her husband. She had entered the world of public work by a back door, that of marriage, and though she may have been literally soiling her hands in the works and challenging the golden rule that married women should not work, she was not in the position of those sullied by earning their own living. Nevertheless she clearly was an enigma for contemporaries, since maternal duties were supposed to absorb almost all a woman's time, energy and interest.

In line with Victorian expectations, Lady Charlotte's ambitions for her own children followed a conventional path. When they were young 'A walk in the works during play hours' with Lady Charlotte in charge was seen as instructive for the girls and boys. As the girls grew older so an active process of feminization took place. Indeed it can be said that, in contrast to many parents, Lady Charlotte's ambitions for her daughters were in a sense more modest than they had been for herself. She wanted at least one of her sons to become a successful ironmaster but her overriding aim for her daughters was for them to make 'good' marriages. Even though Maria helped out with the occasional business letter at a time of family difficulties, she, like all her younger sisters, was destined to become a high Victorian married lady whose business was good works rather than ironworks.

By 1850 Sir John's health worries predominated. In one fortnight the following year he was operated on virtually every day and each time suffered more. Lady Charlotte assumed more and more responsibility and needed unending reserves of patience as her husband's irritability increased with the pain. By the summer of 1852 the future loomed as 'one chaos of darkness'. Now, 'my poor husband's state is so hopeless, although his sufferings may be alleviated; the disease also appears incurable – and the once noble mind is so shattered that it is indeed most trying to bear'. He died on 26 November.

When he died, Lady Charlotte had behind her nearly twenty years of informal training in business. Initially learning on the spot through practical observation, she had also received instruction from a number of highly skilled engineers, craftsmen, scientists and managers. She had read about the business, written about it and dealt with many, many letters about it. To the role of secretary was added that of accountant, personnel officer, representative for the firm, adviser, public relations officer, and, increasingly, deputy director. All of this stood her in good stead for the role she was about to play as the widow actually running the works. Yet her acknowledged public position came at a time when one more curious twist in Lady Charlotte's turbulent personal life meant that she was least disposed to enjoy her hard-won status.

7
The Lady of the Manor

'Manors make the Man.'

In 1846 Lady Charlotte's life had taken a new turning with the purchase of Canford, an 11,000 acre estate and house near Wimborne in Dorset. In many ways this move marked the final stage in the Guest's family journey from Shropshire to Society. It also restored Lady Charlotte's social credibility. The industrialist now had his country seat and, in line with other successful businessmen, could enjoy a new life-style and consolidate his position for his successors. Out of forty-five important country houses built between 1835 and 1854, one-third were for manufacturers. In South Wales Joseph Bailey's retirement led to the amassing of a 12,000 acre estate and by the end of the century the head of the family would be Lord Glanusk. John Guest had married extremely well in social terms but his fortune also derived from heavy industry. Public positions such as being a magistrate gave him respect but despite owning property in Wales, there he remained primarily identified as an ironmaster and one in the shadow of Lord Bute. The Guests needed to distinguish themselves from the works. Lady Bell, wife of an ironmaster who also moved from the vicinity of the works (in Middlesbrough) to a Yorkshire country estate, observed that the distance a man lived from his daily work was in direct proportion to his success in it. By this standard Sir John became fabulously successful.

In addition to renting a London house, the Guests already had Sully House near Barry. Yet though literally the lady of the manor there, Lady Charlotte was passionate in her dislike of Sully. Nor was this 1,000 acre estate suitably prestigious for the ambitious Guests. It had been purchased in April 1836 for £3,500 though it had previously been owned by the sister and brother-in-law of John's first wife, Maria Ranken, and Lady Charlotte had called there with her new husband in 1833 before seeing Dowlais for the first time. The old house (now demolished) was right by the beach at Swanbridge, looking out to the uninhabited Sully Island. It served the function of a holiday home, though Lady Charlotte preferred the fresh mountain air to the damp, mild climate of Sully. For John it was a retreat from work and a chance to shoot pheasant, rabbit and hare. It was also handy for doing business in Cardiff. The children enjoyed the seaside and recovered from illnesses there. They would collect fibrous gypsum and ammonites, encouraged by the amateur geologist William Daniel Conybeare who was the Rector of Sully before becoming Dean of Llandaff (and also married to one of Maria Ranken's sisters). Like many Victorian homes, Dowlais House boasted a fossil collection. Although she enjoyed searching for fossils on the beach, Lady Charlotte 'never disliked any place so much in my life'. For once her imagination would not work. Yet it was clearly a romantic, secluded spot. It inspired the future novelist Charles Kingsley to commit himself to Holy Orders. In June 1841 he and his mother stayed at Sully with Lady Charlotte and he wrote in his diary: 'I have been for the last hour on the sea shore not dreaming but thinking deeply and strongly and forming determinations which are to affect my destiny through time and eternity. Before the sleeping earth and the sleeping stars I have devoted myself to God ...'

Neither did the story of the ghost of Sully House appear to excite her usually fertile imagination. According to local legend an eighteenth-century sea captain had fallen in love with a young woman. Her father disapproved of him and she was married to Colonel Rhys, the owner of Sully House. Undeterred her lover sought her out and three days before the full moon she received a signal and rushed to join him on the beach. So too, unfortunately, did the Colonel. A duel ensued and the Colonel was killed but not before he had placed a curse on the couple, 'as often as yon moon shines upon the scene and wherever your bodies may be at the time, living or dead, may your spirits be forced to return to this spot and enact again this deed'. The couple married but were later deserted by their crew and eventually the ship was burned in sight of Sully. The ghost of the former Mrs Rhys was said to haunt Sully for three days before a full moon.

Lady Charlotte who had 'a horror of the sea' confessed to feeling idle and devoid of energy at Sully. She did, however, start a small school with the Rector. After spending much of the winter and spring there in 1841-2, she was concerned a year or so later lest her husband had 'a mind to add to and so make it more of a permanency'. To her relief this was not to be. In the summer of 1846 the house was let to the coal-owning Powell family and by now energies were being absorbed in Canford.[1]

The search for a suitable home had taken a long time. As early as May 1835 John had told his lawyer that he was interested in purchasing an estate in Border country, not too far from Wales. From this time onwards Lady Charlotte's journal recorded frequent, abortive and usually highly critical comments about viewing gentlemen's residences. They searched in Herefordshire, Gloucestershire, Worcestershire and gradually, as railway developments improved, moved further afield to take in Hertfordshire, Leicestershire, Bedfordshire, Essex, Oxfordshire and Yorkshire. Lady Charlotte was ambivalent: 'For my own part I would *rather* live in the smallest cottage in any part of my own dear beautiful Glamorgan than in the finest palace that could be built at Londesborough,' she wrote after surveying the Duke of Devonshire's Yorkshire estate. Upheaval was not immediately attractive, 'Dowlais seems to have so many useful occupations for me. If I could only do all the good here I ought! And must we so soon leave it altogether? There will never be any home for me like this again.'

Yet continued problems over the renewal of the lease, coupled with family ambitions, increased the pressure to move. As a businessman Sir John may also have wanted to buy an estate which he could develop along the new lines of scientific management in his advancing years. Lady Charlotte was placated by the decision to keep on Dowlais House (Sir John's nephew lived there for a time) and return there periodically.

At the end of April 1845 they viewed Lord de Mauley's estate in the small village of Canford Magna, Dorset. Lady Charlotte was impressed: 'Though not on good land, nor in a fine park, nor in pretty country, the gardens, the house, the villages, the grounds and trees around it and, above all the clear blue river [the Stour] conspire to make it a delightful place.'

In September the house, outbuildings, 5,000 acres of prime land and 5,000 acres of poor land were for sale for £300,000. The railway line from London to Wimborne was almost completed and the history of the manor must have impressed Lady Charlotte. Its former occupants included several remarkable women. Ela Longspée was a principal founder of Salisbury Cathedral. Her father, Walter de Eureux, had been granted the manor by William the Conqueror. It seems that the manor house was first rebuilt in about 1220 (it had been held by a Saxon thane before the Conquest) when the widowed Ela was Sheriff of Wiltshire. An equally illustrious lady of Canford Manor was Margaret Beaufort, mother of Henry VII and founder of two Cambridge Colleges.

The medieval manor became known as 'The Old Grey House'. Some parts of it were rebuilt by the Webb family who purchased it from Charles I in 1611. Fortunately the kitchen wing, known as John of Gaunt's kitchen, (thought to date from the fourteenth century though there is no proof of John of Gaunt having visited it) was retained as a brew house. Sir John Webb was a Salisbury merchant and a Catholic. Lady Barbara Ashley Cooper was a descendant and she and her husband, the third son of the Earl of Bessborough, W.F.S. Ponsonby, had three children. The Guests found that purchasing the estate was a complicated affair due to a trust settlement which divided the estate between these three children.

At the point at which the Guests entered negotiations for the estate, the trust was being wound up by the Court of Exchequer. A decree in Chancery and an Act of Parliament were necessary before the proceeds of the estate could be divided amongst the children since the youngest was not yet of age and the terms of the trust had stipulated this. To make matters worse, a rival offer of £330,000 was made and it was even rumoured that Crawshay might make a bid of £350,000. Since Dowlais also looked as if it was slipping from them, the chance to be assimilated into the landowning class looked bleak. At such times Lady Charlotte resorted to romantic hyperbole. 'I *do* feel like a vagrant and an outcast on the face of the earth. There seems to be no rest for the sole of my foot on it. But God knows best. I do so yearn for a quiet happy place in which to bring up children respectably, as everybody else does.'

Her wishes were eventually fulfilled, though Canford was hardly 'everybody else's' place. One slight compensation in the 'year of harassment' over the purchase was a consultation with the noted barrister Sir Thomas Wilde at Sergeants Inn, something which 'I suppose few women have done'.

After many delays and fears that fresh 'mischief is brewing', the Guests took possession in March 1846 with a down-payment of £5,000. On 11 March Lady Charlotte and some servants set off for the new home. Arriving there the next day all was in confusion. De Mauley (Ponsonby had become the First Baron de Mauley in 1838) had only left that morning and some of his furniture remained. A piano was hired until Lady Charlotte's own arrived and the family began to explore their new surroundings: 'It was a most delicious evening. The western sky was bathed in gold and the air was wild and everything looked beautiful. We walked arm in arm from the turn of the road, all through the village to the front door, both in quiet, subdued spirits, but not unhappy. When we entered the house, Merthyr hung up his hat and I put down my basket and it might have seemed as though we had been settled here for ages and had only been out to take an evening walk.' Canford cost a staggering £335,000 with the purchase of personal land from de Mauley taking a further £19,000. Yet Lady Charlotte felt that 'if it do not prove very ruinous, I am content, for I am quite delighted with the place and like it daily more and more, so that I quite think it worth some sacrifice in the matter or interest of money'.

Not until 5 October 1846 were contracts finally exchanged (the act disposing of the minor's share in the estate was not passed until September). The next day Lady Charlotte wrote: I am fully impressed now with all its responsibilities and trust the cares and pleasures of life may never make me lose sight of them. May Canford prove a blessing to my dear children.'

Between 1825 and 1836 the old gabled house had been replaced by a new one designed by Edward Blore. Sir Walter Scott had got Blore to design his Gothic retreat at Abbotsford in Scotland. This would have appealed to Lady Charlotte as would the mid-Tudor style at Canford with steep roofs and chimneys, mullioned windows and pointed arches. Even after the Guests stamped it with their own distinctive touch, Blore's work could still be seen in the dining room and rooms above it on the east front, and in the whole of the south front.

Not surprisingly for the translator of *The Mabinogion*, Gothic appealed to Lady Charlotte even though the revival was not yet at its height. Gothic arches were evocative of the East and the Crusaders, whilst the romance of towers, battlements and baronial halls suggested a security which the present seemed to lack. The beginning of the Gothic revival dated from the eighteenth century. Horace Walpole had declared that 'one only wants passions to feel Gothic' and the Guests knew his Strawberry Hill house. Lady Charlotte's youth had displayed almost Gothic ingredients of the kind Jane Austen ridiculed and exposed to such effect in *Northanger Abbey*. Her love of medievalism would have led her to agree with Pugin, the author of the architectural pamphlet 'Contrasts' that, by studying 'the real talents and feelings of these wonderful times that art can be restored or excellence regained'.

Travels in Lady Charlotte's early married life introduced her to architecture. On the 1842 Continental tour she and her husband immersed themselves in the study of Gothic architecture which was 'transporting us by magic to the times gone by'. Nuremburg was likened to an illustrated page in a medieval chronicle, the glass and tracery at Prague enthralled her, but she shuddered at the modern tendency to whitewash church interiors in Bruges and was offended by the reconstruction of Wurzburg cathedral which involved 'disfiguring the most precious specimens of Gothic'.

Closer to home, Singleton Abbey in Swansea was built for the Vivians. Thomas Hopper (discovered by George IV when Prince Regent) designed Llanover Court for the Halls and Margam Castle for the Talbots, an Elizabethan Gothic building romantically sited above a (genuine) twelfth-century Cistercian Abbey. The Guests did not want a second Cyfarthfa Castle but they were caught up in the vogue for splendid homes evoking the past. As Philip Jenkins has remarked, 'only a very new community needed to be so anxious to display its antiquity'.[2]

Hopper was the first choice, though his escalating estimates seemed 'alarmingly high'. Soon Lady Charlotte was pronouncing that Hopper 'has not the slightest taste in Gothic decoration'. Such a comment seems unduly harsh but he was past the height of his achievements. More to the point, consultations were underway with Charles Barry, whose politics were preferable and who made his first visit to Canford just after Christmas in 1847. Barry was in the public limelight, having won in 1836 the competition for redesigning the Houses of Parliament after the fire, a task which would take him twenty years to complete. A visit to the robing room of the House of Lords gave Lady Charlotte some ideas for the Great Hall at Canford. Barry had designed Sir John's club, the Reform, in his attractive Italianate style and his private houses included Bridgewater House for the Guests' associates, the Ellesmeres.

His work for Canford began in 1848. Early in May the house was dismantled. By the following February the great hall (one of the largest in a private residence) was heightened and roofed in. Its west window contained shields showing the coats-of-arms of twenty-eight owners of Canford from Longspée to the Guests. The painted and stained glass work was done by Hardman in 1851. The photographer Julia Margaret Cameron recalled the evocative effects of a reading of the medieval tale of St Agnes' Eve in this hall with its casement and shielded scutcheons which could have been the model for Keats's poem. Barry was also responsible for the garden porch leading to the great hall and designed the Victoria tower (still standing today and decorated with the Guest swan crest and the Wimborne coat-of-arms). 100ft high, it was clearly influenced by the Houses of Parliament. John of Gaunt's kitchen was restored and united with the main part of the house, lodges were added, outbuildings restored and the gardens laid out. Between 1848 and 1852 Canford was doubled. Even after 1852, when Sir John died and Barry was knighted, Lady Charlotte used his designs. He was the architect of the mortuary chapel in memory of her husband (and had already designed a mill at Dowlais) as well as designing the splendid Dowlais schools.

Remodelling was generally agreed to be more difficult than building from scratch. Barry's son (who wrote his biography) felt Canford to be his father's best treatment of a Gothic house, combining real comfort and convenience with architectural grandeur. By April 1849 the house was once again being called Canford Manor. The major renovations had caused considerable upheaval. On one occasion Lady Charlotte and her maid came to Canford and stayed in a house without doors to the rooms and were guarded by a night watchman.

Even before the building work and massive bills, there were doubts about the financial expediency of such a venture. In 1847 Lady Charlotte feared that she had become a target for criticism: 'I have made great efforts lately to controul [sic] the expenses, which are become very large and increase rapidly, but I feel it is rather hard that if an economy is to be made it is always something that I had wished to have or do.'

She did not see herself as extravagant, 'I dress meanly. I buy no things for myself. I have no society and I am continually busied in trying to retrench and to administer for the best advantage, such of his wealth as has to pass through my hands, and yet because payment for necessities of life has to pass through me, he considers that I am the cause of expense. I cannot explain, but if I had any spirit left I should remonstrate.'

At this time Sir John was unwell and Lady Charlotte was pregnant with Blanche. The 'first bright days' of her marriage when 'Dowlais and his heart were my only homes' seemed far away. Worried about Barry's mounting expenses, it was agreed in May 1849 that the builders (the large and reputable firm Cubitts,[3] which created Belgravia and much of fashionable Victorian London) should complete his plans at once. The total bill amounted to £30,000, more than twice Barry's initial estimates – and almost one tenth of the cost of purchasing the estate. Not surprisingly, Lady Charlotte had her moments of doubt: 'I fancy sometimes it will make us very poor and be disadvantageous to the prospects of our family, and I fear after all our trouble and expense that it will not be handsome enough to repay us.'

Sir John's interest in the whole proceedings seemed to have waned, though he felt 'bitterly the expense which he has been almost unconsciously led into, and although it is no inconvenience to him, he doubts whether so large a sum, which would otherwise have been put by for the children, ought to be spent in bricks and mortar'.

Yet on reflection the Earl of Lindsey's daughter felt it was worth it: 'This is a reasonable doubt, but it may be carried too far. What tends to the children's comfort and happiness and fitting consideration with their neighbours, may be more than money's worth to them, of course in moderation. The whole thing grieves me more than I can confide to any*one* [authors' emphasis] but this blank paper.'

There were times when she wondered whether they ought to part with Canford. The children had been 'brought up with every comfort. Of course they have an impression that as a family we are very rich,' yet it would be unfair to leave them 'Burdened here with a large house, a large domain and no income'. Fortunately her agonizing was ended by a perusal of the income from rents, which showed that even after deductions there would still be a clear annual income of £10,000.

The house and its interior were completed by March 1851.[4] Some old carved furniture from Uffington was added, Lady Charlotte hoping that in 'Little trifles of this sort I may indulge my taste without being thought to interfere. The things can be burnt or sold again if Merthyr disapproves of them.' Some of the Dowlais furniture bound for Canford was damaged *en route* but the house steward Luff[5] was adept at securing good bargains locally. Lady Charlotte began acquiring items of china, pictures (including a Holbein and a Reynolds) were purchased and more servants were hired. The 1851 census shows a tutor, governess, house steward, coachman, groom, two footmen, a house labourer, nurse, cook, stillroom-maid, three laundry-maids, three house-maids and a kitchen-maid. The kitchen-maid was born in Merthyr, two others were from Dowlais and a fourth was also Welsh. Most significantly, Sir John was described as a landed proprietor.

One of the most unusual features designed by Barry was the cruciform porch built to receive the Nineveh marbles discovered by Lady Charlotte's cousin, Henry Layard.[6] Known as the Nineveh porch it was actually a small museum in the shape of a Greek cross. The Eastern-style traceried windows were designed in a fifteenth-century style and the floor tiles contained Assyrian motifs. Although Lady Charlotte and indeed the country had heard little of Henry in recent years, by mid-century he was a much revered (and reviled) figure. The cousin Lady Charlotte remembered as 'Little Henry Layard', her billiards companion, had grown up with his family in Europe. As a young man he returned to Britain to work in the office of his mother's brother, Benjamin Austen, a successful London solicitor. His Aunt Sara helped Disraeli to get his first novel published. Disraeli's adventures in the East influenced both Henry and cousin Charlotte.

Like his cousin (five years his senior), Henry had also been impressed by the tales of the Arabian Nights, attributing to them the origin of his 'love of travel and adventure'. Not finding a surfeit of either in a solicitor's office, at the age of twenty-two he left London with a companion to travel across the Ottoman Empire and Persia to his uncle in Ceylon.

So much did he enjoy himself that he abandoned his plans to go to Ceylon, travelling instead on his own in Mesopotamia and Persia (he learned Persian and Arabic in Baghdad in surroundings far remote from Uffington House) and lived with desert tribesmen in the Bakhtiari mountains. (His account of his travels later inspired Isabella Bird to explore the same region.) He was especially fascinated by the great mounds on the eastern bank of the River Tigris opposite Mosul (in what today is northern Iraq). These mounds with their cuneiform[7] inscriptions were believed to be the sole remains of the ancient Biblical city of Nineveh, once the capital of the powerful Assyrian Empire.

In 1842 he began three years' work for Sir Stratford Canning (later Viscount Stratford de Redcliffe) based in Constantinople and increasingly allying himself with Canning's anti-Russian (and anti-government) stance. During this time Henry returned to Mosul and made a preliminary report on the recent findings of Paul Emile Botta the French Consul who had recently excavated the large mound Kuyunjik, but not finding anything, had moved on to more successful excavations at Khorsabad. In November 1845 Henry set off to investigate the great mound of Nimrud in the desert. Nimrud or Numroud (Calah in the Book of Genesis) was thought by him at this point to be Nineveh, hence the title of his first book *Nineveh and its Remains* which was actually about Nimrud.[8] Working with local tribesmen and one literate assistant, a Nestorian Christian called Hormuzd Rassam they discovered the north west palace of Ashurnasipal II (883–859 BC).

Canning arranged for the British Museum to give Henry a £2,000 grant (he had no private means) and he continued excavating for the Museum, returning to Kuyunjik and, contrary to Botta's expectations, he revealed what proved to be the actual site of Nineveh and what was probably the largest of all Assyrian royal palaces, the incomparable Palace of Sennacherib (704–681 BC). At the end of 1847 Henry returned to England, his funds of energy and finance temporarily exhausted. Early the next year he re-encountered his cousin, who had heard of the exploits of 'the Ninevite' from Canning. Henry presented Lady Charlotte with a 'Nineveh head', staying at Canford in the spring, a far cry from the tents and mud huts of recent years. Lady Charlotte found the drawings of his finds 'very curious and interesting indeed' and tried copying some of them. Henry lectured to the Canford household in Poole Town Hall and at Dowlais. He showed Lady Charlotte the sculptures in the British Museum and she helped negotiate with John Murray for his work to be published.

Nineveh and its Remains appeared early in 1849. Much of it had been written at Canford. *The Times* described it as 'The most extraordinary work of the present age' (though Aunt Sara had written the review). Running into two volumes with nearly 900 pages, it was an immediate best-seller and was written in an engaging style. Henry's 'discovery is the talk of the day' agreed Mary and Charlotte, and their cousin now became a Paid Attaché in Constantinople (a post Sir John had suggested to Palmerston in 1848). By October he was back in Mosul and within the next two years exposed nearly two miles of sculptured walls. Government money was replaced by private subscription. Prince Albert and Sir John sat on the committee for this, the latter subscribing £100. In 1851 the Trustees of the British Museum provided an additional £3,500. As today's Department of Western Antiquities at the Museum shows, between 1845 and 1851 Henry discovered and explored Nimrud and Nineveh (Kuyunjik and the other main mound of Nebi Yunus), Ashur, Khorsabad and Sherif Khan. Some of the treasures were lucky to reach their destination – fifty cases from Nimrud nearly sank off Ceylon. Henry wrote from England to Henry Ross (in charge of excavations) that his cousin was very anxious 'to have some specimens from Nimroud or from any other place they can be got without interfering with the British Museum … I have promised her to do what I can'. Assyrian sculptures began arriving at Canford in 1849. The long journey had cracked some pieces but not caused irreparable damage. Soon the porch boasted a colossal human-headed bull and lion at the entrance and was decorated with bas reliefs. Assyrian-style cast-iron gates (symbolizing the interests of Sir John and Henry) were added. As the latter had no permanent home in England Lady Charlotte assured him that these precious finds were merely being kept in trust for him.[9]

It is hardly surprising that the two got on so well. They shared a Layard background, a passionate commitment to their work – Henry's working day at Nimrud was frequently seventeen or eighteen hours long – and his father had advised him that 'It would be a great pity not to keep up' his acquaintance with Lady Charlotte. Canford gave him rest and comfort, 'this mild Dorsetshire air does me good and enables me to write'. He loved the rides and nicknamed a view of Poole Harbour, Halicarnassus. He wrote to tell Henry Ross that 'I have been spending a few days with my relations in different parts of England, and am now with Lady Charlotte Guest, at Canford, a fine old mansion in Dorsetshire. These comfortable places and the pleasures of English country life, spoil one for the adventures and privations of the East. I find a great improvement in the upper classes; much more information, liberality of opinion, and kindness towards those beneath them. I think that, on the whole, things in England are much better than could be expected.'

The Guest children loved his company: he regaled them with wondrous stories of encounters with wild boars and dressed up in Eastern costume. Under pressure from her ageing husband's illness, Lady Charlotte had been feeling despondent: 'I do feel my life so uselessly thrown away … my part is to be silent, not morose, but acquiescent. I must seem to be interested and pleased with what others do. I must beware of marring their good deeds, and interests by my restless injudicious meddling.'

Henry's arrival was like a breath of fresh air. Here was somebody who appreciated her interest and welcomed her involvement in his affairs. If there was one thing Lady Charlotte enjoyed, it was assisting in a cause. Her husband got vexed from mere nervous irritability and 'I have no human being to turn to even for support or advice'. Sir John appears to have been more tolerant than many Victorian husbands – even his mercurial wife recognized this much of the time – but the sheer escapism of Henry's life and his sense of fun gave her renewed enthusiasm. As Lady Charlotte played Mozart on the piano so Henry accompanied her, 'more out of tune than ever' on the flute. She even began neglecting some of her regular pursuits: 'I did not go to church this afternoon but sat over the drawing room fire talking with Henry Layard about his public prospects.'

Henry's personal prospects were also of interest: Mary advised him not to get attached to a Miss Allardyce whom he felt under some pressure to marry. According to his biographer Waterfield, in 1853 both Lady Charlotte and Sara Austen were urging him to marry a Miss L. though he felt he could not match her wealthy lifestyle. Waterfield also suggests that he may earlier have aroused the jealousy of Steward Roland who, with his wife Charlotte, helped for a time at Nimrud. Whatever his relationship with her, he did intervene on one occasion when Roland beat his wife. According to Henry Austin Bruce, Layard 'possessed a singularly attractive and impressive face' whilst 'his figure suggested strength and power of endurance'.

Sir John was increasingly concerned about the amount of attention which his own Charlotte was lavishing on Henry. One Sunday in late March 1848 the family went to church and Lady Charlotte stayed behind writing. Afterwards Sir John confronted her with his suspicions – 'It was as though a thunderbolt had fallen at my feet.' For two extremely painful hours he talked seriously to her, 'the wound can never be effaced'. She was horrified by 'these cruel unjust suspicions' and the fervour with which he spoke: 'it was too extravagant, for the moment it really seemed a sort of frenzy'. She wondered 'in the innocence of my heart how little could I have anticipated'. Her husband insisted on a walk but she came home chilled in every sense: 'so cut off from everything. Society, even in the very trifling degree in which I have entered into it seemed gone with the rest now. Canford interdicted, and all the future one prospect of desolation.'

Henry in turn wrote to his aunt that he had been out of sorts and could not account for the 'extreme despression of spirits under which I have been living'. As always, Lady Charlotte maintained a public face, though spent most of the next few days in her room. Henry left within the week. Sir John expressed 'a great desire' that she should forget all that had passed since February (when Henry first visited her in London) and urged her to take an interest in things around her. Within a few weeks 'the long pending cloud of unsympathising chilliness which darkened everything is quite gone' and 'the most perfect communion' was again restored.

Lady Charlotte's passionate endorsement of all that Henry stood for had clearly disturbed Sir John and seems even to have taken her by surprise. It was rumoured that Henry was in love with Lady Charlotte though his biographer has found no positive proof of this. It was not the first time that Sir John had displayed jealousy. Once at Dowlais her intense talks with Charles Babbage had led to a reprimand. His wife had been quite shocked 'at the very notion of such a thing that I was quite overset, and was ill all day'.

Henry continued to spend time with the Guests when in Britain. It is highly unlikely that he was ever told anything about Sir John's talk. In the autumn he joined them and the Aboynes on holiday in Scotland and in the summer of 1851 went straight to Spring Gardens on arriving in the country. 'Poor fellow, he is sadly altered', wrote Lady Charlotte about her exhausted cousin. Parties were held for him but he confessed to Mary that he was 'heartily sick of London and its great places'. He spent much of his time supervising the unpacking of treasures at the British Museum.

Hailed as 'the man that made the Bible true' Henry was lionized by the public. Yet governments viewed his outspoken manner with suspicion and though his fame increased, his fortune did not. He was a free-thinker and, as we saw earlier, a Radical – known as 'the champion of the oppressed', when, in his words, 'to accuse a man of being radical was, in those days, to believe him capable of committing almost any crime'. Determined that he should have a secure future, Lady Charlotte followed his affairs closely. In 1852 he became Under Secretary of State for Foreign Affairs (a remarkable achievement since such posts were usually reserved for an elite circle and 'the man of the people' as the *Daily News* called him, was not even an MP). A week later Lord John Russell resigned. The Tories asked him to remain in office until his successor returned from India. Henry sought Lady Charlotte's advice and she showed 'great repugnance to his joining the Protectionists, even nominally'. It was she who discovered that the

Parliamentary seat of Aylesbury was vacant and Henry won the election there as a Liberal, defeating his opponents by a large majority.

Henry remained a controversial figure, particularly in the conflict between Russia and Turkey which would involve Britain in war in the Crimea. In Parliament he offended the Prime Minister, Aberdeen, by his attacks on Russia's territorial ambitions and his emphasis on Britain's responsibility for Turkey. It was a position Lady Charlotte also supported, though after the declaration of war in March 1854 both she and the Foreign Secretary tried to persuade him to delay his verbal assaults. 'I know he was honest – many think he was imprudent,' wrote Lady Charlotte. Karl Marx, who was impressed by Henry's speeches, even wondered whether he might not unseat the Prime Minister.

First-hand knowledge of the Crimea (where a brother died of dysentery) encouraged Henry to join Roebuck's Select Committee, exposing the inefficiency and incompetence behind the management of war. He helped found the Administrative Reform Association, and denounced government as a closed monopoly of a few privileged families, deplored favouritism and lack of open access to the army, consular and diplomatic services. Competitive examinations for the Civil Service were urged by what *Punch* called 'The Member for Nineveh'. Outside Parliament and, in his new constituency of Southwark, he was a hero. The remaining Merthyr Chartists, some of whom he knew, endorsed the cry for administrative reform as eagerly as Parliament rejected it. He frequently spoke at large public meetings. After six months in India he lectured on the 1857 Indian Mutiny and Lady Charlotte attended his talk, agreeing that the East India Company was quite unfit to 'govern' the country. Between 1861-5 he was Under Secretary for Foreign Affairs and later became a diplomat, spending the rest of his life out of the country. In 1869, at the age of fifty-two, he married. His wife, Enid Guest, then in her mid-twenties, was one of Lady Charlotte's daughters.[10]

The youngest of the Guest daughters also married into a family linked with the Canford years. In 1875 Blanche married Edward Ponsonby, son of Lady Louisa and the Hon. Walter B. Ponsonby, Vicar of Canford. During her first few years in Dorset Lady Charlotte was engaged in a seemingly uphill battle to modify Ponsonby's apparent, and to her mind, dangerous leanings towards Rome.

The living was in the gift of the manor and the church stood close to the house.[11] Lady Charlotte loved its eleventh-century chancel (probably the nave of the original Saxon church) and its fine Norman tower. She had first met the 'agreeable' young cleric in March 1846 but her initial good impressions were soon soured by her conviction that his 'Puseyism is very decided'. She was a Dean's granddaughter and despite the unfortunate examples of some of the clergy she encountered when young, she remained a convinced Anglican who read the Bible and had daily prayers with the household. As mistress of Canford she was aware that not so long ago the manor had been held by Catholics. She felt it her duty to espouse the Protestant faith and maintain a close relationship between manor

1 *Right:* John Guest thought this drawing of Lady Charlotte by the artist Hensel to be more like her than anything that 'has hitherto been done'. It was sketched in Berlin in 1842 while Lady Charlotte was asleep in a railway carriage.

2 *Below:* Lady Charlotte's etching of her family home, Uffington.

3 Lady Charlotte's father General Bertie, later Ninth Earl of Lindsey.

4 Augustus O'Brien (Augustus Stafford), who so charmed the young Lady Charlotte. From a drawing by Eden Upton Eddis.

5 The young, flamboyant Benjamin Disraeli with whom Lady Charlotte became friendly in the spring of 1833.

6 Sir Josiah John Guest (1785–1852), Lady Charlotte's first husband, from the engraving by Richard Buckner.

7 *Above:* Dowlais House and the Works.

8 *Left:* Maria Guest.

9 Ivor Guest.

10 Montague and Merthyr Guest.

11 Montague and Augustus Guest
in Constantinople in 1859.

12 Arthur Guest.

13 *Right:* Enid Guest.

14 *Below:* Blanche, Felicia (Lady Charlotte's sister-in-law), Constance, Katherine Guest.

15 'Poor Lindsey', Lady Charlotte's unfortunate younger brother, Albemarle George Augustus Frederick, Tenth Earl of Lindsey.

16 The youngest brother Bertie (Montague Peregrine), Eleventh Earl of Lindsey, with his sister.

17 *Above:* The furnace tops at
Dowlais Iron Company, from a
watercolour by George Childs,
1840.

18 *Right:* Lady Charlotte
addresses the Dowlais scholars
in the new school buildings
designed by Sir Charles Barry.
On special occasions she
decorated her Society parties,
workmen's soirées and the
schools with evergreens.

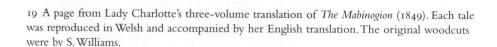

19 A page from Lady Charlotte's three-volume translation of *The Mabinogion* (1849). Each tale was reproduced in Welsh and accompanied by her English translation. The original woodcuts were by S. Williams.

20 Canford Manor, Dorset, in *c.* 1870, the house purchased by the Guests in 1846 and redesigned by Sir Charles Barry.

21 A page from Lady Charlotte's original journal, written three days after her husband's death (on 26 November 1852).

22 Enid Layard (1843–1912), Lady Charlotte's eighth child, who married Henry Layard in 1869.

23 Sir Henry Layard (1817-94), Lady Charlotte's cousin, Enid's husband and discoverer of Nineveh, by G. F. Watts, 1848.

24 Charles Schreiber (1826-84), Lady Charlotte's second husband, from the painting by G. F. Watts, 1857.

25 Painted in enamel colours, the 'Tithe Pig' is in the Schreiber Collection in the Victoria and Albert Museum, London. Instead of giving a pig in payment of tithe, the farmer's wife offers her baby to the clergyman. Bought in Brussels on 20 September 1882 for £4, 'our best find was at Craenen's where we met with an admirable group of the Tithe Pig in good old Chelsea'.

26 The 'Rouen' bottle searched for by the Schreibers in Holland and Belgium, and eventually purchased. The story is narrated in Lady Charlotte's journal. This earthenware wine bottle is now thought to be German and is in the British Museum.

27 *Left:* Palmaroli's painting of Lady Charlotte in Madrid, 1871, signalling the *leitmotifs* of her life.

28 *Below:* Lady Charlotte had an especially fine collection of French Revolutionary fans. This mounted fan depicts costumes of the Revolution showing Officials of the Directory and was purchased in Dresden in October 1880 from Salomon for five shillings. On the reverse is a medallion representing two females joining hands (symbolizing France and Spain) with the inscription 'Paz y union de las Francia Y Espana'. One is crowned, the other wears the Cap of Liberty. In the Schreiber fan collection in the British Museum.

29 An English printed fan leaf of 1740 by S. Clark showing the view from Greenwich Park including the Observatory, people and deer. Bought in 1887 for seven shillings and sixpence, Lady Charlotte added in her notes that at the sides were 'introduced somewhat abruptly and unmeaningly, two small subjects in the Chinese taste'. In the British Museum.

30 Part of an incomplete pack of large, rare and very dramatic *tarocchi* cards from Genoa by F.F. Solesia, printed in blue and ink colours. Usually such cards from northern Italy would have had their names of the court cards and *atutti* in French, but in this pack they are in Italian. From Lady Charlotte's collection of playing cards in the British Museum.

31 Part of a pack of the Bubble Companies – English cards providing a political caricature of the frantic stock market speculations which resulted in the crash of June 1720, bringing down the famous South Sea and other 'bubble' companies. Lady Charlotte possessed an incomplete pack of 'All the Bubbles' cards though Sir A.W. Franks later gave her a complete pack. She also possessed Dutch cards on the subject. The cards illustrated here are in the British Museum in Lady Charlotte's collection.

32 Lady Charlotte receives a unique honour for a Victorian woman – the Freedom of the Fanmakers' Company (1891). Accompanying her is the City of London's other 'Freewomen', Baroness Coutts.

33 *Right:* Cornelia (Lady Cornelia Henrietta Maria Spencer Churchill, eldest daughter of the Seventh Duke of Marlborough), who married Lady Charlotte's eldest son, Ivor, in 1868.

34 *Below:* The Langham Place Shelter erected by Lady Charlotte for the London cabmen in 1886. The *Hackney Carriage Guardian* remarked on her continual and 'extreme kindness and generosity towards cabmen'.

35 *Above:* The elderly Lady Charlotte the year before she died.

36 *Left:* Lady Charlotte and the 1980s: a modern public house at Dowlais is named after the area's best known woman. The pub sign is based on the 1852 Walker engraving of Richard Buckner's painting of Lady Charlotte.

and church (something she had seen flouted in her youth). She was not totally blinkered – she respected eastern religions and acknowledged that in Wales where Nonconformity triumphed, the Dissenters had 'done more for religion in Wales than our church has ever attempted'. She also approved of a 'very good sermon' given by Mrs Backhouse, a Quaker preacher, 'every word well chosen'. Yet, although she had supported Roman Catholic Emancipation in 1829, she was not prepared to countenance high church sentiment which veered towards Catholicism, especially in Canford church. Out of curiosity she had attended a Puseyite service in Regent's Park and 'I did not much like the mode in which the Service was performed'. Edward Pusey was part of the Oxford Movement which was spearheaded by himself, Newman, Keble and Froude. Their 'Association of Friends of the Church' and 'Tracts for the Times' (giving rise to the term Tractarian) sought in the 1830s to revive the doctrine of Apostolic Succession. Many saw this as Popery in disguise, their suspicions confirmed when Newman became a Catholic in 1845. The others remained in the Church of England, posing in some ways a more insidious threat as they encouraged renewed emphasis on ritual.

When the tutor, Mr Milton, showed signs of admiring the Tractarians, Lady Charlotte decided he must go. When it looked as though the beloved governess Miss Kemble might marry him, she despaired that there would be 'but one step I *know* between her and Popery'. Fortunately for the Guests, Miss Kemble valued her job and stopped seeing Mr Milton. Lady Charlotte now concentrated her energies on Ponsonby, reading up on Tractarianism and monitoring his sermons and practices. She noted that he was intoning the service, had introduced a print of the crucifix and candles on the altar of the mortuary chapel, turned towards the congregation in prayer, fasted at Lent and muffled the church bells on Good Friday. He seemed to be like the high churchman in Trollope's *Barchester Towers* who was 'so high, indeed, that at one period of his career he had all but toppled over into the cesspool of Rome'. Lady Charlotte was not the only one to notice that Ponsonby had 'mingled pernicious leaven with the purity of the Gospel'. Mary's husband admitted in his journal that 'he smacks somewhat of Puseyism' but thought it 'nothing offensive'. Lady Charlotte could not agree. The tide of apostasy must be stemmed and 'our people' rescued from 'the contamination' of popish practices. She examined local children in the catechism and did not want alien rituals in the name of Canford. She objected when Ponsonby handed round petitions for the restoration of Convocation. The family tried services elsewhere but a sermon at Wimborne proved to be 'a tissue of absurdities and platitudes delivered in the most pompous manner. Alas where may a good Protestant now find sound doctrine with fervent piety?' Lady Charlotte was fair minded enough to recognize that Ponsonby was intelligent and a good preacher but this just made the error of his ways more apparent. To make matters worse, Maria was being prepared for confirmation.

On more than one occasion the low church Rector of Dowlais was summoned to preach as an example and talk to Ponsonby. The latter must at least have been sincere in his views to have so risked the wrath of his patrons. Eventually in 1850, encouraged by Evan Jenkins (though Sir John was rather less enthusiastic), Lady Charlotte sought an interview with the Archbishop of Canterbury – and 'now I tremble'. Called to Lambeth Palace on 4 August, the same date as that when, as a young girl, she had boldly sought advice from the Lord Chancellor about Lindsey, she spoke for an hour to Archbishop Sumner: 'Being an utter stranger I had of course to apologise for my intrusion on his time etc. and for the liberty I took in coming to ask for his advice.'

Although 'sympathetic with our scruples and the difficulties of our position' the Archbishop could offer no positive help. The use of the crucifix was the only gesture contrary to regulations and even that had not been on the main altar. Nevertheless Lady Charlotte personally confronted the Vicar, itemizing her criticisms, and suggesting that he did not put 'the truly vital parts of Christianity sufficiently forward'. She feared that he might have to leave the ministry. He rather unnerved her by his mild and 'gentlemanlike' response, speaking 'in a most Christian spirit and with a humility that was quite painful to me'. He denounced forms for their own sake and seemed shocked at her accusations of a 'Romanising' tendency. Lady Charlotte judged him sincere but led away by his own convictions and 'on the brink of a precipice'. When the Archbishop called on her in London he was clearly surprised at her bold action in tackling Ponsonby on her own. It was evident that he hardly knew her.

Lady Charlotte's fears were voiced on a national scale that autumn with the Papal decision to restore a regular Catholic hierarchy and divide the country into bishoprics headed by an Archbishop of Westminster. The latter became a Cardinal, the first such appointment since Mary Tudor's reign. The Prime Minister protested and there was a marked popular reaction. It is perhaps difficult today to appreciate how seriously and personally people viewed such developments. When Gladstone heard that Manning had been converted to Rome he felt as if he 'had murdered my mother by mistake'. Lady Charlotte could not recall the country being 'so agitated on any question'. Guy Fawkes celebrations, which had begun to fall into disuse, were revived 'in great splendour almost everywhere'. To Lady Charlotte's surprise and relief, Ponsonby gave an excellent sermon on Papal aggression and they all signed an Address to the Bishop of Salisbury in protest against the Pope's action.

Relief was, however, short-lived. Ponsonby was soon collecting alms from the whole congregation. Although this probably suggests his readiness to try new methods rather than evoking Catholic ideas (the old practice was to rent pews rather than raising money through offertory), the Guests pointedly walked out of the service when the collection plate came round. To make matters worse, Katherine was much impressed by the young Ponsonby and was hastily sent to stay with her aunt. She later married an Anglican priest.

The strength of anti-Catholic feeling against the Papal claims prompted the Ecclesiastical Titles Bill. It sought to ban the adoption of episcopal or territorial titles without Parliamentary approval and the circulation of Papal Bulls. Yet the weak position of the government, which could not afford to alienate Irish Catholic MPs, led to its modification – to Lady Charlotte's disappointment. She also regretted that the Poole MP attacked its violation of the principles of civil and religious liberty (even though he also deplored Catholicism). She feared that such views would not go down well with his constituents though she did concede that 'Members must follow their own consciences in such votes'. The Protestant backlash resulted in anti-Popery disturbances in some towns, particularly those with large numbers of Irish people, who became unfortunate targets.

Although Lady Charlotte had felt that the Rector of Dowlais was a little too vehement in his anti-Catholic sermons, she had her own display of feelings in January 1851 on a return visit to Dowlais. The Guests stayed at Dowlais House where the Spanish Catholic Isabel Hutchins and her husband Edward (Sir John's nephew) were now presiding. Once installed, Lady Charlotte learned that one of the new Catholic bishops, Dr Brown, Bishop of Newport and Menevia, was to arrive the next day, staying with the Hutchins's. She had thought that his visit, for a confirmation in Merthyr, was to have been after they had left. 'I felt I could not meet this man, here, on my ground, my children's birthplace and my own home of so many years standing, where every movement of ours is observed and looked for and commented on, and where in the present state of excited feeling on the Roman Catholic aggression, any seeming favouring of the association on our part might do so much harm.'

Setting an example always mattered to Lady Charlotte. Embarrassed and inflating the incident out of all proportion (she described her husband as 'taking part with my enemies') she was especially hurt when Sir John dined with the Bishop, 'I think I never felt so deserted, so completely cast aside and flung back on myself'. To make matters worse she was eating breakfast the next morning believing Dr Brown to be out, when in he walked. Lady Charlotte promptly left the room. To meet him would have 'neutralised all my previous conduct'. The Bishop was told she was ill. She admitted to herself that her action was discourteous but it revealed the extent of her pride and obduracy, a determination to carry through her actions even if they entailed personal pain.

Poor Edward Hutchins had long received scant sympathy from Lady Charlotte. She felt that he was rather less effective a businessman than did her husband who wanted to encourage Edward as one of his few surviving relatives. After Thomas Guest's death Hutchins had become a partner and in 1850 took control of the manufacturing side of the business. Many of Lady Charlotte's less charitable comments (which she tended to keep to herself) arose from misgivings over his conversion to Catholicism on marriage, coupled with the fact that she felt as though the Guests were the junior partners when they returned to Dowlais House during its occupancy by the Hutchins's, rather than vice versa. It is not entirely surprising that soon after this episode Edward Hutchins sold his partnership and went abroad with his wife. By mutual agreement there was a reconciliation farewell dinner but this was somewhat marred by Pegus, who seemed incapable of talking about anything but the recent Papal assumption of titles. Edward later became a Director of the Rhymney Iron Company.

Recognizing that the future lay with Canford, the Guests paid attention to the estate. Farming methods and management were carefully examined, poor soils analysed and land drained and (appropriately) divided with iron fences. New methods of feeding sheep and cows in sheds were adopted and they both attended lectures on subjects such as potato disease. Lady Charlotte also involved herself in changes in the gardens and was an early conservationist in that she opposed the cutting down of trees unless strictly necessary. Here her 'interference' sometimes conflicted with her husband's 'spirit of improvement'. She wrote out estimates for the farms, discussed railway development with the agent John Pyne who, with his brother-in-law Henry Voss had devised schemes for branch lines, and she opposed the Poole Corporation's plans to take control of the large harbour and impose a fatal toll on clay – pottery was one of the main local trades. In her view the Tory councillors were not 'the fittest conservators' and she spent many hours with 'my head full of Harbours, Mudlands, Coalpits, long work …' after Sir John died.

She also performed the role of Lady Bountiful, as did her successor at Canford, Lady Cornelia Wimborne (after whom the Cornelia Hospital in Poole was named). She became involved in a clothing club, provided costumes for Canford schoolchildren and laid on fêtes for them and the scholars of Hampreston and Kinson. Her journal contains references to the poverty of the Dorset cottagers which 'very justly attracts the attention of all England'. She blamed herself for not providing sufficient aid for one old woman she had met, expressing 'horror and regret' at her own lack of system when the woman died. She 'cried nearly all the rest of the day'. Before purchasing Canford – for a sum which must have seemed obscene to many Dorset folk – she had observed that 'The peasantry are very poorly paid' and deplored the high rents for poor land. Soon after her marriage she had witnessed in London the procession of the Trade Societies to petition the King against the transportation of the Dorchester labourers, known to history as the Tolpuddle Martyrs.[12] The threat to reduce agricultural wages from 7s to 6s a week had been instrumental in the labourers joining together. In some parts of the country wages were closer to 10s, but by early 1847 when the Guests became familiar with Dorset, bad harvests were leaving the people 'wretched and distressed'. Lady Charlotte had long talks with the general agent's wife about relieving poverty, and visited homes noting down facilities (or the lack of them) – 'quite our duty to do it'. The daughter of Uffington slipped easily into the role of helping dependents, reciprocated by their loyalty. Sir John was not always pleased with her pointed remarks about dilapidation and the need for intervention but she felt he should not be screened from the state of affairs. After his death she proudly noted that she had adjusted the labourers' wages 'which I have determined to advance without being asked to do so'. This was essential due to the 'times and the price of provisions'. Doubtless the fact that the neighbouring Sturts of Critchell had just raised their labourers' wages had some influence on the decision.

When Canford hosted an annual agricultural show and dinner for tenants, Lady Charlotte supervised the arrangements for the dinner, noting details 'which would probably have escaped any but female eyes'. After the toasts, prizes and speeches at the 1850 dinner, she took a bold step, having 'set my heart on saying a few words':

I trembled and almost hesitated but there was no time for more consideration. In a moment we should have been scattered. I summoned courage and rose. I saw Merthyr was astonished and the visitors too, but I could not now have retreated even had I wished it. I proposed that another toast should be drunk, the labouring classes, and I said a few words upon the subject and in praise of the peasantry of England above the same class in every other part of the world. Once launched all my diffidence vanished, of course I had never spoken in publick [sic] before, except to my own people at home, in my schools in Wales, but felt when I had once begun that I could have gone on with my subject which is one that I have much at heart for any length of time. But the emotion with which I spoke gave me I think the appearance of being timid. I know my voice trembled, but I know also that every word was distinct and even measured and could have been heard all over the hall. I apologised of course for the unusual step etc. or rather I made a little preface, and my toast was received with all due acclamation.

She doubted whether the Dorset farmers had seen such a lavish event before. More likely they had never seen a landlord's wife make an after-dinner speech. Public speaking by women in the mid-nineteenth century was not common and was especially frowned upon in mixed company. Sister Mary was not even sure about the propriety of attending the Canford dinner for the Poole Mayor and Corporation, though Lady Charlotte soon put her scruples 'to flight', and to her delight Mary even ventured thanks for her health being toasted. Lady Charlotte's 'maiden speech' may not have had the public impact of cousin Henry's fiery words about Russia and Turkey in Parliament but it must have raised some eyebrows and given her a taste of power she was usually denied.

The following year provided an opportunity for Lady Charlotte to bring together many of her interests. Appropriately the Guests promoted excursions by rail (Dowlais Scholars, for example, had been taken to Cardiff on a trip.) In 1851 the worlds of Canford and Dowlais, of agriculture and industry, deference and self-help were all combined in the visit to the 'Great Exhibition of the Works of Industry of all Nations'. It demonstrated to the world Britain's industrial achievements and was the first international exhibition. There were over 100,000 exhibits, including a medieval court designed by Pugin, Dowlais rails (Lady Charlotte supplied a complete series of specimens depicting the manufacture of iron) and six fine arts courts, one of which was a Nineveh or Assyrian court (Henry wrote an eighty-page explanatory booklet to accompany the display). There were two wings, one for Great Britain and the Empire, the other for all the other countries, some of which were beginning to display an industrial strength which would soon challenge Britain's dominant position. In five-and-a-half months over 6 million visitors came to the Crystal Palace (a term coined by *Punch*) in Hyde Park.

Many came through trips organized by workmen's clubs. Dowlais had its own Workmen's Exhibition Club and Lady Charlotte sorted out the arrangements for them to travel by train to London and stay there for several days. She had

attended the opening of the Crystal Palace on 1 May, and her account included
a note of bitter irony at the belated recognition of the industry (in both senses of
the word) of men like her husband 'whose toils erst scorned upon, seemed suddenly ennobled'. She did nevertheless concede that it was a proud moment for
the Queen and country: 'While the nations of the earth were convulsed, she has
called into existence this peaceful meeting, the most gigantic ever known ... as
the wife of the largest manufacturer in the world I could not but feel this to be a
most impressive sight ... the most dazzling sight I ever beheld ...'

Three weeks after this she spent four hours there and at a later date had a guided
tour with the scientist Sir David Brewster. On 21 July she was at Paddington to
greet the Dowlais workers. Her account reminds the modern reader of the scene
on the morning of an England versus Wales rugby international. No sooner had
the train stopped than the brass band struck up. There were just under a hundred
club members but

> they seemed a great many when they were all gathered together on the platform
> – The band was forming in a ring (in the midst of all the passengers hurrying about,
> and scrambling for their luggage) and were on the point of commencing some
> more music when I sent them a message to beg they would wait till they were safely
> esconced in vans, no sooner had they reached which than their cheering and music
> began ... I was almost overwhelmed with the publicity of the new situation in
> which I found myself placed – for our good honest-hearted Welshmen would not
> silence their enthusiasm at seeing me.

The next day 110 Canford employees arrived by train. Lady Charlotte arranged
visits to the Exhibition and to the major sights of London. Henry Layard showed
them round the British Museum and Charles Barry guided them through the
Houses of Parliament. She thoroughly enjoyed her role as travel agent, 'I never
saw people better pleased nor more rational withal.' As she addressed the combined groups: 'the situation struck me forcibly. It was certainly an unforeseen
combination of circumstances which should find me a quiet English individual
and a woman, addressing two hundred people in Westminster Hall.'

Her husband was rather less than delighted when she casually mentioned
her plan for a huge picnic on the lawns of their house at Spring Gardens. 'Yet I
had asked the people, and I felt it would look very odd to put them off,' so the
Canfordians and Welsh workers held their joint picnic, gave speeches and listened
to Henry Layard.[13] Never again would the worlds of Dowlais and Canford be so
clearly combined.

The *Weymouth Journal* devoted one and a half pages to the Grand Fête. At
midday nearly 1,000 tenants were dined, whilst Lady Charlotte 'carved away
lustily'. After a flourish of trumpets she proposed her son's health, 'When I rose
I trembled so violently that I felt I should sink into the earth.' Over 800 schoolchildren were given cake and drinks, their entertainments including acrobats

specially commissioned from London. Lady Charlotte had worn black since Sir John's death but now dressed in white with a splash of red to celebrate 'this great pageant of my eventful life'.

The garden was illuminated, there was a fireworks display (watched by Sir Charles Barry from an appropriate perch in the Great Tower) and a ball for between 700 and 800 guests. At the supper at 1 a.m. a giant cake was produced, but Ivor had already slipped off to bed. His mother showed more stamina, staying until 6 a.m. when the last guests departed. She had been up for twenty-four hours when finally 'Charles and I were left alone in the vast, empty, silent hall' and overcome by emotion and tiredness, she burst into tears.

Ivor's coming of age meant that Canford was now his home. Lady Charlotte even described the following day as the first of his regime. Eleven years to the day on which Canford had been purchased and exactly four years since Sir John had left the manor for the last time, Lady Charlotte left her home. She wrote on this day, 9 September: 'It is all over and the very last act of the Drama is played out.' The girls were especially upset. Enid admitted hating returning to Canford in later years with everything altered and no longer a feeling of going home. Yet the aristocratic Lady Charlotte was a firm believer in inheritance and ancestry. In *Canfordiana*, a magazine printed by the family on the Canford private printing press, she provided witty gems of 'Proverbial Philosophy'. One was 'Manors make the Man'.

Sir Ivor would become Lord Wimborne in 1880, the Wimborne motto appropriately declaring 'by iron, not the sword'. The estate would grow and grow. Lady Charlotte had created her dynasty. Unlike her own background where pride in a more glorious past outshone the present, the Guests placed their hope in a future of aristocracy. When she sat down to write her account of the long and eventful day when her son came of age, Lady Charlotte chose her words carefully: 'my reign terminated magnificently'.

Canford soon won a deserved reputation for entertainment. Not all of this appealed to its hostess, 'These Dorsetshire squires quite freeze up the little spirits I have left.' Rather more amendable were the family Christmases, when, with Miss Kemble's help, the children mounted productions of plays such as *The Merchant of Venice* and they all joined in charades. The drawing room displayed a real Christmas tree (a custom recently popularized by Prince Albert) and Lady Charlotte would don fancy dress for the dances. Family, friends and Welsh acquaintances stayed frequently. Julia Margaret Cameron remarked of her visit in 1855 that: 'Everyone has been charming and everyone has been charmed.' She was impressed by the 'immense capacity' of what must be one of 'the loveliest houses' in England. There was 'sunshine, holiday and midnight revelry all the twenty-four hours round'. Yet even this was exceeded by Ivor's twenty-first birthday celebrations on 29 August 1856.

8
The Head of the Works

'These days of strikes, or sorrow, when women dare to act as Ironmasters!'

When Sir John died on 26 November 1852, Lady Charlotte took over the running of the works as 'sole active Trustee for my life'.[1] She had suffered a harrowing few months as the illness passed through its final stages. By mid-November it was evident that he had only days to live. Leeches were applied to his temples and he began speaking of meeting Charlotte again in heaven. At the same time a young surgeon in Merthyr died of a wasting disease, the Dowlais engineer William Menelaus lost the wife he had married only nine weeks earlier, and the Duke of Wellington, symbol of an era, passed away. Lady Charlotte's journal showed her heightened emotions. On 14 November she wrote:

> I thought myself very wretched twenty years ago – but what was it to the breaking up of all the dear associations and ties of so many years with such a blessed husband! – Ah life! – but the cup is not yet full – probably I have much more to suffer than my weak imagination can now paint – I try to think sometimes that all the great interests that surround me, that the needfully incessant activity of my life, that the care of my children, and my warm interest in schemes for my people here, will lighten the trial for me – but this I believe an unreal and excited feeling. When the trial comes, oh will it not leave me utterly desolate.

At night she slept on a sofa at her husband's feet but there was still work to be done in the daytime: 'It is odd to myself how I can go on with worldly matters when I am on the point of parting with my soul's partner – my (almost) idol for 18 years, in whose existence I have been as much wrapped up as was possible for one individual to be in that of another – I go through all that has to be done – write letters – see everyone on business. It seems a relief to do so.'

On 23 November the Rector administered the sacrament and the boys were summoned from school, 'Last night in my agony I looked out – and there His Works shone brightly – and the moon and stars were up – and the scene seemed glorious, as in mockery.'

The journal continued throughout. On the day of Sir John's death she wrote 'It is all over! I am bereaved,' then added, 'But I cannot help sitting down at once to record it all in order – Not that I can ever forget – but to refresh the memory of my poor children.' It also provided some sort of cathartic release. Although a strong-minded woman, Lady Charlotte would have understood well the words of another Victorian widow, Mary Benson, after the death of her husband the Archbishop of Canterbury: 'Now all is over … I feel exactly like a string of beads, always on one string worn, carried about till they seemed as if they had some real coherence. In a moment the string was cut.'

The burial was at Dowlais: 'My darling was born here – he lived here most of his life – he formed this place. He loved it and was beloved in it.' At the funeral on 4 December workmen were the bearers and Divett, Hill, Bailey, Bircham (the family lawyer), Crawshay and Bruce the pall-bearers. Charles Wilkins described the universal woe in the district amidst the chill November winds, 'The place seemed to have but one great heart. Men and women spoke in the streets with subdued voices, for the hush of death instead of being confined to chamber and mansion seemed to pervade the whole valley.' Work had ceased and *The Times* estimated that 20,000 were gathered for the funeral. Mourners included Henry Layard, Pegus and Brownlow Layard, the latter immersed in mesmerism. Before another year was passed he would have committed suicide, yet another tragic figure from that Rectory household of Uffington.

Lady Charlotte heard the Rector's funeral service in the church her husband had built. 'My sorrow is much deeper than mere tears – though many are called to my eyes – that I find I am able all through to go on with everything that is required of me.' Jenkins took as his text, Chronicles XV, verse 13 'The Lord Our God made a breach upon us.' He stressed that John Guest was 'not only the high and noble-minded Master, but also the kind friend and tender-hearted Father of his people'. Obituaries also emphasized the blend of old-style paternalism with forward-thinking industrial enterprise. The *Gentleman's Magazine* praised the man of business and his recognition of the duties as well as rights of property. *The Times* compared the Guests to the Arkwrights and Peels, portraying Sir John as a man to which 'this country owes so much of her wealth and prosperity', whilst for Lady Charlotte there was praise for the 'moral and social improvement that has taken place in the population connected with the Dowlais works. Identifying herself with the people, she acquired their language, translated and published their national traditions, and directed her well-deserved influence to the establishment of schools and other institutions for the education of the working classes.' A huge memorial tablet would soon be placed in the church, emphasizing that Sir John was 'Happy in his domestic life, Prosperous in his Business.'

Lady Charlotte moved into a new room in Dowlais House facing her husband's burial place and the hills she loved. Not until 8 December were all her children together. Ivor arrived then from Europe, exhausted by travel and grief. Although *The Times* had used the past tense to describe Lady Charlotte's activities, her days were soon 'crowdedly occupied'. On the day of the funeral she wrote, 'And now all the poetry – all the happiness of my life is gone – The Work begins …'

Although in practice she had borne much of the recent responsibility for the Works, she was now propelled into a more public and onerous position, and was uniquely placed running such a vast industrial concern in mid-century. Throughout these months it is Lady Charlotte's loneliness which echoes through the journal. She lacked close friends outside her family. In February 1853 Mrs Vivian visited her from Swansea, the first lady she had received since her 'affliction' and she poured out her heart to her. In previous centuries widows had managed their husbands' businesses in a number of trades ranging from printing to millinery. This had become much less common by the end of the eighteenth century. When, in the 1790s, Matthew Boulton had written to his partner about the sale of an ironworks he had reported that it was being sold because 'many of the company are females, who do not find it convenient to carry on such extensive concerns'. As Davidoff and Hall have put it, by mid-century 'inconvenience had changed to social catastrophe'. Nevertheless Lady Charlotte could utilize the informal experience she had gained in her husband's lifetime though, like Lucy Thomas of Waunwyllt who managed her late husband's colliery, opened up two drift mines and built up the Welsh steam coal trade, she was operating in an especially male-oriented world.[2]

By the end of the century Lady Charlotte would be matched by a few other women industrialists. For example, Amy Dillwyn (of the Swansea family known to the Guests) would take over the ailing Spelter works (as a single woman), turn round the family business and make it one of the largest producers of zinc in the United Kingdom, and like Lady Charlotte would be hailed as 'one of the most remarkable women in Great Britain'. But it was a difficult period for the Dowlais works, the huge profits of the earlier years (£172,747, for example, in 1847) had been reduced to under £4,000 by 1850 and the following year showed a loss (of over £30,000) for the first time.[3] The 'heady' days of the British iron trade appeared to be over. In 1858 one of the four big local works, Penydarren, would close. Protracted worries over the renewal of the lease had played havoc with the Company's planning and financial position and seriously affected morale.

The Dowlais lease had long been a 'plague spot' which seemed 'to throw a gloom over everything'. A year before the expiry date, Lady Charlotte had expressed her sorrow at John's position – 'It was his creation and through almost overpowering difficulties he carried it through and made it prosper'. Bute had brought in a new mediator, John Clayton, Town Clerk of Newcastle upon Tyne and solicitor to his north-eastern property. Although there were rumours that Crawshay might take over Dowlais, no suitable successor could be found. With no agreement the Guests could see little point in continuing and in December 1847 made an emotional journal to Dowlais. As they approached and saw the familiar fires from afar: 'I gave a shout and pointed to the spot. I could not speak for my heart was as though it would burst, but Merthyr understood me.'

Few might have guessed that what Lady Charlotte was describing so fondly was an ironworks: 'There had been most brilliant fairy rings from the columns of steam up the clear sky, all day, and now the golden tints from the fires upon the steam were hardly less beautiful, certainly more grand.'

She begged for one last walk into the works: 'I wanted once more, while they were in full operation, to go through the dear old works, leaning as of old on my husband's arm. I knew it to be my last day at Dowlais, at Dowlais in its glory … I knew that I would never see them in their old activity again.'

Although it was 21 December, the shortest day of the year, Lady Charlotte described it as the longest day of her life.

Edward Hutchins, who could never quite do the right thing, had made arrangements for a dance. Such an event seemed 'a profanation' to Lady Charlotte. In a line which evokes Voltaire's poem on the Lisbon earthquake, she asked 'How could they dance whilst Dowlais was crumbling?'⁴ By February 1848 three of the furnaces were blown out and engines were about to be dismantled. Some miners had already been discharged. In this month the *Mining Journal* declared that 'The hitherto thriving mining town of Dowlais … will be, I fear, ere long marked by little else, than a heap of deserted ruins.' Yet affairs were about to take another dramatic turn.

The spring of 1848 was a volatile time. The toppling of Louis Philippe from the French throne had been followed by reports of revolts in a number of other major cities. On 20 March, six weeks before the lease expired, Lady Charlotte left Canford to visit Lady Portman in Bournemouth. One of the other visitors was busy talking about rumours of a revolt in Berlin and casually ended her conversation with the throwaway line, 'And there is a report in the paper that Lord Bute is dead and that he died suddenly at Cardiff Castle.'

For once, Lady Charlotte's composure left her: 'I shrieked rather than exclaimed, "Lord Bute!". My agitation was so great that I could hardly breathe. The tears stood in my eyes and for many minutes I trembled violently.' She rushed to the reading rooms but could find no news about it. Arriving back at Canford she found Sir John already informed: 'It appears he was at the height of his glory.' He had brought his son and heir to Cardiff for the first time, seemed in good health and had been boasting that he would make Cardiff a second Liverpool. Within a few hours he had died of a heart attack. With some wit Lady Charlotte wrote about her feelings: 'For years, ever since I married, Lord Bute has been *the* person to thwart and annoy us, perhaps I should say he was the only enemy I felt conscious of possessing. It was the continuation of an old feud and his conduct towards us was certainly more like a persecution than anything else. Now to feel that one's only enemy was removed, so suddenly was awful indeed … It is an awful thing when one's only enemy dies suddenly.'

Lord Bute, who had been elevated into the seemingly immortal wicked Lord of the 'Mabinogi' world – 'The man one had been pursued by all one's life' – was suddenly 'no more than the dust under one's feet' and it was quite a shock to realize that at last he was 'powerless to harm or help'! His massive funeral, accompanied by thirty-one carriages, drew larger crowds than had the funerals of the last two kings. Yet not one leading ironmaster was present. John Patrick, his successor, was only one year old. Negotiations for the lease now passed into the hands of the trustees. A settlement was reached on 21 April, ten days before it was due to expire.

If the Bute-Guest feud was reminiscent of ancient rivalries between Norman Barons and Welsh Chieftains, then the reception which greeted the Guests on returning to Dowlais after the good news had been received was like the triumphal return of a feudal lord from battle. In the emotion of the moment – 'restored to Wales, to Dowlais, to home' Lady Charlotte even turned the early Guests of Shropshire into Welshmen. The renewal would rescue thousands from want and ruin so that Sir John's 'return to the home of his ancestors is surely one of those occasions in which all may join together to rejoice'. A gigantic procession over a mile long greeted them. 'The whole of the population of this most populous place seemed to have come out to welcome us ... Truly they had brought us right royally home.'

Sir John's speech carefully mentioned his wife's particular attachment to Dowlais which prompted her to stand up in the carriage and give three cheers for '*yr hen wlad*' (the beloved land). Lady Charlotte made a pledge (in her journal), marking the Guest side of the feudal oath of reciprocal obligation: 'May we indeed be enabled to do them good, and under a reviving trade have it in our power to minister to the necessities etc. not only bodily but mental. May we by our care and unceasing attention to their improvements in every respect, in some measure justify the warmth their reception has evinced towards us. It is a heavy responsibility.'

Yet despite the jubilant reception for the Guests at the restoration of Dowlais, there was still a delay over boundaries. An Act of Parliament had to be passed to clarify the new leasing power. Even this was not to proceed smoothly. The final irony was that by the time the new lease had been drawn up and approved, Sir John was too ill to sign it. On 24 November as he lay dying, Evans had appeared with the lease: 'I quite exclaimed and the tears filled my eyes. The lease *He* had been troubled about – that had cost us all so much anxiety and vexation – that he had expected to arrive from day to day – then it was only waiting for his signature – and he could never see it – never hold a pen again!'

Always superstitious, Lady Charlotte saw it like a curse in an ancient story: 'Not one of the Proprietors of the old lease, not the Lessor, remained – except dear Merthyr! He was the last surviving of the old arrangement – Oddly enough I had always felt that none of the old people would ever put their hands to the New Covenant – and so it must be now!'

Two days later Sir John died. The new lease was finally signed by Lady Charlotte on 18 January 1853. Its terms were reasonable, the renewal fee now reduced to £2,000, and it was granted for fifty-two years.[5]

John Guest's will had been made in November 1837. By this Lady Charlotte was appointed sole executrix and sole trustee and guardian to the children. On her suggestion a clause was added to the effect that if anything should happen to Sir John and 'I should be such a fool, which however seems to me to be too absurd to contemplate, as to form a second connexion, I must first become an outcast from him, from his house, and from my own poor children.' This was, Lady Charlotte explained to her journal, because 'I have suffered so much from a step-father myself that I should feel very sorry if there were a possibility Merthyr could in a moment of anxiety or illness be led to happiness or fortune, in a like manner'. An amendment in July 1847 endorsed Lady Charlotte's business position, giving her greater latitude in selecting her sons for the works and greater discretion in distributing property: 'the management of his property, for the children, should be committed to my charge, unshackled by the authority of the Trustees. I feel very much touched by this mark of confidence ...'

On 9 September 1850 Sir John made a new will and early in 1852 added two codicils. Lady Charlotte was given control over the freehold estates and provision for a life annuity. She, Divett and Clark were executors and she was guardian for the children during her lifetime. Her trusteeship of the Dowlais Estate was for the period of her widowhood. Sir John left £500,000 in his will. The five sons were to inherit the works with equal shares after a long period in which their parents had feared for the future of the Dowlais lease.

Within a few weeks of her husband's death Lady Charlotte was choosing the new Stipendiary Magistrate for Merthyr Tydfil, grappling with coal calculations and viewing work as her way of coping: 'Nothing but the strong excitement of hard mental work and the resolution to perform what he left me to do, can keep me up at all.' She would rise at 7 a.m. and spend the first hour of the day writing her journal and a works journal,[6] noting all business transactions. The exertion paid off: 'My spirit never sinks (thank God) but sometimes I think my body will for a time at least — and yet I am wonderfully strong — the fact is that I have (besides all the thought and direction) so much to learn, so much to set up — so much to revive that I used thoroughly to know but now seems to have faded ...' In May she wrote that she was 'growing hardened' from extreme suffering and incessant work.

Lady Charlotte was in an anomalous position. Widowhood made a dramatic change in the status of Victorian women. It was accompanied by elaborate rituals. Heavy mourning, black clothes covered in crêpe, no ornaments and a widow's cap and veil were *de rigueur* for a year and a day. Second mourning (simple black clothes) followed and even in the third year and beyond many women continued to wear black accompanied only by sombre colours such as grey. Despite carrying on a huge business, Lady Charlotte strictly adhered to etiquette. When the Vicar at Canford removed the mourning drapes from the church in March 1853 Lady Charlotte made enquiries about royal custom. On discovering that important Dorset families such as the Eldons and Shaftesburys maintained mourning for at least a year, the drapes were replaced. She continued to wear black and letters were edged with black until the end of December 1853, over a year after Sir John's death. She was still in deep mourning in February 1854 when Mary was urging her to wear less lugubrious clothing though, as we shall see, her sentiments were by now not exactly corresponding with her outward apparel — her personal thoughts were no longer exclusively dedicated to Sir John's memory. It was only on Easter Sunday that she began wearing lighter clothes. Interestingly the period of mourning tended to be longer for women than for men who had to continue in the public world of business whilst many middle and upper class ladies could withdraw from society for a year. Lady Charlotte's first set dinner (for a large group of relatives) was not until Christmas 1853 and London Society was not resumed until the following year when she saw the opera *Fidelio*. Even then 'I muffled up going and coming – and sat at the back of the box and so escaped notice.'

John Guest's era had witnessed the emergence of the new breed of industrial manager and he was fortunate in having a strong, loyal and experienced management team which had become more clearly structured over recent years. George Clark (joint executor) gave advice too. Yet, although in most aspects of her life Lady Charlotte seems to have been remarkably fortunate in her timing, for once she was at a disadvantage. The iron trade was changing rapidly, fierce competition making it an unpropitious moment to change control from above. On balancing accounts with the accountant, James Walkinshaw, early in 1853 she wrote: 'every day brings with it unforeseen difficulties and expenses – and at times I confess I do not see my way to make iron (even at the advanced price) without a loss.' Imported ores now accounted for about half the total pig iron now made at Dowlais. Heavy capital investment in a new plant was overdue though now gradually undertaken, for example six new puddling furnaces were started. Lady Charlotte now read only 'matters pertaining to my trade and my general position'. This included Matthias Dunn (the famous colliery viewer of north-west England) on the workings of collieries, and Mill's *Political Economy*. Characteristically she called in one of the country's top experts, Nicholas Wood of Newcastle, to survey and report on the mineral workings at Dowlais. With the exception of the sinking of two new pits (not achieved until 1857) his proposals were accepted and some improvements made in haulage. Lady Charlotte was anxious to increase coal production: 'I shall not rest till it is done.' Wood suggested modifying the wasteful pillar and stall method of extracting coal. The alternative longwall system (which maintained a continuous working face and meant that all coal could be removed in one extraction) was in its infancy but after enquiries into its success in the north-east, it was tried at Dowlais.

Lady Charlotte made trips underground, 'It is my desire to make myself as well acquainted as circumstances will permit with the workings of our mines', and in November she saw the longwall system for herself. An agent gave her lessons on the coal mines and after each trip she studied colliery maps. On her fourth visit she encountered a small trapper boy who, when asked his age, declared he was 'going his nine'. She determined to find him 'an easy berth above ground, poor enfant' wanting him to know that this was because he had told her the truth (boys under ten were legally banned from operating trap doors or doing any work below ground). The original version of the 1842 mines bill would also have barred Lady Charlotte from visiting mines but had been amended to allow women to enter but not work underground. In November 1853 she spoke to the manager Menelaus about the renewed practice of using girls to pile iron at night. Although this was temporarily abandoned, the practice soon resumed and in the mid-1860s Menelaus opposed proposals to ban 781 Dowlais women and girls from night and Sunday working (this was made illegal in 1872).

When the puddlers begged not to be compelled to light furnaces on Sunday evenings, Lady Charlotte, unlike John Evans, wanted to acknowledge that right. She was anxious to ensure a regular supply of labour at a time when many men were emigrating. She also appreciated that 'what with repairing the furnace and one thing and another they get very little of the Sunday to themselves'. She believed that the fairest approach was 'to speak to them, to hear their grievances and concede what they wish'. Furnace lighting was soon changed to Monday mornings.

In June 1853 colliers and miners met to discuss the Company's new rules for dealing with those who left without leave, another safeguard against loss of labour. Lady Charlotte's conciliatory approach to labour relations was at its most evident at this stage and contrasted with the more autocratic style of John Evans. As she explained, 'of course we adhere firmly to our own plans – But I do not like to treat the people de haut en bas – They are generally very reasonable – and a few firm, kind words often puts matters on the proper footing and in the right light with them.'

There was some concern about the methods of paying wages. In the early 1840s the Company had tried paying men individually through the offices in response to the Mines and Collieries Act, which outlawed the payment of wages in public houses. The new system did not, however, prove popular. By 1852 John Evans was complaining to Lady Charlotte that its failure was increasing the amount of drunkenness. Just before Christmas 1852 the system of payment was further reformed by changing payday to nine times a year. Although in practice workmen had advances on their wages known as 'draws' to tide them over between pay, the system of long pay was especially regretted by tradesmen. Lady Charlotte now began to take further the plans begun in the 1840s to ensure that men were paid individually rather than in lists. For those engaged by contractors, wages were to be paid out in the schoolrooms rather than the public houses. She supervised the new arrangements personally. On the first day, to the dismay of several sleepy clerks and even greater consternation of those who were late, she was at the forge office by 8 a.m. She then worked on the arrangements for the mills and furnaces. By June 1853 all colliers were being paid separately and £11,000 was being paid out in gold, silver and copper.

From early in 1853 ironworkers were seriously feeling the pinch as the price of provisions rose rapidly and fast outstripped wages. Acknowledging that this was a real hardship, Lady Charlotte was ready to enquire into the situation though she preferred not to interfere with trade and thought it wiser to leave it to find its own level. She was wary of schemes for buying provisions and selling them to the men as this smacked too much of truck – the firm had kept a company shop between 1797 and 1823 and again from 1828 until the outlawing of the system in 1831. H.A. Bruce suggested a cooperative store managed by a committee of workmen and supported by their own funds. Lady Charlotte was wary of proffering any advice about putting earnings into potentially unstable ventures and preferred to let the men make their own decisions about how to use their wages.

Wages had in fact increased several times over the past year. Sir John had granted a 5 per cent increase on returning to Dowlais in September 1852, and all four of the local ironworks had provided a further increase of 5 per cent in December. None of this was sufficient to stem rapid inflation and in March 1853 a further rise of 10 per cent was given at Dowlais which led Crawshay's men to come out in May for a similar advance, which they won. A fourth rise of 10 per cent was granted by Dowlais in June. Lady Charlotte was not keen on this increase but it was heralded by rises from Hill and Thompson, and knowing that labour was scarce there seemed little option but to follow.

By mid-June the ironmaster Anthony Hill was anxious that the four works should coordinate their movements. After meeting him, Lady Charlotte wrote 'I do not know whether the moment has come to stop any further rise of wages – but I am quite confident that if the four works would agree to act together – and keep faith with each other it would be better for them.' Although much historical emphasis has been placed on the reputed rivalries and hostilities between the big ironworks, relations between them tended to fluctuate according to a number of factors, not least of which was the trade cycle. As Martin Daunton has shown, in boom times they were very much in competition with each other but in upturn and downturn periods there was greater incentive for combination, especially to exercise some collective control over wage rises. They were also prepared to supply each other with coal and iron ore in times of need. Yet, unlike their neighbours in Monmouthshire, the Glamorgan ironmasters had no formal association or mechanism for adopting a common approach and, as they tended to lurch from co-operation to conflict and back again, depending on the state of the market, their separate workforces were able to utilize to advantage this lack of consistent agreement and sometimes play off one works against another, which in turn forced the employers concerned into closer if uneasy alliances with each other.

On 28 June Anthony Hill wrote to Lady Charlotte suggesting a meeting of the trade. Interestingly his letter actually asked her to instruct John Evans about her wishes for the meeting, not mentioning meeting her directly. Yet Lady Charlotte's reply made it clear that she would be in London with Evans and attend herself. In fact the meeting which was to cause her so much worry took place at her home, Spring Gardens, on 1 July. It encapsulated the difficulties which even an intelligent and determined woman could face when confronted with a group of masters who were used to working in concert (as well as competition) with each other. Hill (Plymouth), Crawshay (Cyfarthfa) and Forman (Penydarren) were present. The Penydarren colliers were striking for a wage increase. The meeting discussed whether their employers should give in to them and the wisdom of making an agreement against a further advance as a precaution to counteract the knock-on effect which one increase seemed to have on neighbouring works. It was suggested that Penydarren's loss of profits could be covered by the other three companies rather than capitulating to the strikers. Robert Crawshay feared that his father would not concur, so Hill and Forman jointly proposed that all four works stop all or part of their operations until the Penydarren men returned. Lady Charlotte's voice was now heard: 'I was horrified – and ventured to remind them of the necessity of a month's notice at least to our men – To this they assented and said the month's notice could be given forthwith – Then I remonstrated strongly against the injustices of such a proceeding – and spoke warmly in praise of our men and their conduct "ought not the men, in the Works that were working, to be at least spoken to and the position of affairs brought before them?".'

Hill then suggested that the three companies tell their men that no further advance could be made and that if the Penydarren men did not return to work in a week, the other concerns would close down a week later. 'I remonstrated once more – It seems to me monstrous to tell our steady good men that unless (as it were) they *compelled* their refractory neighbours to go to work we would revenge it upon them and throw them out of bread – But they were all against me – even *Evans* – they said it would never come to that, – that with the month's notice – if not within the week – all would be at work – that only strong measures could be of any use.'

It was a baptism of fire! Lady Charlotte's life-long belief in the importance of the ruling class setting a good and honest example to others seemed to have no meaning in their environment. She objected to any form of intimidation and compulsion, especially if it meant using other people to bear your own responsibility. Yet she felt extremely ill at ease in this public arena and protest was not easy. Although she saw that she had to be as tough as the next person, this experience and the politics and pressure of group dynamics were foreign to her: 'I was overwhelmed and bewildered, I suspected my objections might arise from a woman's weakness, and succumbed for the moment – with extreme reluctance.'

Hill wasted no time in putting the proposals in writing. Alderman Thompson (Forman's partner) had arrived late but although initially he seemed 'startled at the violence of the proposed measures' it was in his interest to get his men back to work, so he too accepted them. It was presumed that there was complete agreement, the Monmouthshire masters were to be asked to cooperate and the meeting ended with Lady Charlotte 'in a state of horror – which would have been agonizing had I not felt that until I signed the document I was not pledged to it actually, and could, after reflection, withdraw'.

Reflection made her even more uneasy about the implications of the agreement – 'That I should be a party to daring the men (as it were) to a strike, seemed to me appalling.' What if they called their bluff and did not serve their notice? They were innocent people who should not be used, 'What had our men done? but work steadily, behave respectfully, act reasonably, during times of much difficulty and temptation – should I not deserve to lose that confidence which I have always studied so carefully to inspire them with – and that confidence once shaken I knew I should never

Lady Charlotte's draft letter to Alderman Thompson.

regain it – No – the thing could not be – and I had determined to stand free from all partaking in it – It was unjust, wrong and could not prosper.'

Failing to intercept Hill or Crawshay at the station, Evans was sent to the City the next day to 'free me at once from anything like participating in the compact'. Once Lady Charlotte's views were known a new meeting was arranged for 4 July but in the meantime, to her annoyance, the Penydarren men were told that if they were not in work in a week, the other ironworkers would be given notice. To this the men replied that 50,000 out of work would prompt a rebellion.

Lady Charlotte was blaming herself for not having sounded more resolute in the meeting. Her first lesson in dealing with the combined masters was proving more difficult than handling the workmen and she felt keenly her position as the sole woman:

I deserve some punishment for having been so weak … and though I might plead the extenuating circumstances of being a woman and in argument *alone* against the opinion of five experienced men of business who hurried matters unduly to an assumed conclusion, yet I cannot but own that I had the *power* to say no, which I ought to have exercised on the spot … I hope I shall take warning and act better and more confidently another time – It was my first trial of the kind, and I must confess to having been a good deal agitated at the outset at even seeing men, whom since my sorrow, I had not met before.

On receiving a strong letter from Thompson she drafted an equally strong reply (opposite), though the arrival of the Penydarren manager, another Mr Martin, enabled her to show him rather than send the letter. It stressed that it was completely wrong to hold innocent men responsible for the actions of their neighbours and, she deplored such an aggressive course of action. To make matters worse, Evans now seemed to be 'almost veering round again to advocate the sterner course' but she wrote (in words very similar to those used in her letter to Thompson) that 'I know I am right in this that it would have been opposed to common justice and prudence for me to have given our men notice, or to have threatened them to do so – and having acted conscientiously and, I believe justly, the results must take their own course.'

Yet, this proved to be the beginning rather than the end of the affair. Although keen to rejoin the children at Canford, Evans advised her to 'remain at my post'. By 8 July the Penydarren men were back at work with a new increase of 7 per cent. Three days later the Plymouth workers came out for an increase which they got (10 per cent on top of the June increase) as did Cyfarthfa a little later. Whilst she was not prepared to resort to blackmail, Lady Charlotte was similarly unimpressed by the inconsistency of her fellow employers. Her reactions over the next few weeks were informed by her determination not to chop and change course as they did. She was also beset by concern that she had not stood up sufficiently to the ironmasters and must now ensure that they did not see her as weak or indecisive. She had already angered them by refusing to sanction their agreement but she had annoyed herself even more by her behaviour in their presence. From now on she would show her strength. Thus on 11 July she wrote of the likelihood of Dowlais following suit and requesting a further increase:

It will be a question whether we should give it or resist it – But of one thing I am quite resolved. If the men threaten, or make any demonstration of a strike – I will resist them to the end – Every wheel in these works shall stop simultaneously if I see any indication of a compulsive course being followed. I am not afraid of the men – and all the more I have declined all aggressive meanness towards them, the more I shall feel not only justified, but bound, to resist any movement of this kind on their part – I will be their master …

In the midst of the strike which followed, Kitson from the London House visited Dowlais and told the people that it was now 'a question of who shall be master, the proprietor or the workman and that in this state of things she will not concede to outside pressure'. Lady Charlotte's comment was in part a declaration of her position *vis-à-vis* the men but it was also intrinsically linked to her memory of the troubled dealings at Spring Gardens. She badly wanted to win back her credibility and in her works journal wrote 'my line of action is taken and must and shall be firmly pursued'.

Rumours abounded that Dowlais had granted the advance. Sitting on her own in Dowlais House (*Ty Mawr* as it was called in Welsh, the Big House) in an increasingly confrontational atmosphere she learned that the colliers had met on 20 July and resolved to strike if they could not obtain the advances granted elsewhere. The Dowlais men felt vulnerable as they were the last works to be paid and had not yet actually received their June increase. They were now seeking an extra 7.5 per cent or 10 per cent to give them parity. Twenty-seven years earlier when the other works had reduced wages, Dowlais had sustained the rates of pay and the Company had gained the reputation of paying the best wages, a position they were now in danger of losing. Evans tried to explain that iron was down 20*s* a ton and that if they could not accept the June increase alone, they should serve their notices. He conceded that within the month affairs might improve sufficiently to justify their remaining, but would not promise anything. Watching from a distance Lady Charlotte described the deputation as 'All respectable, intelligent fellows'.

The men would not accept Evans's pleading and on 21 July the strike began. Whilst Henry Layard was making increasingly bellicose Parliamentary speeches, Lady Charlotte was writing dramatically in her journal, 'My question was Peace or War? and he [Evans] answered War!' She deliberately went to the Works to sanction personally the stopping of thirteen blast furnaces. The ironstone miners continued working but about 1,500 colliers were on strike.

Lady Charlotte was convinced that she was in the right. When, a little later, Monmouthshire workers threatened to strike, she wondered how Edward Hutchins would respond at the Rhymney Ironworks – 'He was educated in an atmosphere of justice.' She was no more prepared to be intimidated (as she saw it) by the men than by the masters and the state of the market was very different from the good times of the 1840s. She believed that the increases in the other works had been given on the plea of them becoming equal with Dowlais. The men, however, argued that Evans had promised them that they would have the same advances as other works, something he now denied. Most importantly, Lady Charlotte believed that the men had broken their side of the contract. Since works had been in the habit of poaching labour from each other, written agreement existed whereby workers could only be released from work after a written discharge. Supported by the Stipendiary Magistrate and the MP, Lady Charlotte felt that this breach of contract justified the Company in withholding wages. In fact the strike broke out three days before payday and although there had been 'draws' on account, the colliers had been forfeiting their wages for the past six weeks. On 22 July the statutory month's notice was given.

In the past Lady Charlotte's behaviour towards the workforce had been predicated upon an understanding of deferential loyalty. This new turn of affairs was alien, just as taking decisions without even the tacit support of her husband was new. She wrote: 'The isolation of my position is I believe my greatest trial.' In mid-century and in mid-life (and what turned out to be in between two marriages) she had not only become iron*mistress* of the world's largest concern of its kind but had taken over at a time of strained labour relations. A small contingent of police was drafted in, though she refused to house them in the stables. That would have made her look nervous and afraid of the men, 'which I am not in the slightest – for indeed I never saw the people more civil and better behaved'. She noted the 'acuteness' of her own workmen who, when told that the trade could not afford further increases, asked why Hill had therefore given unsolicited a 10 per cent rather than 7.5 per cent rise.

After further negotiations she refused to let the colliers work out their notices. She would not contemplate any increase above the June rise. Constantly aware of her sex, she recognized her peculiar position, 'a woman here quite by myself among all these wild fiery spirits – But thank God I am well – and quite up to all my work and all the exertion that the situation requires.' On 25 July she impressed on Hill the 'necessity of the other Ironmasters giving their assistance in fighting this great battle and he quite agreed with me that it ought to be so'. Yet, as the *Merthyr Guardian* wryly observed, the trouble would never have happened had the three masters who gave the original increase and thus provoked Dowlais to follow, held back collectively. To make matters worse, the other ironmasters were now adopting a new tactic and retracting their problematical increases! All three gave notice of the withdrawal of their most recent advances, threatening to suspend all operations at the end of the month should the men refuse to work. As the newspaper recognized, it was impossible to tell what labour was worth in the market, workmen fixing one rate and employers another. Certainly the cavalier and opportunistic actions of Hill, Crawshay, Thompson and Forman fuelled an already volatile situation.

Quite apart from the implications of this latest volte-face, Lady Charlotte now had new problems. As the local press put it, 'Large numbers of working men are continually on the wing.' In August a gentleman at the Castle Inn, Merthyr was seeing as many as a hundred men nightly who were anxious to emigrate to Australia and a better life. There were also legal obstacles from an unexpected source, the puddlers. These highly skilled men exercised considerable control in the works. Richard Fothergill had been supplying Dowlais with some Scotch pig iron to tide them over. The puddlers now refused to puddle Scotch or Tyne pigs without increased pay. Since they were paid by the ton earnings were adversely affected as it took longer to puddle this new iron. Scotch pigs anyway fetched 2s 6d more than Welsh pigs. Attempts to compromise failed and the puddlers left work. The Company was taken to court over the issue. Lady Charlotte sought legal advice in London. Evans was worried that losing the case could mean that the men's assent might be needed in future before prices were fixed for alterations in the mix of iron. As he put it in a letter to Lady Charlotte (who was spending a few days at Canford): 'capital will loose [sic] all the influence it aught [sic] and must command'. The Company lost the case as it was deemed that they had broken their side of the contract by expecting a different quality of iron to be puddled. Evans added at the end of his letter, 'I fear that my letters are very annoying to your ladyship, and am very sorry that I have not got it in my power to write on a more interesting subject …' Lady Charlotte was now watching her daughters dress dolls and play weddings 'which mightily diverted them, but seemed to me extremely dull'. Affairs at Dowlais were quite the opposite.

Although the Company lost the case against the puddlers they won a court action against a collier who, in a test case, sued for his loss of wages.[7] In this instance it was deemed that the collier's wages had been justifiably forfeited since he had broken his side of the contract. As the date for the end of the month's notice approached, Dowlais was producing about one-third of its usual output. The colliers had already reduced their demands to 5 per cent (not wanting to return empty handed) and their wives had deputized Evans for a draw. On 18 August Lady Charlotte received a deputation of colliers anxious to at least secure their forfeited money. She still refused to grant any increase (despite being compared to the biblical David) though did concede that they could have a small sum on account if they went back to work with the remainder following in due time.

The strike had shown Lady Charlotte's capacity for playing politics. Although a letter from the chemist and scholar Thomas Stephens to *The Times* claimed that Lady Charlotte was the scapegoat of the ironmasters, this was true only in so far as they had provoked the unfortunate series of events which had led to the strike. From this time onwards Lady Charlotte's position was one of increasing independence and resolution. Whereas the Rector seems to have been softened by the strike and its effect on the people – anxious to mediate he had burst into tears when Lady Charlotte threatened to stop the entire works if need be (more as a threat than as a serious intention) – she had correspondingly emerged toughened by the experience. In sorting out who was to continue in employment after the notices expired Lady Charlotte talked to all heads of departments and gave personal instructions to about twenty men for paying off workmen they could not afford.

On 18 August Merthyr tradesmen called a meeting. It was chaired by Thomas Stephens. According to the press, 3,000 to 4,000 attended though few were colliers. A joint memorial to the ironmasters of the district was read out deploring the strike and lamenting its effect on trade, but hoping that amicable relations could be restored between masters and men. Perhaps surprisingly, two of the leading local Chartists were prominent in this meeting. Yet both were tradesmen – Henry Thomas was a master cooper and William Gould a grocer – and both would become leading figures in years to come in the transition towards Reformism and conciliation which reached its height in 1868 with the election of the Nonconformist Liberal

MP for Merthyr, Henry Richard. Gould criticized the employers for not giving wages according to the market price of iron but also blamed the colliers at Dowlais for 'striking rashly'. He stressed that their strike took place in an establishment 'which was principally ruled by a lady, whose excellent qualities all willingly acknowledge, and whose claims to their good wishes could scarcely be overstated (Applause). No lady in the kingdom had such cares to bear as Lady Charlotte Guest. He (Mr Gould) wished this to be distinctly understood, that the meeting sympathized with her, as did workmen in general (Applause).'

Not for nothing did a recent appraisal of the Dowlais strike label it 'The Respectful Strike'.

Lady Charlotte's reply endorsed many of the sentiments in the memorial reiterating that 'the welfare of Masters and Men are identical' and her aim to act always with firmness and justice. Her reply was read out at a reconvened session of the meeting on 23 August and received a much warmer response than that from Anthony Hill.

Increasingly anxious about the fact that the colliers were not drifting back to work, Evans suggested using strikebreakers. Convinced, however, that the strike was about to end, Lady Charlotte was intent on returning to Dowlais herself rather than bringing in workers from elsewhere. She left London at the end of the month and, as so often on her returns to Wales, her arrival was dramatic. No sooner had she got out of the carriage at Cardiff than John Evans's nephew greeted her with a letter:'The Colliers had gone to work and the Strike was over!' The breaking point had come when the tradesmen combined to raise £170, out of which they offered a small sum to each collier who returned to work between 1 and 12 September. The temptation was clearly too great for about 300 colliers who went back immediately, and in just over a week 600 had returned and men from other works were again seeking employment at Dowlais.

The strikers had not been unionized. Despite the brief appearance of the Miners' Association in the coalfields in 1844, South Wales at this time was not a centre of union activity and indeed John Guest had discouraged this. In some respects it is surprising that the colliers were able to hold out for as long as they did. Desperate for money, not supported by other Dowlais workers and lacking the structure of organization and leadership from a union, they somehow remained on strike for six weeks. Lady Charlotte's resolution and consistency must have seemed to them much more like obduracy, whilst the prospect of starvation finally enticed them back to work with a pitifully small sum and no new rise. They returned on Lady Charlotte's terms. The summer of 1853 did however encourage them to use the strike weapon as a bargaining tactic in future. In October, for example, they complained of a lack of colliery rails and threatened to come out again unless these were supplied immediately.

In order to maintain the status quo, Lady Charlotte stayed away from Dowlais for a while, going to Sully instead. On 1 September she wrote 'and so, thank God this harassing phase of my life, the Strike, was closed'.[8]

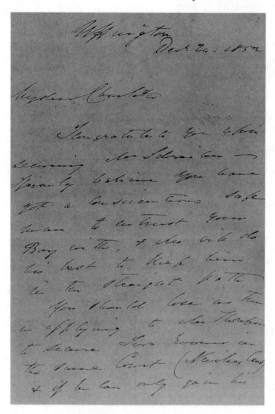

Left and opposite: Mr Pegus writes to Lady Charlotte about the new tutor.

Her description of Dowlais on 13 September suggests the resumption of a calmer period: 'The Progress up valley was delicious – quite like a dream of Lotus land.' The colliers now applied for the money which had been legally declared forfeited. Lady Charlotte used this to extend her leverage, stating that she would give half in a week and the rest when justified. They agreed and (according to her) 'we parted with the warmest expression of affection and goodwill'. Yet she relented on learning that up to 300 men would receive nothing since their previous draws had already covered the part-payment she proposed. She therefore agreed to the whole sum being paid out, not missing the opportunity to emphasize that 'I had now put the fullest trust in them and their good intentions.'

With the strike behind her, she now settled back into the routine of daily management – 'to which I shall devote myself with all my own ardour – I am calm and contented now – and can own and appreciate many beauties of the "Present" but when I look to the "Future" my heart quails – for I see nothing but misery everywhere'. This misery was not, however, a reference to the economic privations of the Dowlais people. It referred to something much more personal: her growing involvement with the new tutor, Charles Schreiber, and the secret hope for a future with him.

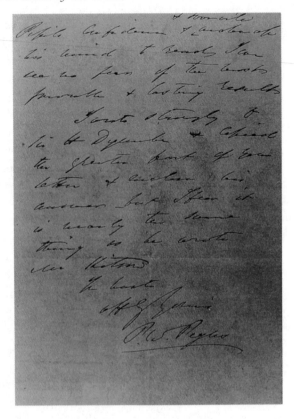

Charles Schreiber had walked into Lady Charlotte's home and life only twenty-four days after her husband's death. On 14 December she had written that she needed to place Ivor with 'some Cambridge man' now that he was home and needed preparation for university and a tutor whilst there. Six days later, on returning from her husband's vault in Dowlais church, she had to compose herself to receive Mr Schreiber. Ironically it was Pegus who had, as in the days of Mr Martin, selected the new tutor and unwittingly provoked a new emotional drama for his stepdaughter. Born on 10 May 1826, the son of Lieutenant Colonel James Alfred Schreiber of Melton, Suffolk, Charles came from a family of German origin (on his father's side). His father, a cavalry officer in the battle of Waterloo, had died in 1840 when he was at Dedham school. His mother, Mary (née Ware of County Cork), was still alive.[9]

Lady Charlotte's first impression of this intelligent young Fellow of Trinity College, Cambridge was that 'he seems altogether to be a very desirable man for the office – I like what I see of him very much'. This innocent statement must have caused her some amusement later as would have Pegus's congratulatory letter, approving of her appointment of this 'conscientious safe person' who would keep her boy 'in the straight path'. There were few journal references to Mr Schreiber over the next few months. Recently widowed and in mourning, Lady Charlotte would, in ordinary circumstances, have had little opportunity to get to know well her son's tutor, a young man in his twenties who was her employee. Yet Lady Charlotte's life was no respecter of ordinary circumstances. As in a contrived melodrama, the one permissible situation developed which gave her the chance to get close to the tutor. He fell dangerously ill. Having spent so long by the bedside of a dying man, Lady Charlotte was used to emotional scenes and providing comfort – it seemed almost as if she were back with John. On 19 June when signs of fever were first evident, she wrote:'I should really grieve if anything should happen to him. He is such a very nice person and we like him so very much.' By 23 June he was worse and keen to see her:'I felt a little prudery about it at first – for it is very difficult for me who was (comparatively) a young woman last year to feel and believe myself, as I am, an old woman now.' He was, however, in 'agony of mind' and 'all his youthful, unrepented sins came thronging before him' – in his delirium he seems to have told Lady Charlotte all about a former attachment to a young lady. His mother was summoned from Ireland and one of his brothers came too.

Yet by mid-July he was recovering and it seemed to Lady Charlotte that his young life had been saved after her earnest prayers at his bedside. He now asked her to remind him of what he had suffered when he thought he was dying:'I was so nervous and felt so deeply that I could scarce say anything I wished … I think if there was ever a pure, uncorrupted spirit it was his … Another mind is added to the very few I value and am interested in – I pray God may be instrumental for its good.' When he left with Ivor for the south coast she wrote, 'I am now left quite alone, not one mind near with whom I can exchange one idea.' By August she was beginning to betray her new feelings in her journal entries. When she discussed with Maria the minds of those possessing practical wisdom, she confessed that in addition to the four they singled out, 'I could I believe have added a fifth but I forbore'. Whilst Dowlais was plunged into distress with the strike and Lady Charlotte experienced a sense of alienation from her workforce, she spent a few days at Canford. There she walked with the girls and Charles Schreiber on 'an evening never to be forgotten'. The romance she had sought from her youth had come back into her life just when she least expected it. She had never fully wiped out the memory of that early tutor Mr Martin. Now, no sooner had her husband died than another tutor, as if by providence, had appeared in her home in need of comfort. Her sense of destiny was once more confirmed.

Once the strike was over, she was keen for Mr Schreiber to join her at Dowlais, 'I find thoughts of my own desolation will rise up in every picture of the future' and she confessed that 'my mind is in a very unhealthy, unsettled state – even work does not seem to bring the relief it ought'. From this time the journal entries became cryptic, due to fear lest somebody else read them, and because of the guilty confusion in the mind of a woman whose husband had not been dead a year but who was becoming increasingly attracted to a man fourteen years younger than herself. The old moods of depression interspersed with short bouts of delirious happiness returned and, as was usually the case when her thoughts were troubled, her sentences became riddled with dashes, hiding as much as they revealed. She had long talks with Maria, who declared that she had never known her mother in so strange a mood. As time wore on, Maria was increasingly upset at her mother's deepening relationship with Mr Schreiber, who was closer in age to herself than he was to Lady Charlotte. In 1911 Blanche and Katherine read their mother's journal for this period. Blanche read it 'with mixed feelings of admiration and regret'. Katherine added that she admired her mother's great business activities but 'was grieved to read how soon my dear father's memory was effaced'. At one point Lady Charlotte became concerned about Katherine's interest in the Schreibers (particularly the student brother, Henry). She hoped she was not too interested 'for that indeed would be fearful and would add most materially to my embarrassment'. She even feared that Katherine was becoming too fond of Charles himself. Katherine added the word 'absurd' to this specula-tion when she eventually read the journal.

As the references to Charles increased, so Sir John virtually disappeared from the journal. Yet Lady Charlotte was not likely to expend much feeling on what was now past. She generally succeeded in burying thoughts with those who died and, as we have seen, her half-sister Elizabeth was successfully exorcized from her writings once she had died. On the anniversary of Sir John's death she knelt beside his coffin, then wrote: 'What can I say more! Now I have but one hope and cling to that with passionate tenacity.' She added a line from Longfellow's 'A Psalm of Life', 'Learn to labour and to wait' (she had given Charles a volume of Longfellow's poetry).

Although Charles and Ivor were now installed at Cambridge, Lady Charlotte was beginning to contrive for them to spend some time together. When Ivor had a dental appointment in London the couple spent 'the quietest, happiest hour I have known for some time', no doubt hoping that Ivor would not return too soon to Spring Gardens. She expended much energy on waiting anxiously for the mail and was plunged into unreasonable despair if nothing arrived from Cambridge. Like a teenager experiencing her first romance, she treasured the mementos Charles gave her – a silk handkerchief and one of his medals which she wore constantly. Even dinner with Pegus could have its moments. She feared his 'careless manner' but he talked about Cambridge and the evening was 'very pleasant'. She began planning trips to Cambridge, though recognized that Ivor might not wish to see her so soon. Lady Charlotte had always been disdainful of even a moment wasted when she might be improving herself in some way. Now she indulged in the new pleasure of day-dreaming about Charles, allowing herself to 'be idle and think'. For his part, although intellectually inclined, Charles seems to have spent much of his time indulging in active sports such as hunting and tired quite easily, though Lady Charlotte's amused references to his 'hopelessly sleepy fits' may say more about her indefatigable energy than about Charles being lethargic.

Although she was only enjoying some deserved happiness after a long period of anxiety about her ailing husband, Lady Charlotte was concerned to maintain (in public) a sense of propriety, even though this was increasingly difficult. The journal's hints of the snatched hours they spent together suggests that behind the façade of control was a passionate woman who had simply fallen in love.

In November she wrote from London, 'sometimes I tremble at the risks I ran and wondered what would be the end – but then came thoughts of comfort and hope'. Her increasingly furtive actions necessitated much planning and it was not only in the works that she now needed to 'trust to my ingenuity'. She wrote (deliberately ambiguously) that she was 'resorting to contrivances to try to get a little spare time to myself'. In mid-November James Walkinshaw, the accountant, was hastily dispatched to the City in a bid to get him out of Spring Gardens. Ivor had conveniently fallen ill (her favourite child had a mild attack of English cholera but even this did not seem to worry his mother unduly). In the midst of descriptions of purchases was the word 'ring' and soon after this Charles received a signet ring from her.

After the strain of recent times, her hair had turned grey then white. With some humour she wrote about her attempts at rejuvenation. 'I have spent a curious morning! My white hair (which had no business to become white yet awhile) has been undergoing the process of being made black again! – what a thing for a woman not very old, to own in her own journal.' Charles, 'the only authority at least whose opinion or feeling on the matter I care for' endorsed the transformation. Unfortunately Maria and Katherine were rather less enamoured of the change and Lady Charlotte had to placate her daughters by promising that something would be done to make her 'look as old and venerable as possible'.

Charles spent Christmas 1853 at Canford and there were euphemistic journal references to the brief snatched periods they had alone: 'In my room for the medal – but only for a moment', and an awkward interruption by a maid who came unexpectedly into the drawing room: 'I shall not easily forget Hillyard coming in to enquire about some game to be taken to Wales! But it was all right.' Like a rebellious daughter she wrote, once again euphemistically, that 'after 10 when the coast was clear I was very happy for nearly an hour'. Whenever possible she dispatched the family on long walks. In February she recorded staying in a hotel in London (Spring Gardens was rented out for the season) but to her dismay her brother Bertie's future father-in-law was also staying there and this 'very much disturbed some of my calculations'. In the same month she spent a week at Cambridge, a place she had loved since childhood. She stayed at the Bull Inn with Merthyr but managed 'some time in peace' with Charles in his rooms at Nevilles Court. The coming together of his two worlds clearly unnerved him. 'He is out of spirits and seemed quite unhinged.' By April Mr Schreiber had given way to Charles S. or C. in the journal (yet only now was she abandoning her deep mourning clothes) and before long he would be Charles or Charley. She was now writing more openly, though found it tantalizing, 'even to be prohibited from saying here all it would be such a relief to write'. On 30 May she declared that the new ring she had been given would never leave her.

As the possibility of married life with Charles increased, so the attractions of continuing to run a complex ironworks waned. What had once fired her with enthusiasm now became a duty. In March 1854 she went round the Dowlais Schools which 'I thought but right to visit before leaving'. Once such tasks were finished 'I felt emancipated for a while'. An especially severe cholera outbreak at Dowlais in 1854 kept her away – on the advice of the Rector and others. She finally returned to the grief-stricken community on 11 November. The home which in the past had been viewed through rose-coloured spectacles and had once been called by her 'a dream of Lotus land' now looked 'more dull and dirty and dismal than I ever saw it'. And whilst some survivors from the epidemic were preparing to seek a better future across the seas, Lady Charlotte was also now planning to move away.

As early as December 1853 she had wondered what the other executors would say if 'the home be gladdened'. Would Divett consent to her working on? Although soon after Sir John's death she had written, 'I seem to feel that he has gone on a journey – and that he has left me behind for a little while to put all in order ere I leave and follow him', by January 1854 she was asking Francis Bircham whether it might be possible to sell the works.[10] Her journal mentioned the increasing competition from the Middlesbrough iron trade, certainly a factor that could not be ignored (and probably the excuse she gave the lawyer) but this was not the real reason. The outbreak of the Crimean War made an imminent sale impossible (Russia had been their key customer) but renting out the works was mooted. Meanwhile Lady Charlotte increasingly consulted with H.A. Bruce (who now helped Kitson with the London management) and George Clark. Misinterpreting her mounting consternation, John Evans declared that the job was 'too much for any man to do – much more a lady'. Her personal response was like that of many men: she felt that the whole enterprise would be much easier with 'the aid of a kind heart to commune with when the day's work was done'.

Recognizing that this would be unacceptable to others, she wrote: 'I must toil on till either I can transfer all the charge or till my spirit quite breaks.' In the spring of 1854 she felt duty bound to remain in charge until her youngest son was twenty-five and got his share of the inheritance. Yet that meant another twelve and a half years. Meanwhile Canford was about to pass to Ivor. Needing to find a new abode, she reverted to a false innocence in the journal – perhaps because it concerned a public (though personal rather than domestic) occasion. She went to view Reigate Priory which was to be let and wrote that, since she could not go alone, 'I availed myself of Mr Schreiber's being in town – and asked him to be my escort'. Considering that this trip was made on the day of her brother's wedding and she had declined attending the occasion on the grounds that she had not entirely abandoned mourning, her action and writing were somewhat less ingenuous than she pretended.

A future with Charles Schreiber necessitated some economizing. By June Lady Charlotte was trying to 'look my affairs boldly in the face – I must retrench and perhaps go abroad for a year or two'. She sold her pony carriage and ponies and had her life insured with three companies (for a total of £15,000) to 'make a suitable provision for one I love'. Not surprisingly this move rather baffled the lawyer, Francis Bircham. At the start of Ivor's second year at Cambridge his tutor resigned, thus permitting a 'great feeling of freedom and release from restraint'. Charles then put his mother in the picture. By mid-December 1854 Lady Charlotte was writing 'all on earth I look forward to is the retiring, into private life in a very quiet, humble scale'. The impossibility of such a lifestyle for herself does not seem to have occurred to her. Her feelings were now dwelling on the future and allaying the misgivings of her children.

Like a national figure she announced her retirement from politics, telling a meeting of Poole corporation politicians that in future she would 'abstain from all interference in Politicks [sic]'. Yet as with so many people for whom political activity is a way of life, she could not keep away for long. Her decision to keep her distance had been because this was one of the few areas in which she disagreed with Charles, 'Now Charles has always been a Tory – or as they call it a Conservative – My feelings being quite the other way.' Used to calling the Tories 'the enemy' the adjustment was not easy. At first the couple determined not to talk politics at all but this proved impossible. Lady Charlotte was relieved to find that Charles was not opposed to Palmerston, even though he would not pledge himself to 'any of those advanced Liberal measures, which I look on as essential in the present day'. She sought out possible seats for him, but when he stood as a Tory candidate for Cheltenham in 1859 (and was narrowly defeated), she refused to canvass for him or join him in the constituency until the very last moment. For once in her life she kept so low a profile that she was simply referred to as 'the lady in the white bonnet'.

A few years before this there had been a gap in the journal. It lasted from the end of December 1854 to April 1855. It was the first time Lady Charlotte had abandoned the journal since 1833. She later mentioned that there was a 'memorable scene' at Mary's when she broke the news of her impending marriage. On 10 April 1855 the wedding of Lady Charlotte and Charles Schreiber took place in London.

Part 3

LADY CHARLOTTE SCHREIBER

9

The Traveller and Collector

'We had some sport in our chasse among the shops.'

In 1953 Mr O. Van Oss addressed fellow members of the English Ceramic Circle[1] with a paper which was 'an act of piety – almost an essay in hagiology – devoted to the memory of the lady who has the best claim to be considered our patron saint'. This person was none other than Lady Charlotte. Yet at the end of 1856 she had described her situation as 'retired into private life, in a very small house – spending a comparatively small sum of money as we are saving all we can to pay off debts'. Although the word 'comparatively' is more significant than 'small', it is none the less true that Lady Charlotte's lifestyle had altered considerably. Yet in this chapter we shall see how her affairs would change gear yet again, transforming the former 'iron lady' into one of the world's leading collectors of ceramics.

Marriage to Charles Schreiber in April 1955 had signalled a new start, with a 'fresh, young, pure, enthusiastic, *beautiful* being'. After all the upsets of recent years the honeymoon in Paris was spent in 'a state of happiness that it would be vain for me to attempt to describe'. Even sight-seeing was, for once, forfeited as they were 'so wrapped up in each other's love'.

Family problems soon interrupted their passionate bliss. A letter from Merthyr's tutor in Rome brought 'the awful announcement' that his charge was critically ill with pleurisy. Charles returned home to collect Maria and Katherine whilst Lady Charlotte and her maid travelled by sleeper and steamer to Rome, 'lovely as is every object by which I am surrounded I am sick at heart with every kind of apprehension'. Charles had to spend his twenty-ninth birthday without his new wife. Merthyr had been a sickly child and was now dangerously ill for some days, though he had improved by the time Lady Charlotte reached him. The Schreibers stayed with him for a few weeks and Merthyr-born artist Penry Williams acted as the family's guide round the city and Vatican.

The journal was suspended during the second half of 1855, probably due to Lady Charlotte having a miscarriage. New Year brought a resolution to resume writing. The bond between C.E.S. and C.S. as she sometimes called them, was strong: 'It is impossible for two people to be happier together or (I believe) to love each other more.' The month before writing this came a second miscarriage: 'We hoped we were to have been blest with a little pledge of our love – but are disappointed – It is a trial, especially to him who loves children so much.' A third attempt to have a child of their own failed in August 1858. Lady Charlotte's ten children can have been no real compensation for Charles. Despite or because of the intense emotion generated between their mother and her young husband, relations with the new stepfather were fraught. None of this was helped by the need to economize. Canford was now Ivor's (his coming of age celebrations had cost £1,000). In September 1856, after the Government purchased Spring Gardens at the 'very inadequate' price of £4,500, the family moved to 130, Marine Parade on Brighton's sea-front – 'as small as we can cram in to' – and reduced the number of servants. Since Sir John had died Lady Charlotte had been receiving an average of £5,700 yearly (paid quarterly) exclusive of Ivor's expenses and the maintenance of Canford.[2]

By February 1856 she had already overspent by about £6,000. A third of this was covered by her husband's legacy, the rest borrowed on the security of an insurance of her life. She now applied to Clark and Bruce 'to receive the largest allowance for myself and the children that the Will authorizes'. The following spring the Schreibers decided to 'retrench and go into a cottage outside London'. The 'cottage' they finally chose was Exeter House, Roehampton (for £550 a year) with a paddock of sixteen acres. Further financial concern was caused by Monty, who had run up a £700 debt since joining the army two years earlier. Charles had some income from land in Suffolk but also borrowed £2,000 from his brother Brymer.[3]

To make matters worse, all was not well at Dowlais. Despite the Company being left to the Guest sons, George Clark was not prepared to let Ivor join him. There were financial worries too. Towards the end of 1857 Lady Charlotte consulted lawyers and bankers about borrowing £25,000 to meet problems there. There had been heavy capital investment recently and further improvements were needed. A more secure future was ultimately guaranteed. Dowlais had been experimenting with soft iron under the direction of Henry Bessemer and in August 1856 took out the first licence to use his patent. Commenting on the way in which the puddling process could now be superseded through the application of cold blast to pig iron, Lady Charlotte added prophetically that if worked out satisfactorily, it 'must revolutionize completely our present system of iron making'. A Bessemer Converter was erected and in 1865 Dowlais started rolling steel rails.

Added to financial worries were domestic upsets. Charles's mother died of cancer (aged seventy-eight) in 1857 and Lady Charlotte's own mother died the following year. The Pegus family had all but disowned Charlotte when she remarried. Not one of them had attended the wedding and, somewhat ironically, it was Edward Hutchins, so often the target of Lady Charlotte's criticism in the past, who gave her away. Another source of former disapproval, the Rev. Ponsonby, officiated. Mary ignored her sister for a year and relations with Pegus once more plummeted. For three years the Schreibers did not meet him even though he had originally discovered the young tutor. Pegus had assumed 'a bad and insulting tone' when told of the marriage plans and for some time Uffington was out of bounds to her children: 'I wish them to have as little intercourse as possible with a man who had made such efforts to promote discord between me and my family and who has taken such an inimical part against me.' As late as 1862 Enid told Monty that she dared not visit her grandparents 'as the M. I am sure would never have heard of such a thing'.

On remarrying Lady Charlotte had once more to be presented at Court. She seems to have enjoyed the 1856 season and, with advice from Lady Somers (sister to her friend Julia Margaret Cameron) held a ball to which 'all that came were of the best and nicest of London's Society – but it was a little too thin'. She feared it might break up too early but dancing continued until nearly 4 a.m. Lady Charlotte was working hard to be seen and once more accepted. The Schreibers rode together in Rotten Row in the mornings and saw Prince Albert there. These Hyde Park rides were 'the brightest part of my London existence.' She attended Court on the Queen's birthday and presented Katherine.

She had been concerned about her reception, having remarried quite soon after the death of her husband; Charles was considerably younger than herself, had no title and not yet even access via Parliament. Lady Charlotte commented that: 'A great deal had been said to make the children uncomfortable as to doubts of how I should be received on account of my second marriage. All this had been set at rest by the result – They must now be content to believe that my position is as good if not better than ever – and Charles himself appears so popular that on that head also they must feel satisfied.'

Although she couched this in terms of her children's concern, there had been personal apprehension about 're-launching' herself, particularly since the couple needed to curb any extravagance. When they went to Goodwood races for example, the carriage demanded 5 guineas for 5 miles so was turned away whilst they sought another 'of more reasonable pretensions'.

From her more modest base in Roehampton (and with her son presiding at Canford) Lady Charlotte began to meet a new social group, moving in artistic circles. One neighbour was the singer Jenny Lind, now Mrs Otto Goldschmidt. One of the most popular entertainers of her day – her portrait appeared on chocolate boxes, matchboxes and pocket handkerchiefs – her singing was much favoured by the Queen. It was said that on three occasions the House of Commons was unable to vote because so many Members were listening to this 'Swedish nightingale'. Although she now spurned publicity, Lady Charlotte found that Jenny Lind was 'most agreeable and made no fuss at all about singing' to her and her family. Constance and Blanche used to sing for her and she also instructed Katherine's young daughter.

The success of Lady Charlotte in these later years can be gauged by a comment from the daughter of Lady Westmoreland, Lady Rose Weigall, in November 1866. She singled out three people at Lord Stafford's ball: 'The Prince of Wales was very civil and came up twice to speak to me. He danced away all night. I never saw anything so pretty as the Queen of Denmark still is, although it is an unhappy face, and she looks like a person who has gone through a great deal of anxiety and trouble. We both like Lady Charlotte Schreiber the best of all the people there. She is agreeable and very kind to me.' Lady Charlotte would surely have been delighted to have been described with such company. She had succeeded in moving amongst the 'top people'.

Although Lady Charlotte remained married to Charles for longer than she had been wedded to her first husband, in the eyes of many this new match was both precipitate and unsuitable. If her first marriage had raised some aristocratic eyebrows, then her second was definitely a *mésalliance*. It provoked 'much trial and inexpressible opposition'. Although Lady Charlotte was marrying a member of a respectable Suffolk family, she was breaking the golden rule that the man should be older than his spouse. In fact she was reversing it, and not long after her considerably older husband had passed away.

According to Lady Charlotte's journal, John Evans retired to Sully due to ill-health. His granddaughter Phoebe (herself the daughter of Lady Charlotte's godchild) tells a different tale. Her recollection is that he resigned from the Works because he was so disgusted with Lady Charlotte's marriage. Like the Guests, Evans had come to Wales from Shropshire (in the same year as Lady Charlotte was born) and had 'really loved his friend' John Guest. Phoebe Simons's account is not strictly accurate – she extended the fourteen-year gap between Lady Charlotte and Charles to twenty years and thought they married only six months after Sir John's death, a measure of the sense of impropriety felt by those close to the family. There was quite a telling incident at Ivor's twenty-first birthday celebrations at Canford when an elderly farmer proposed the health of 'Mr Schreiber and Lady Charlotte *Guest*', with his neighbours plucking at his coat in vain whilst he repeated his words. There is also a popular myth at Canford today that Lady Charlotte married the gardener. In Phoebe Simons's words, by marrying Charles, Lady Charlotte was 'quite distinctly outcasted by everybody'. We have seen how former Society friends such as Lady Hall now spurned her whilst Henry Layard 'cannot forgive my marriage', and 'altogether kept aloof from us …'

When Enid married Henry Layard in 1869 she wrote that: 'None of us had a happy home and we were all glad to get away.' She referred to 'fighting' after Charles entered the household, and the sisters communicated in a secret shorthand. In 1860 Lady Charlotte noted that Charles was relaxed when with his own relatives, but with her own family 'I cannot but constantly feel in dread lest some chance sentiment or contradiction may lead to unpleasantness'.

What distressed her most of all was the difficulty her eldest child had in adjusting to her stepfather. At the wedding Maria had signalled a truce by telling Charles she 'hoped all unpleasantness would now be quite forgotten and that they should be fast friends asking him to call her by her christian name'. Yet over the next year nothing improved and 'her manner has been our one great trial'. Lady Charlotte praised Charles's forbearance though eventually Maria's 'continual contradiction and the assumption of authority over us all produced some effect – and his replies became (on one or two occasions only) a little more decided'. The journal depicts Maria as 'touchy', 'dictatorial', 'sullen', 'brusque' and 'uncompromising'. For Lady Charlotte, who had carefully cultivated self-possession and kept her inmost feelings veiled from the world, it was always difficult to comprehend how her own daughter could be so transparent and give vent to her temper so easily. By summer an injured silence existed between Maria and Charles and Lady Charlotte felt *she* was being shunned. A year later there was 'no syllable of discussion with her on any subject whatsoever'. Yet there were parallels between this eldest child (now twenty-three) and her mother. Both had seen their younger sibling inherit the family home by virtue of his sex; both felt keenly the effects of their own mother marrying someone with whom they clashed violently; and both had lost their fathers and felt rejected and lonely after the new marriage. Yet despite her early experience, Lady Charlotte's sympathy was entirely with her new husband whilst Maria turned so 'savagely against me with such a deepening and relentless energy'.

The children clearly grieved for their father. Any respect for Charles was challenged by his youth and having been a family employee. Although a superior tutor in intellect and duties, he had nevertheless been a paid tutor and other tutors had been somewhat disposable. Since Charles lacked an authority of his own it followed that Lady Charlotte's responsibility as a parent was redoubled. Selecting or approving appropriate careers for her sons and suitable marriages for her daughters now rested firmly on her shoulders. Ironically, given her own personal history, the solution to Maria's problem lay in marriage.

After a particularly difficult exchange between Maria and Charles (with Katherine intervening on her sister's behalf) Maria declared she would have to leave home. Lady Charlotte appealed to the lawyer Richard Du Cane, who now handled her legal entanglements with Uffington. He discussed the matter with Maria, who expressed contrition and 'I felt that my child was restored to me'. Lady Charlotte suspected that Maria rather liked Mr Du Cane. In some ways this posed difficulties – he was a cousin of Charles's and belonged to his generation. Would Maria's brothers, sisters and friends approve of a match with a solicitor? Unlike ironmasters, the income of such professionals ceased when they stopped work. Yet at last it seemed as though Maria had found somebody she admired and the interest appeared mutual. After a little match-making – Lady Charlotte ensuring that Richard's seat 'happened to be next to Maria's' at the theatre – the couple became engaged and relations between Maria and Charles visibly improved. Maria and Richard married on 9 August 1859 (there was a marriage settlement of £75,000, £10,000 of which was Maria's) and so reconciled did she become with her family that before long the couple moved to Ashburton cottage next door to the Schreibers.

Lady Charlotte was also attracted to the Little Holland House set where Julia Margaret Cameron's sister, Mrs Prinsep, presided over a coterie of artistic and literary figures, including an artist-in-residence, G. F. Watts. Watts did portraits of both Lady Charlotte and Charles. It was here that in April 1857 Lady Charlotte first met Tennyson, and he told her about his poem 'Geraint and Enid'. The Tennysons were friendly with Julia Margaret Cameron. Julia's photographs illustrated the second volume of *The Idylls of the King*. She was a neighbour of Lady Charlotte's at Roehampton and her daughter was a close friend of Lady Charlotte's eldest daughters. In October Tennyson stayed at Julia's home and Lady Charlotte joined them one evening:

'He talked a great deal about Welsh literature – and I who have forgotten all the little I ever knew about that and everything else, felt quite ashamed at my own ignorance.'

This was the new Lady Charlotte Schreiber, now physically and increasingly mentally removed from Wales. On another occasion she joined a gathering of Pre-Raphaelites, including Holman Hunt and Rossetti, to converse with Tennyson. After most guests had left he read his *Morte d'Arthur* and 'that really was a pleasure'. More than once Lady Charlotte reversed the usual male to female gesture and presented Tennyson with roses. She described his 'Geraint and Enid' as 'extremely beautiful'. Late one summer night when Lady Charlotte was in bed, her neighbour Julia arrived at her house with Tennyson. Meeting Lady Charlotte at the garden gate they persuaded her to return to the Camerons 'to see how nicely I have converted my conservatory into a sitting-room for Alfred'. Tennyson placed his large black sombrero on Lady Charlotte's head and later presented her with a signed copy of *The Idylls of the King*. In 1864 she visited him on the Isle of Wight. Edward Lear was present though not overjoyed at such events – 'I find all that quiet part of the Island spoiling fast,' he wrote. 'Add to this Pattledom has taken entire possession of the place ... Guest, Schreibers, Pollocks and myriads more buzzing everywhere.'[4] Lady Charlotte and some of her children printed some of Tennyson's works on the Canford private printing press. For example they produced 'The Victim' in 1868 and a beautiful red leather copy of *Morte d'Arthur* for which Ivor sketched the original ideas for the exquisite illustrations by the Hon. Mrs Fox Strangways. There was also a bound copy of Tennyson's and Lady Charlotte's Geraint tales.

Amongst the 'beautiful people' gathered at Little Holland House in the summer of 1857 was a young lady with an enchanting singing voice, Georgina Treherne. The following year she returned and spent some time at Exeter House. Lady Charlotte presented her at Court. Merthyr, a Cambridge student, now confessed that he had loved Georgina for a year and a half. Perhaps remembering her own youth, Lady Charlotte did not intervene, sensibly recognizing that there were 'so many shipwrecks following on the checking of early natural affections'. Pegus, always susceptible to young, beautiful women remained 'charmed' but after her wealthy landowning father objected to the match, Lady Charlotte began to 'see and mistrust the mysteriousness of the young lady's conduct'. It was agreed that Merthyr should delay an engagement until he was twenty-one and he went to Germany to study metallurgy. Soon Lady Charlotte's suspicion of the 'young lady's duplicity and flightiness' was confirmed. When she visited Little Holland House Georgina remained closeted alone with Lord Ward in Watts's studio. Lady Charlotte wrote to Merthyr, Georgina was dispatched by her father to Switzerland and the romance was over. Lady Charlotte was relieved that 'the young lady's character' (she seemed reluctant to name her in writing) 'had been unmasked in time, and that my dear son had been saved'.

Although the Camerons were to remain friends (Maria was a bridesmaid at young Julia's wedding and Enid taught the sons music for a time) Lady Charlotte's attitude towards Little Holland House was changing, particularly with the need to maintain the respectability of her unmarried daughters. When Katherine and Julia went there alone without telling Lady Charlotte, mother and daughters stopped talking to each other for a time and Lady Charlotte wrote, 'I know there cannot be a worse place to go alone than Little Holland House, amidst artists and musicians – and all the flattery and nonsense which is rife in that (otherwise) most agreeable society.'

Although one son had been saved, the fourth Guest son was much less fortunate. Augustus was a lively young man and his photographs suggest that he was the most dashing of the boys. He had started at Trinity College, Cambridge in 1858 (interestingly the four sons who went to university went to Charles's college, though Arthur transferred to Peterhouse). Augustus, Arthur and Merthyr seem to have inherited their mother's love of the stage and were active in the University Amateur Dramatic Club. Augustus's forte was in playing comic parts. Work seems to have taken second place and he failed his first-year examinations. When supposedly studying for 'resits' he was shooting with Ivor in Wales. Yet Lady Charlotte regarded him as 'a great sunbeam in the house' which may suggest that he was more conciliatory towards Charles than some of the family. He spent six months with Merthyr in Germany in the summer of 1860, returning 'full of fire and spirits and (innocent) mischief'. He returned to Cambridge and, according to Enid, was 'more or less a favourite of the Prince of Wales'.[5] He attended the fateful farewell dinner for the Prince in December where proceedings were interrupted by the news that his father Prince Albert had died.

Yet on 23 May 1862 Augustus Frederick Guest also died. He was twenty-one. The cause of death was rheumatic pericarditis and congestion of both lungs. He died at Canford in the presence of the faithful Luff. Having survived the precariousness of being an early Victorian baby and the diseases so prevalent in Merthyr, it was especially tragic that he should be struck down in the year he came of age. What adds a particular twist and sadness to the episode is the possibility that Lady Charlotte or, more likely, Charles, was a carrier of the infection which led to his illness and death.

On 7 March Lady Charlotte had heard that Ivor had scarlet fever at Königsberg. She left immediately to nurse him. Charles accompanied her but returned alone in early April. Ivor was now recovering though his mother had a mild attack of the fever. It is difficult to piece together exactly what happened and the precise timing, since Lady Charlotte's journal was suspended during this period. It seems, however, that Augustus acquired a streptoccal infection from someone who had, or was a carrier of, scarlet fever and, as a result of this, after a short delay the infection spread to the joints which became swollen (rheumatic fever) and the lining of the heart (rheumatic pericarditis), the latter proving fatal.

It was not Augustus's death alone which caused Lady Charlotte to cease writing, since there had been a gap since 23 September 1859. During the unrecorded period she had become a grandmother. Alice Maria Du Cane was born on 1 April 1861 and, eight days later, Katherine married the Curate Cecil Alderson. Montague Albemarle

Bertie, son and heir at Uffington, was born and Pegus died. All of this was recollected when Lady Charlotte wrote a brief résumé of the period in her journal on 1 January 1863. Yet it is what she does not say that stands out. She admitted, 'How long it is since I have written here – months, nay years! and now I am going to force myself to try and write again, though indeed with sad heart and broken spirits – Alas, how much of sorrow I have gone through since last I wrote here in September 1859.' Otherwise there is no mention at all of the loss of her son.

Augustus was buried at Canford yet there is no memorial tablet inscribed to his memory, though lavish tablets commemorate other family members and even Luff. Nor for many years could Lady Charlotte bring herself to mention Augustus in the journal and even then the terse references show her determination to put on a stoical front. The first acknowledgement of him came in September 1873, over eleven years after his death, and the poignant entry suggests something of the inner torment she battled against. She visited Heidelberg and it was 'connected in my mind with very sacred memories – my dear boy having staid [sic] there so many happy months – It was a trial to go there – but these feelings should be mastered – at all events in appearance.' Five years later came an oblique reference to the date of his death, 'my saddest anniversary'. By 1880 she was less severe on herself, 'I mooned and wept over a book that I had just received, The Memoirs of the Cambridge A.D.C. which had many notices of my dear, dear boy and recalled many memories. But he is at rest.'[6]

There is a further gap in the journal from the start of 1863 to May 1869. It seems that the volumes covering this six-year period have been lost since previously Lady Charlotte had provided updates for gaps in subsequent volumes. The entries for May 1869 are preceded by no such summary and no explanation is given for the very different emphases in the new journal – in content and format. The eighteen regular journals were now replaced with smaller, mostly soft-covered notebooks which could be carried more easily on travels. The first extant number of the 'Ceramic Memoranda' set the pattern for those to follow. In addition to entries for the day were accounts of purchases. The journal had become a vehicle for recounting travels collecting china abroad (between 1869 and 1882) and the period between trips was either summarized or ignored. Entries were often written up a few days later with Lady Charlotte staying up or rising early to write. They nevertheless capture the impulsive and compulsive spirit of the collector.

Unfortunately the six-year gap makes it impossible to establish precisely how, why and when the Schreibers became such passionate pioneers of china-collecting. Certainly by May 1869 they knew what they were doing. Collecting often seems to run in families and Ivor was a collector of fine arts (including silver and furniture) and his interest may have initially been stimulated by his European tour. Enid later collected jewellery. She was given a sixteen-diamond bracelet by the Turkish Sultan and also possessed a bracelet made up by Phillips Brothers, London from a seal found by Henry, most probably at Nimrud. Merthyr and Monty also collected. The latter left his badges, tokens and passes to the British Museum, and his interest in china led to the two-volume publication of his mother's 'Notes Ceramic' (journal entries) described as 'Confidences of a Collector of Ceramics and Antiques' in 1911 soon after his death (completed by his assistant Egan Mew). Although eliminating some personal details such as Charles's toothache and the tribulations of Lindsey, it is a very rich source for the collector of porcelain, earthenware, enamel, glass and much else. In his introduction Monty suggested that his mother began collecting seriously in the mid-1860s. Fortunately, a copy of the Schreiber catalogue of the couple's English collection survives, personally annotated by Lady Charlotte (it was given to A.W. Franks of the British Museum). It matches her acquisitions to the pieces and reveals that she purchased the earliest piece in the collection, a pair of square Chelsea pedestals (with the supports moulded as griffins) for £15 in June 1864. A number of items now in the Schreiber collection housed at the Victoria and Albert Museum in London were bought in southern England, Bath, London and elsewhere over the next few years. This catalogue also reveals a European trip in 1867. Two Bristol jugs were acquired from an Amsterdam dealer and purchases were made in Paris, Cologne, Hanover and Hamburg. A pair of branch candelabra (damaged) which had been part of a service given by George III and Queen Caroline to her brother the Duke of Mecklenberg-Strelitz got snapped up in Hamburg. The Schreibers were definitely abroad in August and September 1867 whilst young Enid's journal for that year reveals that she stayed at Canford, then had several months with Miss Kemble at Langham House, Portland Place, the Schreibers' new home.[7]

Although the full force of 'china mania' only seems to have gripped Lady Charlotte in the 1860s, she had long been interested in collecting. It was, after all, an age with a reverence for counting, collating and classifying, whether it be species, census statistics or keeping journals. For Lady Charlotte the transition from the Dowlais fossil collection to china also symbolized the shift from the world of production and utility to that of leisure, from concern with invention, change and the future to art, appreciation (in both senses of the word) and a new kind of admiration for the past. It was a move which had more in common with her own class than her earlier industrial interests had shown.

At Canford (which was itself conducive to building up collections of beautiful objects) Lady Charlotte had taken over her cousin Edgar Layard's collection of stuffed birds from Ceylon. Some interest in antiques (though this word is not used) had also been apparent during her first marriage. Sir John does not seem to have shared this. For example, when Lady Charlotte persuaded him to visit a York collector she saw 'one or two trifles I might have liked but Merthyr was so afraid of losing the train that I hardly caught a moment to glance at them'. Charles would always have risked missing a train for the sake of china, something which gave him and Lady Charlotte a rare sense of partnership at a time when so much emphasis was placed on employment for men and leisure for ladies. The Schreibers defied this duality and turned leisure into hard but enjoyable and rewarding work.

Sir John did enjoy paintings, though Lady Charlotte did not find those at Dowlais House really to her taste. She frequently reiterated that she was no judge of paintings. She seems initially to have seen this as her husband's interest but later the comment assumed a different meaning, that is, that *unlike* other branches of fine arts, notably china-collecting, she did not view herself as an expert on paintings. Sir John gave Lady Charlotte Penry Williams's *Procession To The Christening* as a wedding present and this sat on her desk. They bought a portrait at the famous Strawberry Hill sale of 1842 and later purchased many pictures for Canford. The accomplished picture-cleaner and dealer Alexander Barker obtained thirty-seven pictures for them at one Phillips sale in 1849 and ten Italian primitives from another sale. Lady Charlotte was especially interested in anything with family connections and they purchased from Bertie Mathew (heir of the Duke of Ancaster) a Reynolds painting of her father.

By the 1850s, Lady Charlotte's knowledge and interest in china was increasing. She requested some Cochin-China eggs through the Dowlais Iron Company's links with India and in October 1852 received a letter from Poole asking her as 'a collector of Old China' whether she would be interested in viewing the collection of a local man who had recently died. The exodus from Canford in 1856 involved taking furniture and 'a good deal of my much valued China' to Spring Gardens 'for besides that I am fond of seeing it and having it with me, there is nothing that sets off a house to so much advantage'.

Perhaps the greatest incentive came from foreign travel. The Guests had visited Dresden in 1842 and in terms which might be said to parallel the steps in acquiring expertise, Lady Charlotte outlined the stages from the unglazed brown of 1708, to the first attempt at white, experiments with blue and then 'the rapid strides of improvement from good to better and from better to perfection. Lucky the alchemist, who failing in discovering the philosopher's stone, hit upon so delicate an invention.' The Victorian diarist and poet A.J. Munby described (somewhat disparagingly) the contemporary lady of leisure as the Dresden china type of lady. Appropriately enough, Dresden helped stimulate Lady Charlotte's interest, but in such a way that the chance of a good piece of porcelain would in future years produce a seemingly boundless energy and activity, far removed from the Victorian couch. The Guests also visited Sèvres (in 1851), 'here some of the specimens were clever, and ingenious and elaborate – but all wanted the *taste* of older times'.

Lady Charlotte never forgot the gypsy at Uffington who had foretold that it would be her lot to travel 'much and far' but it was marriage to Charles which finally provided the chance for sustained travelling. Unlike Sir John, Charles did not work for his living and he shared with his wife a love of fine arts and new places. In October 1857 they attended the Art Treasures Exhibition in Manchester, the city's answer to the Great Exhibition, and the first real opportunity for the public at large to view pictures, sculpture and ornamental art belonging to private collectors. The Ancient Masters section alone included over 1,000 entries.

Wealthy employers and landowners sent workers there on special outings and the average daily attendance was about 9,000. Lady Charlotte noted how much it meant to Charles: 'Having no profession, no pursuit at this particular moment, I cannot describe how pleased I was to see how heartily he threw himself into the spirit of all around him.' She viewed this visit as 'quite an epoch in our history'. On both a national and personal level it revealed just how seriously something of genuine interest could be pursued. The Schreibers spent five full consecutive days at the exhibition examining the pieces to the accompaniment of Hallé and his orchestra. One day there was a great rush prompted by a (false) rumour that Florence Nightingale was present. Lady Charlotte had contributed three of Penry Williams's paintings. Following their sustained art lesson, the Schreibers visited the Potteries and were shown over Minton's works by his nephew.

By 1869 the opportunities for travel abroad had increased. Three daughters were now married and the youngest, Blanche, was eighteen. Although Charles became MP for Cheltenham in 1865 he did not stand again at the 1868 election. Foreign travel probably helped divert Lady Charlotte's mind from the death of her son. It was a welcome release from responsibility after the demands of managing Dowlais and the tension surrounding her second marriage. Her active mind and past history suggested that she needed fresh stimulation. Although she was fifty-seven by the date of her first recorded ceramics tour she was hardly one to be deterred by age.

As with so many of her ventures, the timing was perfect. The passion for china-collecting had not yet caught on and collecting by non-professionals was in its infancy. George IV had collected French porcelain and so stimulated interest, but as yet, there was little serious and systematic collecting.[8] The Schreibers were interested in the less well-researched collection of ceramics which meant that the field was wide open to them; and though not professionals in the sense of earning their living from this source, they were never mere dilettantes.

Wonderful bargains could be picked up at this time. With an abundant supply and very little demand, there was no great need for fakes (though they were not unknown), and anyway the market did not remain static. Such a new art also meant that there was little accumulated knowledge available and they had to learn by trial and error. There appears to have been only one serious book available with photographic illustrations, Chaffer's *Keramic Gallery* (1872). Few collectors' books existed though Lady Charlotte had possessed a copy of Joseph Marryat's *Collections Towards a History of Pottery and Porcelain* (covering the fifteenth to eighteenth centuries) since 1853.

Part of the secret of her success lay in her capacity for research developed in her work on *The Mabinogion*. Indeed the notes accompanying the Schreiber collection are reminiscent of those in the Welsh work, with their emphasis on historical allusions. Whenever possible Lady Charlotte read up on a subject, perused old sales catalogues and attended factories and potteries. At Sèvres, for example, the Schreibers made careful enquiries about dating, gilders and decorators, so sharpening their ability to attribute pieces correctly. They also visited many museums and sought out local experts, sometimes using interpreters. Lady Charlotte always made the most of opportunities. When she learned that the Director of the Musée Céramique was travelling on their train from Rouen, 'we commenced our attack' and showed the captive traveller the collecting basket. In 1879 Dr Schneider, an authority at Fulda, visited them and through him they viewed antiquities being shown to a royal party. The Dresden Museum was an old favourite and being known there Lady Charlotte was admitted even when it was closed to the public. Fétis, the Belgian collector, art critic and librarian at the Royal Library in Brussels, became a friend. They researched in libraries and attended exhibitions, including the Paris Exposition of 1878.

Lady Charlotte's networks of well-connected acquaintances proved a valuable entrée. She and Charles travelled armed with letters of introduction. In 1874 the Queen of Holland invited them twice to her palace. In the same year they visited the Earl of Salisbury's château at Pûy (Katherine had married Lady Salisbury's brother, and her son Augustus, christened in memory of Augustus Guest, was staying there at the same time). With such contacts they were well placed to visit private houses and sales. Henry Layard was now a diplomat in Spain and this helped open doors, though Lady Charlotte observed that residents benefited most since dealers bargained for them with the grandees who were gradually selling off their treasures. During one visit to Henry and Enid the Schreibers were joined by Henry Cole. (It was Cole who had organized the Great Exhibition and whose Museum of Manufactures formed the nucleus of what would eventually become the Victoria and Albert Museum.) Colin Minton Campbell (Thomas Minton's nephew and manager of the works) was also in the party.

Sometimes the Schreibers' research took a practical turn. In 1870 their persistence prompted the proprietor of the Fulham works to investigate the old office ledgers where were found the notebooks of John Dwight, the seventeenth-century potter who claimed to have discovered 'the mystery of transparent earthenware'. The first porcelain factory in England dated from 1744. The Schreibers joined in excavations at the site in Bow (now, in 1868, the home of a match factory), and specimens of the different stages of early manufacture and old moulds were uncovered. They purchased the 'memorandum books' of John Bowcocke, who worked there in the eighteenth century.

Although Lady Charlotte's collection is well supplied with Bow china, her focus was on the rarer products rather than on the blue and white wares of Bow's heyday. Indeed, like any good collector she had an eye for what was currently unfashionable and might prove a good investment for the future. Fortunately for her, much middle-class taste veered towards modern wares, old items often being associated with poverty, whilst the interest in older china which began to develop tended to favour the oriental blue and white. Lady Charlotte was disparaging about this 'ridiculous rage now in England' popularized by Whistler and others.

Although Monty acknowledged that Charles was a great help in identifying and collecting china, he maintained that in reality his mother was 'the leading spirit, *she* was the fine judge'. His loyalty was unquestionably towards the memory of his mother and, like the rest of his family, he may have been less than favourably disposed towards his stepfather. John Mortlock (who owned a London china emporium) confirmed that Lady Charlotte was the superior partner, claiming that nearly all he knew about china was learned from her. It is nevertheless worth noting that Lady Charlotte wrote of purchases and judgement in the plural tense which she would not have done had she felt that decisions were hers alone. Occasionally an independent opinion was registered – a pair of buckles bought in Paris were thought by Charles to be Chelsea-Derby though Lady Charlotte disagreed. Expert opinion later concurred with his view. Certainly the Schreibers seem to have worked well as a team just as that other prolific diarist, Beatrice Webb, had a 'partnership' with her husband, Sidney. When Charles had bronchitis Lady Charlotte recorded missing 'my own dear companion very much' adding that: 'It seems that as if we do not fully understand or enter into anything unless we see it together.' Their taste was harmonious though there were occasional references to items which one prized more highly than the other.

As in the past, Lady Charlotte combined her ability for single-minded obsessive interest with her business acumen. The couple only bought if they thought the price right and the following extract gives some notion of how they struck deals. In this case they were in Brussels and the journal describes part of one day's work in March 1874:

> We strolled into Stroobant's shop on the Boulevard d'Anvers before going home to dinner: He is so dear that we have never been able to buy anything of [sic] him, nor expected now to find anything à notre portée. It was a sort of forlorn hope. He showed us a very fine Chelsea figure of Justice, 15 inches high, and quite perfect; we asked the price – £20. For us this was out of the question; there was nothing else in our line and we came away. Old Stroobant followed us out into the street – Would we make an offer for the figure? We declined to do so because, we said, we could not come anything near the price he asked and therefore it would be useless. He then said he thought we might have the figure for £14 – a vast reduction! We said we would consider it and call again in the evening. When we did go he was out; we went a second time and saw Madame, and left her with a note saying we would give £12 10s and would call on Monday for an answer. We overhauled the figure again and were satisfied that it was very fine. This little transaction occupied most of the evening.[9]

The next day they returned to the shop. Stroobant had left word that as they were old customers (they were actually old browsers rather than customers) they should have the figure at the price they offered. This figure (now thought to be Derby) is in the Schreiber collection. It dates from about 1765 but is now slightly damaged.

In 1869 (with the exception of Germany) 'as a *rule* we have bought at about half the English market value and in some cases at much less', Milanese dealers possessed 'taste but only a little knowledge' a heady combination, 'one *might* make great trouvailles there'. In Amsterdam they got a perfect Bristol figure of a youth holding a comb for £7 since the dealer did not know what it was. They were able to take advantage of the scant knowledge of English china amongst many European dealers: indigenous European or oriental china was more in vogue on the Continent and the Schreibers recognized that they could obtain Bow, Bristol and other figures much more cheaply there than in their native country. Nevertheless they had to work hard to track down supplies of eighteenth-century English china, and by no means all places they visited yielded results. For example, Lady Charlotte discovered that 'English china seems unknown in Florence'. In a sense she was reversing the trend – in the previous century noblemen had ransacked Europe to bring back European treasures to fill their country houses. Now this nineteenth-century noblewoman was combing Europe, not just for European china but, wherever possible, for English samples which she could bring back home.

Between May 1869 and October 1882 the Schreibers made twenty-three Continental tours. The length of their stays varied from short visits of a month or so to long ones of about four months. Most years they made at least two trips abroad, the first generally in the spring or perhaps encompassing a more ambitious summer tour from early May to August. Later would follow the autumn tour which tended to end in mid-November. In 1874 they went abroad three times, whilst in 1877 and 1878 they were away for more months than they were home. Blanche was married in April 1875 and, as Lady Charlotte explained, she now had no home ties and 'my dear husband and I are free to roam as we will'. Once Charles became MP for Poole (1880) they had to wait until the end of the Parliamentary season before fleeing the country. The later tours were slightly less frenetic than previously and this is reflected in the journals, which revert to a more daily routine of writing and recording home affairs after the rather breathless stopgaps between trips which had for a time sufficed for recounting life in Britain.

The Schreibers became familiar with much of the map of Europe, showing more geographical adventurousness as time wore on, doubtless stimulated in part by the need to find new markets as the passion for collecting spread to the countries they had once appeared to monopolize. Thus from Belgium, France, Germany and Holland, the mainstays of their original collecting trips, they branched out into countries such as Portugal, Poland, Denmark and Sweden.

Charles was a keen huntsman and the language Lady Charlotte used to describe these European trips became that of the chase. In Venice they were 'hunting the curiosity shops'. She described how they 'fell into a snare' at one dealer's, referred to 'our best hunting grounds' and numerous 'forays'; the aggressive language suggests almost ruthless energy and activity. After the French word 'chasse' the most frequent description was that of 'ransacking' towns and shops. They arrived in Gouda 'barely in time to save daylight enough to ransack the old dealers' stocks'. They 'prowled'

Seville and 'swept' the Quai Voltaire in Paris, whilst their thoroughness is suggested in a reference to the first day's 'operation' in a new town and by an entry beginning 'Determined to beat up Holland in detail, and find if any English china was to be met with there'. Nor was the language inappropriate: two weeks in Belgium and Holland in 1876 produced ninety-one pieces to be sent home. There were also mining metaphors. For example they 'struck a new Vein' in 1875. With her propensity for foreign languages Lady Charlotte quite often substituted words such as the French 'trouvailles' in preference to the more mundane 'finds'. Shops were usually called 'curiosity shops' but she sometimes called them 'prenderia' in Spain

She was unsparing in her criticism of shops with worthless goods. After all, one of the benefits of keeping a journal is that it permits frankness. More than one dealer was pronounced 'mad' in the journal. Yet they returned year after year to some: Eva Krug at Rotterdam would pack up their goods and dispatch them by sea, and other dealers exchanged pieces with them or looked out for what they wanted. When two old ladies were reluctant to part with a dinner service in Utrecht, Lady Charlotte left instructions for Van Gorkum to keep an eye on it. A Bruges dealer gave them a 1641 Lambeth Whit-Wine jug found on the Ostend coast, and in gratitude the Schreibers took him specimens of Samian ware. Sometimes they took goods bought in one country or city to receive an expert second opinion elsewhere. The relative prosperity or decline of the dealers can be charted through their travels. When they visited the Barcelona house of the jeweller Carrera they were 'charmed at such indications of prosperity and think it augurs well that its tradesmen are able to inhabit such quarters'.

If dealers got too expensive they were simply struck out of the address book. Pieces surplus to the Schreibers' collection were sometimes sold to dealers; at a time when it could be very difficult to get instant credit abroad, even for the Schreibers, it was a handy way of obtaining extra foreign currency. The dealers came to understand their needs and made arrangements with them. For example, many Dutch dealers were Jewish and in October 1882 the Schreibers were in Leuwaarden during the Feast of Tabernacles. In order to circumvent the problem of doing business on a holiday, Lady Charlotte agreed that the salt-glaze teapot she wanted should be a 'present'. The understanding was that she would send the dealer the payment once his religious observance was over. So eager were some dealers to see them back in town that they would appear at Lady Charlotte's hotel sometimes even before breakfast. In March 1874 a Rotterdam dealer presented himself at the hotel and 'what was my astonishment and delight when he displayed before my bewildered eyes no less than 5 beautiful Bristol figures'. He thought them Chelsea and after some 'parleying' (a rather more genteel word than 'bargaining' or 'haggling') she had them for £32. They are in the collection and include a figure of a boy with a hurdy-gurdy and a girl dancing.

The hours the Schreibers worked are impressive, especially when it is remembered that Lady Charlotte was close to seventy by the time of the last 'chasse' in 1882. There are descriptions of walking round shops for seven or eight hours a day and most of this time (usually between midday and 7 p.m.) they would be clutching precious and heavy items. Sometimes they combined walking with travelling by carriage and even when assured that they would find nothing in a town being scoured for the first time, they would discover something hidden away. Lady Charlotte claimed that walking restored her strength and it was invariably Charles who flagged first. He seemed to suffer from headaches and colds, relieved by poppy heads!

They were used to their punishing routines, but Lady Charlotte's maid got rather a shock when she had to substitute for Charles. After walking from 1.30 to 5.30 for the sole purpose of ascertaining that nothing could be found – a need only intelligible to the committed collector – the exhausted maid had to be sent home. A 'normal' day's work was not interrupted by rain or snow: the 'faithful old water proof' served well. A long day in one town would be succeeded by rising perhaps as early as 4 or 5 a.m. to catch a train somewhere to begin again. From large centres such as The Hague day trips were conducted to mop up any finds in surrounding areas. Sir Joseph Joel Duveen (the international art dealer who founded Duveen Brothers) told Monty that whilst looking for objects in Holland he heard of a wonderful cache in a remote village. Just as he neared it a triumphant Lady Charlotte was being driven away. London dealers admitted that they stood little chance if she was known to be anywhere in the vicinity of good china. The Schreibers reached Bremen at 3 a.m. on one occasion, and went to bed at 4, but were soon with the dealers; the following day they visited fourteen shops in Hamburg. Nor did the work end when they returned to the hotel. China had to be carefully examined, washed and recorded, and numerous letters written to arrange future itineraries, sales at home, and deal with commissions for family and friends.

They returned time and again to some city hotels but were not always able to stay where they wanted. At Arnhem they were tormented by mice, fleas and mosquitoes in their rooms. It was a far cry from the comfort of Canford. Once in Valladolid, where the hotels were either full or dirty, they spent the night in an omnibus parked in a yard. Lady Charlotte mentioned that the maid was frightened and did concede that she herself remained quite still, 'for it did not seem to me that we were altogether safe. Although the gates were supposed to be locked men now and then came in and out of them, as if in a bad dream – and sleep seemed to be impossible, from the stamping and neighing of horses and mules, the crowing and cackling of cocks and hens, and above all, the tinkling of a bell attached to a very restless, playful goat.'

Unlike some diarists, for whom life seems to have been composed of one gargantuan meal interspersed by brief interludes, Lady Charlotte was never bothered about recording details of meals. She might mention something exceptional and was amused at Zutphen when a menu offered 'Dukes with Champions' (Ducks with mushrooms) but 'I am no epicure, nor care what I eat'. Rather than recounting food, Lady Charlotte's journal gave details of china purchases in a way which enables us to consider why it is that people collect and how, then and now, once hooked, their energy and enthusiasm know few bounds.

Today it is easy to underestimate just how difficult, hazardous and lengthy were many of their journeys through Europe, journeys which are now covered in comparative luxury at speed. Fortunately; 'A Railway always does me good.' They never wasted time. When Charles got left behind at Gouda station when changing tickets he spent the extra half hour dashing back into town to look at stock. Many of their train and carriage journeys were demanding: they had sixteen changes between the Hague and Brussels – in one day. They generally travelled first class and often saved precious time by using sleepers, where Lady Charlotte was responsible for waking up Charles and any fellow travellers. Porters would recognize them 'laden as usual, almost to inconvenience'. Lady Charlotte's red velvet bag went everywhere, as did the collecting basket. Feeling the weight of individual items such as their Chelsea figures, it is difficult to imagine how they managed, let alone how most items survived intact. Some goods didn't, and were repaired by Mintons. Although most buys were shipped home, the Schreibers tended to keep their most precious finds with them.

They were remarkably lucky with customs officers, though there were some nasty moments. Not surprisingly given the history of Alsace-Lorraine (annexed to Germany in 1871 after the Franco Prussian war) it was difficult to cross the border there. All their Venetian glass had to be opened and examined in 1873. In the same year Belgian officials were told that their goods were *objets d'art* and so were not opened, though 'we have so many boxes and baskets full of china etc. that it will be a miracle if all arrive safely in England'. Since there were usually some incomplete or broken pieces officials tended to accept the Schreibers as collectors exempt from tax. Lady Charlotte was much amused at the Belgian border when one official dismissed the china as modern and worthless. (She did add that if her hand box and red bag had been searched as well as the collecting basket, he might not have been so convinced.) Occasionally they had to pay a small tax. Only once was anything irretrievably lost or stolen – Lady Charlotte's pocket was picked at Toledo after buying some buckles and ornaments.

They were not just indulging in a hobby. Some goods were later sold for profit which helped finance further ventures, and pieces which were duplicated were sold, usually in sales held by Christie's, Sotheby's, Phillips and Bonham's. In 1875, for example, Lady Charlotte received letters from Christie's 'on account of our sale – not quite so successful as I could have hoped, though many things did marvellously well'. In March 1872 she disposed of 132 lots of miscellaneous china and enamels for just over £200.

So, what exactly were the Schreibers looking for? Their name today is largely associated with the impressive Schreiber collection which takes up much of Room 139 of the Victoria and Albert Museum. Yet this represents by no means the sum total of their collecting years since the 1,800 pieces cover only their English ceramics. The European specimens went to relatives, though Christie's sold some.* The Schreibers sometimes branched out: in addition to buying fans

---

* See Appendix 5B.

they obtained a cinquecento jewel for £8 in Paris thanks to the 'ignorant French dealer', and they spotted bargains for others. After seeing a 1760s' gold watch with Prince of Wales feathers which formerly belonged to Charles Edward the Pretender, Lady Charlotte wrote to the Windsor Castle librarian. She was asked to purchase it for £80 (it was on sale for £100), did this and then discovered that the buyer was Queen Victoria. They also helped find items for Ivor.

Yet, as Appendix 5A shows, the major concentration was on building up a comprehensive and interesting collection for the future. They were compulsive buyers. When the London dealer Kerridge brought Lady Charlotte a salt-glazed stoneware teapot and cover depicting the capture of Portobello on one side and a figure of Admiral Vernon on the other (one of her fans commemorated the same event), she felt it to be 'very desirable, very ugly and very dear'. He wanted £5 'but of course I must have it'.

They tended not to collect medieval or Renaissance work, not least because their financial resources were not unlimited. Nor did they appreciate very modern designs, 'vile' modern French taste or 'modern trash' in general. Even Minton was a little too modern for their liking, 'Minton does wonderful things but he cannot attain to the tone of the old people.' They were charmed by ceramics of the second half of the eighteenth century where, interestingly, their preference for the more restrained styles – for example, a fondness for the Chelsea of the 1750s rather than the lavish and ornate gold anchor period – may have clashed with contemporary taste but is appreciated today.★

A recent book on enamel boxes has described Lady Charlotte as 'the doyenne' of English collectors of eighteenth-century *objets d'art*. The Schreiber collection includes many types of Battersea enamels such as wine labels, sacred plaques and snuff boxes. Although she usually paid a few pounds for such items, one day in Utrecht she spent £35 on Battersea enamels. One of her greatest 'trouvailles' was an enamel figure of the Emperor Charles V on a globe, purchased for 100 florins (equivalent to about £8.33 today). Careful research revealed that it had been the boss from the plume of a suit of armour given by the Emperor to a sixteenth-century Harlingen man who had built an orphanage. Sarlins offered them £100 for this treasure and when he realized that they would not part with it, admitted that it was worth £250.

Wedgwood had been heavily exported to Europe in the eighteenth century and the Schreibers picked up some good bargains, including a dinner service (155 pieces) and dessert service for £15 in Holland and a black coffee set with Etruscan decoration signed Wedgwood and Bentley. One of their most curious and protracted purchases was a gourd-shaped tin-glazed earthenware bottle painted with a lake scene and tulips in bright polychrome. In March 1875 Charles had taken some china into Holland for shipping home and Lady Charlotte amused herself by writing up an account of the bottle.[10] She entitled this 'The Adventure of a Bottle'. Written in the third person it is a parody of the novel of sensibility with echoes of

---

★ See Appendix 5A.

Sterne's *A Sentimental Journey*. It is also reminiscent of the style of some of the pieces Lady Charlotte had helped compose for the family magazine *Canfordiana* produced by the Canford press. It traced the fate of the bottle from the time Charles purchased it in Holland in February 1873. The Hague painter Bisschop had not considered it of value and, the Schreibers therefore sold it to an amateur via a Utrecht dealer. On returning to Utrecht that autumn they discovered that the customer had returned it as it was not Delft. Charles repurchased it then sold it in a sale for £18.

The following summer at the Musée Céramique in Rouen, 'oh horror! oh despair! What should meet their eyes, set on the most conspicuous shelf in the very place of honour, but bottles exactly similar in style, shape and decoration to that which they had once possessed and in an evil hour had sacrificed! ... And now indeed there was wailing and gnashing of teeth! It was almost more than Amateur nature could endure.' In more sober tones in her daily journey Lady Charlotte admitted that they had sacrificed something very valuable – 'These things will happen to the best regulated Collectors – but alas ...' Her story presented the couple as sadder and wiser. Yet in Brussels that autumn Lady Charlotte suddenly espied the long lost and much lamented bottle 'whose very history is a romance'. They paid 40 francs for it and were told that it was by the celebrated Italian decorator of Rouen ware, Denys Dorio. As a postscript to this, in 1935 the expert W.B. Honey reattributed the piece to Germany (Harau) and the decoration to the Nuremburg painter Johannes Heel.

This incident, with its implicit rejection of hasty action repented at length and reward for perseverance also shows how, despite the story involving more than one country, the Schreibers were nevertheless operating within a fairly small world of *cognoscenti*. Yet this world was beginning to expand and soon others, both amateur and professional, would join the trail. By 1874 Lady Charlotte was complaining that 'the ideas the Dutch have formed now of prices is ridiculous' and two years later she remarked on the number of London dealers 'flitting about' The Hague. A rare note of disenchantment began to creep in: at Ghent the shops were 'never so ill supplied with fine things, and what little they have is very dear' and at Prague in 1877 a Vienna dealer was picking up all that was worth having. They had themselves helped stimulate what would become very big business.

Americans were now starting to pay 'great attention to antiquities'. One was Mrs Moore who was in Europe buying pieces for a museum her husband had started. She was fervently buying goods but Lady Charlotte was not impressed by her money or her sense, 'She has little knowledge and I do not think her selection will be a very interesting one'. She felt sorry for her, though, as it was not easy for a woman to travel on her own, and understandably she rather clung to the Schreibers. She had a habit of popping up wherever they went, even in Scandinavia.

The more interest in collecting old china, the greater the temptation to produce forgeries. In 1873 the Schreibers saw reproductions being made at Marseilles at Ferdinand Gaidan's workshop 'some of them (his Satsuma, his Fäience Emaillée etc.) most successful'. They heard about *contrefaçons* in Alsace-Lorraine, and forgeries produced aroundTournai but painted in Paris and passed off as good Sèvres. Four years later they visited a Monsieur Bock at Tournai. He had a room full of biscuit figures 'done from the old models and also a quantity of white vases of the old Sèvres forms' which followed this route.They tracked some of it down in Paris; Lady Charlotte felt sure that it would not deceive a true connoisseur. They also found copies of Sèvres at a pottery at St Amand employing about 400 people.To this source could be traced forgeries ofWorcester china using imported china clay.They saw a forged Worcester plate at the 1878 Paris Exhibition, 'very derogatory to our English reputation' and the Schreiber collection includes a pair ofWorcester teacups purchased in Bordeaux for £1 10s and bearing a forged Sèvres mark. Lady Charlotte's descriptions of the production of fakes provides vital information for historians of china and today's collectors. Frank Herrmann, writer on ceramics, stresses that her 'evident familiarity with every variant of fake and forged mark must have been almost unique' at the time.

Very occasionally the Schreibers were themselves deceived. In 1876 they purchased for £6 a silver gilt ring reputed to have belonged to Pope Pius II, said to have been found on his tomb. In Paris, this and a wax head of Marie de' Medici (both purchased in Amsterdam) were pronounced forgeries by the expert Davilliers, 'So they cannot be admitted into the collection, but must take their chance at Christie's.' Spanish vases bought in Madrid were later discarded after a Parisian admitted making their covers. Lady Charlotte was always her own most serious critic.Amongst the numerous purchases at 'my beloved Dresden' in 1869 were a silver copy of Luther's wedding ring (£7 10s) and an enamel flacon, apparentlyVenetian. Both were forgeries so 'I look back to our short stay with anything but pleasure'.Yet significantly none of these forgeries had been in their real area of expertise, English ceramics. When in 1873 a little figure they had purchased and believed perfect was examined and its fingers found to be damaged, Lady Charlotte declared it to be 'a drawback on our supposed good buying – and rather a censure on our circumspection'.

On some trips travelling companions from England joined them. In 1874, for example, Sir Tatton and Lady Sykes teamed up with the Schreibers,[11] and occasionally Ivor and Cornelia met them in Paris. They took Bertie with them a couple of times, though he was a bit of a liability as he tended to wander off without warning.When not engaged in frenetic searching for china they would visit cathedrals and comment on architecture (Lady Charlotte's intolerance of Catholic practices had not abated). If possible, they would attend Protestant services and the English church at The Hague was a familiar spot.There were definite preferences amongst cities:Vienna might rank next to Paris in scale of buildings but Lady Charlotte felt 'no love or sympathy for it'; the city was 'all show and modern tinsel'.Venice, on the other hand, was 'the pick of the whole earth'.

Running through the journals for these years is an infectious sense of adventure. Whereas purchasing gowns was always 'a troublesome business', searching out old china was pure pleasure. Just how far Lady Charlotte had moved from her former interests can be gauged by her dismissive comment on a French mining town

– 'utterly uninteresting'. Delay in England for any length of time was greeted with impatience.

Yet the Schreibers did not waste time in England. They avidly discussed china with the family. When Merthyr, his wife Theodora and the Wimbornes arrived in London, 'We flew to the enamel cabinets and saw and talked all we could.' They attended fine arts exhibitions and collectors visited them. One Frenchman who spent three days examining their collection was especially intrigued by their Sèvres medallion of the Chained Negro with its inscription of 'Ne suis-je pas un homme, un frère?' This had been officially suppressed in France as inflammatory.

Despite their wanderlust and eagerness for bargains abroad, they still collected at home even though it tended to be more costly. Although Monty's volumes give the impression that the overwhelming source of their collection was western Europe, a survey of Lady Charlotte's annotated catalogue actually reveals that they bought rather more in England than may previously have been recognized. Taking a random sample of six pages from this catalogue, with a page each from the sections of Bow figures and enamels, Chelsea figures, Derby, Worcester, Chelsea scent-bottles and Staffordshire salt-glaze, only twenty-three out of the sixty-two items listed on these six pages were actually acquired on the Continent. The other thirty-nine, that is, well over half, came from sales and shops in England. Lady Charlotte bought regularly from London dealers such as Partridge, Wareham, Bulton, Dalgliesh, Brookes, Jacobs and others. She received a number of gifts – a glass scent-bottle from one of Mr Pegus's sisters, for example, as well as presents from her children and pieces from A.W. Franks. Some exchanges were made. A pair of Chelsea dwarfs inspired by a Callot drawing came to the Schreibers from Emerson Norman, a Norwich dealer, who received in return two Bow vases with damaged flowers (which had cost £5) and a Chelsea-Derby cup and saucer (also £5). The Schreibers travelled to sales in different parts of the country and kept in touch with collectors such as William Edkins of Bristol. Although the great china-collecting days ended with Charles's death, Lady Charlotte continued to make some purchases and, for example, viewed and bought from the sale of china at Christie's in 1885 the collection of her late friend Lady Hopetoun.

In the introduction to her catalogue of the Schreiber collection Lady Charlotte explained that the most valuable addition they ever made was in the autumn of 1868. Then they acquired all the Bristol and Plymouth porcelain which had passed to descendants of William Cookworthy, the Plymouth apothecary who had patented the hard-paste Plymouth porcelain 100 years earlier. His descendants 'willingly ceded' their treasures to the Schreibers so that they would not be dispersed.

By concentrating on European travel, the 'Notes Ceramic' edited by Monty convey the impression that Lady Charlotte almost invariably paid ridiculously low prices for the pieces she acquired. Although this was in many ways true, especially in the early years in Europe when they would pay the equivalent of a few shillings or pounds for beautiful examples of eighteenth-century British products, it was not so often the case in their country of origin. It may well have been less easy to barter and bargain in such home terrain where dealers were also familiar with the wares. And in order for us to estimate the value of the prices they were paying we need to multiply the figures by about thirty-two. Using the annotated interleaved volume of the catalogue and Lady Charlotte's accounts, a rather more complex picture emerges of their spending. The most expensive purchase recorded by Lady Charlotte was a set of Bristol figures of children representing the seasons for which she paid £380 to Sanders of Hammersmith in March 1873. Dating from about 1775, the figures bear the modeller's mark 'T'.[12] Sanders also provided the single most expensive item, the most significant piece of Chelsea in their collection. This was the large, ornate group of gold anchor Chelsea known as 'The Music Lesson' but described by Lady Charlotte as a shepherd and shepherdess. For this she paid £364 at Sanders' sale at Christie's. It shows a shepherd boy teaching a shepherdess to play the flute. He has his arms around her, behind is a hawthorn bocage. The study is modelled (with alterations) on Francois Boucher's painting *L'Agréable Leçon*. Lady Charlotte provided an engraving of this with the collection. In 1770 it had been sold for £8. By the end of the nineteenth century it was worth about £500. The Schreibers paid out sizeable sums especially to London dealers. They gave Cavallo, for example, £55 for a Worcester vase and £75 for a Chelsea vase.

Being back in Britain also enabled Lady Charlotte to catch up with her growing number of grandchildren. The height of enjoyment does, however, seem to have been the combination of family, travel and collecting made possible by Henry Layard's diplomatic career and marriage to Enid. Everybody, including it seems from her journal, Enid herself, had been surprised by Henry's declaration of attachment and Enid and Monty had nervously composed a 'very laconic and unsatisfactory' letter to explain the situation to Lady Charlotte. Soon after their marriage Henry became the first accredited Minister in Spain since its 1868 revolution. Despite the turbulent political situation – the Liberal military Republic was threatened by political factions and in particular the opposition of the right wing Carlists – the Schreibers wasted no time in visiting the Layards. It was a risky time to travel. One night a 'small émeute' took place opposite the hotel they had just left in Seville, killing four and wounding twelve. Undeterred they returned again in 1871 when the monarchy was briefly restored, still collecting china and courting danger. At Madrid Lady Charlotte sat for the portrait artist Vincente Palmaroli Y Gonzalez. It is a remarkable picture, depicting Lady Charlotte like a stately widowed señora, surrounded with her life's symbols: porcelain, a fan, the poem of 'Geraint and Enid' (Augustus's nickname had been Geraint) whilst in her hands is a piece of needlework. The Schreibers travelled south with the Layards and briefly visited North Africa.

Their return journey was one of their most eventful. In the wake of the Siege of Paris and end of the Franco-Prussian War, radical French Republicans had set up on 25 March 1871 an elected assembly known as the Paris Commune.

In late May the government (which had fled to Versailles) finally crushed the Communards. It was estimated that 20,000 were killed, about 13,000 were imprisoned and another 7,500 transported. With their knack for being at the centre of action, the Schreibers reached Versailles on 1 June. They travelled in a small market cart pulled by a sturdy horse, feeding off bread, cheese and *vin ordinaire* as they made their 'triumphal entry in the Cart into Versailles'. With difficulty they found some cramped lodgings. They were determined to see Paris. They drove in the woods around St Cloud, learning afterwards that they were full of fleeing Communards, probably 'more fearful of us than we of them'. They saw people bricking up open spaces and cellars as precaution against arson attacks from the *Pétroleuse* who were rumoured to be coming to Versailles. They finally got into Paris on 3 June.

> It was a city of the dead, no life or animation, scarce any one in the streets, not a conveyance to be seen; altogether a most melancholy sight, the Tuileries and other public buildings still smoking … We called at the Lille et d'Albion, where we used to lodge, and found it shut up, but the maid in charge gave us sad accounts of alarms that had been suffered all round from the insurgents. We went also to some of the dealers we had been used to buy of. Mme Caillot and Mme Oppenheim had both died of fright or anxiety. Poor old Fournier had lost his reason …

One woman's house had been threatened with fire so she had hidden her goods. At Mme Flandin's they found some dishes to match their maroon Chelsea set: this was the first sale the shop had seen for months. 'While we were with her there was a great noise in the street, a brougham was going by. We found it contained the celebrated Roussel [a Deputy who had joined the Republicans] who had just been captured. The escort had difficulty in protecting him from the fury of the people. As we returned along the deserted Champs Elysées we met some prisoners, bound and strongly guarded, with a little crowd hooting and menacing them. The whole scene was impressive and very sad, but I would on no account have missed it.' The next day they went to the Gare du Nord and so home.

A third and final visit to the Layards in Spain in 1872 was conducted amidst rumours of bandits stopping trains, and what Lady Charlotte described as 'very alarming accounts of several Carlist risings' proved well-founded. There were troops at stations and 'a revolution may any day be expected'. Yet despite the perilous state of the country they got home safely, though Lady Charlotte worried about her daughter, who at one point had to flee Madrid with the former Regent.

By 1877 Henry had been posted to a new trouble spot. He was now Ambassador in Constantinople. Although Turkey and Russia were at war and the Russians soon advancing on the capital, Lady Charlotte was determined to visit. Meanwhile Enid was enciphering important documents and nursed some of the hundreds of thousands of refugees pouring into the city (St Sophia Mosque held 5,000 of them) and started a smallpox hospital. Not until the Russians were within 8 miles of

Constantinople was a preliminary treaty signed. In mid-June 1878, thanks largely to Henry's work, the Congress of Berlin secured the peace terms. Like good media journalists, the Schreibers were in Berlin *en route* to Turkey. At one Embassy reception the Prime Minister Lord Beaconsfield (formerly Disraeli) 'subsided into an armchair beside me where he remained a long time', and 'We talked of old times – of Spain – of the East and it was very pleasant'.

As a teenager Lady Charlotte had met Lady Macdonald who had ridden on horseback through Russia and the Caucasus. She had written innocently in her journal 'Her enthusiasm for the East nearly approaches mine', and she had dressed up as a 'grave Turk'. Now the Schreibers travelled through Tsarist Russia where Lady Charlotte was appalled by the degraded state of the peasants. They arrived at Turkey in the French mail boat with about 2,000 sheep, some cows and a few passengers. Based at the Embassy's summer residence at Therapia for the next few weeks, Lady Charlotte fulfilled her dreams of the Bosphorus and bazaars, set foot in Asia, watched the Dervishes whirl and declared St Sophia superior to any ecclesiastical building she had ever seen. Whilst Charles innocently found himself in the Green Parlour (the harem) when visiting Princess Nazli, Lady Charlotte admired the Golden Horn from the Embassy at Pera (partly designed by Charles Barry) and compared the Forest of Belgrade to the Welsh Vale of Neath. When they reluctantly left, Lady Charlotte commented: 'Poor devoted country! How will its sad history end – the Turks are so very much the best of the population, if they could only be decently governed – But Russian intrigue will never leave them alone, and one trembles for the future.'

Before long, however, Lady Charlotte was to be trembling for the future of her own husband. In April 1883 Charles's lungs became congested. After her own son's experience, she must have been especially worried. Neither sea air at Folkestone nor three months on the Isle of Wight really cured him, so doctors recommended a sea voyage. On 26 October the Schreibers sailed from Dartmouth to Lisbon and once there decided it best to extend the trip to the Cape of Good Hope. This was a brave and unselfish move since Lady Charlotte always found even Channel crossings unpleasant. Yet she saw the long voyage in the *Hawarden Castle* as her duty. In mid-November they anchored in Table Bay. Charles was better but not really fit.

For once Lady Charlotte's appetite for travel, for adventure, for novelty had abandoned her. Worry about Charles dominated every thing and she could not even find china collectors to divert attention. The couple travelled in the vain hope of better health At Ceres Lady Charlotte disapproved of her landlady's treatment of a young black house-boy and wrote: 'I have taken care to have him restored to his rights (which are of older date than ours) and have pleasure in looking at him.'

It was increasingly 'hard to assume constant cheerfulness, while the heart is almost breaking'. The medical opinions were worrying and at the end of January they felt it best to return home. Both found the tropics oppressive and were relieved to dock once more at Lisbon. They stayed there in January and February with Charles getting steadily worse, his condition exacerbated by the cold. It was a far cry from the few happy months they had spent in Portugal in the 1870s when they had travelled round the country together and discovered the Elysian Fields – 'of all the exquisite spots I have ever visited in my many wanderings this was by far the most exquisite' had been Lady Charlotte's words then.

Charles died early in the morning on 29 March 1884. He had contracted tubercular peritonitis. Lady Charlotte wrote: 'And now it is all over. The 11 months of anxious care and watching are past – and he is gone.' She and her maid Emma Moody were alone in a foreign country. She supervised her husband's body being placed in a coffin in the vaults of the English cemetery, mechanically wrote letters and attended the funeral service. The clergyman and his wife, the English Consul and his daughter, the English doctor and Moody were the only other mourners: 'I felt stupefied as if in a dream'. She travelled to Madrid, still aware how much more fortunate she was than if she had been 'a poor forlorn creature' without wealth or connections. Her grandson, Dacre Du Cane, met her in Paris to help the next stage of the long journey home. In May Charles's remains were shipped home and placed in a vault at Canford, alongside the body of Augustus who had died twenty-two years earlier.

Charles Schreiber remains a shadowy figure, not least because our knowledge of him is largely refracted through the writings of someone who was herself such a strong personality. Given the family hostility it is difficult to assess him fairly from chance comments made by Enid or other Guest children. Unlike John Guest who has received attention from industrial and political historians (though, surprisingly, as yet no biography) Charles's life is less well-known. He can be briefly heard through his House of Commons speeches and amongst the pamphlets which belonged to George Clark of Dowlais is a copy of a lecture Charles delivered to members of the Church of England Association at Cheltenham Town Hall in 1860. The subject was Venice and its history from the fifth century AD. His conclusion was topical and dramatic: an impassioned plea for a return to true liberty and the triumph of Garibaldi. Yet even here the influence of Lady Charlotte can be seen – when describing the intricate methods for electing the Doge, it was to Hallam that he urged his audience to turn.

Yet if Lady Charlotte helped shape some of Charles's interests, there were some (like his political beliefs) which remained his own. Perhaps more importantly, there were others which they discovered together and their joint contribution to the collection of ceramics is considerable. Deprived of her partner Lady Charlotte had written in Lisbon, 'and so ends my life on earth'. Back in England she now added 'I think I must give up the idea of trying to keep a journal. Why should I keep one? I have nothing to remember but what I should wish to forget – everything is so painful now.' Yet, largely because her journal was her oldest surviving friend, she could not relinquish it and, despite her loss, she and the journal were busy for some years to come.

10

The Elderly Widow

'This winding up of life …'

On 1 June 1884 Lady Charlotte noted in her journal how, 'I go on calmly and I daresay people could never guess that I had an ever present sorrow at my heart.' Her children were not so easily deceived. When Enid visited her mother the day after she had returned from Lisbon she wrote: 'We felt very nervous as to how we should find her notwithstanding that those who had seen her had told us she was curiously calm – This we found her and she set off telling us all about her and Mr Schreiber's journey to the Cape and back, and every detail of his death.'

She told Enid that she had known for some time that he was slowly dying but that when she lost all, she 'had to do every thing and to be like a stone'.

Long years of practice enabled Lady Charlotte, now seventy-two, to present a stoical front but she found that her private grief increasingly engulfed her. Fortunately some of this was released through her journal. In September she wrote, 'I think my misery gets worse and worse.' Some of her comments are strangely reminiscent of the forebodings of her youth.

Unused to protracted solitude in recent years or staying in one place for long, she was also free from obligations and recognized that the best means of coming to terms with her situation was via work. 'I feel as if I must break down if I have not constant employment.' Little Elizabeth Pegus, her husband John, Augustus and now Charles had been taken from her. Each previous loss had presaged a spurt of energy and immersion in some absorbing subject. Charles's death produced a similar result – 'Work is such a strengthener' – leading to an intense period of cataloguing and the feverish pursuit of fans and playing cards. The Schreiber collection of English ceramics was the first result of her reserves of energy, the product of years of joint effort, and its presentation to the public was Lady Charlotte's way of acknowledging their years collecting together and perpetuating her husband's memory.

In the process she once more found some purpose in life. Henry Layard informed the South Kensington Museum (now the Victoria and Albert)[1] that the gift would be made to them. An unpublished memorandum by A. W. Franks reveals that it went there on his advice and Lady Charlotte agreed that it would be of use to the nation there. Early in June she felt 'bound to begin my Catalogue in right earnest … I rather shrink from the task, which will be a very laborious one – But it is not

the labour I dread – it is my own insufficiency to execute it as it should be done.'
She was painfully aware how much easier it would have been with Charles but, as of
old, work was her palliative, 'the only thing that now gives any relief to my sadness'.

Some years earlier the Schreibers had briefly contemplated having pieces
photographed and privately printed. They had done a little cataloguing. Now
a far more ambitious project developed, necessitating selecting, labelling and
presenting a vast collection for public scrutiny. It required a comprehensive
printed catalogue. Within a few days of starting work on her Bow china, Franks
secured the assistance (for 2s 6d an hour) of George Harding, a London dealer.
He spent about three hours each weekday evening working with Lady Charlotte
at Langham House. The catalogue eventually contained 1891 entries, each item
carefully researched and described.[2] The aim was to bring together objects typical
of ceramic art rather than simply showing their beauty or variety. Lady Charlotte
added some appropriate pieces to what they had already gathered – 'If I go on at
this rate my morning walks will become very costly', she observed in the early
stages of cataloguing, though consoled herself with the knowledge that such purchases were for the Museum rather than for herself.

By January the two largest rooms in the house were cleared and china laid out
on seven long tables. Lady Charlotte arranged illustrations, prints to accompany
pieces based on paintings and drawings and had photogravures of herself and
Charles inserted into the catalogue. The Venice and Murano Mosaic and Glass
Company provided coloured mosaics of them based on Watts's pictures; these still
look down on the collection today though apparently Lady Charlotte never liked
them. She checked catalogue numbers, chased up queries, visiting places such as
the Whitefriars Glass Works and the London Library, and did the proofs.

Her eldest grandchild, Alice Du Cane, compiled the index. Lady Charlotte
approved of Alice's interest in cataloguing, 'a great resource for a girl at home
who has nothing particular to do'. She was delighted when the shy Alice became
engaged to the equally retiring Alex Henry Hallam Murray. Hallam worked in
his father's publishing business and Alice was to become 'a shareholder or partner
in the business'. The Preface was daunting, 'I quite shrink from undertaking this
task – small as it seems – and it weighs sadly on my now shattered spirits.' It kept
hovering 'like a nightmare'. George Clark thought he was helping by sketching
out some ideas but 'He has mistaken most of my points.' She finally wrote a brief
Preface, emphasizing that the collection's formation had been 'a labour of love'.

In October the collection was moved to the Museum, a wrench which cost
some tears 'but I am most grateful that I have considered it a fitting monument to
my poor darling – I feel sure it is what he would have approved of'. She visited
the Keramic Gallery (first opened in 1868) and made suggestions about display.
There remained the correction of the index: 'If there had been such things in
Solomon's time he would have said "Oh! that his enemy should write one".' On
Boxing Day 1885, a year and a half after embarking on the task, the Schreiber
collection was opened to the public. Fifty copies of the catalogue were presented

to the Museum. Both collection and catalogue have been invaluable to historians and collectors of ceramics. Bernard Rackham (who worked in the Museum at the end of the century) compiled his own catalogue of the collection between 1915-30, benefiting from advances in knowledge such as chemical analysis which could now test porcelain paste for the presence of phosphates and so show that the body contained bone-ash. Such expertise could confirm or amend Lady Charlotte's earlier attributions. Thus indirectly the Schreiber collection continued to inform long after the lives of its compilers.

Lady Charlotte and Harding now began cataloguing the Continental china. The next year Harding succeeded to his brother-in-law's business (the Schreibers used to buy from him) and began tempting Lady Charlotte with expensive items. They included a Battersea enamel tea caddy which he believed cheap at £400, 'How prices have changed', she wrote, 'since we used to buy these things! – £50 would have been a very high price in those days.' He also bought part of the collection of Octavius Morgan (who lived up to his name and died aged eighty-five). Lady Charlotte found it impossible to resist the salt-glaze jug with a portrait of Charles Edward; having become so used to a large collection she now felt justified in buying a little more.

Over the last few years her interest in ceramics had been shared with Augustus Wollaston Franks. His visits to Langham House were a great treat: 'Beyond my own family there is nobody that it gives me so much pleasure to see.' Franks was the only non-family member invited to Lady Charlotte's first dinner party after Charles's death (held in 1888). Lady Charlotte and Franks were two of a kind. Franks was fifty-eight when Charles died and had worked for the British Museum since 1851, was now Keeper of the Department of British and Medieval Antiquities and Ethnography (which included ceramics) and an avid collector. His wide-ranging interests included heraldry, Anglo-Saxon rings and seventeenth-century tokens. He possessed 3,000 brass rubbings and 80,000 book plates. Somehow he also found time to write on many subjects, and was admired as an archaeologist and as an astute identifier of fakes. Director of the Society of Antiquaries (and later President), he was Senior Keeper from 1886. A bachelor, he has been described as a 'quiet, grey, dreamy man with extremely perceptive taste, an unexpected sense of humour and the most selfless modesty'. His acquisition for, and gifts to, the British Museum (he bequeathed 3,330 pieces) make him one of its most significant figures and benefactors. He found the space to advise Lady Charlotte on china, fans and playing cards. They frequently gave each other gifts, their friendship founded on mutual respect and a real understanding of the pleasure provided by *objets d'art*. In July 1887 Lady Charlotte and Franks made a selection of fans and fan leaves worth reproducing 'for the little book I am meditating'. This 'little book' became what one reviewer called 'an elephant folio', one of the huge volumes she produced on fans using photolithography.

Like other fashionable young ladies, Lady Charlotte had long possessed fans. Her mother gave her a feather fan when she was nineteen. During the collecting years of the 1870s and 1880s a number of fans and fan leaves were acquired but as collectors' pieces rather than as accompaniments to fashion. From the late 1870s Lady Charlotte had been buying groups of fans (dealers would send batches on approval) as well as making individual personal purchases. She often spent only a pound or less on a fan though occasionally paid £20 or £30 for something special.[3] She prided herself on her Revolutionary fans from France depicting scenes such as the fall of the Bastille and the making of Louis XIV's will, and she wrote in April 1887: 'I am now getting almost a complete history of the French Revolution.' One of her main suppliers, Captain Wundt, praised her French collection in an article in the *Queen*.

Just as collecting china had revealed historical and political issues so was it possible to focus on this aspect of fan-collecting (Lady Charlotte's earliest historical fan dates from 1727). A number of her fans used political satire. One depicted the separation of England and America by showing a cow being milked whilst having its horn sawn off. Sometimes the same issues were reflected in china, fans and playing cards* since in all three areas Lady Charlotte specialized in the eighteenth century. Most of her fans were printed. Printed fans had appeared in London in about 1725 and made fans much more accessible and popular.

A fan could be produced for almost any occasion and for all sorts of reasons.† Some were instructional, teaching history, geography or scripture by packing masses of information into tiny writing or pictures. One French fan showed a scene from Lady Charlotte's cherished *Waverley*. She also possessed a few modern fans such as the bullfighting examples obtained by Enid. Lady Charlotte's collection included music and dance fans (with printed music and verse), fortune-telling fans and pastoral scenes inspired by Watteau and others. Commemorative fans not only celebrated royal marriages but immortalized events ranging from battles to ballooning. One of Lady Charlotte's fans shows a rustic poking a balloon with a stick whilst another prepares to use a pitch-fork. (Balloons were seen as weird and wonderful in the eighteenth century. Professor Charles's unmanned hydrogen balloon had actually been shot at and attacked with pitch-forks by suspicious onlookers.)

Lady Charlotte was not the only British contender in this relatively new field of collecting. Lady Foley and Robert Walker of Uffington (Berkshire) were fan-collectors too, and Lady Charlotte purchased from Walker's sale in 1882. Yet by the 1890s the *Observer* was describing her as 'one of the most eminent fan-collectors in Europe' and, unlike most collectors, she did not restrict herself to the fans of her own country. She eagerly followed up clues about origins and painters, reading history books and the few studies available about fans such as S. Blondel's *Histoire des Eventails* (1875) and visiting exhibitions and museums. At the British Museum she secured some help in checking old newspaper advertisements. Monty passed the fan leaves he had collected

---

* See Appendix 6B.

† See Appendix 6A.

to his mother. Her offspring can have had little difficulty knowing what to buy for her birthday. Many fans and fan leaves came from her children and grandchildren. One of the latter, Dacre Du Cane, conducted a surrogate 'chasse' on her behalf in Paris.

Her personal maid, Emma Moody, (who eventually received £100 from Lady Charlotte's will) had soon discovered that service with Lady Charlotte meant a life of variety. She had already travelled extensively with her mistress and now inserted fan leaves into books and read aloud books and articles relating to fans for an hour each morning. When Lady Charlotte began cataloguing in 1885 she had forty-eight English fans, and her manuscript catalogues eventually ran to thirteen volumes on fans. In the autumn and winter of 1886 she catalogued and indexed but could only manage to cover about three fans a day. (Maria helped catalogue German fans.) By Christmas the English fans were completed but they, like the French, Dutch and others, kept increasing.

Now that Hallam Murray was part of the family, the obvious publishers were John Murray. William Griggs did some experimental photography and Harding worked with Lady Charlotte on preparing the hook on English fans and fan leaves. The need for a Preface revived old fears. 'I find it so difficult now to put two words together and what little power of writing I ever had is now quite gone and I don't know how I shall ever get over the task I have set myself.' Her self-confidence was fast evaporating, exacerbated by deteriorating eyesight which made close work such as deciphering the writing on fans taxing and troublesome. She was still, however, sharp enough to detect errors in the proofs.

The manuscript was delivered on July 1888. Text describing the fans was followed by their reproduction in a sepia tone. There were 104 fan leaves and fifty-eight mounted fans (which had cost over £3 each to photograph). Lady Charlotte commented, 'It is a great step to have got so far – and I feel it to be an immense relief'. Before Christmas she received the first copies, splendidly bound in red-tooled leather with family coats-of-arms and drawings of fans in the corners. The press reaction was, on the whole, very favourable. *The Times* regretted that it was a limited edition costing 7 guineas but recognized that making it less of a volume deluxe and reducing the size of the illustrations would have diminished their effectiveness.

With help from Arthur Du Cane and Enid, work proceeded now on a companion volume on European fans. A Mr Heath who had written about French Revolution fans for the *Illustrated London News* also gave advice but was soon dismissed as he was 'too diffuse and dilatory'; he 'raked up endless details'. Lady Charlotte was not above such an approach herself, but by this time (1890) her sense of working against time militated against self-indulgence. She chose instead Alfred Whitman, an assistant at the British Museum (Prints and Drawings Department), who had helped with the previous volume.[4] Most of the 153 fans reproduced were French, reflecting the fact that there were over 130 *maîtres éventaillistes* in Paris by 1773. There were also Italian, Spanish, German and Dutch fans. This volume (with a one-paragraph Preface) appeared in August 1890. In the meantime

Lady Charlotte lent fans to English and European exhibitions, including one art exhibition in aid of the Girls' Friendly Society and Recreation Rooms for Working Girls (causes which especially interested her).

In 1878 the Worshipful Company of Fan Makers had attempted to revive interest in fans in Britain, displaying 1,284 fans from all over the world. The exhibition did not result in a significant revival of the indigenous trade though Enid was interested in creating a society to encourage and patronize fan-painting and Lady Charlotte discussed this with Colonel Sewell, Clerk to the Fan Makers.[5] She possessed a few hand-painted fans herself. One painted flower fan was made by Miss Tregellis of Kingsbridge (a descendant of William Cookworthy, whose Plymouth and Bristol china the Schreibers acquired in 1868). Of greatest sentimental value was the silver wedding present from the Dutch artist Kate Bisschop. Not completed until 1887, it was a landscape design depicting Canford like a romantic castle in the background. In the centre of the fan Cupid turns the leaves of a book, one showing the anniversary date of 10 April 1880.

To help encourage the trade's revival Lady Charlotte offered prizes (through the Fan Makers) for the best fan designs. She gave £10 for the best depiction of the Queen's jubilee (Miss Churton's winning prize showed Victoria in her coach *en route* to Westminster Abbey) and Margaret Tyssen-Amhurst won the competition on Chaucer, showing the procession of the Canterbury pilgrims. On 17 December 1891, the Fan Makers awarded Lady Charlotte the Freedom of their Company, Angela Burdett-Coutts, herself a 'Lady Freeman' of several companies, was at the presentation ceremony. The Company had been established since 1709 to protect the interests of English fan makers and apprentices. Eighteenth-century records show women fan makers such as Sarah Ashton as Guild members, but women's influence had declined in such areas: Baroness Coutts and Lady Charlotte were the only two 'Freewomen' of full standing in Victorian England and Lady Charlotte the only one honoured by the Fan Makers. The *Standard* commented how even the most conservative of municipal institutions might now demonstrate modern ideas.[6]

Increasingly conscious of her own mortality, Lady Charlotte decided that her fans should go to the British Museum. Old age and the influence of Charles's Disraeli-style beliefs had intensified her sense of nationality: 'My Darling' used to say what pleasure it gave to collect national objects 'for the benefit of the country'. The fans (and not just the British ones) were presented to the Prints and Drawings Department in 1891 and Lionel Cust published for them two years later a 128-page catalogue containing descriptions of 734 fans and fan leaves, including many which had not featured in the folio books. Yet the total collection was still larger since Lady Charlotte kept back some fans for her children and the Museum took only those she did not already possess. They also received her etchings of 1830–34 (now bound) and some German engravings. 'My love for the dear old Museum seems ever to increase', Lady Charlotte wrote, and she frequently walked there, talked to Franks, consulted books in the reading room and experts in Prints and Drawings. She was disappointed that cousin Henry had not received better treatment from the Trustees and incensed that Franks was not publicly rewarded, and tried to exert influence via her son-in-law Edward Ponsonby, now Personal Assistant to the Speaker of the House of Commons. Franks was eventually knighted. He also turned down offers to become Director of the British Museum and the Victoria and Albert Museum.

There was something of the magpie about Lady Charlotte in these later years though her hoardings were ultimately for others. Increasingly the collector gave way to the accumulator. She possessed old political handkerchiefs of the French Revolution, collections of antique jewellery, buttons, horn boxes and metal boxes.

In 1880 she paid over £10 for some packs of playing cards in Munich admitting that 'I am so inexperienced as yet, in this branch of collecting that I do not know if they are worth anything.' It soon became a subject which 'occupies me very much'. Playing cards had been in use in Europe for centuries – by the fifteenth century they were well enough known in England for their importation to be prohibited, but the 'Devil's Picture Book', as the Puritans called them, did not gain respectability for some time.[7] By the 1670s England had non-standard geographical packs depicting county maps, and Pepys possessed packs showing the Popish Plot and Glorious Revolution of 1688. Lady Charlotte's collection encompassed such subjects. She had standard packs of fifty-two cards with four suits and variations on this, plus non-standard cards in which the message in the pictures or use of pictures dominated. The latter especially fascinated her, particularly historical-cum-political satires. Her packs of English cards revealed, amongst other things, the depth of anti-Catholic feeling in Tudor and Stuart England. Some packs concentrated on instruction, providing, for example, geography lessons. The early erroneous belief in a four-continent world had produced a neat division into four suits. There were also fortune-telling, phrenology cards and a host of gimmicks.★

Although she enjoyed the occasional game of piquet, the national French card game using a thirty-two card pack (and possessed piquet playing cards and a fan depicting the game), Lady Charlotte's interest in cards was chiefly as a collector. Starting so late in life she did less personal collecting than with other objects, becoming largely a recipient, collator and cataloguer, receiving consignments from Stiebel in Frankfurt, Olschki in Venice, Miss Millard in Teddington, and others. Her family secured some packs and she exchanged cards with collectors. She did still make some purchases personally, viewed collections at Sotheby's, visited the Worshipful Company of Playing Card Makers and read up on the subject. She studied not only William Chatto's *Facts and Speculations on the Origin and History of Playing Cards* (1848) and the Rev. Taylor's 1865 volume on cards but also perused more obscure French and German books and articles.

In April 1885 she began the slow task of ticketing individual packs to provide a systematic catalogue. Her twenty-five manuscript volumes of notes describe her

★ Appendix 6C

packs and often give details of individual cards. Most of this is in Lady Charlotte's own hand though sight problems made her slow and disdainful of her ability – 'stupid and uncertain' was her harsh self-criticism. She still followed up references meticulously in places such as the Society of Antiquaries, the Bodleian Library in Oxford and elsewhere. A visit to a member of the Nelson family in Parkstone near Canford and some hard bargaining yielded a rare Cavalier pack satirizing the Commonwealth in return for £25 and a tray bearing the Nelson coat-of-arms.

Increasingly, however, she became an armchair collector, her compulsive cataloguing helping to fill the time. The journal betrays her intense loneliness. She described much of her cataloguing as 'sad solitary work' yet was pleased when Franks gave her some of his cards as 'I should be so glad to be of some use to somebody'. Franks had hoped that Lady Charlotte might exchange her little box of gold ornaments for his European cards. At first she resisted from sentimental attachment to her pieces. She then added a codicil to her will bequeathing Franks the box, but finally relented and handed it to him. In return she received over 170 packs which, to her embarrassment, were of greater value than her own offering.

In September 1887 Lady Charlotte stayed in Italy with Enid and Henry. The collector Sylvia Mann has pronounced Lady Charlotte's collection of Italian cards as 'the finest in Europe today'. Tarot cards (today associated in Britain with divination) had originated in the medieval Italian states as a game. Fifteenth-century Ferrara had, for example, been familiar with what is known as *trionfi*. To the regular pack of fifty-two cards was added a fifth suit of emblematic designs always trumping other cards. The game became known as *Taroccho*. Lady Charlotte's collection included *tarocchi* cards of northern Italy (seventy-eight in a pack) and allied games of *Minchiate* (ninety-seven cards) from the Florence area and smaller *tarocchini* cards from Bologna. In a Milan antique shop Lady Charlotte purchased nearly fifty packs and some single cards which had belonged to the owner's son. 'Indeed I came away quite triumphant. It seemed a dream. I had never had such a chance before and could hardly realize my good fortune.' They were unsorted and revealed three packs engraved by G.M. Mitelli. Enid described how her mother 'pounced' on them. On her next visit in 1890 she spent several hundred pounds on some Mantegna cards. 'Staggered by the price' – both what was asked and what she gave – she added 'my collection will be quite rich and I nearly ruined!' She was now more prepared to part with money for the sake of the collection as she felt her life to be drawing to a close. Her published works on cards includes two sets of *tarocchi di Mantegna* (now not considered to be designed by Mantegna or strict tarot cards though nevertheless rare and important fifteenth-century emblematic cards).[8]

Lady Charlotte found that she not infrequently had to pay £10 for a pack of cards. Unlike the halcyon days of china-collecting, prices were now competitive and she had to compete with collectors such as 'my rival' George Clulow, Isaac Falcke, Captain E. Rimington Wilson, and others. She had not lost her appetite for bargaining though, and relatives strategically placed in European cities were instructed to offer less than the going price.

Her three volumes on *Playing Cards of Various Ages and Countries* were published by Murray in the same format as the fan volumes. Frank helped select 'reproductions of curiosity and interest' for the first volume of English, Scottish, Dutch and Flemish cards (144 plates in all). Lady Charlotte still personally supervised arrangements and had cataloguing help from Whitman. Her manuscript notes include extracts from books reminiscent of the copying exercises of Uffington.

The first volume (costing £3 13s 6d) appeared in 1892. Sets of cards were reproduced by photolithography 'so as to bring within the reach of students objects that are often rare and costly and which throw light on the manners and customs of former times'. (Interestingly, one modern book, *A Handful of History*, utilizes Lady Charlotte's English cards as a means of teaching school history via visual aids.) The Preface ended with acknowledgements to Franks. A year later a second volume covered French and German cards with early examples printed from wooden blocks. They included a famous Stukeley pack of forty-eight cards of which no other example is known. This had been discovered in the binding of a fifteenth-century book and presented to the Society of Antiquaries.

The third volume was published posthumously. Countries not already considered (most significant of which was Italy) were reproduced here. Lady Charlotte's will had entrusted 'my friend' Sir Augustus Wollaston Franks with seeing it through the press. With characteristic modesty his Preface omitted the fact that her collection had been boosted by his own rare packs. Her cards now went to the British Museum and, in accordance with her will, a catalogue was compiled (by Freeman O'Donoghue in 1901) itemizing 1,066 packs, 376 of which were German. The British Museum already had a good collection (it had issued its own catalogue by Willshire in 1876) so only took packs which would not be duplicated. The rejected packs were returned to the executors and a two-day sale held at Sotheby's in May 1896. *The Times* claimed that this was the first occasion in which old playing cards were in sufficient number to justify an independent sale. The auction (which included some old games) centred on the sale of a *tarocchi di Mantegna* pack which raised £120. The entire proceedings only raised just under £400 for 277 lots. Many were French and German packs. The English cards included the War of Spanish Succession and Marlborough's victories which were bought by the Fine Arts Society.

Lady Charlotte also bequeathed her books on cards to the British Museum and her 141 games (catalogued by Whitman), many of which were similar to packs of instructional cards. Almost half were Italian games, many engraved by Mitelli, and came to Lady Charlotte from Henry Layard. The collection included some German engraved games and about a dozen French games. The majority were in sheet form (some were seventeenth-century) and many showed cartoon-like figures, the object being to compete and complete a tortuous course. Many were hand-painted and twenty-three were free-standing (mostly board) games. Amongst the English examples were some topical issues such as a Game of Russia versus Turkey.

Since Lady Charlotte had difficulty resisting anything which might have some relevance to her interests, her collection included some slightly risqué *cartes à rire*. Henry Layard was shocked when she insisted on buying some 'immoral' cards and commented that 'Collectors seem insensitive to all feelings of decency.' She wrote to reassure him: 'As for the objectionable cards: I have already promised you that I will not even look at them, but as soon as I have made my usual minute descriptive catalogue of them, I will put them away in a drawer and lock them up, quite out of sight.' In November 1892 the Worshipful Company of Playing Card Makers (established in 1628) granted Lady Charlotte the Freedom of their Company.

When not collecting fans and playing cards, Lady Charlotte kept busy in other ways. When she (like her contemporaries) said she was doing work, she meant needlework. She made clothes, screens, even curtains. Women had once been members of the Embroiderers' Guild and important in ecclesiastical workshops, but when the Guild was reformed in the mid-Tudor period its membership became exclusively male. Yet, just as fans were mainly used by women (possibly explaining why fan painting tended not to attract the best-known artists) so embroidery, whether done by working-class girls on new machines or performed as a ladies' accomplishment, had become feminized and perceived as a craft rather than an art. However, the 1870s saw attempts to reinstate ornate secular needlework as a decorative art. In 1872 the School of Art Needlework began modestly above a bonnet shop in Sloane Street, London with twenty 'impoverished genteel ladies'. It soon grew, moved to Exhibition Road and became the Royal School with Princess Christian of Schleswig-Holstein its President. Its committee of eminent ladies included Lady Charlotte, who joined soon after the School's foundation. (When she first saw the Bayeux Tapestry in 1874 she described it as 'the most magnificent thing I ever saw or ever imagined – No Needlework was ever like it for spirit or design and execution, rude as the Stitches often are – I wish our School of Art may ever produce anything half as good.')

Its founders were Lady Helen Welby (an accomplished needle woman related to Felicia Bertie) and Lady Marion Alford (author in 1886 of a book on needlework as art). Pre-Raphaelites such as Burne-Jones and William Morris did designs for the school and Jane Morris's sister taught there. By 1882 an average of twenty ladies were constantly employed. Some embroidered, others designed patterns, did repair work or prepared work for sale or amateurs – lady amateurs could complete items in their own homes. The staff were female and, according to the *Magazine of Art*, committee workers showed much interest in the workers' welfare and working conditions. Art needle work was in part a reaction against the craze for Berlin wool-work (embroidered in wool or canvas from patterns drawn on squared paper) so popular with middle-class women. It was ornamental, drawing on medieval embroidery and emulating the seventeenth-century crewel work (utilizing twisted two-play worsted yarn) revived by William Morris. Rather than encouraging individuality, it stressed the value of careful copying and disciplined study and was one of the few forms of respectable work in which gentlewomen in 'reduced circumstances' might engage, earn a living and not lose status. Lady Charlotte applauded its combination of application, skill and respectable opportunities for needy women, as well as its promotion of things medieval and its education of public taste.

The school flourished and although its publicity stressed gentility rather than commercialism, its workers' skills did help raise the standing of embroidery. In 1875 Lady Charlotte was 'still busy in bringing into a little order the affairs of the Needlework-School'. She attended committee meetings, helped with the Christmas party and contributed items to a special exhibition of Ancient English and Other Art Needlework (and sat on its organizing committee). Charles's death saw her withdrawal and resignation from the committee (in April 1887) though she continued to lend embroidery and lace-work. She had done some lace-work herself. Late nineteenth-century Britain saw a revival of the trade, stimulated by lace-making associations, and Lady Charlotte was lucky enough to visit the Government Lace School in Venice where fifty women received free tuition.

It was, however, the Turkish Compassionate Fund which gave her a real chance to further 'work' for a productive end. During the Russo-Turkish war, Henry Layard had alerted Baroness Coutts to the plight of Turkish refugees. Like the Baroness, Henry had a banking interest, having founded the Ottoman Bank in London in 1856. He now wanted to secure the support of this extremely wealthy bank-owner who had already displayed her generosity and formed a model sewing workshop in East London. Baroness Coutts appealed for aid through the *Daily Telegraph*, setting up a Turkish Compassionate Fund with £1,000 to help 'these cruelly treated Moslems'. Within a few weeks the money had trebled. A yacht sailed to Constantinople with medical equipment, food and blankets. For her support for the Turks, Baroness Coutts and Enid (now presiding over a team of women helpers in Constantinople) were, along with Queen Victoria, the first women to receive medals from the Sultan.

Both Lady Charlotte and Baroness Coutts had for many, many years been interested in the Turks and now combined forces through their work for the Turkish Compassionate Fund. The Guest offspring also helped: Maria organized a concert, Arthur developed retail outlets in America, and Constance, Blanche and Monty held bazaars. From April 1880 Lady Charlotte was treasurer of the Fund. Turkish refugee work was sent over from Constantinople and Lady Charlotte also helped develop markets, drawing on her business experience of past years. No opportunity was lost for gaining a customer. Mr Harding the cataloguer was pressed into selling, Mrs Moore persuaded to win support from the American Minister's wife in Rome, Lady Marlborough (Cornelia's mother) sent embroidery to the Queen of Portugal, whilst Lady Marion Alford as Vice President of the Royal School of Art Needlework could hardly refuse and helped sell to the Rothschilds. Lady Charlotte recognized the value of royal patronage. The Princess of Wales purchased some embroidery and dresses were sent to the family of the Crown Princess Frederick in Germany. Lady Charlotte devised a pattern for a dress combining a popular Turkish design with Swedish crowns, suggested by a visit to the Swedish Royal Chapel in Stockholm where she had studied the ceiling during 'an interminable sermon'. This was adopted not so much for aesthetic reasons as from a realization that it might interest the young princess in Sweden and so extend sales 'which latter seem to have been increasing to a wonderful degree'.

Although she was clearly very successful in bringing in money, Lady Charlotte remained cautious: 'I work on and on, and *will* work, but I am not easy much less am I confident.' She sought to win over the retail trade. A friend persuaded the upholsterer Maple to order £50 worth of embroidery work and she got commissions from Marshall and Snelgrove and Howell and James. Department stores were rapidly becoming big business. The most successful outlet proved to be the Regent Street store, Liberty's. Arthur Liberty had called his original shop East India House. He was always interested in goods with an eastern flavour and sold coloured eastern silks before expanding into items such as rare embroidery. He also persuaded English firms to experiment with eastern dyeing techniques which led to the distinctive Liberty fabrics so familiar today. In the early 1880s sales from Turkish work through Liberty's were worth about £50 a month but in May 1884 they became sole agents. They put Turkish work on permanent display and sales shot up. By this time the Fund's account at Coutts had already reached £13,000, over £9,000 of which had been accounted for by Lady Charlotte. In the mid-1880s she would visit Liberty's (which was close to her home) about twice weekly.

Hardly a week went by without journal references to some aspects of Turkish work – getting the weekly accounts ready for Constantinople, banking cheques, cataloguing for exhibitions at home and abroad. The ever-versatile Moody found herself deputizing for Lady Charlotte at bazaars. Gradually, however, the strain began to tell. Lady Charlotte admitted that: 'At times it entails upon me a good deal of attention and more writing than is good for my eyes.' In 1887 she ceased to be the Fund's treasurer.

In the last few years Lady Charlotte's accounting skills had not been restricted to the Turkish refugees. Retail and charitable work were also combined in a scheme rather closer to home. In May 1885 Cornelia explained her plans to provide respectable lodgings for young women employed at shops and other businesses in the City of London. Cornelia, Lady Wimborne lived until 1927 and spent many years doing good works. As châtelaine of Canford she held meetings for Poole working girls, was involved in projects for estate workers and founded schools and churches. She became associated with a Cambridge Mission set up by Trinity College, Cambridge involving sisters and nurses working with laundry and factory women. Increasingly she devoted herself to the Church of England and in later life wrote books such as *The Daily Walk* (1925), a book of devotions for every day of the year. She owned a theology bookshop in Bond Street. Lady Charlotte did not agree with her daughter-in-law's politics. 'Old Whig as I am I have no sympathy with the Primrose League' was her response to Cornelia's huge fête for the Tory Primrose League at Canford in 1885. Despite its increasing anachronism, Lady Charlotte clung to her Whig label (partly to distance herself from Gladstone and in particular his foreign policy) but she was happy to engage in philanthropic work with Cornelia. The Wimbornes' London home, Hamilton House (renamed Wimborne House) was in Arlington Street. Here Lady Charlotte, Cornelia and her sister Fanny met with other ladies to plan their home for working women.

The Guest daughters had all made 'good' marriages. Quite apart from their large families, their status prevented them from working for a living. The sort of philanthropic work in which Lady Charlotte's daughters and daughters-in-law engaged permitted active involvement in public life and gave them some sense of worth independent of their husbands. Yet there was perhaps rather less overlap between their private worlds and those of the people they visited or patronized than had been the case when Lady Charlotte lived in Dowlais. For ladies like Cornelia, married to an eldest son and herself from a high-ranking family, religious duty and commitment could be combined with an appropriate benevolence, but tended to be maintained without too much personal identification.

Lady Charlotte's family became involved in various charitable schemes. Maria's early work for the hospital for incurables at Putney had stimulated concern for aiding hospitals in later life. Enid distributed daily meat dinners to unemployed workmen in a large mission house in Paddington when she was not helping Turkish refugees. Blanche was a District Visitor in Lambeth – 'she is always on charitable work intent' wrote Lady Charlotte – and she promoted Irish cottage industries. She also sang at charity events organized by sister Connie in support of causes such as Sunday evening recreation 'for the people'. As the wife of a clergyman, Katherine's involvement was statutory, expected as a matter of course and centred on the Rectory at Holdenby.

Occasionally Lady Charlotte accompanied her daughters. She went with Blanche to a large tea-party at Lambeth and with Constance to a public house kept by the uncle of a boy she was helping, 'so had a new peep into life by going there – admirable and well ordered, the publican quite an old gentleman'. She also visited the relatives of servants, helped secure work for some and gave financial aid to others. She contributed to Baroness Coutts's charity for children, supported Jewish elders who provided meal tickets for the needy and gave some of her own '*inartistic* work' to the Ragged School movement.

The plan to house respectable women shop workers materialized in June 1886. The dramatic growth of the retail trade in these years would help contribute to their being close on one million women shop assistants in England and Wales by 1914, their numbers increasing by over 50 per cent in the last thirty years of the nineteenth century. Larger stores often had their own living-in facilities but many shop and other city workers had to find their own lodgings. The last years of the century saw some attempts to help these vulnerable young women through establishing clubs such as Mabel Morgan of Hammersmith's Enterprise Club. In 1887 the magazine *Work and Leisure* ran a competition for practical suggestions for erecting and managing dwellings for single women at 10s to 15s a week. Ordinary lodging houses were often inadequate and the Churchill Home which emerged from Cornelia's plans saw itself filling a gap. It was described as 'A Restaurant and Lodging House for City Workwomen' Lady Charlotte researched the subject, visiting a number of institutions including a YMCA, a girls' home and The Welcome in Jewin Street, run by a 'very clever woman of business'. After viewing one young men's club, she wrote (in terms reminiscent of her Dowlais days) that such places 'do the greatest possible good in giving homes and rational amusements to young workmen – I wish there were many more of them'. By March 1886 suitable premises had been found at Chiswell Street near Finsbury Square. Lady Charlotte supervised the fitting up of the cubicles in this five-storey building (a former warehouse) then laid on 'a sort of supper' for the workmen. She was disappointed when Cornelia did not approve of her providing music for them. She did, however, secure the services of the Welsh harpist Mr Thomas, for a benefit concert in aid of the home. He had first performed publicly at Spring Gardens and was now harpist to the Queen.

Although Lady Charlotte now preferred not to attend formal events and so did not go to the official opening, she could not resist attending the workmen's tea. Cornelia was the home's official treasurer but it was her mother-in-law who actually handled the accounts (with Coutts). Since the Wimbornes tended to be in London only during the season, Lady Charlotte shouldered quite a lot of responsibility. Not that she minded. She evidently enjoyed showing people around, soliciting financial support and on the first day was in evidence. She gave the young women free meals as the food was delayed by ten minutes. A few days later she found Lady Tavistock 'holding a sort of religious meeting with the singing of hymns' to which the diners were invited. The veteran Lady Charlotte had her doubts 'I wonder if this will answer or will frighten the girls away?' She took along two of her grandchildren to help with evening classes when subjects such as geography and French were taught and Moody's sister, the aspiring actress Miss Tennison, gave recitals.

Personal involvement always appealed to Lady Charlotte. Over the next few days she served daily meals between 12 and 2 p.m., 'rather amused at my new vocation'. The restaurant boasted facilities for 1,000 (250 could be managed at one sitting). After a slow start many began to use the facilities. The managing steward, Mr Haines (who also helped procure and repair fans), was soon complaining that he was over-worked. The superintendent, Miss Rolfe, was overwrought. Both told Lady Charlotte that they had never known such a busy fortnight in their lives. Cornelia was abroad and Lady Charlotte had to reassure them. Miss Rolfe was concerned because Haines appeared to be showing too much authority; she was on principle opposed to having a man on the premises. The committee therefore decided to run the home with an all-female staff and Lady Charlotte had to hand Haines his letter of dismissal.

Early in 1887 an eye operation forced her to give up the home's accounts. The avid reader and keen needlewoman had long been concerned about her eyes. As a serious twelve-year-old prone to fear the worst in a life which appeared to offer few attainable goals she had written, 'my eyes feel less strong everyday and the small beadwork I am now doing, does not at all improve them. What should I be without sight?' She was to see for many more decades, though she was short sighted and refreshingly free from self-consciousness about this. When the shy young Amy Dillwyn of Swansea made her Court debut in 1863 she discarded her glasses for the occasion, despite the inconvenience. She wrote in her diary that Lady Charlotte was there and 'wore her Spectacles all through everything at the drawing-room which struck me as being rather an idea for there were heaps of short-sighted people there'.

Lady Charlotte's later writings frequently commented on her failing eyesight. In February 1886 she consulted an oculist at Canford because he happened to be visiting Ivor. Her language now began to betray her concern. Monty's visits were 'bright spots on the dark background' and she despaired when further consultations did not 'throw more light on my case'. By the beginning of the following year both eyes were affected with glaucoma which was (and remains) widespread amongst older people. Baroness Coutts also had glaucoma and an iridectomy performed by the same surgeon as Lady Charlotte. Critchett was a famous eye surgeon but could not arrest the disease. Not wanting any fuss, Lady Charlotte kept quiet about the operation (on one eye). There followed an enforced six-week sabbatical. Even the journal was suspended; Maria acted as 'secretary'. As there was little sign of real improvement Lady Charlotte soon abandoned her latest project, photography.

In 1886, aged seventy-four she had enrolled at the Regent Street Polytechnic for photographic lessons. Her erstwhile friend Julia Margaret Cameron had only taken up the subject when forty-eight and became a famous photographer. Lady Charlotte wanted to understand the processes involved in photographing her fans and hoped to do some herself. Forty-four years earlier she had experimented with the precursor to modern photography, the camera lucidor.[9] George Clark had shown her how to operate this drawing contraption which relied on reflected light, but her first efforts to use it on a European tour were abortive. This was hardly surprising since even the 'father of photography' John Guest's fellow Whig MP, Fox Talbot, had failed with it. His efforts to sketch the scene at Lake Como had 'only left traces on the paper melancholy to behold'. This had spurred him on to experiment how natural images might imprint themselves permanently and effectively on paper.

Yet, unlike most of her interests, the elderly Lady Charlotte abandoned photography without very much perseverance or regret. After a few lessons she was describing it as 'very fidgetty [sic] work'. She hoped to do 'as much as possible before total dark – perhaps for ever'. The state of her eyes soon decided against investment in expensive photographic equipment. By September 1888 there was 'a constant mist before me and my difficulty in reading constantly increases'. She heard of a Wiesbaden oculist, said to perform wonders, and the next year took the brave and progressive step of visiting Dr Julers 'to have my eyes electrified'. To Julers's surprise the new electrical treatment appeared to have little effect on this tough old lady. Most people would 'bound out of their seats' when it began but not Lady Charlotte. A course of treatment followed but did not seem to help much, and to make matters worse she was now forced to use an old Chelsea walking stick as rheumatism made her fear that 'All hopes of recovering my loco-motive powers are at an end.'

Yet failing eyesight did not spell inactivity. Although intensely miserable in the few years after Charles's death, especially on Sundays when she recalled how they used to sit hand in hand in church – she now preferred to sit in the park rather than revive memories in a service – she had regained some of her old spirit by the late 1880s. In September 1888 Enid recorded dining with her mother who had arrived in London from a month in Scotland with the Wimbornes (helping with Cornelia's confinement). She had travelled all night, arriving at 8 a.m. and then went 'about London all day and was not a bit tired. At 75 she is a marvel of strength'.

She now believed that her main objective should be to do what was possible for her children. Grandchildren stayed with her and she helped her children and even distant relatives with any financial problems. She was not unlike an employ-ment agency: if a grandson or nephew failed in business it was to Lady Charlotte they turned in hope that she would activate her wide circle of acquaintances and contacts. Barely a day went by without her seeing at least one or two daughters or sons. Blanche and Maria lived nearby and Sunday evenings were usually spent with Blanche's family. Ironically, given the animosity which once existed between Maria and her stepfather, she was the only one (with the exception of Miss Kemble) to remember Lady Charlotte's silver wedding anniversary. Monty saw his mother whenever possible and Arthur (whose marriage to Adeline Chapman had broken up) visited in between trips to America. She visited her children in the country – Merthyr was Master of Hounds and he and Theodora spent most of their time fox-hunting. Merthyr was as accident-prone as ever. Theodora's mother, Lady Westminster, lived with them (she was ninety-four when she died), and Lady Charlotte once described their meeting as 'the lame and blind leading the rather more aged but equally active.'

By 1887 even the youngest daughter, Blanche, was forty. Lady Charlotte was now a great-grandmother. Cornelia's youngest (father to Revel Guest) was born in August 1888 and Lady Charlotte now had forty-two grandchildren. When Katherine suffered from a nasty gnat bite and was confined to the house for over four months, she stayed with her mother. Lady Charlotte then paid for her to convalesce in Bournemouth. Whilst Katherine went out in a bath chair her eld-erly mother walked beside her with a shade over her eyes and a thick black veil.

She returned to her favourite city, Venice. In 1875 the Layards had bought a home called Ca'Capello on the Grand Canal. They retired there nine years later.

In 1887 Lady Charlotte travelled with them after their summer holiday in England. At Vicenza they were greeted by the metal designer Cortelazzo who was then 'constantly backwards and forwards and stays in the house when in Venice',[10] and Lady Charlotte observed his devotion to his patron, Henry. She helped correct proofs for Henry's book about his early travels and examined the treasures of the Correr Museum. Many well-known figures called: the Stracheys, Elizabeth Barrett and Robert Browning's son, Pen, and the Gregorys. Sir William Gregory had been the Layards' 'best man'. He had married in 1881 the Anglo-Irish Augusta Persse, forty years his junior. In later years she would become linked with the Renaissance of Irish culture, a sort of latter-day Lady Hall in her espousal of 'Celtic dawn' and national culture. Lady Charlotte now sought Lady Gregory's help in translating a German book on playing cards and together they traced a sixteenth-century double-winged fan lent by Guggenheim.

Leaving Venice in mid-November, Lady Charlotte dreaded returning home. Travel had once more rallied her spirits and fused many of her old interests. She confessed to feeling more like her old self than she had done for three and a half years. Her rides in gondolas and her walks around Venice had reinvigorated her.

For some years Lady Charlotte had been without her own landau. She sometimes borrowed a carriage from Ivor or Blanche but more often walked about London or took a cab. As her eyesight deteriorated she found herself increasingly relying on cabs, and their drivers interested her as a hard-working and deserving group of men. Today some of the most exclusive parts of central London, such as Brompton Road and Warwick Avenue, boast dark green buildings in the middle of the road. The windows tend to be blacked out and they look like a mixture between overgrown dolls' houses and pagodas. They are the taxi drivers' refuge, the shelters where they can rest and eat cooked meals. Now only thirteen remain but in the 1890s there were forty-one and about 3,500 cabmen frequented them daily.[11]

The first shelter was built in the early 1870s at Palace Yard, Westminster, financed by subscriptions from the Houses of Parliament and much welcomed by the early cabmen with their horsedrawn vehicles. They were run by the Cabmen's Shelter Fund and Arthur was on its committee. He had presented the wooden shelter at Vauxhall station. In August 1885 Lady Charlotte spoke to her son about the possibility of erecting a shelter close to her home. It would be:

a pretty offering from me to a class of men, whose services I have so frequently profited by – and from whom I have never experienced anything but civility – When I hear accusations against a class – I often think there must be faults on both sides – and whereas we are told that a soft answer turned away wrath, on the other hand rough language often leads to retaliation – We are too apt to disregard the feelings of others if not quite of our own class and forget that at all events they are our fellow creatures.

She then discussed her plans with the fund's secretary and visited three shelters. Permission had to be sought from the local vestry and water laid on. The cost (before fitting up the two rooms) was £175. The Langham Place shelter was finally opened in March 1886, resplendent with potted plants. Henry Layard spoke on behalf of Lady Charlotte and read out a letter from her. Arthur and a cabman then made speeches.

Having erected shelter 38, Lady Charlotte suggested reading matter for its users. She proposed *The Times* but the men were more keen on three papers for the same price. Anxious that her shelter should have 'the most useful and suitable papers' she compromised by giving them *The Times* and the *Daily Chronicle* so that they could have 'both sides of politics'. Some months later she decided to add an illustrated paper: 'So I pitched upon the *Sporting and Dramatic News* as being suitable.' She used to call in at the shelter and was pleased at its popularity. Impressed by the widespread use of umbrellas in Italy, she sent to Rome for a sample. When umbrellas (from the Italian 'ombrello', meaning a little shade) were introduced into Britain from Paris in the late eighteenth century, their early users were viewed as eccentric even though such protection from the elements had its origin in classical times. Now the cabmen enjoyed their use.

Lady Charlotte also supported their recreational activities, giving money for excursions and attending their entertainments with her grandchildren, Ola and Nellie Du Cane. She inaugurated a tea-party at her own shelter. Blanche and Edward sang at the first one. Long, red woollen comforters (scarves) were knitted daily for the cabmen, and Lady Charlotte found that this was something not dependent on sight. She was responding to an appeal in the press for comforters and mittens for cabmen and now knitted six or seven weekly. The Ragged School children had previously received her knitted work and now 'I should be only too glad if I could be of use to these poor hardworking men in this way.' Being of use mattered as the world she had known seemed to change and the people she loved departed. The fear of being an elderly, forgotten widow goaded her into persistent activity, even though her large family and reputation belied such fears. Knitting helped keep her hands active and, most importantly, prevented total idleness 'which of all things I most thoroughly abhor'. This was written in her seventy-ninth year. The men of her shelter and at the Pickering Place shelter were periodically bombarded with the results of her 'eternal knitting' usually receiving parcels of four dozen comforters at a time. She also provided yearly donations to the fund. In 1893 for example, the fund's eighteenth report showed that although most subscribers gave a few pounds, Lady Charlotte's 'constant supply of newspapers and a large quantity of warm wraps and comforters' had, as usual, been accompanied by a gift of £150.

In April 1889 the Ponsonbys bought 17, Cavendish Square. It was actually Lady Charlotte who put up the money, borrowing £6,000 from Guest and Company (paying back the first instalment of £500 plus interest in August 1890). In 1892 she gave the house to her son-in-law. The lease of Langham Place had been due for renewal in 1890 and Lady Charlotte had decided to sell it at auction (it fetched £14,000) and accept the invitation to live in four rooms in Blanche's new home. It was this move which prompted her gifts and sale of European china. Christie's took this in May and held a two-day sale in March 1980.* They also sold furniture (Constance received some treasured china cabinets). Thirty cases of china (mostly Oriental and European) went to Canford and Merthyr had most of the remaining English china. Lady Charlotte kept her saltglaze (which eventually went to Blanche) and a few favourites. It was a big upheaval. Langham Place had been home for twenty-four years. In June she moved out, going first to the Ponsonbys' home at 1, Queen Anne Street until the new house was ready. In the autumn she accompanied Maria's family to the Wimbornes' seaside home at Branksome Dene.

At first she felt disoriented and depressed at Cavendish Square. Her loss of independence coincided with no longer being able to see faces. Yet she was determined to appear sociable. She went to the theatre for the first time in many years, though sadly all was 'in a mist'. She took her granddaughter, Ola, to a ball, tried a 'crush' reception at Lady Salisbury's and in January 1891 attended the wedding of Ivor's daughter Corise to Lord Rodney. At a garden party at Marlborough House she saw another elderly widow, Queen Victoria. She dined with her family: at Maria's she was entertained by Oscar Wilde, 'who is always very amusing and full of anecdotes'. It must have been trying to participate in events she could no longer see and frustrating not to be able to work as she liked. She related a poignant little tale about herself. She detected something on the floor and thinking that an item had dropped which might get crushed, she asked Mr Whitman to rescue it and tell her what it was. 'Only a sunbeam' was his reply.

The 1888–90 volume of her journal contained many more crossings out than were usual. Recently effort seemed to have replaced enjoyment in keeping a journal. It was one more duty to perform, even though it allowed space for thoughts and feelings. In April 1887 she wrote 'I must force myself to write again – but I do so with a very heavy heart. I am so utterly out of spirits and everything seems to require a greater effort from day to day.' Yet the journal represented unbroken contact with the past and though it was increasingly difficult to write 'the old habit is strong upon me – and I must indulge in making a few notes even though I can *scarcely* see to write them and cannot see to read them when written.' She saw herself as an anachronism yet would not completely accept that infirmity could sap all energy: 'I have almost over lived all regrets – almost all feelings – and I am surrounded by every comfort and luxury – it is a feeling of hopelessness and want of energy that I can neither account for nor describe.'

Not surprisingly, at a time when life expectancy was significantly lower than it is today, Lady Charlotte now thought each new year would be her last. She always liked to complete things properly and so bade farewell to the places that mattered.

---

* Appendix 5B.

In 1890 she visited Uffington where memories of Ariosto and Hallam 'crowded in on me' in the cherished second avenue. She paid a final visit to Dowlais where literary memories combined with more practical experiences and then she saw Venice for the last time.

On 22 February 1891, sixty-nine years after her first self-conscious lines in her pocket book, Lady Charlotte made her final entry in her journal. The writing now spilled over the lines, it had gradually got larger and more difficult to decipher, with some lines running into each other. The careful phrasing of that last entry displays the tacit understanding of diarists that they are writing both for themselves and, if not for posterity, then at least for their loved ones to read; ' – and here I close a journal which I have kept for very many years – I can no longer see to write or to read what I have written – I am thank God perfectly well in health though growing feebler every day – and I feel confident the end cannot be far off – I am most kindly cared for by all that are dear to me and I bless them for it … and now adieu to all.'

Lady Charlotte's life was not yet finished though for somebody so used to structuring and recording her daily details, the demise of the journal must have intensified the sense of awaiting the end. Some of her old determination nevertheless persisted. One of her grandsons later recalled how she could still identify and describe Battersea enamel by its feel. Nor did blindness stop her knitting, reciting Chaucer aloud or taking exercise by walking up and down the room. She went out with Blanche in her carriage in the afternoons. A Mr Upton read *The Times* and part of a book to her for an hour each lunch-time and she still supervised some of the work on the playing card books. Her younger sister Mary died from heart disease in August 1893 and the following year her cousin and son-in-law Henry, one of the men she had most admired, passed away. Enid, who had spent the last twenty-five years constantly with Henry, wrote simply in her journal (in words reminiscent of Lady Charlotte's account of Charles's death): 'I turned to stone.'

After staying at Branksome Dene in October 1894, Lady Charlotte had hoped to return to London for the winter. Illness forced her to go instead to nearby Canford, her former home. A doctor was called on 18 November and from that date she remained in her room, though she still knitted for the cabmen. Gradually she became weaker. Her lungs were congested. Doctors attended from Wimborne and Bournemouth, then her own London physician, Dr McLagan. She was in her eighty-third year. Most of the family visited and Maria and Blanche stayed on. On 15 January 1895 Lady Charlotte died.

She was buried at Canford on 24 January, the same day as Cornelia's brother, Randolph Churchill, died. So crowded had been Lady Charlotte's life that her obituaries concentrated on the achievements they saw as most relevant to their readers. *The Times* focused largely on her latter years, emphasizing her talents as a collector, the recent books and her work for the London cabmen and Turkish refugees; there was no mention of *The Mabinogion*, today her most remembered achievement. In contrast, Welsh newspapers recounted her twenty years at Dowlais, her marriage to John Guest, work for the iron trade and 'monumental' translation of the work which formed the 'real basis of modern Romantic writing'. The *Cardiff Times* added that one of her 'chief claims to respect and reverence rests on the enlightened interest and zeal which she always evinced in the improvement of the social condition of the workmen and their families connected with the Dowlais works'. The long, reverential and deferential obituary from the *Poole Herald* summed her up as 'one of the most eminent and one of the most remarkable women of the century – a lady of great artistic tastes and literary ability, combined with which she possessed, to an almost phenomenal extent, all those administrative faculties which are necessary to success in great business enterprises'.

Determination and sustained application were common to all Lady Charlotte's undertakings so that, to use her own words, she did 'reach an eminence' in whatever she decided to pursue.

Timing was important. Lady Charlotte married John Guest when Dowlais was at its height; she witnessed at first hand some of the major formative events of modern history, such as the Congress of Berlin. And although women of the nineteenth century led lives which, with hindsight, may appear restricting and stultifying to the modern woman, the exact timing of Lady Charlotte's life did give a woman of her social class, an advantage over those born slightly earlier or later.

Born soon after the libertine excesses of the late eighteenth-century high-life hedonists such as Lady Seymour Dorothy Worsley, early nineteenth-century aristocrats like Lady Charlotte remained sufficiently close to this world (and its more serious side of ladies of letters and blue stockings) to retain a little latitude in freedom of expression. Moreover, unlike the middle-class lady, anxious to demonstrate aspiring gentility, Lady Charlotte's class had no need for emulation. She was, irrefutably, a lady. Paradoxically her daughters did not and were not encouraged to enjoy the limited freedom and opportunities which Lady Charlotte had carved out for herself. As Guest children, they were products of the new industrial society and grew up in highly stratified mid-Victorian Britain. They sought to re-engage with a landed society which was being overtaken by one created by wealth (ironically symbolized by their own father), and Lady Charlotte was also anxious that, through her descendants, she might recoup the glory that had once been the Berties but which was now merely a history story. Had Lady Charlotte been born twenty years later, it is likely that her life would have been more restricted, and it is no coincidence that the daughter whose life most closely approximated to that of her mother's (yet who significantly had no children to cope with) was Enid. Not only was she married to someone of her mother's generation, but she lived for most of her life outside Victorian Britain.

Young women in the 1880s like Lady Charlotte's grand-daughter, Alice Du Cane, might have expected to have greater freedom and opportunity than Lady

Charlotte had possessed in her youth. Yet the end of the century was not a propitious time to be born into the aristocracy. Rather, it suggested opportunities for the educated, ambitious, intellectual middle-class woman who was now pushing at the doors marked politics and professions. Although Lady Charlotte survived all these periods, she was perhaps fortunate in being born early in the century before the full force of Victorian domesticity. In this sense time was on her side.

So, although the bells had not been rung when a baby girl was born at Uffington House in 1812, when an elderly widow died at Canford Manor in 1895, church bells were deservedly muffled and flags were lowered. Lady Charlotte's life, but not her influence, had been finally 'wound up'.

APPENDIX 1

LADY CHARLOTTE'S FAMILY

The First Earl of Lindsey was Robert Bertie (who was also the Twelfth Lord Willoughby De Eresby). Queen Elizabeth I and the Earl of Essex were his godparents. He was knighted after the capture of Cadiz and became Lord High Admiral of England. In 1605 he married Elizabeth (daughter of the First Baron Montague of Boughton). He became the Earl of Lindsey in 1626. As General in charge of the King's forces at the Civil War Battle of Edgehill (1642) he was fatally wounded and died soon afterwards at Warwick Castle. The title passed to his son, Montague, who had also fought at Edgehill and in 1649 assisted Charles I to the scaffold. He was Lord Great Chamberlain during the early years of the Restoration but died at Campden House, Kensington in 1666.

It was his second son, Charles Bertie (the first of several generations of the same name), who acquired the Uffington Estate from the Second Duke of Buckingham in the early 1670s. Here he laid out the impressive avenues of trees and 'in the afternoon of my age' built Uffington House, which he called not 'a fine house: but I hope it will be big enough for a younger brother's family'. He commissioned the Neapolitan artist Verrio (who also worked at Burghley House) to decorate the walls of the great staircase and the ceiling with the 'Fall of Phaeton' from Ovid's *Metamorphoses*.

Lady Charlotte's own father succeeded to the title of the Ninth Earl of Lindsey at the death of his kinsman the Fifth Duke of Ancaster. Born in September 1744 he entered the army and became a General in 1803. He was MP for Stamford between 1801-9. He became the Ninth Earl on 8 February 1809, when he was sixty-four and widowed. His first marriage to Eliza Maria Scrope (née Clay) had been childless but within months of succeeding to his title he had remarried. His second wife was Charlotte Susanna Elizabeth Layard, born in 1780 and descended on her father's side from a distinguished Huguenot family – they had fled France at the Revocation of the Edict of Nantes in 1685. Her grandfather had been physician to George III's mother. Her father was the Very Reverend Charles Peter Layard DDFRS and her mother Eliza Ward. Layard became the Rector of Uffington in 1798. He was a Prebendary of Worcester Cathedral, Chaplain in Ordinary to George III and Dean of Bristol. It was said that his advancement was due to his sister who had married the Duke of Ancaster after being governess to the Duke's younger sister. He published a prize poem on charity, a poetical essay on duelling and a volume of sermons, though was best remembered in Bristol for selling off the Cathedral's bronze eagle (in 1866 his granddaughter Lady Charlotte presented a brass eagle lectern to Uffington Church). Charlotte's mother was twenty-nine when she married the Ninth Earl of Lindsey, (then in his sixties) at Greenwich on 18 November 1809. Her brother, Brown Villiers, had become the Rector of Uffington in 1803. He was married twice and had twelve children.

Lady Charlotte was born in 1812 and on 17 September 1818 her seventy-four-year-old father died. His second eldest child, the feeble Albermarle George Augustus Frederick, was four. His godparents included the Prince of Wales, later George IV. He became the Tenth Earl and when he died unmarried in March 1877, his younger brother Montague Peregrine (Bertie) became the Eleventh Earl. He had married Felicia Welby (who lived until she was ninety-three) and their son and heir Lord Bertie (Montague Peregrine Albemarle, who later became ADC to the Governor of New South Wales) was born in September 1861, succeeding to the title in 1899. In 1883 the estate consisted of 4,790 acres worth £9,286 per annum. Uffington House was burned down on 20 December 1904.

Lady Charlotte's mother had remarried on 14 April 1821. Her second husband was the Reverend Peter William Pegus, born in 1791. They were first cousins, his mother, Mary Anne, being a sister of the Countess of Lindsey's father. She died in 1858 and Pegus died just two years later. They had two children, Maria Antoinetta known as Mary (1822-93) and Elizabeth (1824-37).

APPENDIX 2

Date of Birth	Name	Explanation of Name	Date of Marriage	Spouse	Year of Death	Additional
3 July 1834	Charlotte Marie	1) Lady Charlotte 2) Maria Ranken	1859	Richard Du Cane. Cousin to Charles Schreiber. Solicitor.	1902	Had ten children (including twins). Alice, Arthur and Dacre in particular helped with Lady Charlotte's fan collection. Lived at Park Crescent, London, though when first married became neighbours of the Schreibers at Roehampton.
29 August 1835	Ivor Bertie	1) Ifor Bach, hero of Morlais Castle. 2) Family name.	1868	Lady Cornelia Henrietta Maria Spencer Churchill. Eldest daughter of 7th Duke of Marlborough. Mother, Lady Frances Vane OBE, d. of 3rd Marquis of Londonderry. Died 1927 and lived in Merley House after Canford was sold in 1923. Brother was Randolph Churchill whose son, Winston, used to play at Canford as a child – and once had to stay in bed for three months after jumping from a bridge there.	1914	Eldest son became Baron Wimborne 1880. Lived Canford Manor. Nine children. Ivor Churchill was their heir (and married into the Duke of Westminster's family). Youngest son Oscar Montague – father of Revel Guest.
29 January 1837	Katherine Gwladys	1) Lady Carbery, a godmother and also a family name. 2) A Welsh name. Gwladys helped bring Christianity to Britain.	1861	Rev. Frederick Cecil Alderson, youngest son of a judge. Rector of Holdenby, then Lutterworth. Resident Canon of Peterborough Honorary Chaplain to King Edward VII. Died in 1907.	1926	Nicknamed 'Cattws' as a child, later known as Kate in the family. One of her children was named after her little brother Augustus.

18 January 1838	Thomas Merthyr	1) Sir John's brother. 2) 'The term of endearment by which for now near five years I have called my husband.' Place of residence.	1877	Lady Theodora Grosvenor, Sister of 1st Duke of Westminster, 8th d. of 2nd Marquis. Died in 1924.	1904	Lived Inwood House, Master of Hounds (Blackmore Vale). One child.
28 February 1839	Montague John	1) Family name. 2) Sir John.	Did not marry.		1909 (on a visit to Sandringham on Edwards VII's birthday.)	Known as Monty. MP. Published a two-volume book on his mother's ceramic journals. Also a collector.
12 August 1840	Augustus Frederick	1) & 2) Names of 'first' loves. Also named after godfather the Duke of Sussex.	Did not marry		Died on 23 May 1862, aged twenty-one of rheumatic pericarditis. A Cambridge student.	Nicknamed Geraint as a child after one of *The Mabinogion* heroes.
17 August 1841	Arthur Edward	1) 'In honor of my old friend and ally, King Arthur.' 2) Sir John's nephew.	1867	Adeline Mary Chapman youngest d. of David Barclay Chapman of Rochester. She divorced Arthur, and remarried in 1899 Cecil Chapman of Metropolitan Police Magistrate (her cousin).	1898	Died aged fifty-six, only three years after mother's dead. Two children. MP. Director of London & South West Railway and Taff Vale Railway Co.

11 July 1843	Mary Enid Evelyn	1) Lady Charlotte's half-sister. 2) After 'Geraint and Enid' in *The Mabinogion*. 3) A Welsh name.	1869	(Sir) Austen Henry Layard, PC CGB DGL. Discoverer of Nineveh. MP. Diplomat in Spain and Turkey. Lady Charlotte's cousin. Died 1894.	1912	No children. Enid helped Henry in his work. Painter and sculptor.
17 October 1844	Constance Rhiannon	1) Chaucer and the Lady Constance of De Vere. 2) Pwyll's wife in *The Mabinogion*.	1869	Charles George Cornwallis Eliot. Youngest son of 3rd Earl of St Germans. Captain in Grenadier Guards. Equerry to Prince Christian. 3rd Earl of St Germans 1865. Died 1901.	1916	Known to the family as Connie. Seven children. She was in attendance on Princess Christian in Lady Charlotte's later years.
25 August 1847	Blanche Vere	1) Chaucer's Duchess of Lancaster. Wife of John of Gaunt (connection with Canford). 2) Family name.	1875	Edward Ponsonby, son of Walter William Brabazon Ponsonby (brother of Lord de Mauley) and Vicar of Canford 1846–69. Edward became 7th Earl of Bessborough. His mother, Lady Louisa, was the only d. of the 3rd Earl of St Germans so Blanche's mother-in-law was sister to Constance's husband. Barrister. Sec. to Lord Robert Grosvenor at the Treasury 1880–84. Personal Secretary to Rt Hon. Arthur Wellesley Peel. Died 1920.	1919	Blanche became Hon. Sec. of Princess Victoria's Auxiliary for the Inspection of the YMCA Recreation Huts for soldiers in the First World War. Their eldest son, Vere, edited Lady Charlotte's journals (abbreviated version). Lived at 17, Cavendish Square with Lady Charlotte in her last years.

APPENDIX 3

A

The following stanzas were written by Rees Lewis (Ab Tudful) a Merthyr printer. The accompanying English translation has been provided for this book by Dr Aled Rhys Wiliam. It should be noted that the poet's admiration for Lady Charlotte outstripped his inspiration and literary ability. His lines were printed on small cards. A similar twelve-verse *englynion* was composed by the same poet to celebrate the birth of Ivor Bertie Guest in 1835.

1. Dyngarwch! cafwyd di'n goron-urddas
   Ac harddwch i ddynion;
   A'th goledd gwaith ei galon,
   Yw llaesu briw, lleshau bron.

1. Philanthropy! thou art seen as a crown
   of dignity and beauty for humanity;
   to lessen inquiry and heal the breast
   is thy cherished heart's ambition.

2. Rhenaist ddeubarth o'th rinwedd-orenwog
   I'r rian brydferthwedd;
   Dy des ei mynwes a'i medd: –
   I'w galon rhydd ymgeledd.

2. Thou has shared the better part of thy
   celebrated virtue
   with this lady of fair countenance;
   her bosom is full of thy warmth;
   it gives succour to the heart.

3. CHARLOTTE GUEST
   yw Nest fy nydd, – haelfrydedd
   Yw hwyl frwd ei hawydd;
   Rhoddi yn fad rhwydd i'n fydd
   O'i channerth mawr a'i chynnydd.

3. CHARLOTTE GUEST
   is my latter-day *Nest*: generosity
   is the ardent temper of her desire;
   freely does she give us of her support and
   prosperity.

4. Gesyd wylwyr yn gyson-i holi
   Helynt y tylodion;
   Yn gofrestr yn nhir estron
   Gwyr ei bryd ynt ger ei bron.

4. Constantly she sends her scouts to
   ask the welfare of
   the poor; listed in foreign lands, the people of
   her concern are near to her heart.

5. Baich y gwan, ei rhan a rydd – i'w symud,
   A dwys ammod beunydd:
   I'r dall mae'n oleu'r dydd,
   I ugeiniau y mae'n gynnydd.

5. She gives her share to shift the
   burden of the weak,
   with solemn covenant every day;
   to the blind she is daylight;
   to many she is prosperity [lit. progress].

6. Cydymdeimlad mad, hi a'i medd-i bawb,
   Mae'n boen ac anhunedd
   Os gwel yn ddiymgeledd
   Un gwr syw o gyrrau'i sedd.

6. She has sympathy for everyone –
   suffering and sleeplessness are hers
   if she sees a single person
   destitute and homeless.

7. Ymddifaid mewn llaid a llwch, – a gweddwon
   Mai gwyddus mewn tristwch,
   O'i rhadau yn fflau a fflwch,
   Dyd iddynt er dedwyddwch.

7. Orphans in mire and dust, and widows,
   as is known, in sorrow – to them
   for their happiness she gives of her
   bounteous blessings.

8. Lin a gwlân yn lân ar led, – rhag anwyd
   I'r gweinion didnodded;
   Diwyrgam y daw eurged
   I'r llu a'i gloes o'r llaw gled.

8. Linen and wool all around against the cold
   for the weak and unprotected;
   directly from the open hand
   comes a golden gift. For the crowd
   in its woe.

9. O'i mêl ddil a'i gwin hilia wiwfwrdd llawn
   I frydd llwyd rhag traha;
   Gyru o'n plith gur ein pla,
   Neu hoyw gysur i'n geisia.

9. With honeycomb and wine she prepares
   a fine full table for a myriad grey from
   outrage;
   to cast from our midst the pain of our
   affliction
   some comfort for us doth she seek.

10. Eur addysg oreu roddiad-weinydda,
    O'i nodded a'i chariad;
    Ein plant a feddant yn fad
    Hoff urddau o'i hyfforddiad

10. With patronage and love she ministers
    the finest golden gift of education;
    our children will derive high office
    [lit. 'favoured orders']
    from her schooling.

11. Yr eiddig Bendefiges-urddasol!
    Hardd iesin Arglwyddes!
    I'n byd lwydd a'n bywyd les,
    Yw dymuniad da'i mynwes.

11. A zealous, noble peeress –
    Beauteous, glorious lady,
    whose heart's desire is our worldly success,
    and benefit in our lives.

12. E ddengys y rian ddengar-ffordd nef
    Ffwrd o nwyfiant daear: –
    Hon a'i gwaith, gan Dduw fo'n'gâr
    A'i hagwedd iddo'n hygar.

12. The lovely lady shows heaven's way –
    away from the world's excitement;
    may she and her work be friends with God
    and her aspect pleasing to Him.

B

Education at Dowlais 1820-55

(Attendance figures in brackets show the attendances on 12 February 1849.)

Infants

Dowlais Infants (expanded in mid-1840s from department in girls' school) (140).
Gwernllwyn Infants founded 1845 (145).
Gellifaelog Infants founded 1847 (131).
Banwen Infants founded 1848 (51).

All had trained teachers and assistants, and cost pupils ½*d* weekly.

Day schools

1820 purpose-built school established for boys and girls though as early as 1814 Guest was discussing plans for a school with his (rather more reluctant) partner, William Taitt. Mr and Mrs Beattie Goodyer were teachers until dismissed in 1825. Replaced by Thomas Jenkins. New girls' school 1828. 1844 schools reorganized and junior and senior day schools developed.

Boys: (upper 45, lower 142). Subjects included three R's, religion and chemistry and mensuration for upper boys. In 1847 the Dowlais Iron Company employed thirty-two out of fifty-six who had left upper school. Paid 2*d* weekly. Hirst in charge (got his teaching certificate in 1847), also three Masters.

Girls (112): Taught three R's, geography, history etc. brought in own sewing on Fridays. Paid 1*d* weekly, found own copy books. Three mistresses (two with certificates).

September 1855, Opening of new Dowlais Central Schools

Seven schoolrooms. Accommodated 650 boys and girls and 680 infants.

Adult schools

October 1848 adult evening school for young women. Seven paid teachers. Met October – April (127). Free. Took women workers, servants and daughters of workmen. Three R's, geography, history, needlework etc. Adult male classes (upper twenty-three, lower ninety-three) only for youths and men working for the Dowlais Iron Company. Five paid teachers and Superintendent. Upper class developed out of fee-paying small mathematics class. Also small advanced morning class for men at library. Dowlais Drawing School from 1853 for twenty-six men – taught technical drawing by master and skilled engineer.

Sunday schools

Seven schools – boys and girls (Welsh and English) and adults (three Welsh, one English) *c.* 2,500 attendance by early 1840s.

APPENDIX 4

A: *THE MABINOGION*

Translated by Lady Charlotte. Source for all tales except 'Taliesin': Red Book of Hergest, Oxford.

Tale	Type	Extant Translations Welsh to English	English and Continental Versions	Publication date – Lady Charlotte's Translation	Some Key Features
1. The Lady of the Fountain – Iarlles y Ffynnawn or Owain	Arthurian Romance (Arthur, British King, Court at Caer Llion). It seems that although similarities between this and following two chivalric tales, each had a different author and they did not evolve as a group.		Ywayne and Gawin (English) British Museum and in Ritson's *Metrical Romances*, vol. 1 12th c. Chevalier au Lion (French) Chrétien de Troyes. This and his *Perceval* and *Erec et Enid* are French reworkings of Welsh originals. Also German verse form by Hartmann von der Aue, Danish version 12th c. or 13th c. Swedish version Icelandic Saga.	1838 1st part	Hero's knightly obligations. Valour and forgetfulness, remorse. Theme of regeneration strong probably 10th-11th c. no later than end of 12th c., though not dated with certainty.
2. Peredur the Son of Efrawc – Peredur ab Efrawc	Arthurian Romance	Owen Pughe had a translation which he showed to Scott in 1800.	English Metrical Romance (Thornton MS). Perceval le Galois (French). Chrétien de Troyes metrical and prose versions, German poem c. 12th c. Wolfram (Schulz trans. this) Icelandic Saga. (In 1842 Sir Frederic Madden of the British Museum provided Lady Charlotte with French references to the Roman de Perceval and alerted her to the Icelandic Perceval Saga.)	1839	Less well-constructed story than other two. More episodic. Lot of Norman-French features. Duty of vengeance. Seems to be based on 6th-c. Chieftain. Proving of hero crucial. Outline paralleled in Chrétien de Troyes' poem but also contains some native features.
3. Geraint the Son of Erbin – Geraint ab Erbin	Arthurian Romance	Col. Vaughan lent Lady Charlotte his copy of Geraint ab Erbin from the Peniarth MS (that is, the White Book of Rhydderch-Peniarth MSS 4,5)	*Erec et Enide* (French) metrical Romance, Chrétien de Troyes. German version, Hartmann von der Aue. Icelandic Saga. Used as basis for Tennyson's *Geraint and Enid* (Lady Charlotte's trans.).	1840	Seen as more refined story. Arthur more evident. Geraint's devotion; need to win back his lady. Enid's patience. Least mythical.

Title	Notes	Translation / Reference	Date	Description
4. Kilhwch and Olwen Ystori Kilhwch ac Olwen neu Hanes y Twrch Trwyth	Native Welsh tale. Earliest Arthurian tale in Welsh.	Sir John Bosanquet (Justice Bosanquet) had made a translation of at least part of this tale and lent it to Lady Charlotte.	1842	Performance of seemingly impossible tasks to win lady's hand. Focus on Twrch Trwyth, ferocious wild boar. Long list of heroes. Arthur's court at Celliwig in Cornwall. Earliest written record of Arthurian cycle. Romance, folklore and fantasy. Long tale.
5. The Dream of Rhonabwy – Breuddwyd Rhonabwy	Native Welsh tale, Arthurian.		1843	Took shape later than others (excepting Taliesin). Episodes purely Welsh. Specific location Powys. Includes 12th-c. historical figures and splendours of Arthurian court (though not chivalric). Retrospective and ironic. Complex narrative including first Welsh use of dream motif. The most literary of the tales.
6. Pwyll Prince of Dyved – Pwyll Pendevig Dyved	One of four Branches of the Mabinogi. Distinct but linked Welsh tales seemingly with one common final author. Each of Lady Charlotte's translated tales ends with the colophon, 'And thus ends this portion of the Mabinogion' (it is the end of this tale which gave rise to this title).	Jones's *Welsh Bards. Cambrian Register* 1796, 9, 1818. By Owen Pughe.	1843	Set in South Wales. Pwyll making good initial mistakes by proving himself. Son Pryderi comes in to all for tales. Wife Rhiannon euhemerized horse goddess. 2nd half of 11th c.
7. Branwen the Daughter of Llyr – Branwen Verch Llyr		Owen Pughe had translated it.	1845	Set North Wales and Ireland; one of most popular, Cauldron features. War between Ireland and Wales. Has been suggested may contain elements developed in primitive versions of Grail legend. Informative about habits and customs of Wales.

Tale	Type	Extant Translations Welsh to English	English and Continental Versions	Publication date – Lady Charlotte's Translation	Some Key Features
8. Manawyddan the Son of Llyr – Manawyddan Vab Llyr	Mabinogi Branch	Welsh Bards. Cambrian Register		1845	South Wales includes episodes in England. Manhood of Pryderi. Simpler tale. Combines old myths and contemporary life. Includes famous story of mice in wheat. Stress on gentle and generous behaviour. Short notes by Lady Charlotte. Also has 'Wasteland' theme which comes in Grail legend.
9. Math the Son of Mathonwy – Math Vab Mathonwy	Mabinogi Branch	Cambrian Quarterly 1829 and 1833. Owen Pugh. (His source for this was not the Red Book.)		1845	Math magician and King of Gwynedd. In 3 parts. Math had been seen as great mythological character – the 'Celtic Zeus' (Rhys).
10. The Dream of Maxen Wledig – Breuddwyd Maxen Wledig	Historical Independent Tale.	Y Greal. 1806. Text only.		1849	Independent version of the story also in Geoffrey of Monmouth's Historia. Composite figure based on Spanish Magnus Maximus who commanded Britain and in AD 383 dispossed Gratian as Emperor. Concerns his arrival and departure from Britain. Union of powerful Rome and beauty of Wales.
11. Here is the Story of Lludd and Llevelys – Gyfranc Lludd a Llevelys	Historic Independent Tale	Y Greal	English translation of the edition of it in the Myvyrian Archailog, vol. II, by Rev. Peter Roberts in 'The Chronicle of the Kings of Britain'.		Shortest tale. Was inserted into the earliest Welsh version of Geoffrey of Monmouth's work. Expansion of Triad telling of three of the invasions of Britain. Celebrated King Lud was brother to Caesar's opponent, Cassivelaunus. Extols virtues of the British Celts. Includes magic.
12. Taliesin Hanes o'r Mangofion	Later. Different source from others. Prose and Poetry. Not in Red Book. Taliesin Williams supplied by Lady Charlotte with inexact translation from Iolo MS. She also used the William Morris MS in London.	Cambrain Quarterly 1833. Owen Pughe from inexact copy of 16 MS – not Red Book. Provided by Taliesin Williams and 'very defective' according to Price.		1849	Taliesin was a 6th-c. Welsh Bard. His works were collected in c. 1275 into a MS now known as the Book of Taliesin but the 'Hanes Taliesin' (a prose account of his adventures and the Book of Taliesin poems and others) only dates from the 16th c.

B

A list of some of the books which Lady Charlotte possessed in 1852 relevant to *The Mabinogion*.

Date if/as given in inventory

	2 Welsh Bibles
	Sermons in Welsh
	Book of Common Prayer in Welsh
1820	Richard *Welsh Nonconformist Memorial*
1836	Rees on the Welsh Saints
1792	Llywarch Hen, *Heroic Elegies*
1789	Dafydd ap Gwilym, *Barddoniaeth*
1804	Davies, *Celtic Researches*
1840	Davies, *History*
[1632?]	Davie, *Antiquae Britanniae Rudimenta*
1815	Daivies, *Agriculture of South Wales*, 2 vols
1843	Evans, *Blodau Ieuanc*
[n.d. given though 1784]	Jones, *Relicks of the Welsh Bards*
	Jones, *History of Wales*
	Jones, *Hanes y Nef a'r Ddaear*
1805	Jones, *History of Brecknock*, 2 vols
1830	Jones, *Y Bardd*
1584	Lhuyd, *History of Cambria*
1849	Stephens, *Literature of the Kymry*
1825★	Prichard, *Welsh Minstrelsy*
	Prichard, *Adventures of Twm Shon Catti*
1831	Prichard, *Eastern Origins of the Celtic Nations*
1799	Sir William Jones, *Works*, 8 vols
1801	2 supplementary vols
1836	Roscoe, *Wanderings in North Wales and South Wales*
1825	Merrick on Glamorgan Antiquities (folio)
1807	Malkin, *South Wales*
1779	Pennant, *Tour of Wales*
1841	*Derivations from the Welsh Language*
1801	Myvrian, *Archaeology of Wales*, 3 vols
1805	Y Greal Cynnulliad
1829	*Cambrian Quarterly Magazine*
1793	*Cambrian Register*, 3 vols
1820–2	Cambro-Briton
1822–43	Translations of the Cymmrodorion Society
	Owen Glendower, A Romance
1825	*Life of King Arthur*
1841	C.H. Smyth, *Le Pays de Galles et son Language*
1829	Sainte-Palaye, *Memoirs sur L'Ancienne Chevalerie*
1836	'Charlemagne', an Anglo-Norman Poem
1841	*Graal, Le Roman du Saint*
	Peredur ab Ebranc MS copy
1841	Percevell of Gales Transcription (Thornton MS)

★   Prichard is not to be confused with James Cowles Prichard. He was Thomas Jeffery Llewelyn Prichard – his book *The Adventures and Vagaries of Twm Shon Catti, Descriptive of Life in Wales* (1828) is recognized as the first Welsh novel.

1819	Hazlitt, *Political Essays*
	Hazlitt, *Lectures on English Poets*
1821	Hazlitt, *Lectures of the Age of Elizabeth*
1821-2	Hazlitt, *Table Talk*
1775	Chaucer, *The Canterbury Tales*, 1775 ed.
	Hallam, *Literature of Europe*
	Hallam, *Europe in the Middle Ages*
	Hallam, *Constitutional History of Europe*
1833*	Gambold, *Welsh Grammar*, 3rd ed.
	Richard, *English & Welsh Dictionary 1798-1805*
	Owen, (Owen Pughe) *Cambrian Biography*
1832	Pughe, (Owen Pughe) *Dictionary of the Welsh Language*, 2 vols
1810†	Richardson, *Dictionary of English, Persian and Arabic*
1811	Richardson, *Grammar of the Arabic Vocabulary*

Also other books in French, German and Italian.

*   1st edition of this dates from 1753.
†   1st edition of this dates from 1727.

APPENDIX 5

A

A description of some of the English porcelain, earthenware, enamels and glass in Lady Charlotte's collection, including examples of individual items.

i) *Porcelain*

a) *Bow*. Essex, soft-paste. Edward Heylyn and Thomas Frye (celebrated engraver whose prints Lady Charlotte collected) took out patent in 1744. First porcelain factory in England. Managed by Frye until 1759. Closed *c.* 1776 and the moulds moved to Derby. Used bone-ash as an ingredient from 1748. This reduced risk of collapse in the kiln and has become a means of identifying Bow. Works known as New Canton. Creamy colour of porcelain; early white wares of mid-18th c. often decorated by applied moulded sprigs. Schreiber collection includes the early period *c.* 1750-52. Large number of figures 1755-8 period inspired by Meissen. See for e.g. figure of gallant kissing his hand copied from one of a pair of Meissen figures modelled by J.J. Kaendler. Original figure supposed to represent Augustus the Strong, King of Poland and Elector of Saxony, blowing a kiss to a lady of the Prussian Court. Sold to Schreiber as Dresden in Amsterdam 1873 – cost £5.

b) *Bristol*. Soft-paste. Founded 1749 in Bristol using soapstone as an ingredient but within a few years had transferred to Worcester. Hard-paste: (see Plymouth) produced hard-paste porcelain after Plymouth factory moved to Bristol *c.* 1770. See for e.g. set of four figures emblematic of the seasons c. 1772 or later, sign of zodiac on each. Cost £28 from Mrs Haliburton, Richmond.

c) *Chelsea*. Soft-paste. Earliest wares milk white, very translucent glassy paste and little decoration. (Triangle period.) See for e.g. Goat or Bee Jug (1745-9) based on a Sprimont silver original (Sprimont was the Chelsea manager). Schreibers especially interested in this and in succeeding raised anchor phases. Collection includes figures, vases and wares for domestic use. See the large rabbit tureen of red anchor (*c.* 1742-56) purchased at Rotterdam 1876: 'It has suffered much. Still it is a noble piece.' Offered for £5 but £4 accepted. Rabbit crouches with a lettuce leaf in mouth *c.* 1755. See also their Chelsea 'toys' – scent bottle in form of a girl holding a basket of flowers *c.* 1760. Purchased Paris 1874 for £7.12 and brought back from Germany by dealer Oppenheim. Some scent bottles and other pieces (e.g. *c.* 1750 a group of Hercules and Omphale) have since been attributed to the unknown factory probably based in London *c.* 1749-54 and known as the 'Girl in a Swing' factory.

d) *Chelsea-Derby*. In 1770 the Chelsea factory was acquired by William Duesbury and John Heath of Derby. Chelsea style was largely abandoned. More subdued colours now predominated. See for e.g. pair of statuettes of musicians purchased in Paris 1830. Sold to Lady Charlotte as Meissen and after bargaining paid £9. Often difficult to distinguish from Chelsea. Group known as 'The Tithe Pig' in which farmer's wife offers her baby to the clergyman in place of pig for tithe payment, was originally catalogued as Chelsea but later reattributed to Chelsea-Derby by Rackham. Cost £4, 1882.

e) *Derby*. Soft-paste. Made in Derby by 1750. William Duesbury was associated with the factory in 1756, and Heath. Many figures imitated Meissen. Some of the best were in white biscuit.

1786-1811 Crown Derby period proper. See pair of custard cups and covers *c.* 1800 Bought Rotterdam 1872, sold to the Schreibers as French Fürstenberg.

f) *Longton Hall.* Soft-paste. Staffordshire, mid-century. Run by William Littler. Similar to other Staffs. wares. Rich blue tends to be used as background. Some vessels formed of overlapping leaves or simulate melons e.g. pair of soup plates painted in bright underglaze blue, rim of each moulded in relief and overlapping leaves. One purchased from Lady Hopetoun's sale and the other a gift from Franks. Also a pair of sugar bowls with covers and stand each in form of a melon. Purchased Utrecht 1879.

g) *Lowestoft.* Suffolk 1757-*c.* 1802. Utility wares. See mug painted in blue with dragon, Chinese style *c.* 1770.

h) *Plymouth.* Between 1745-55 the true china clay (or kaolin) had been discovered. In 1768 William Cookworthy took out a patent for hard-paste porcelain produced at Plymouth until 1770, then in Bristol. See figure of an Indian woman, emblematic of America, one of a set of continents. Purchased in London 1869 from Carter (he called it Chelsea) for £6.

i) *Spode.* Josiah Spode (1733-87) established pottery at Stoke-on-Trent, after death, son carried on. Porcelain not produced until early 19th c. Bit too modern for Lady Charlotte's liking but September 1869, for example, purchased little Spode violet basket from Exeter *c.* 1820 for 3*s*.

j) *(Welsh) Swansea.* Cambrian pottery at Swansea established 1764. Porcelain not made there until 1814 when Lewis Weston Dillwyn took over. He lost no time bringing founders of Nantgarw works, Billingsley and Walker to Swansea where they worked for three years. Plate with painting of Swallow of Otaheite given to Lady Charlotte in 1868 by Dillwyn family.

k) *Worcester.* Soft-paste. Founded 1751 and following year incorporated the Bristol soft-paste factory. 1751-83 known as Dr Wall period after a leading partner. Soapstone used in the porcelain. 1765-75 adaptation of oriental designs. 1760 Chelsea painters went to Worcester and began elaborate decoration, influenced by the French royal factory at Sèvres which had replaced Meissen in leading European fashion in second half of 18th c. Neo-classical designs popular about 1780 and modified Sèvres introduced by Thomas Flight *c.* 1783. Martin Barr taken into partnership 1792. See Worcester vase and cover in imitation of Chinese porcelain *c.* 1770, figures of Chinese lady and boy. Also dish *c.* 1765 open-work, oval, middle panel surrounded by crimson scrolls with canary yellow birds among bushes. Purchased London 1894 for £4 10*s*.

ii) English Earthenware

English earthenware included Lambeth. Delft (the potteries began *c.*1660), also 17th c. Bristol Delft; Fulham Stoneware (in 1671 John Dwight of Fulham took out a patent) and Staffordshire salt-glazed ware. The most famous was, and is, the pottery of Josiah Wedgwood (1730-95). Wedgwood had been apprenticed with his brother at Stoke. He entered partnership with Thomas Whieldon, a Staffordshire pottery-maker of tortoise-shell, Astbury and other types of ware and soon dominated the market and developed a fine green glaze. From 1759 he was based at Burslem and in 1769 in partnership with his cousin Thomas Bentley built the famous Etruria works for the manufacture of ornamental wares. They produced green and yellow glazed 'cauliflower' wares and creamware known as Queens Ware from *c.* 1765, enamelled either in the factory or at Chelsea or by outside enamellers. Alternatively they might be transfer-printed at Liverpool. Ornamental output included marbled wares and unglazed stonewares. See Appendix 6B for stoneware. Wedgwood includes two plaques of Louis XVI and one of Marie Antoinette (Based on Jean-Baptiste Nini's terracotta relief). Purchased from Mme Flandin for £19; 'an outrageous sum but they are very fine'. Louis XVI had given them to an Italian family from whom Mme Flandin had purchased them.

iii) Painted Enamels

Painted enamels made of metal (usually copper covered with enamel) produced in the 15th-c. Italian states and later spread to France, especially Limoges. By the beginning of the 18th c. small personal items such as snuff boxes were enamelled in Germany. In England enamels were produced at Battersea in the mid-18th c.

a) *Battersea Enamels.* York House, Battersea London. 1753-6. Factory run by Stephen Theodore Janssen. Battersea began transfer-printing which was soon extended to porcelain decoration. Very skilled craftsmen such as Ravenet were employed. The works closed in 1756 when Janssen became bankrupt. Lady Charlotte's collection includes a range of painted enamels e.g. Battersea painted plaque of Paris giving the apple to Hibernia, purchased 1874 at Rennes for 16s, coloured enamel pegs (4s) and a pair of candle sticks bought for after rejecting a similar damaged pair costing £20! Lady Charlotte listed twenty-five types of Battersea enamels in her collection but Rackham later attributed some of the individual items to Staffordshire.

b) *Bilston Enamels.* Staffordshire. Produced japanned snuff boxes with enamel decoration on lids, 1740-50. Large number of painted enamels between 1760s and 1780s e.g. two medallions (painted) with boys at play – taken from 18th c. book of engravings. Purchased Paris 1881, cost £21 (a high price for the Schreibers to pay abroad). Lady Charlotte thought them to be Battersea, Rackham believed Staffordshire (greater knowledge about the engraver Robert Hancock led him to attribute a number of enamels in this way). See also Appendix 6B.

iv) Glass

The Schreiber wine glasses all belong to the group known as Jacobite glass. They were made for the use of the many 18th c. secret societies supporting the House of Stuart. Mottoes and emblems decorate them. In 1882, for example, Lady Charlotte purchased a goblet in Worcester depicting Charles Edward in tartan dress c. 1750. It cost £6.

B

Examples of the Schreibers' European collection which can be viewed in England include, at the British Museum, a drug or spice jar painted with the arms of the monastery of San Geronimo de Buenavista, Spanish Talavera 17th c. and a mid-18th-c. Spanish Alcora tiled plaque depicting St Michael slaying the dragon (presented by Lady Charlotte to Franks). At the Victoria and Albert Museum (but not in the Schreiber Collection) are two fine Italian Este figures 1783 (originally in the Countess of Bessborough's collection). Probably modelled by Jean-Pierre Vanon they depict the Virgin Mary and St John. The Museum also possesses an enamelled copper plaque by Alexander Fromery of Berlin. It depicts the flight of Stanislas Lesczynski from Danzig (c. 1734) when Danzig was besieged by Imperial forces supporting the claim of the Elector of Saxony to the throne of Poland. Lady Charlotte visited Danzig in July 1876 and commented how 'The grouping of the fine old buildings and spires from some of the points of view, rising above the ramparts, most striking, reminding us of our Little Berlin enamel of the flight of Stanislas "De Dantzig à Bar".'

In March 1890 Lady Charlotte sold many items after leaving Langham House. The two-day sale at Christie's included some English porcelain and Wedgwood wares but the majority of the 217 lots were European porcelain. This included a small number of oriental items (the rest went to Ivor), Mennecy and a substantial section of Dresden (many teacups and saucers). Italian porcelain included Nove and Doccia teapots and covers. There was also a Buen Retiro tureen and cover.

APPENDIX 6

A

Some examples of the variety of fans in Lady Charlotte's collection.

1. *Political.* A printed English fan leaf depicting The States of Europe Playing at Piquet. Female figures representing France, Spain, Sardinia, the Empire, Saxony, Russia and Poland are playing the French game of Piquet. Britain, Holland and Prussia are seated but watch. Captions accompany the characters. For example France says 'I make the hand and play first' whilst Britain declares 'I'm preparing though I don't play, but if I'm nettl'd I'll take up the cards.' Towards the right a man in civilian dress comments on the game; further right are the Sultan of Turkey (on horseback) and the Shah of Persia. One chair is empty – that of the Pope. He is 'in the wings' declining to take part although his chair awaits him. This sophisticated political cartoon was long thought to depict the period when Innocent XI was Pope and John Sobieski of Poland triumphed over the Turks at Vienna. Lady Charlotte dated it to Innocent XI's time (1676-89) because of the pontifical coat-of-arms and Lionel Cust accepted this, dating this fan leaf as the oldest in the catalogue. Recent research, however, questions this. Evidence from France and the fact that the countries depicted would not have been part of Innocent XI's concern (for example Sardinia and Prussia) suggest that it is more likely to be representing the Polish War of Succession 1733-8. The Pope then was Clement XII and the subject would have been the exploits of Stanislas Lesczynski (also depicted on Lady Charlotte's enamelled copper plaque – see Appendix 5B). He was received in Warsaw on the death of the rival candidate to the Polish throne, Augustus of Saxony. France supported Spain and Sardinia upheld Lesezynski's claims. An article by Dr Isabella H. Van Eeghen ('The Polish War of Succession and the Fan' in *Fans* Newsletter of the Fan Circle no. 10, January 1970), examines this issue and suggests that the fan probably dates from the end of 1734 or early 1735. Lady Charlotte purchased this much-treasured and rare item in December 1879. Another English fan leaf was used to promote the deposed Ferdinand VII of Spain and stir up anti-French sentiment in the 1790s. Napoleon Bonaparte had banished the Spanish King in 1808.

2. *Marriage.* An English fan leaf attributed to M. Gamble of London celebrates the marriage of the Crown Princess Anne (daughter of George II) with the Prince of Orange in 1734. A dove carries a love letter and the couple are symbolized by a rose bush in full flower and an orange tree full of fruit. This is known as the 'Orange Fan'. All female members of European royal families received marriage fans. Written on the paper mount of this one is 'The Orange Fan with an Ode set to Music, Tune Let's be Jolly fill our Glasses'. Twenty verses of this are printed.

3. *Mourning.* English fan leaf 1760, very plain, the only decoration being an oval medallion in the centre with a female figure scattering flowers on a tomb. This was supposed to have been executed in memory of the Duke of Cumberland (brother of George III) who died in 1790.

4. *Commemorative.* Mounted English fan of 'Mr Thomas Osborne's Duck Hunting Party', September 1754. Obtained by Lady Charlotte in September 1880 from Elizabeth Birch whose father worked at the British Museum. Decorated on both sides (etched and coloured by hand), the fan shows the garden and duck-hunt at the pond on one side and the guests and their

festivities on the other side. Each lady guest was later presented with a fan commemorating the occasion. Tommy Osborne was a well-known London bookseller who held this party at his new Hampstead home to ingratiate himself with local society.

5. *Topographical.* English unmounted fan leaf by S. Clark of Greenwich Park – see illustration. Fans of the Neo-classical period depicted European views popular with those on the Grand Tour e.g. an Italian fan showing a view of Venice during the yearly celebration of the 'Marriage of Venice with the Adriatic'.

6. *Cabriolet.* A French fan consisting of two bands of unequal width representing Parisian life. In 1755 Joseph Child had introduced (into Paris) an elegant horse-drawn two-wheeled cart; known as a cabriolet it became 'all the rage' and was depicted on many items.

7. *Revolutionary.* Officials of the Directory – see illustration. Other fans included depictions of the taking of the Bastille (also celebrated in a centenary souvenir fan of 1889) and a Royalist fan showing the King and Queen with the words 'Lache Qui T'Abandonne'.

8. *Classical, Mythological.* An English example showing Charles Edward Stuart supported by Mars (Cameron of Lochiel) and Bellonia (Flora Macdonald) – a memorial to the Jacobite Rebellion of 1745.

9. *Church.* English chapel fan showing a family at the Resurrection (from a picture).

10. *Historical Victories.* Many of these depict battles, e.g. a large number of the Peninsular Wars. Not surprisingly since Ivor married Cornelia Churchill, there are six relating to the Marlborough family, e.g. one unmounted fan with nineteen verses of a song composed after the Battle of Malplaquet (1709) in which it was wrongly rumoured in France that the First Duke of Marlborough had been killed. Lady Charlotte's Dutch fans included one of the 'Zoutman' fans which commemorated the 1781 Dogger Bank battle between Zoutman and Sir Hyde Parker, commanders of the Dutch and British navies. Kate Bisschop did some research in Holland for Lady Charlotte, finding out information about Zoutman and other Dutch subjects.

11. *Advertisement.* New Opera fan for 1797. English mounted fan showing the seats of the Opera House with all their occupants. Lady Charlotte noted that very few people, even of the highest rank, had more than one place, and few had a box to themselves (though the Princess of Wales and the Duchess of Marlborough had two apiece). She obtained this fan in September 1883 for £1 2s 6d from Mallet in Bath. It was of especial interest to her since it included the name of Mrs Schreiber, the 'not very amicable' third wife of her husband's great grandfather alongside Lady Milsington who was the only child of the last Duke of Ancaster and a Bertie by birth!

B

Some examples of historical-political subjects which Lady Charlotte collected.

A. Anti-Gallican badges

The Anti-Gallican Society was formed in 1745 to discourage the importing and consumption of French produce and manufacture. Janssen (of Battersea enamel fame) was its President.

1. A badge of the Society made of gilt metal in rococo style with colourless paste set in silver. It is engraved with the Society's emblems and on the reverse has the coat-of-arms of William Plumer of Bakesware, MP for Herts in mid-18th c. British Museum.

2. Enamel badge of the Society, oval-shaped, depicting St George on horseback piercing with his spear a shield showing the arms of France. On either side of the escutcheon are figures, the lion rampant of England and the double-headed eagle of the Empire. Above, amidst flags and military trophies is Britannia holding a sphere. Below is the Anti-Gallican motto, 'For Our Country'. Purchased London, 1880. Lady Charlotte believed this to be Battersea, Rackham thought this and the next item were Staffordshire. Schreiber collection, Victoria and Albert Museum.

3. Similar badge to 2 though this one was printed red and a purplish black. Purchased London 1884 for £3. Schreiber collection, V&A.

4. Liverpool earthenware jug painted red with arms, supporters and crest of the Society. *c.*1775. Cost 2s 6d, from Marseilles, 1870. British Museum.

B. John Wilkes

Lady Charlotte's list of books consulted for the catalogue included *North Briton* no. 45, 1763. Wilkes libelled the King in this journal. The cry for Wilkes and Liberty was popular among the 18th-c. London crowd. Having experienced exile in France and the Tower of London, the return of Wilkes as MP for Middlesex in 1786 gave rise to London riots, which culminated in the 'massacre' of St George's Fields after Wilkes's imprisonment.

1. Enamel box of Wilkes with printed transfer of Britannia holding up the Cap of Liberty and crowning the British lion with a wreath. Britannia leans on a scroll inscribed no. 45. Purchased in Brussels. Schreiber collection.

2. Impressive figure of Wilkes. Lady Charlotte thought Chelsea but reattributed by Rackham to Derby. He stands beside a pedestal on which are scrolls with 'Magna Charta' and 'Bill of Rights' written on them. At his feet is Cupid with a cap of liberty and a volume entitled 'Lock' [sic] on Govt. *c.*1765 commemorating the public support for him of 1763. This has a companion figure of General Conway who spoke in Parliament against the government on questions linked to Wilkes's case. Schreiber collection.

3. Industrial pottery. Wedgwood teapot and cover depicting Wilkes the patriot flanked by small seated figures of Liberty and Britannia. On reverse is allegorical subject – young man approaching Liberty represented as a woman swooning into arms of Wilkes robed as Lord Mayor of London. She has a pike and cape and scroll with 'Magna Charter Bill of Rights' and shield hearing Union Jack beside her. *c.*1775. Lady Charlotte explained that Wilkes was Lord Mayor then and his popularity so great that his friends displayed various articles with his effigies. Purchased Walford, Oxford £1 5*s*, 1876. Schreiber collection.

C. The Excise Bill

1. Fan leaf of Sir Robert Walpole's Excise Bill 1733. Caricature sketch based on the agitation caused by the bill. A male figure (Poultney) displays a scroll in each hand entitled 'Liberty and Property' and 'No Dutch Politicks. Down with the Excise'. Above him is a medallion portrait of Cardinal Wolsey. To the left is a prostrate monster on whose body are the words 'Printing, Salt, Malt' etc. and other items. Lady Charlotte quoted from a contemporary book on caricature which suggested that ladies of the period were so interested in politics that caricatures were introduced on to their fans. The reference to Wolsey is that he, like Walpole served his master and sold his country. Published by M. Gamble. He sold it for 2*s* 6*d*. Advertisements for this fan said it would be useful for meetings for nominating MPs, no. 3 in vol. I of *Fans and Fan Leaves*. Lady Charlotte also possessed a fan leaf caricaturing Walpole's Parliamentary Motions in 1741. Quite 'the gem of my collection' it came from Franks in 1887.

2. Pear-shaped salt-glaze stoneware (Staffs.) *c.* 1765 with 'Liberty and Property. No Excise' on it, the motto made popular when Walpole's Excise Bill was abandoned. Lady Charlotte explained that the motto was still in use in 1763. From Edkins, Bristol cost 4*s*, 1881. Schreiber collection.

D. Titus Oates

1. Two packs of cards on Titus Oates and other Popish Plots 1658-1679 plus packs concentrating especially on this plot to murder Charles II which was disclosed to the King and government in 1678 with Oates as the major informer. Such packs reveal the strength of anti-Catholic feeling in England and mix truth and fiction liberally.

2. Lambeth Tiles in Schreiber collection cover some of the same events as those on Ace of Hearts and King of Hearts in Titus Oates cards.

C

Some examples of packs of non-standard cards in Lady Charlotte's collection.

1. *Political Caricatures.* See illustration of 'All the Bubbles' pack of 1720. Other political packs included one of the 1710 Trial of Dr Sacheverell, the Rump Parliament, and 'All the Popish Plots'. See Appendix 6D for Titus Oates.

2. *Heraldic.* Scots pack depicting the arms of the Scottish peers in 1691 engraved by an Edinburgh goldsmith. This pack sold for £10 at the 1896 sale. A pack of the heraldry of English peers cost Lady Charlotte £6 4s 6d in 1880.

3. *Transformation.* English pack of 1828 with court cards depicting Homeric characters, printed by E. Olivatte of London. Only the suit marks are coloured in the pip cards, thus highlighting their double purpose. In such packs the pips themselves became an integral part of the design. Lady Charlotte called them 'grotesque' or 'fanciful' cards. Her collection also included the 1806 pack on a classical theme of J.G. Cotta (a German bookseller who published a series of transformation cards) and his 1810 pack (thought to be designed by C.F. Osiander) also using classical subjects.

4. *Fancy Games.* Modern English pack of forty-five cards entitled 'The Game of Parliament'. The cards are divided into Conservative and Liberal, each card caricaturing a Member of Parliament. They are blue and yellow (respectively) on the reverse. Each Parliamentary party has a card containing its programme and the object is to get this passed. Portraits of Randolph Churchill (Cornelia's brother) and Gladstone are on the front of the game. A similar game of 'Cabinet Council' includes cards representing MPs for Diddlesex, Brokenhead etc. The pack called 'Victorian Cross' concerned events in the Crimean War. A French game of the Revolution consists of thirty-one triangular cards which, placed together, form the Bastille.

APPENDIX 7

LADY CHARLOTTE'S FAMILY TREE

Lady Charlotte Elizabeth BERTIE (b. 1812, m. 1833, d. 1895) = Josiah John GUEST (b. 1785, d. 1852)

Charlotte Maria GUEST (b. 1834, m. 1859, d. 1902) (issue) = Richard DU CANE

Katharine Gwladys GUEST (b. 1837, m. 1861, d. 1926) (issue) = Frederick Cecil ALDERSON

Montague John GUEST (b. 1839, dunm. 1909)

Arthur Edward GUEST (b. 1841, m. 1867, d. 1898) (issue) = Adeline Mary CHAPMAN

Constance Rhiannon GUEST (b. 1844, m. 1865, d. 1916) (issue) = Charles George Cornwallis ELIOT

Ivor Bertie GUEST (b. 1835, d. 1914) = Lady Cornelia Henrietta Maria SPENCER-CHURCHILL

Thomas Merthyr GUEST (b. 1838, m. 1877, d. 1904) (issue) = Lady Theodora GROSVENOR

Augustus Frederick GUEST (b. 1840, dunm. 1862)

Mary Enid Evelyn GUEST (b. 1843, m. 1869, dsp. 1912) = Austen Henry LAYARD

Blanche Vere GUEST (b. 1847, m. 1875, d. 1919) (issue) = 8th Earl of BESSBOROUGH

Corisande Evelyn Vere GUEST (b. 1870, m. 1891, d. 1943) (issue) = 7th Baron RODNEY

Ivor Churchill GUEST (Lord Wimborne) (b. 1873, m. 1902, d. 1939) (issue) = Alice Katherine Sibell GROSVENOR

Frederick Edward GUEST (b. 1875, m. 1905, d. 1937) (issue) = Amy PHIPPS

Lionel George William GUEST (b. 1880, m. 1905, d. 1935) = Mrs Flora DODGE (née BIGELOW)

Frances Charlotte GUEST (b. 1869, m. 1894, d. 1957) (issue) = 1st Viscount CHELMSFORD

Elaine Augusta GUEST (b. 1871, m. 1st, 1898, 2ndly, 1933, d. 1958) = Ernest Amherst VILLIERS / = Robert Lewin HUNTER

Christian Henry Charles GUEST (b. 1874, m. 1911, d. 1957) (issue) = Frances Henrietta LYTTELTON

Rosamond Cornelia Gwladys GUEST (b. 1877, m. 1899, d. 1947) (issue) = 2nd Viscount RIDLEY

Oscar Montague GUEST (b. 1888, m. 1924, d. 1958) = Kathleen Susan PATERSON

Bertie Warner GUEST (b. 1925, m. 1949) (issue) = Margaret Rose HENDERSON

Patrick Henry GUEST (b. 1927, m. 1951) (issue) = Juliet Marian JAMES

Cornelia Rowena GUEST (b. 1928, m. 1st, 1949, m. 2nd, 1957) (issue) = Hugh Dearman JANSON / = Peter Frederick Arthur DENMAN

Revel Sarah GUEST (b. 1931, m. 1963) (issue) = Robert Alan ALBERT

NOTES

INTRODUCTION

1. Throughout this book Lady Charlotte's husband is referred to as John (and Sir John after he received his Baronetcy in 1838) rather than Josiah as this is how he was known. The journal uses the more familiar nickname of 'Merthyr' but, with the exception of journal quotations, this has not been used to avoid confusion with the town and constituency.
2. For example she features in Jack Jones's *Off To Philadelphia in the Morning* (Hamish Hamilton, 1947) and Alexander Cordell's *Land Of My Fathers* (Hodder & Stoughton, 1983). In 1986 she was one of the central characters in Made In Wales Stage Company's production of Michael Bosworth's *The Poor Girl*.
3. Over 3,000 people lost their jobs when the works closed in 1930. The Ingot Mould Foundry made its first cast in 1958. Hoover came to Merthyr after the Second World War and in the same year as the Foundry closed it was announced that the UK Hoover office would move from London to Abercanaid, Merthyr.
4. The term 'journal' is used to describe Lady Charlotte's manuscript as this is the word she used. It perhaps suggests the recording of thoughts over time (as well as events) more effectively than the term 'diary' which can often mean the diurnal recording in a book with allotted space. The freer, more discursive nature of Lady Charlotte's writing seems to fit better the term journal. Some of the original manuscript volumes are missing (vols I, II, IV and V) but are covered in the typed version. See Chapter 8 for information about a works journal in the 1850s and Chapter 9 for Montague Guest's two-volume edition of the ceramics journals. Some loose sheets of pencil notes also exist with the original journals.
5. Compare the similar situation of the diarist Jeanette Marshall (1855-1935), daughter of a London physician, in Zuzanna Shonsfeld *The Precariously Privileged* (OUP, 1987).
6. D'Israeli praised the journal which gave 'an account of a man to himself and where a *single observation* becomes a clue to past knowledge in his hands, restoring to him his past studies and his *evanescent existence*' (Lady Charlotte's emphases).
7. This exists in seventeen volumes, some difficult to decipher because of typing on both sides of thin paper. It is, however, extremely useful as it includes observations made by Monty and other Guest children on reading their mother's words years later.

CHAPTER I

1. Her etchings were published in 1889. They included Uffington House and church, the Gateway of Trinity College, Cambridge, Lindsey House (on the west side of Lincoln's Inn Fields, London) and copies of drawings in Hallam's and Scott's works, one of which took her over sixty hours to execute.
2. Albermarle disappeared soon after this. His father, the Rector, caught up with him and forced him to go to sea. He escaped but before long was incarcerated in Clerkenwell gaol having stolen a watch from his landlady and cashed cheques under false names in strings of hotels. He later married this landlady, a sixty-year-old with money but 'of bad character'. When the

marriage failed, he returned to beg money from the Rector. In the last mention of him by his cousins (in Mary's diary) he was on the verge of being transported.

3. When her mother was dying Lady Charlotte wrote, 'I know she fretted much about my marriage.'

4. She later gave both 12 July and 13 July as anniversaries. Perhaps John proposed on 12 July and they became formally engaged on 13 July.

CHAPTER 2

1. See below.

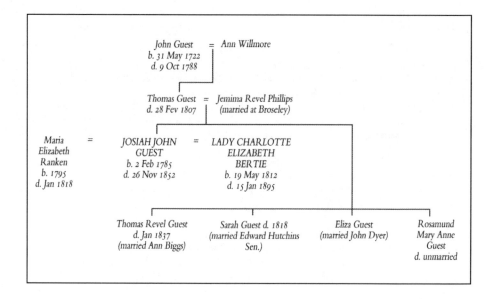

2. There were some methods of birth control in use (especially the condom – rubber was vulcanized in 1843) but most were unreliable and the condom too much associated with prostitution to be thought 'decent'.

3. Lady Charlotte tried breast-feeding several of her children but was told that it was at risk to her own life so reluctantly gave it up (and thereby the contraceptive effect of lactation). The sixteen-year-old who nursed Maria was a 'dear healthy girl' newly married with a baby of four months. For a while the doctor stayed in the house to look after Lady Charlotte.

4. When first pregnant she visited the Rector's wife and was dismayed by her baby's continual crying – 'I pity her for I did not think the noise agreeable.' She added, with suitable decorum, 'I hope it was not a foretaste of a not-very-remote futurity.' In common with her contemporaries Lady Charlotte did not use the word 'pregnant' and would instead refer to 'delicate' or 'weak' health.

5. In fact Martin's career was not doomed. He became Chaplain to the Bishop of St Davids in 1840 and was Rector of South Somercotes in Lincolnshire from 1848. He eventually became Honorary Canon of Lincoln and was the author of several religious works. He died in 1864.

6. Mary thought her 'a nice ladilike [sic] person' and punctilious in the management of the children. One German governess, a 'tiresome vulgar woman', annoyed the Guests by seeking to eat with them. 'She has given herself great airs and has been very disagreeable.'

7. Ivor's tutor in Paris complained of his temper and waywardness. After a stiff letter from Lady Charlotte he resigned. She discovered later that he had a reputation for visiting gaming houses. The following year his wife wrote Lady Charlotte a begging letter. £20 was sent but further help refused.

8. He also paid for Brownlow's election expenses in 1841. Lady Charlotte received begging letters from distant impecunious relatives such as Mrs Pope whose clergyman husband had financial problems. Her response was usually generous.

9. Lady Charlotte learned of Elizabeth's death on reading a paper in a Bristol inn. Always fatalistic, she had just heard a preacher utter the words: 'You may scarcely have risen from your knees here when you will go home and hear of the death of your favourite child.' Elizabeth drowned in a canal half a mile from her home.

10. Huntly's diary recorded his feelings on meeting Mary: 'this day should be marked in letters of gold', he wrote after one meeting; whilst Mary wrote how she later took him to see her fossil collection and they returned engaged.

CHAPTER 3

1. About fifty of the voters resided in Aberdare. In 1837 there were 582 voters, 776 in 1841, 872 in 1847 and 938 by 1852. In the 1831 census the town of Merthyr had 103 males over twenty in the professional and educational category and 1,270 in trade and handicrafts.

2. Cornelia signed the 1889 petition against women's suffrage published in the journal the *Nineteenth Century*. Yet despite her anti-feminist stance she was involved in politics. Although she eventually supported the Liberals, in Lady Charlotte's time she was a staunch Tory. She became a Dame in the Primrose League (formed in 1883). In 1910 she was named in a petition and court case after electoral malpractices involving intimidation of tenants. This lost her son Freddie his seat as MP for East Dorset. Freddie was Chief Whip to Lloyd George. Lady Charlotte's own sons were interested in politics. In 1880 two were Liberals and two Tories. Sir Ivor and Arthur were Tories but, unlike their Liberal brother, Montague, they were unsuccessful Parliamentary candidates then.

3. The decision to build a workhouse was passed by a majority of only one in June 1848.

4. In the 1880 Poole election Charles Schreiber's election expenses amounted to £2,015 1s 5d, £91 8s 10d of which was paid to Lady Charlotte. Expenses included the hiring of detectives and repair bills for the Committee Rooms.

5. The 1880 Poole election demonstrated resentment against the Canford control of the seat. There were 'frequent incendiary fires in the heaths and plantations'. There were also threats that Charles Schreiber would not reach his pre-election Parkstone meeting safely. Lady Charlotte tried to allay her fears by concentrating on her stoneware collection (see Chapter 10). Charles received a bloody nose from a stone but no further injury. He won by just six votes and a petition was threatened but not filed. Lady Charlotte also scrutinized electoral registers in the hope that some known opponents of the Canford interest could be disqualified before elections.

6. This was the only actually contested election at Merthyr between 1832 and 1868 when Guest's successor, H.A. Bruce (son of Bruce Price) Senior Trustee of Dowlais and later Lord Aberdare, was defeated by the Liberal Nonconformist Henry Richard (with the support of ex-Chartists) and Richard Fothergill (Merthyr now had two Members). In 1837 Guest polled over half the votes.

7. See Gillham's thesis (cited in Bibliographical Note) for further details.

8. Roger Gammage, Chartist and author of an 1854 book on the movement, praised Hume who 'often spoke with a boldness that contrasted markedly with the milk-water speeches of the Whigs and their supporters'. In 1848 Hume sponsored a 'Little Charter' advocating a modified form of the Peoples' Charter. The Merthyr literary scholar, Thomas Stephens, invited Guest to a meeting in support of this.

9. Lady Charlotte's old associate, Charles Kingsley, helped create an influential and misleading picture of Kennington Common in his novel *Alton Locke* (1850).

10. For details of Henry Layard see Chapter 7.

11. This refers to the mythical incident *Brad y Cyllyll Hirion* (Treachery of the Long Knives) in the wars between Anglo-Saxons and Britons (Welsh).

12. A Mechanics Institute was formed in the 1820s with weekly lectures mostly on mining and metallurgy.

13. Some years later Emily Talbot, reputed to be the richest heiress in Britain, maintained a number of schools. The children of Groes Day School were invited annually to a tea party in the servants' hall at Margam Castle. There Miss Talbot presented them with lengths of cloth to be made into dresses and suits. In the 1950s Angela John attended this Groes Primary School.

14. With the inception of George Clark's control in 1856 the Dowlais schools were officially placed under government Inspection and began receiving grants. The total number of scholars did not include the 400 Catholic schoolchildren.

CHAPTER 4

1. In 1830 Lady Charlotte recorded visiting a mother and daughter in Stamford: 'the young lady (who fell to my share) [was] so insipid and provoking, that after going through the ordinary commonplace topics, and questions to which I scarcely received answer I was much tempted to begin, as Lord Byron would have done, with one, two, three, four, five, six, seven'. She was much happier visiting the Stamford bookseller to order Arabic and Persian dictionaries.

2. In 1840 Caroline Norton visited Lady Charlotte. Her divorce case was infamous and her attempts to reform the law had just resulted in a new law about the custody of infants. Lady Charlotte remarked that her visitor seemed 'very subdued and melancholy' adding 'I feel to pity for her greatly'.

3. By 1848 Ferdinand's bouts of insanity resulted in his abdication. Prince Metternich had in practice been managing affairs for some time. The Guests took an opera box at La Scala with Count Orsini. They attended a Court Ball which reminded Lady Charlotte of medieval Welsh Literature: Owain being entertained in the castle of the yellow man. She was introduced to the Empress.

4. The waltz was new then (introduced by the Prince Regent in 1816) and *The Times* warned parents against exposing daughters to 'so fatal a contagion'.

CHAPTER 5

1. Lady Charlotte's translation appeared in seven parts from 1838-45 and was then printed in a handsome three-volume edition in 1849. The Quaritch one-volume reprint (English only) was in 1877 with a facsimile by Spread Eagle publications a century later. Lady Charlotte's translation appeared for Dent in the Temple Classics series in 1902 and in Everyman's Library in 1906. Leslie Norris, a native of Merthyr, edited a reproduction of Lady Charlotte's translation for the Folio Society in 1980. Jeffrey Gantz's version of *The Mabinogion* (Penguin, 1976) was reprinted in 1977, 1978, 1979, 1981, 1982, 1984 and a new edition appeared in 1985. The standard modern translation is acknowledged to be that by Gwyn and Thomas Jones, published by the Golden Cockerel Press in 1948 and in the Everyman edition in 1949. Throughout this chapter the spelling used by Lady Charlotte has been retained. Thus for example Kilhwch is given rather than the more correct Kulhwch or Culhwch.

2. William Morris claimed that he began reading Scott at the age of four! Alfred Nutt in 1902 described *The Mabinogion* as the greatest 'fairy tale the world has ever known' – with the exception of the finest Arabian Nights tales.

3. There is a problem in dating enhanced by the absence of contemporary dates within the material, also a lack of radical change in the Welsh language over a long period.

4. Patrick Ford's translation (for the University of California Press) in 1977 – from the White Book of Rhydderch – was the first in over a hundred years to include 'Taliesin' (from Elis Gruffydd's sixteenth-century chronicle).

5. W.J. Gruffydd linked the word to the development of Pryderi (see Appendix 4A). Alfred Nutt believed that the bardic apprentice was styled a *Mabinog* and the material he had to master, *Mabinogi*. Yet another interpretation links the word to the family of the divine Maponos. Some scholars – for example Gantz and Norris – erroneously attribute the adoption of the

title *Mabinogion* to Lady Charlotte despite William Owen Pughe having used it earlier. It is a tribute to the wide influence of her version that its title has remained. She did, nevertheless, appear to use the title somewhat loosely herself referring for example to the Romance of *Bown* as a 'Welsh Mabinogi' (or romance).

6. Dr James Cowles Prichard, author of *Eastern Origins of the Celtic Nations* (1851), a scholar who emphasized the Indo-European origins of the Celts and adjudicated at the 1848 Cymreigyddion.

7. We shall use the names Tegid and Price as did Lady Charlotte.

8. Taliesin Williams and Price edited the Iolo MS in 1848 for the Welsh Manuscripts Society. The Iolo MS eventually became part of the Llanover Collection.

9. Rose Crawshay sought to extend her patronage via English Literature. She founded a prize competition open to women of any nationality (the trust still exists) for writing an essay on Byron, Shelley or Keats.

10. The Llandovery printing and publishing firm had been started in 1829 by William Rees of Tonn.

11. It is possible that Evan Jenkins did this translation as the Rector of Dowlais translated Henry's lecture on Nineveh (given to Dowlais workers) into Welsh. At one of the 'evenings for the People' at which Henry spoke about Nineveh, the Rector had translated some of his talk into Welsh. Rees had been present and published the Welsh edition – which referred to Lady Charlotte and the people of Dowlais in the Preface.

12. The fact that Stephens was the new 'rising star' of Welsh literature may in part account for Lady Charlotte's move (after the publication of her work) to other fields of interest.

13. This is accompanied in print by 'Breuddwyd y Bardd' ('The Bard's Dream') unattributed but very similar in style so likely to have also been the work of Tegid and Lady Charlotte.

14. Her copying of the 2,288 lines of the Thornton MS (loaned from the library of Lincoln Cathedral) took her six days. She acknowledged that it was difficult to decipher. In 1911 the Arthurian scholar Roger Loomis took one month to complete the same task. In addition to all the work she published, Lady Charlotte's Deed Box includes the English translation of 'Amlyn or Amig' ('The Friendship of Amlyn and Amic'), the text of 'Y Saeth Ddoethion' ('The Seven Wise Men') and a few lines of 'Ystorya Bown O Hampton' ('The History of Bevis of Hampton'), translated from Tegid's manuscript.

15. Lady Charlotte and Mary coloured Perceval tracings and the Reverend Kingsley, a keen amateur painter, helped colour the facsimile of Perceval.

16. A Diplomatic edition of the Text of *The Mabinogion* and other Red Book tales was edited by John Rhys and J. Gwenogvryn Evans in 1887. Here Lady Charlotte's work is described as belonging to the 'pre-scientific age' but performed 'with great success'.

CHAPTER 6

1. John Guest had opened a bank at Cardiff in 1823 with a Merthyr branch. In 1825-6 when sixty banks collapsed as the public lost confidence in provincial banks, depositors demanded gold for bankers' notes. He met the rush but soon abandoned this venture.

2. Entries for the month leading up to Ivor's birth in 1835 included the following references to the works:

29 July	I could not resist going up to the top of the furnace and then climbing the hill.
3 Aug	Watched the removal of the cylinder from No. 1 engine.
7	In the works.
8	" "
9	(Felt the baby's birth was imminent.)
10	Balancing the books. In the works.
11	In the works.
16	To top of new furnaces.
19	To the engine.

21   (John left for London).
22   To the furnaces.
23   " "
29   Ivor's birth.

3. An inventory of Lady Charlotte's personal books in the early 1850s revealed that they included
   the following: Roget's *Bridgewater Treatise* (1840) Kidd's *Bridgewater Treatise* (1833) and his
   Outline of Minerology, Faraday's *Chemical Manipulation* (1842), Ferguson's *Lecture on Mechanics*
   (1805), Whewell's *Dynamics* (1832-4), Blunt on mechanical drawing, Gurney, Gregory and
   Griffiths on chemistry, Hodgkinson on cast iron, Scrivenor's 1841 *History of the Iron Trade*, De
   la Bêche's *Mining Processes* (1851), Parliamentary reports on mining districts, a German study of
   the Dowlais works and works of the political economists McCulloch and Malthus.

4. The Dowlais women defended their right to work as a letter to the Welsh press (*Y Glorian*) in
   March 1867 shows. By the mid-1860s they were working at night again. Menelaus was loath
   to prohibit this, arguing that they were more active and showed greater aptitude than men.
   They were also considerately cheaper to employ. Ironically the law of 1872 which banned
   women's night work at mines was introduced by Henry Bruce, Home Secretary and Senior
   Trustee of Dowlais. Sir John's first wife, Maria, had opposed Sunday working but the need to
   keep the furnaces in blast meant that it tended to continue. See Chapter 8.

5. See Edgar Jones *GKN* vol. I, p. 60, cited in Bibliographical Note to Chapter 6 for the annual
   profits (adjusted by the index of commodity prices). The railway boom of 1836-7 when nearly
   1,500 miles of railway lines got Parliamentary approval formed the basis for the ensuing high
   profits. In 1837 profits were £129,160 (adjusted to £136,967). In the mid-1840s the management
   structure was carefully developed. Subcontracting was largely discontinued and a hierarchy
   of agents, overmen and managers created, all directly employed by the Company. As early as
   1830 Dowlais was shipping more iron by canal than Cyfarthfa though supremacy was not fully
   established until the mid-1830s. The peak year for Dowlais was 1847. By mid-century Dowlais,
   Cyfarthfa, Ebbw Vale and Nantyglo accounted for just over half of the Welsh iron shipments.

CHAPTER 7

1. In 1856 John Evans retired to Sully. Ivor later inherited it and made it over to his eldest son in
   1895. The estate was sold at auction in 1914.

2. One of the most romantic of all Gothic castles was to be Castell Coch, the medieval red castle
   transformed for the Third Marquis of Bute and ironically to provide the setting for twentieth-
   century films about the Arthurian legend.

3. William Cubitt and son also built Osborne House on the Isle of Wight, Queen Victoria's
   treasured retreat. To Lady Charlotte it resembled a workhouse rather than a palace.

4. A serious fire at Canford in 1884 destroyed the staircase, part of the hall and items such as
   Buckner's portrait of Sir John. Romaine Walker and Touraine embellished the new stairs in
   1887-8 and a west wing was added with smoking and billiard rooms.

5. John William Luff was an interesting example of Guest patronage resulting in social mobility.
   Born in Woolwich in 1837 he entered the Guests' service in the 1840s and was in turn a
   footman in livery, butler, house steward and land agent. He was later Mayor of Blandford for
   four successive years and his son married a general's daughter. Lady Charlotte: 'I delight in
   such instances of advancement by means of integrity and brains but it is too rare'. When he
   died in 1893 a memorial plaque was erected in Canford church paying tribute to his 'high
   principles, cultivated tastes and refined mind'.

6. He was christened Henry Austen Layard but in deference to his uncle reversed his name to
   Austen Henry.

7. Wedge-shaped letters or characters used by the Assyrians, whose public records were engraved
   on stone.

8. His book *Nineveh and Babylon* (1853) recognized that Kuyunjik was the true Nineveh.

9. Towards the end of Henry's life there was some criticism of his right to have so disposed of
   marbles, the Museum claiming that it owned all the antiquities. Sir Henry pointed out that

had Sir John Guest not financed their transportation they would have been lost to Great Britain. The gateway figures at Canford were sold when it became a school in 1923 and are now in the Metropolitan Museum in New York. The porch became the school tuckshop and in 1958 seven reliefs from Sennacherib's Palace were found embedded in the wall.

10. Lady Charlotte hinted that rumours of Henry being jealous of her second marriage circulated in London.

11. Canford Magna had a population of about 900. The living included Kinson Parish. Longfleet was also in the gift of the manor.

12. Sir John later became foreman of the Grand Jury at the Dorchester Assizes.

13. Henry presented Mr Howard (who led the Dowlais club) with science books to help his weekly instruction class in chemistry – a token of thanks from the club members. The trip seems to have been exclusively organized for the workmen.

CHAPTER 8

1. The other trustees were George Clark and Edward Divett. Henry Bruce later replaced Divett.

2. Recent research questions whether Lucy Thomas really merits the title of 'Mother of the Welsh Steam Coal Trade', since her husband was still alive at the time the significant contract was signed. This does not, however, detract from her success as a (widowed) businesswoman over the next decade.

3. Edgar Jones's figures adjusted by the index of commodity prices give figures of £178,848 for 1847, £4,906 for 1850 and a loss of £42,715 for 1851.

4. Voltaire's poem on the 1755 disaster ended with the line 'Lisbonne est abîmée, et l'on danse à Paris' ('Lisbon is devastated and Paris dances').

5. There was a sliding scale for bar iron and reasonable rates for coal and ironstone used and sold.

6. Between 6 December 1852 and 11 April 1854 a works journal recorded technical details and everyday work. It covered much of the same ground as Lady Charlotte's own journal. Nevertheless, despite some identical statements, there are differences between the two versions and some of the accounts in Lady Charlotte's personal journal are longer and more intimate. Some original statements in the works journal are not, however, replicated in her own. She often wrote up the two of them at the same time, e.g. 4 July 1853: 'Up early, wrote journals etc. before breakfast.'

7. For details about the court causes see Havill (cited in the Bibliographical Note). A third case against the Company in which the puddlers sued for compensation for their three weeks' wages was dismissed.

8. Always concerned to put the record straight, she wrote to the *Merthyr Guardian* to contradict claims that Evan Jenkins had been carrying out instructions as her spokesman. She also prepared (with the help of Charles) a draft article on the strike for *The Times*, though eventually used Bruce's statement instead.

9. Charles's great-grandfather was Carl Schreiber of Durlach who settled in England in about 1720 and married a Berkshire woman. His father (who was born in 1789) was a Justice of the Peace. Charles went from Dedham to Cheltenham College (later becoming first President of the Cheltonian Society), and entered Trinity College, Cambridge as a Pensioner of sixteen. He became a Scholar in 1847, got his classics degree in 1850 and his MA was awarded in 1854, winning a gold medal (worth 5 guineas) for the best Greek ode 'in imitation of Sappho'. This was one of three gold awards annually awarded to Cambridge undergraduates. In 1880 he became a Senior Chancellor's Medallist. In all he won fifteen prizes at Cambridge

It seems that he lost one brother in the same year as Lady Charlotte was bereaved. George Alfred (aged twenty-six) had been serving in the army in Calcutta. According to the 1841 Census George and Charles were both aged fifteen at that time and may possibly have been twins. Charles had four younger brothers – William, Henry, Brymer and Arthur. The last two were also army officers, Brymer distinguished himself at Khartoum. There was one sister, Mary, who married the Rev. Henry Thomas Glyn. They lived in Dorset. A nephew of Charles's became Curate of Canford at the end of the century.

10. It was valued at £400,000 (excluding stocks of iron and raw materials). Atkinson and Baber (see Bibliographical Note, Chapter 6) warn against too Smilesian an interpretation of the success of the Welsh iron industry. In place of the emphasis on the individual self-made ironmaster they stress the geographical and geological factors which over time made: 'The decline of the works of the north-east rim as inevitable as their rise and prosperity.'

CHAPTER 9

1. The English Porcelain Circle (which became the English Ceramic Circle), was founded in 1927.
2. According to the will Lady Charlotte was granted a life annuity of £4,000 and a further £600 when not living in one of Sir John's houses.
3. When Charles married he became one of the principal landowners of the 927-acre farming village of Willisham, Suffolk through a family settlement.
4. Julia Margaret Cameron (née Pattle) now lived in the Isle of Wight. Sir Frederick Pollock was a barrister. The Guest was, appropriately enough, Enid.
5. Albert Edward became King Edward V in 1901. The Guest sons remained in communication with the Prince after his period at Cambridge and Lady Charlotte attended events at which he was present, e.g. a breakfast at Hatfield House in 1874. The west wing of Canford was built to accommodate the Prince of Wales and other aristocratic friends of Ivor's, whilst Monty died at Sandringham in 1909 on a visit to the King on his birthday.
6. This book recalls student productions such as 'A Thumping Legacy' in which Augustus appeared on stage dressed as a proctor accompanied by two bulldogs. This was described as the 'hit of the evening' and the author (the editor of *Punch*) thought it perhaps 'the most genuine spontaneously funny thing I have ever seen on any stage'. Augustus was elected the society's auditor in 1860 (Merthyr had earlier been stage manager) and continued to act. In the year he died he played Ralph Recklen in 'Twice Killed', sharing the stage with his brother Arthur.
7. Langham House was viewed by the family in December 1864. It was rented to them by Mr Jones of Pantyglas, Wales.
8. A. W. Franks (who played a major role in Lady Charlotte's later years) collected porcelain but he worked in the museum world. Another travelling and collecting couple were the Eastlakes. Charles Eastlake was President of the Royal Academy, Secretary of the Fine Arts Commission and between 1855 and 1865 Director of the National Gallery. Lady Eastlake was a translator, writer (and journal keeper) who enjoyed travelling in order to collect. Yet the Eastlakes (who were friends of Henry Layard) poured their energies into painting not ceramics. Compare also Lady Charlotte's life with that of Lady Dilke who wrote eight volumes of art history, was active in women's trade unionism and, like Lady Charlotte, married a forty-eight-year-old man when twenty-one. Her second husband was the younger and notorious Sir Charles Dilke.
9. Monty relied on a typed version of the journals and some of the transcriptions of names were incorrect, differing from Lady Charlotte's spelling. The latter has been used here for dealers' names.
10. In Bessborough vol. II it is claimed that Monty wrote up this story. Since the Earl of Bessborough relied on the typed version of the journals (see note above) he would not have been able to tell that the writing was in Lady Charlotte's hand. Monty did, however, add some dates.
11. The Sykes rented Langham House for a year in 1876. They had discovered in their English home a cache of English china wrapped in a newspaper of 1792 (a period when there were French invasion scares).
12. Lady Charlotte (and others) believed that the mark 'T' represented the modeller Tebo. It is now thought that it may instead have stood for a family of modellers called Toulouse.

CHAPTER 10

1. The South Kensington Museum changed its name in 1899. It had included the Science Museum as well as what became the Victoria and Albert Museum.

2. C.H. Read made transcripts of the marks for engraving (and was rewarded with silver candlesticks) whilst R.H. Soden-Smith from the South Kensington Museum and Arthur Church helped identify some pieces. Church, Professor of Chemistry at the Royal Academy of Arts, paid tribute to Lady Charlotte in the Preface to his *English Earthenware* (1884). 'I cannot refrain from placing (foremost) the Lady Charlotte Schreiber, whose large, instructive and splendid collection has been generously given to the South Kensington Museum since the following pages were written, although in past years I have been accorded many opportunities of studying its treasures.'

3. She paid £31 for a marriage fan of Louis XVI (purchased from Lady Louisa Dalton).

4. Whitman was left £50 in her will and described as her 'Secretary' as well as a museum assistant.

5. In the late 1860s an attempt to encourage painted fans by holding a competition amongst students in the female schools of art had received support from Queen Victoria, Cornelia and others.

6. An article in the *Citizen* in 1894 claimed that nobody took a keener interest in fan making than Lady Charlotte. It also described her as 'a painter and exhibitor of fans' though there is no evidence from the journals that she ever painted fans herself.

7. Two centuries later duty was still levied on playing cards and not until 1960 was it totally removed.

8. Sidney Colvin of the British Museum thought these cards were reprints not originals and that the specialist book which Lady Charlotte had consulted was itself inaccurate.

9. The camera lucidor had been invented in 1807 by William Wollaston. A four-sided prism, it aided drawing the correct perspective of views and objects. The prism was positioned over the drawing surface and presented a reflected image of the view which its user (usually an artist) could then sketch.

10. Antonio Cortelazzo was famous for his Renaissance-style metal work. Henry encouraged him to produce his own signed works rather than forging Renaissance pieces. He secured commissions for him (including one from Lord Wimborne). Cortelazzo bought a country villa which he decorated with sycophantic tributes to Henry.

11. At their height there were sixty-three shelters though apparently only thirty-two in operation at any one time. Some have recently been restored and gradually reopened. Charles Schreiber had exerted himself on behalf of another group of public servants, the postmen. He had argued in Parliament against deductions from their wages because of Christmas presents. Thanks to his intervention the system was reformed. The postmen sent a wreath to his funeral.

BIBLIOGRAPHICAL NOTE

Lady Charlotte's journal has been the principal source for this book. It is now kept in the National Library of Wales (NLW). Readers keen to follow up further information about Lady Charlotte's life and times should, however, find the following sources of interest.

Most illuminating (though out of print) are the two volumes edited by the Earl of Bessborough which reproduce extracts from the journals: *The Diaries of Lady Charlotte Guest* (John Murray, 1950), and *Lady Charlotte Schreiber 1853-1891* (John Murray, 1952). Lady Charlotte's Deed Box in the National Library of Wales (NLW) contains her extracts from D'Israeli's *Literary Character* and manuscript versions of *The Mabinogion*. The diaries of her half-sisters, Mary and Elizabeth Pegus, and of Mary's husband, Charles, Tenth Marquis of Huntly, are at Northamptonshire Record Office – Wickham 12/2. Enid Layard's diaries and letters are in the British Library Add, MS 58173 and 46153-70. Montague Guest's two volumes, *Lady Charlotte Schreiber's Journals, Confidences of a Collector of Ceramics and Antiques* (The Bodley Head Press, 1911), cover the collecting years.

Introduction: See also R. Halsband (ed.), *The Selected Letters of Lady Mary Wortley Montagu* (Penguin, 1968 edn), Christopher Hibbert (ed), *Queen Victoria in her Letters and Journals* (Penguin, 1985 edn), Leonard Woolf (ed.) *Virginia Woolf. A Writer's Diary* (Triad Grafton Books, 1985 edn), Norman and Jeanne MacKenzie, *The Diary of Beatrice Webb* vol. 1 1873-1892. *Glitter Around and Darkness Within* (Virago, 1986 edn). On women's journals see Cynthia Huff, *British Women's Diaries* (AMS Press, 1985), *Women's Studies International Forum* (vol. 10 No. 1, 1987) (special issue on personal chronicles and autobiographical writings), and Judith Schneid Lewis, *In the Family Way. Childbearing In The British Aristocracy 1760-1850* (Rutgers University Press, 1986), also the Letts Catalogue *Letts Keep A Diary, A History of Diary-Keeping in Great Britain* (1987) and Sarah Gristwood, *Recording Angels: The Secret World of Women's Diaries* (Macmillan, 1985). See also Eric Homberger and John Charmley (eds), *The Troubled Face of Biography* (Macmillan, 1988) and Deborah Epstein Nord, *The Apprenticeship of Beatrice Webb* (Macmillan, 1985).

Chapter One: For the general background see F.M.L. Thompson, *English Landed Society in the Nineteenth Century* (Routledge & Kegan Paul, 1963), and for the local area F. Earle and A. Willis, *A History of the Parish of Uffington* (Printing Craft Ltd). For accounts of the education and interests of young ladies see D. Gorham, *The Victorian Girl and the Feminine Ideal* (Croom Helm, 1982), and Jeanne Peterson, 'No Angels in the House: The Victorian Myth and the Paget Women', *American Historical Review* (89,3,1983), and Wanda Neff, *Victorian Working Women* (Cass Reprint, 1966). R. Blake's *Disraeli* (Methuen edn, 1969), includes the quote about Lady Charlotte and B. Disraeli, *Sybil or the Two Nations* (1845, Penguin, 1980 edn) the other Disraeli quotes. The description of the latter is quoted in G. Waterfield, *Layard of Nineveh* (John Murray, 1963).

Chapter Two: For early nineteenth century Merthyr see Charles Wilkins, *The History of Merthyr Tydfil* (*Merthyr Express*, 1867) – more lively than accurate, and the works of Gwyn A. Williams, especially *The Merthyr Rising* (Croom Helm, 1978). I.G. Jones's lecture, 'Communities. The Observers and the Observed' (University College, Cardiff, 1985), provides fascinating descriptions of who surveyed what and when. For contemporary accounts see the *Cardiff and Merthyr Guardian* (*Merthyr Guardian*), Jules Ginswick, *Labour and the Poor in England and Wales 1849-1851*, vol. III (Cass,

1983), based on the *Morning Chronicle* letters, and C. Carus *The King of Saxony's Journey Through England and Scotland* (Chapman & Hall, 1846).

Margaret Stewart Taylor *The Crawshays of Cyfarthfa Castle* (Robert Hale, 1967), introduces us to Rose Crawshay. L. Davidoff, C. Hall, *Family Fortunes. Men and Women of the English Middle Class 1780-1* (Hutchinson, 1987), provide many insights into the constraints yet adaptations of married women. The writings of Mrs Ellis, Queen Victoria and others are shown in J. Horowitz Murray, *Strong-Minded Women* (Penguin, 1984). The Dickens-Cruikshank correspondence is extracted from M. House, E. Storey (ed) *The Letters of Charles Dickens*, vol. 2 (Oxford University Press, 1909), and Lady Holland's words from the Earl of Ilchester (ed), *Elizabeth, Lady Holland to her Son 1821-5* (John Murray, 1946). The MS Dillwyn Diaries were kindly lent by Richard Morris. The G.T. Clark correspondence includes the letter to Lady Huntly, NLW MS 15029. For the 'Rectory Affair' see the *Stamford Mercury*, 4 August 1843.

Chapter Three: For women's involvement in nineteenth-century politics see Jane Rendall (ed.) *Equal or Different. Women's Politics 1800-1914* (Basil Blackwell, 1985), and Beatrix Campbell *The Iron Ladies* (Virago, 1987).

For Merthyr Politics see the works of I.G. Jones, especially his 'Health, Wealth and Politics in Victorian Wales' in *Communities: Essays in the Social History of Wales*, (Gomer Press, 1987), and Glanmor Williams (ed.), *Merthyr Politics. The Making of a Working Class Tradition* (University of Wales Press, 1966). Contrast Gwyn A. Williams's two articles in the *Welsh History Review* (WHR) 'The Making of Radical Merthyr 1800-36 (vol. 1. 1961) and 'The Merthyr Election of 1835' (vol. 10, 1981), with C.L. Gillham 'The Politics of Sir John Guest 1825-52' University of Wales MA (1972). See, too, I.W.R. David 'Politics and Electionary Activities in South East Wales, 1820-52' University of Wales MA (1959), and E. Ball 'Glamorgan Members During the Reform Bill Period', *Morgannwg* (X, 1966) and Raymond Grant *The Parliamentary History of Glamorgan 1542-1976* (Christopher Davies, 1978) and Hansard third series. See also A. Farquharson, *The History of Honiton* (Devon & Somerset Steam Printing Company, 1868), and T. Davis Jones, 'Poor Law Administration in Merthyr Tydfil Union 1834-1894, *Morgannwg* (VIII, 1964). See D.J.V. Jones, *The Last Rising* (Clarendon Press, Oxford, 1985), Angela V. John, 'The Chartist Endurance. Industrial South Wales 1840-68', *Morgannwg* (XI, 1971), Dorothy Thompson, *The Chartists* (Temple Smith, 1984), and T. Morley '*The Times* and the Revolutionary Crisis of 1848' (Thames Polytechnic, PhD, 1985). Newspaper material includes the *Merthyr Guardian* and *Hereford Times* 1835, and *Northern Star* 1839, 41. See, too, the Bute MS XX in Cardiff Reference Library, Dic Box 6, Section 1, Home Office Papers at PRO 8045/454 and Poole Borough Archives VLP 171 Poole Election 1880, and Poole Elections 1859-85 Poole Municipal Archives, also T.A. Macdonald 'The Electoral History of Poole', University of Bristol M. Litt (1981).

For education see Leslie Wynne Evans, *Education in Industrial Wales 1700-1900* (Avalon Books, 1971), and *idem* 'Sir John and Lady Charlotte Guests' Educational Scheme at Dowlais in the mid-nineteenth century', *NLW Journal* (vol. IX no. 3, 1956). See Dowlais Iron Company (dic) letters at the Glamorgan Record Office, D/DG correspondence, section 1, boxes 2, 4, 5. Parliamentary papers include: pp 1847 XXVII; pp 1842 XV; pp 1845 XVIII; pp 1851 XLIV 1; pp 1846 XXIV, pp 1850 XXIII; pp 1856 XVIII, pp 1857 XVI, and pp 1877 LXXVII. The presentation address to Matthew Hirst is in Cyfarthfa Castle Museum, Merthyr Tydfil, and the Rules of the Dowlais Friendly Society, 1837 and address by Bruce to the Young Men's Mutual Improvement Society in Merthyr Tydfil Reference Library.

On social welfare see K.T. Weetch 'The Dowlais Ironworks and its Industrial Community 1760-1850. A Local Study in Economic and Social History of the late eighteenth century and early nineteenth century'; London University Msc. (1963), G.P. Smith 'Social Control and Industrial Relations at the Dowlais Iron Company 1850-1970', University of Wales Msc. Econ., (1981). For public health see Huw Williams (ed.) *Public Health in Mid Victorian Wales*, vol. 2 (University of Wales Press, 1983), and articles on Merthyr in *Llafur*. For comparisons with elsewhere see the following: John Vivian Hughes, pamphlet on *Emily Charlotte Talbot (1840-1910)*, F.C. Mather, *After the Canal Duke. A Study of the Industrial Estates Administered by the Trustees of the Third Duke of Bridgewater in the Age of Railway Building 1825-72* (Clarendon Press, Oxford, 1970).

For paternalism see Patrick Joyce, *Work, Society and Politics* (Harvester Press, 1980), and D.A. Reid 'Labour, Leisure and Politics in Birmingham 1800-75', University of Birmingham, PhD, (1985). For rational recreation see Peter Bailey *Leisure and Class in Victorian England. Rational Recreation and the Contest for Control 1830-85* (Routledge & Kegan Paul, 1978). See, too, William N. Bruce (ed.), *Sir Henry Layard. Autobiography and Letters*, 2 vols (John Murray, 1903), Dot Jones, 'Self Help in Nineteenth Century Wales: The Rise and Fall of the Female Friendly Society'; *Llafur* (vol.4 no. 1 1984).

Chapter Four: For etiquette and the organization of the London Season see Leonore Davidoff, *The Best Circles* (Croom Helm, 1983). The correspondence between Lady Charlotte and Charles Babbage is in the British Library MS 37191. See also the Marchioness of Londonderry (ed), *The Letters From Disraeli to Frances Ann, Marchioness of Londonderry 1837-61* (Macmillan, 1938), R. Nevill (ed.), *The Reminiscences of Lady Dorothy Nevill* (Methuen, 1919), Tresham Lever (ed), *The Letters of Lady Palmerson*, (John Murray, 1957), Lady Greville, *The Gentlewoman In Society* (The Victoria Library, 1892) and R. Weigall, *Lady Rose Weigall* (John Murray, 1923). It is helpful to compare the material in this chapter with Carol Dyhouse's account of 'Mothers and Daughters in the Middle-Class Home, (1870-1914)' in Jane Lewis (ed), *Labour and Love. Women's Experience of Home and Family 1850-1940* (Basil Blackwell, 1986). The rhyme is in the hands of Lord Eliot at Port Eliot.

Chapter Five: Especially useful for this chapter has been Rachel Bromwich's article '"The Mabinogion" and Lady Charlotte Guest', *Transactions of the Honourable Society of Cymmrodorion*, (THSC) (1986.). See, too, Meic Stephens (ed.), *Oxford Companion to the Literature of Wales* (Oxford University Press, 1986). Arthur Johnston, 'William Owen Pughe and the Mabinogion', *NLW Journal* (X, 1958), quotes from the Scott MS in the National Library of Scotland and from the W. Owen-Pughe MS in the NLW. See, too, Marion Henry Jones, 'The Letters of Arthur James Johnes 1809-71', *NLW Journal* (X, 1958), and additional letters, ibid (xiv, 1965); Glenda Carr, *William Owen-Pughe* (University of Wales Press, 1983). See Rev. C.C. Southey (ed.), *The Life and Correspondence of Southey* (vol. 2, 1850); the 1851-2 volume of the published letters of Sir Walter Scott, and Jack Simmons, *Southey 1774-1843* (Collins, 1945).

For the Welsh inventive spirit see the works of Prys Morgan, for example *The Eighteenth Century Renaissance*, (Christopher Davies, 1981); Tony Curtis (ed.), *Wales: The Imagined Nation. Studies in Cultural and National Identity* (Poetry Press Wales, 1906), Gwyn A. Williams, *The Welsh in Their History* (Croom Helm, 1983), Philip Jenkins 'The Creation of An "Ancient Gentry" Glamorgan 1760-1840,' *WHR* (12, 1984) in which it is claimed that Lady Charlotte attempted to 'create a Cymric counterpoise to Scott' and Ian Haywood, 'The Making of History: Historiography and Literary Forgery in the Eighteenth Century', *Literature and History* (vol. 9, 2, autumn 1983). Relevant manuscript letters in the NLW are: MS Autographed Letters, 964E, 1848-9, 1849, 965E, 1857. Letters between Lady Charlotte and Thomas Stephens; 1564a, 1837 Lady Charlotte's letters to the Liverpool Cambrian Society; 1805E, four letters to Walter Davies; 13182E six letters 1837-41 to the Cymreigyddion Y Fenni. The correspondence between Lady Charlotte and Sir Frederic Madden is in the British Library MS 2842 (1839) and 2843 (1842), also a letter to Charles Babbage in 1837, MS, 37190. The NLW has the sheet music for the 'Bard's Journey to Bala' – XM 1621 J921Y6, whilst the printed poem is in the British Library. The ode dedicated to Lady Charlotte appears in R. Garlick and R. Mathias, *Anglo-Welsh Poetry 1840-1980* (Poetry Wales Press, 1984). The letter from John Evans of Machynlleth comes from DIC op. cit., letter 81, 28, July 1840.

Material on the Llanover connection includes Jane Williams (Ysgafell), *The Literary Remains of the Reverend Thomas Price, Carnhuanawc*, 2 vols (Rees, 1854); J. Stephen Williams, '"Carnhuanawc" (1787-1848) Eisteddfodwr ac Ysgolhaig', *THSC* (1954); Mary Ellis 'Anghard Llwyd 1780-1866' pts I and II, *Journal of Flintshire Historical Society*, vols 26, 27 (1974-6) and Mair Elvet Thomas, *Afiaith Yng Gwent* (University of Wales Press, 1978). Maxwell Fraser has written a number of articles on the Llanover connection in the *NLW Journal* and *THSC*, the article on 'Lady Llanover and her Circle' in *THSC* (pt III, 1968) includes the Lady Greenly quote. See D. Rhys Phillips, *Lady Charlotte and the Mabinogion* (Camarthen, 1921) and the *Western Mail* April 1921 on the authenticity of Lady Charlotte's work. Further information about the significance of 'The Mabinogion' can be found in Matthew Arnold, *Lectures and Essays in Criticism* III (part of the Complete Prose Works of Matthew Arnold, R.H. Super (ed.) (University of Michigan Press, 1962). Arthur Johnston, *Enchanted Ground. The Story of Medieval Romance in the Eighteenth Century* (Athlone Press, 1964) gives the quote from Loth. W.G. Gruffydd's claim about 'devilling' can be found in his *Rhiannon*, (University of Wales Press, 1953). The subject has attracted much interest from Arthurian scholars. See for example Roger Loomis *Wales and the Arthurian Legend* (University of Wales Press, 1956). The Mrs Ellis and Ruskin quotes come from Horowitz Murray op. cit. and the description of Lady Charlotte as Welsh is in H.C. Adams (ed), *Cyclopaedia of Female Biography* (R. Forester, 1866).

Chapter Six: Invaluable to an understanding of the daily running of the works are the original letters to and copies from the company. There are thousands of letters in the Dowlais Iron Company Records at the Glamorgan Record Office [GRO] D/DG Correspondence. A number of letters written to or from Lady Charlotte have been used in this chapter, especially those of 1852. The London House correspondence (now available in catalogue form) has also been useful and the Institute of Civil Engineers Report and Menelaus's Report D/DG, section E, box 4 is the same collection. Fortunately a useful selection of the DIC correspondence is available in M. Elsas (ed.), *Iron in the Making. Dowlais Iron Company Letters* 1782-1860 (GRO and Guest Keen Iron and Steel Company Ltd 1960). Also extremely helpful are Edgar Jones's beautifully illustrated *A History of G.K.N. volume one: Innovation and Enterprise 1759-1918* (Macmillan, 1987) and John A. Owen, *History of the Dowlais Iron Works* (The Starling Press, 1977 edition). See too M.J. Daunton 'The Dowlais Iron Company in the Iron Industry 1800-50', *WHR* (vol.6, 1972-3), Michael Atkinson, Colin Baber, *The Growth and Decline of the South Wales Iron Industry 1760-1880* (University of Wales, 1987) and David Jones, 'Lady Charlotte Guest. Victorian Businesswoman', *History Today* (vol. XXIII no. 1, January 1973), Lady Bell, *At the Works* (Virago edn, 1985), and Anthony Hyman, *Charles Babbage. Pioneer of the Computer* (Oxford University Press, 1982). Roebuck's story is recounted in the *Poole and Bournemouth Herald*, 17 January 1895. The quotation about Mrs Gladstone is in Esther Simon Shkolnik 'Petticoat Power: The Political Influence of Mrs Gladstone', *The Historian* (vol. XLII, no. 4, August 1980). To understand the geography of Dowlais a personal visit is better than any book.

Chapter Seven: For Canford see Alan J. Miller, *Stories From Dorset History* (The English Press, 1987), with its very readable story, 'The Blue Stocking of Canford' and Norah Parsons 'The Manor of Canford Magna* (Purbeck Press, 1974). For architecture see Rev. Alfred Barry, *The Life and Works of Sir Charles Barry* RA FRS (John Murray, 1956), Jill Franklin, *The Gentleman's Country House and its Plan 1835-1914* (Routledge & Kegan Paul, 1981), Mark Girouard, *The Victorian Country House* (Yale University Press, 1979 edn) and Royal Commission on Historical Monuments: England, County of Dorset, vol. 2, South-East, pt. 2, 1970. Barry's plans for the exterior and interior of Canford can be seen at Dorset Record Office. See also the 1851 Census, Philip Jenkins, *The Making of A Ruling Class. The Glamorgan Gentry 1640-1990* (Cambridge University Press, 1983), W.D. Rubenstein *Men of Property* (Croom Helm, 1981). The quotation about a high churchman comes from Anthony Trollope, *Barchester Towers* (1857). See the Maybery Collection, NLW 2236, 2339, 2340 and the DIC letters for December 1852 for the search for houses. For Sully see Glyn M. Jones and Elfyn Scourfield, *Sully. A Village and Parish in the Vale of Glamorgan* (published by the authors, 1986). This includes the Kingsley quotation.

For Henry Layard see the readable biography by Gordon Waterfield, *Layard of Nineveh*, op. cit. See too the Layard papers in the British Library, especially MS 38978 and his autobiography, op. cit. See R. Moorey, P. Parr, *Archaeology in the Levant Sculpture* (Trustees of the British Museum, 1983), and Layard's speeches in Parliament on the *Prospect and Conduct of the War* (John Murray, 1854) and his *Nineveh and its Remains* (John Murray, abridged version of 1867). R.D. Barnett 'Canford and Cuneiform: A century of Assyriology' *Museums Journal* (vol. 60, no. 8, November 1960) is informative. The Gladstone quotation is given in Asa Briggs, *Victorian People*, (Penguin, 1970 edn) See, too, Olive Anderson, *A Liberal State at War* (Macmillan, 1967), and for the Great Exhibition, Asa Briggs, op. cit.

Chapter Eight: Details of the funeral are reproduced in a diagram of the cortège in Cyfarthfa Castle Museum. The sermon preached in Dowlais church was published in English and Welsh by Rees of Llandovery. See, too, the *Gentleman's Magazine* (vol. XXXIX, pt I, 1853) and *The Times*, 9 December 1852. Ivy Pinchbeck, *Women Workers and the Industrial Revolution* (Virago, 1981 edn) discusses the role of widows. Mary Benson is quoted in Katherine Moore, *Victorian Wives* (Allison & Busby, 1985 edn) Sir John's 1850 will and the 1852 codicils are in DIC D/DG 165.

For the renewal of the lease see John Davies, 'The Dowlais Lease 1748-1900' *Morgannwg* (XXIV, 1980) and his book *Cardiff and the Marquis of Bute* (University of Wales Press, 1981). See, too, M.J. Daunton op. cit., and Edgar Jones op. cit. Sources include NLW Bute Papers 70. Letter Book 1845-6, Bute MS VI no.41038, VI no. 11034 Cardiff Public Library and the Coal Reports of 1851 and 1853 (in family hands). The DIC reports and letters, especially D/DG London House correspondence are useful for the 1852-5 period. See, too, *Mining Journal* February 1848. The Matthew Boulton quotation comes from Davidoff and Hall op. cit.

For the 1853 strike see Elizabeth Havill, 'The Respectful Strike' *Morgannwg* (XXIV, 1980). This uses the works journal – Glamorgan Record Office microfilm reel no. 129. It is useful to compare this with the extracts in Bessborough, vol. 2. op. cit. See, too, the *Merthyr Guardian* and *The Times* for August-September 1853, Elsas op. cit. and NLW Stephens MS 13182E. See also J.P. Addis, *The Crawshay Dynasty* (University of Wales Press, 1957) and David Painting, *Amy Dillwyn* (University of Wales Press, 1987). The information about Mary Evans comes from a transcript of the unpublished writings of Miss Phoebe Simons in Cyfarthfa Castle Museum. A little information about the Schreiber family can be found in J.A. Venn, *Alumni Cantabrigienses* (vol. V, Pt II 1752-1900. Cambridge University Press, 1953), *Who's Who in Suffolk* (1935), the eighteenth edition of Burke's *Landed Gentry*, and the 1841 Census for the parish of Melton, Suffolk. The Suffolk Record Office holds the wills and probates of Charles's parents – SRO HB 76 (932).

Chapter Nine: The best way to appreciate Lady Charlotte as a collector is to go to Room 139 in the Victoria and Albert Museum, London and view the impressive Schreiber collection. The official museum catalogue (1986) describes it as 'still one of the finest groups anywhere of eighteenth century English porcelain'. Lady Charlotte's Catalogue of the Schreiber collection of English Porcelain, Earthenware, Enamels etc. (Eyre & Spottiswoode, 1885) and Bernard Rackham's versions – Catalogue of the Schreiber collection (London) 1915: vol. 1924: vol. III enamels and glass; 1928, 2nd edn of vol. I; 1930, vol. II earthenware – are unfortunately all out of print and there is no current catalogue for the collection. Rackham was the Assistant Keeper in the Department of Ceramics at the Museum and he updated the catalogue. His 1915 volume retains the same numbering as Lady Charlotte's, but his later volumes depart from this as a result of altered attributions. This later edition of Rackham's work is used as the basis for the classification of the collection today. For this chapter a combination of all the catalogues has been used, relying especially on the interleaved annotated version of Lady Charlotte's own catalogue in the Department of Medieval and later Antiquities at the British Museum. Montague Guest's 2 volumes op. cit. have also been extremely useful. This work has been described by Frank Herrman as: 'Probably the earliest and most interesting account of the formation of a great ceramic collection that we have'. It includes many illustrations of pieces retained by the family. Herrmann's own book *The English as Collectors*, (Chatto & Windus 1972) pays some attention to Lady Charlotte, whilst W.B. Honey's *Old English Porcelain*, (Faber & Faber, 1977 edn) contains a number of illustrations from the Schreiber collection. See also O. Van Oss 'Lady Charlotte Schreiber', *English Ceramic Circle Transactions* (IV, 1957); *Country Life* Fine Arts Number 29 January, 12 February 1981 for articles by Frances Russell; *The Times* 23 October 1976 for an article by Sally Kevill-Davies and *Antique Dealer and Collector Guide* July, August, September 1983 for articles by Anton Gabszewicz. See J.V.G. Mallet, 'Collecting and the Study of Chelsea Porcelain' in Margaret Legge, *Flowers and Fables. A Study Survey of Chelsea Porcelain 1749-69* (National Gallery of Victoria, Australia, 1984). See, too, Christie's Catalogue of the Collection of Foreign Porcelain. March 25-26, 1890.

For European history see James Joll, *Europe Since 1870* (Weidenfeld & Nicolson, 1973) and Waterfield op. cit. which includes the quotation from Layard's letter to Blanche. See also Judy Rudoe 'The Layards, Cortelazzo and Castellani: new information on the diaries of Lady Layard',

Jewellery Studies (vol. 1983-4), Enid Layard's diaries op. cit., Phoebe Simons transcript op. cit. and Charles Eastlake Smith (ed.), *Journals and Correspondence of Lady Eastlake*, vol. II (John Murray, 1895). Charles Schreiber 'A Lecture on Venice' (1860) is in the NLW. See, too, F.C. Burnand, *The 'A.D.C.' being Personal Reminiscences of the University Amateur Dramatic Club*, Cambridge (Chapman & Hall, 1880) for the Guest sons. For a fictional comparison of three generations of nineteenth-century women, see the novel *Hester* by Margaret Oliphant, published in three volumes (Macmillan, 1883-8, Virago edition, 1984).

Chapter Ten: For fans see Lady Charlotte Schreiber *Fans and Fan Leaves, English* and *Fans and Fan Leaves, Foreign*. (John Murray, 1888 and 1890) as well as the manuscripts for both in the Prints and Drawings Department of the British Museum (only the volume of English fans is in Lady Charlotte's own hand). This department contains her fan collection. Its catalogue was compiled by Lionel Cust in 1893. There are also thirteen vols of MS notes of fans and fan leaves by Lady Charlotte. See, too, The *Queen*, 6 December 1879; *Art and Letters*, January 1888; *The Times* 20 September 1889; *The Saturday Review* 13 August 1889 and *The Spectator*, 13 August 1889. Modern works include Mary Gostelow, *The Fan* (Gill & Macmillan, 1974), Nancy Armstrong, *A Collector's History of Fans*, (Studio Vista, 1974) Hélène Alexander, *Fans* (Batsford, 1984) and Susan Mayor, *Collecting Fans* (Studio Vista, 1980). Further information can be gleaned from the *Bulletin* of the Fan Circle (International) no. 1 1975. The world's first museum devoted exclusively to fans opened in Greenwich, London 100 years after Lady Charlotte's first volume appeared in print.

Some information on Franks is gleaned from his unpublished autobiographical memorandum 'The Apology of My Life'. See, too, David M. Wilson, *The Forgotten Collector. Augustus Wollaston Franks of the British Museum* (Thames & Hudson, 1984). For playing cards see Lady Charlotte's three volumes of *Playing Cards of Various Ages and Countries* (John Murray, vol. 1 1892; vol. 2 1893; vol.3 1895). Her collection is in the Prints and Drawings Department, British Museum, as are her games and the volumes of MS notes on her cards and one volume of extracts from books, newspapers etc. The catalogue to the collection was compiled by F.M. O'Donoghue in 1901. See, too, the Sotheby Wilkinson and Hodge sale catalogue for 1-2 May 1896 and *The Times*, 4 May 1896. See, too, George Clulow, *The Origin and Manufacture of Playing Cards* (Macgibbon & Kee, 1966). Eleven of the fourteen chapters in, J.R.S. Whiting's *A Handful of History* (Alan Sutton, 1978) use Lady Charlotte's cards to illustrate historical events. See also *Antique Collector* April 1981 and John Berry's notes to accompany 'Popular Pips. The Art of the Transformation Card' exhibition at the Guildhall Library London 1987.

For embroidery see the *Magazine of Art* 1882 and Rozsika Parker, *The Subversive Stitch: Embroiderers and the Making of the Feminine* (Women's Press, 1984), Edna Healey, *The Life of Angela Burdett-Coutts* (Sidgwick & Jackson, 1978), Diana Orton *Made of Gold. A Biography of Angela Burdett-Coutts* (Hamish Hamilton, 1980) and Waterfield op. cit. for the Turkish Compassionate Fund. For London lodgings for women see Martha Vicinus, *Independent Women. Work and Community for Single Women 1850-1920* (Virago, 1985) and Ted Ward's unpublished paper ' Selected Aspects of the Life and Works of Lady Cornelia Wimborne 1847-1927'. For Amy Dillwyn see Painting op. cit. and H.P. Arnold for *William Henry Fox Talbot. Pioneer of Photography and Man of Science* (Benham, 1977) from whom the quotation is taken. Rudoe op. cit. discusses Cortelazzo. See, too, the Layard papers op. cit. and Mary Lou Kohfeldt, *Lady Gregory*, (Andre Deutsch, 1984). For the cab drivers see *Hackney Carriage Guardian*, 1893.

Obituaries include *Cardiff Times*, 19 January 1895 (see, too, 12 January 1895), *Poole and Bournemouth Herald*, 17 January 1895, *Merthyr Express*, 19 January 1895 and *The Times*, 16 January 1895. Lady Charlotte and Charles Schreiber's wills have been consulted. Mrs Oliphant's *Hester* was reprinted by Virago in 1984 with an interesting introduction by Jenny Uglow.

INDEX